342.7308 SPEAKING

Speaking of race, speaking of

Speaking of Race, Speaking of Sex

Speaking of Race, Speaking of Sex

Hate Speech, Civil Rights,
and Civil Liberties

Henry Louis Gates, Jr., Anthony P. Griffin,
Donald E. Lively, Robert C. Post,
William B. Rubenstein, and Nadine Strossen

with an introduction by Ira Glasser

NEW YORK UNIVERSITY PRESS
New York and London

"War of Words: Critical Race Theory and the First Amendment" by Henry Louis Gates, Jr., is adapted and expanded from "Let Them Talk," *New Republic*, September 20 and 27, 1993. Reprinted by permission of *The New Republic*, © 1993, The New Republic, Inc.

Several passages in "Racial Myopia in the Age of Digital Compression" by Donald E. Lively originally appeared in an article entitled "Reformist Myopia and the Imperative of Progress: Lessons for the Post-Brown Era" (46 *Vanderbilt Law Review*, 865 [1993]), and are reprinted by permission of *Vanderbilt Law Review*.

"Regulating Racist Speech on Campus: A Modest Proposal?" by Nadine Strossen is reprinted by permission of *Duke Law Journal*, in which a previous, fully footnoted version (1990 *Duke Law Journal*, 484 [1989]) appeared.

"Racist Speech, Democracy, and the First Amendment" by Robert C. Post is reprinted by permission of *William and Mary Law Review*, in which a previous version (32 *William and Mary Law Review*, 267 [1991]) appeared.

NEW YORK UNIVERSITY PRESS
New York and London

© 1994 by New York University
All rights reserved

Library of Congress Cataloging-in-Publication Data
Speaking of race, speaking of sex : hate speech, civil rights, and
    civil liberties / Henry Louis Gates . . . [et al.] ; with an
    introduction by Ira Glasser.
        p.   cm.
    Includes bibliographical references and index.
    ISBN 0-8147-3070-1 (alk. paper)
    1. Hate speech—United States.   2. Freedom of speech—United
States.   3. Racism in language.   I. Gates, Henry Louis.
KF9345.A75S67   1994
342.73'0853—dc20
[347.302853]   94-36519
                          CIP

New York University Press books are printed on acid-free paper, and
their binding materials are chosen for strength and durability.

Manufactured in the United States of America

10   9   8   7   6   5   4   3   2   1

Contents

Contributors

Henry Louis Gates, Jr., is W. E. B. Du Bois Professor of the Humanities and chair of the Afro-American Studies Department at Harvard University.

Ira Glasser is the executive director of the American Civil Liberties Union.

Anthony P. Griffin, a practicing attorney in Galveston, Texas, was general counsel for the NAACP and was removed in 1993 for his representation in a First Amendment case of a Grand Dragon of the Texas Knights of the Ku Klux Klan. He is the recipient of the first Justice William J. Brennan, Jr., Award presented by the Thomas Jefferson Center for the Protection of Free Expression.

Donald E. Lively is professor of law at the University of Toledo.

Robert C. Post is professor of law at the University of California, Berkeley.

William B. Rubenstein is the director of the Gay and Lesbian Rights Project of the American Civil Liberties Union.

Nadine Strossen is professor of law at New York Law School and the president of the American Civil Liberties Union.

Speaking of Race, Speaking of Sex

Introduction

Ira Glasser

Sometime near the end of the second Reagan administration, news stories began to appear about a burgeoning phenomenon on American college campuses: codes of conduct that prohibited and punished speech that demeaned or denigrated people on the basis of race, sex, religion, sexual orientation, or other such characteristics.

Free-speech advocates, long accustomed to defending speech they hated, were nonetheless somewhat unprepared for this development, in large part because its impetus came from the political left, and in some cases from people they considered their public-interest allies.

As Anthony Lewis has pointed out, repression of speech in America has historically come mostly from the right. The Sedition Acts of 1798 and 1918; suppression of slavery abolitionists in the South prior to the Civil War; the Palmer raids in 1920; the arrests of union organizers during the first quarter of the twentieth century; the tyranny of McCarthyism in the 1950s; the arrests of civil rights marchers and anti-war protesters in the 1960s—all were examples of minority dissenters seeking social change and being suppressed by an entrenched government seeking to maintain and consolidate the status quo.

The recent movement to restrict so-called hate speech—words that reflected racial or sexual bigotry—is different. The call has come mostly from liberals, arising initially on college campuses and in law schools and being led mostly by law professors who saw themselves as advocates of equality. Suddenly, free speech and equality were pitted against each other, as if they were antagonists. This was a new development and it caused much agony and soul-searching.

Until this startling development, free speech and equality had been assumed to be comrades in a common struggle. For example, when Fred

Shuttlesworth, a black minister and civil rights leader in Alabama, was arrested and convicted in the late sixties for leading an orderly protest through the streets of Birmingham, his conviction was overturned by the U.S. Supreme Court as an unconstitutional form of censorship. His case was not unique. As veterans of the civil rights movement such as Andrew Young and Hosea Williams often said and still say, the First Amendment was a critical weapon, a prerequisite, in the fight for equal rights and equal citizenship.

And so it was. Every time Martin Luther King, Jr., marched for freedom, protested for the right to vote, paraded across bridges or down Main Streets in the South, every time black and white arms were linked together, every time a demonstration was organized to dramatize Southern oppression to the rest of the country, the First Amendment came to the rescue. Every one of these initiatives was met with resistance, arrests, repression, and censorship. And most of the early court cases that beat back this resistance and gave the civil rights movement room to function and flourish were First Amendment cases.

So it was with more than a little bewilderment that free-speech advocates confronted these new efforts to restrict free speech. Many of them were advocates of equality as well; some were veterans of the civil rights movement who had first learned about the First Amendment in the context of civil rights marches. They saw equality and free speech as mutually reinforcing, twin pillars of a singular value system. For them, free speech was a necessary though far from sufficient precondition of equal rights. And, conversely, equal rights to freedom of speech had always been an integral part of the fight for equality. A wholesome, if not always perfect, marriage.

Now came these new advocates, calling for a divorce. For them, free speech, or at least its excesses, had become an adversary of equality. What the Constitution and the civil rights movement had bound together, they sought to tear asunder.

They posed several interesting questions. If bigots are allowed to use harsh words and epithets to subordinate and marginalize people on the basis of race or sex, doesn't that deny equality? Don't such words wound people? Aren't they intended to wound people? If so, shouldn't such words be considered not speech, but rather an assault, designed to injure, meant to intimidate, intended to deny equal access to public spaces and public benefits? If these messages have little to do with ideas and everything to do with attempts to keep people down, to deny equal citizenship, shouldn't they be treated as torts, as actions that can be prohibited and punished rather than as ideas that should be exchanged and debated? And can't that be done without endangering First Amendment rights more broadly, without opening the door to wider restrictions of whatever a majority—or the government—finds offensive? Aren't we smart enough to make such distinctions?

Certainly the new advocates of speech restrictions thought they were smart enough. They still do. Law professors like Catharine MacKinnon built entire careers constructing elaborate legal theories designed to remedy sexual harassment, curb sexual extortion and discrimination, and reduce the frequency of rape by restricting First Amendment rights. Other law professors, such as Mari Matsuda, Charles Lawrence, and Richard Delgado, made similar arguments with respect to race. Still others, like Thomas Grey, drafted narrow, carefully written speech codes designed to restrict as little "legitimate" speech as possible.

One such code was enacted at Stanford. It was narrower than other campus codes. But even this narrowest of all the campus codes prohibited "insult" on the basis of sex, race, color, handicap, religion, sexual orientation, or national and ethnic origin, defining "insult" to include any words directed at individuals that "by their very utterance inflict injury or tend to incite to an immediate breach of the peace."

These standards, even though much narrower than most of the campus codes passed or advocated during this period, were nonetheless problematic. What would happen if campus police or any government had the power to arrest people for words that "tend to incite to an immediate breach of the peace?" We don't have to speculate. We've had laws like that in the past. Civil rights demonstrators were often arrested and stopped from peaceably parading because the sight of black and white folks marching arm in arm was highly likely to incite white Southerners to immediate violence.

In New York in 1970 anti-war demonstrators were arrested because their views incited construction workers to violence.

And countless people have been arrested for words of protest and peaceful assemblies that incited the police to violence.

In all these cases, the First Amendment was successfully invoked to require the government to protect, not arrest, peaceful protesters. Throughout the South, courts ruled that peaceful parades could not be broken up because people who would be offended might become violent. In the New York case, the police were ordered to curb the violence instead of arresting the targets of the violence.

These cases recognized that it would be disastrous to establish a legal principle that permitted restricting what one person said because of the violent reaction of another person. But that is exactly what the Stanford code did. Those who drafted this standard may have had a very narrow class of insults in their minds, but the language of the code itself was broad and insufficiently defined. As Eleanor Holmes Norton (a black lawyer, veteran of the civil rights movement, former chair of the Equal Employment Opportunity Commission, and now a member of Congress) has said, "It is technically impossible to write an anti-speech code that cannot be twisted against speech nobody means to bar. It has been tried and tried and tried."

Even more dangerous is that part of the Stanford code that blurred the line between action and speech by prohibiting words that "by their very utterance inflict injury."

The mere fact that words are used as an integral part of a crime does not immunize that crime from prosecution. A threatening, midnight phone call is not protected by the First Amendment. Blackmail uses words; extortion uses words; murder threats use words. No one has ever suggested that such crimes are somehow protected by the First Amendment because words are involved. When the chief judge of the New York Court of Appeals was recently indicted and convicted of threatening his former lover and her daughter, no First Amendment defense was available despite the fact that every element of his crimes involved letters or telephone calls, that is, *words*.

But once we get beyond clear threats and intimidations and enter the realm of speech that denigrates or insults or vilifies or causes emotional distress, blurring the line between speech and action becomes dangerous. If such speech is considered to be conduct that, like an assault, can be subject to legal restrictions and punishments, then a great deal of speech we want to protect will be in jeopardy. Although all speech is a form of conduct and all conduct sends a message, generally blurring the legal line between speech and action will necessarily open up large fissures in the First Amendment.

This is a problem that the new advocates of speech restrictions did not address. Nor until recently have their opponents. As Henry Louis

Gates, Jr., points out in this volume, the initial response of many free speech enthusiasts to the new wave of speech restrictions was merely to invoke the First Amendment like a mantra without fully coming to grips with the arguments being made in their behalf.

Primary among these arguments was the notion that words were deeds and could be punished as such. The idea that words are deeds was first articulated in the context of the philosophy of language by Ludwig Wittgenstein. But the transfer of this idea to the world of law and politics is highly problematic. In a seminal 1993 book entitled *"Speech Acts" and the First Amendment,* Frank Haiman, a professor of communications at Northwestern University, deconstructs this idea and provides the most complete analysis and rebuttal yet of the attempt to blur the boundaries between speech and action and between morality and law.

But for at least five years before Haiman's book was published, law reviews were filled with articles constructing the legal and moral foundations for a new jurisprudence that would fundamentally change the First Amendment as we now know it. During this time speech-restrictive codes spread rapidly on college campuses, and gained many enthusiastic followers. In 1993, this movement culminated in two books—*Only Words* by Catharine MacKinnon, and *Words That Wound: Critical Race Theory, Assaultive Speech and The First Amendment* by Mari J. Matsuda, Charles R. Lawrence III, Richard Delgado, and Kimberlè Williams Crenshaw. Taken together, these two books present a strong challenge to First Amendment jurisprudence and to those of us who believe that the principles of free speech and equal rights are mutually dependent partners, not antagonists.

This challenge cannot be met, as Professor Gates says, with sound-bites, one-liners, or the ritualistic invocation of First Amendment homilies. It can be met only through reflective analysis and by taking the arguments of those who favor speech restrictions seriously. For in fact, their arguments provide us with an opportunity to rethink and reexamine why we believe what we do and decide whether there remains a sound basis for our beliefs. This book does that.

The essays that follow cover a lot of ground, in different yet overlapping ways.

Henry Louis Gates, Jr., the W. E. B. DuBois Professor of the Humanities at Harvard University, focuses primarily on the book *Words That*

Wound and critically examines each premise that supports the authors' proposals to restrict racist speech.

Nadine Strossen, my colleague at the American Civil Liberties Union, where she serves as president of the national board of directors, is professor of law at New York Law School. Her essay responds specifically to Charles Lawrence's work and more generally to the many proposals to regulate speech on campus, examining their likely, if unintended, consequences.

Robert C. Post, professor of law at the University of California at Berkeley, begins by stating his commitment to both freedom of expression and to the fight against racism. He focuses on the First Amendment as it relates to the value of democratic self-governance, and sees this value as primarily responsible for the development of First Amendment safeguards. He then assesses the implications of limiting these safeguards in order to ameliorate the harms said to be caused by racist speech.

Donald E. Lively, professor of law at the University of Toledo, criticizes the new advocates of speech restrictions not so much from a First Amendment perspective but rather from the perspective of racial progress. He argues that the "racist speech management strategy" disregards history, does not even address the main sources of stigmatizing speech, and diverts scarce reformist resources away from "the nation's unfinished racial business."

Anthony P. Griffin, a practicing lawyer from Galveston, Texas, recently received wide national publicity for representing local Klansmen in a First Amendment case against the Texas Human Rights Commission, after which he was dismissed from his position as general counsel of the Texas NAACP. He approaches the problem through a series of three fables, mixtures of fact and fiction.

Finally, William B. Rubenstein, an attorney who directs the ACLU's Lesbian and Gay Rights Project, addresses the debate from a lesbian/gay perspective and argues that the First Amendment has been responsible for more progress for lesbians and gay men than the Fourteenth Amendment. Like Professor Lively, but from a highly specific perspective emphasizing the particular problems of "coming out," Rubenstein shows why an interest in equality requires devotion to the First Amendment, and why it is a mistake to pit free speech against equality.

Although these essays make a variety of arguments from a number of different perspectives, one theme seems worth extra amplification. The new advocates for speech restrictions do not desire to suppress social change but rather wish to advance it. Unlike those who arrested abolitionists for advocating an end to slavery or who put Martin Luther King, Jr., in jail to stop him from his campaign to end Jim Crow laws, the new advocates for speech restrictions seek racial justice and claim that carving out exceptions to the First Amendment will advance the cause of equality. Even if they were right, we might argue that sacrificing free speech rights is too high a price to pay, and that other methods must be found. It would not be the first time that the Constitution was judged to be a justifiable obstacle to an otherwise commendable goal.

But if they are not right—if in fact the effort to restrict speech will likely damage the cause of racial justice instead of advancing it—then the harder question of whether it is worth placing the First Amendment at risk in order to advance equality need not be asked.

Moreover, it would be pointless to place free speech in jeopardy if doing so is also likely to damage the effort to achieve equal citizenship. That is precisely the argument William Rubenstein makes with respect to the rights of lesbians and gay men, but it is an argument that is equally powerful, though for somewhat different reasons, with respect to race. This point is made or implied in most of the essays that follow, but it is worth emphasizing, on two levels.

First, the attempt by minorities of any kind—racial, political, religious, sexual—to pass legal restrictions on speech creates a self-constructed trap. It is a trap because politically once you have such restrictions in place the most important questions to ask are: Who is going to enforce them? Who is going to interpret what they mean? Who is going to decide whom to target?

The answer is: those in power. And what possible reason do minorities have to trust those in power? Why should minorities be willing to entrust the majority with the authority to decide who should be allowed to speak? As Donald Lively points out, "First Amendment history indicates a tendency to transform minority protective rules into methodologies that consolidate the dominant group's advantage."

How could it be otherwise? If people in power were deeply hostile to racial injustice, would it continue to exist? Conversely, if people in power are indifferent to racial injustice or responsive to others who are indifferent, why would minorities want to entrust their rights to them?

Recent First Amendment history reinforces Lively's point. Several cases are cited by Nadine Strossen in her essay. Especially notable was a rule adopted by the British National Union of Students in 1974, in part to curb campus anti-Semitism. The rule barred speakers who were "openly racist and fascist." One year later, the rule was invoked to disrupt speeches by Israelis and Zionists on the ground that Zionism was a form of racism.

Similarly, during the year that the University of Michigan speech code was in effect, ostensibly to create a safe harbor for blacks, there were more than twenty cases of whites charging blacks with racist speech, and the only two cases in which the rule actually resulted in punishing racist speech involved speech by or in behalf of blacks. In one of those cases, a black student was punished for using the term "white trash." Is that what the new advocates of speech restrictions had in mind? Not likely.

One can therefore reasonably expect that if a rule is passed allowing a college administration—or the mayor of a city—to ban speakers if they denigrate people based on race or religion or sex, the most frequent targets of such bans are likely to be the very minorities the ban was ostensibly designed to benefit.

Had such laws existed in the late 1950s and early 1960s in the South and been held invulnerable to First Amendment challenge, surely Martin Luther King, Jr., and his colleagues would have been their most frequent victims. And if college codes banning speakers who denigrated people on the basis of race had existed in the early sixties, surely Malcolm X would have been the speaker most often banned.

None of this ought to be surprising, because those in power do not usually represent minorities and are not, when it comes down to hard cases, primarily responsible to minorities. Most university presidents will tend to be responsive to alumni, to donors, and to the majority of students and their parents. Why relatively powerless minorities would want their own speech subject to the permission of those in power is difficult to fathom.

A strong First Amendment is therefore especially important for minorities living in a society where power is not evenly distributed. For minorities, establishing rules that permit the banning of offensive speech is like using poison gas: it cannot be employed against your enemies without having it blown back on you. And in most contexts, those who maintain or tolerate the structures and beliefs of racism have the more powerful fans. They will seize upon the poison gas and blow it back on minorities; they always do. That is why it is politically naive and strategically foolish for minorities ever to support legal restrictions on speech. As Lively says, the risk is not that speech codes will achieve so little for blacks, but that they risk losing so much.

Beyond the strategic importance of maintaining strong free speech rights for minorities, there is the larger question of coming to terms with the persistence of inequality.

The problem that gives rise to this debate in the first instance is not free speech but racial injustice. The free speech problem is derivative: it arises as an imagined remedy for racial injustice.

Taking the new advocates of speech restrictions seriously therefore requires us to bear witness first to the sorry state of racial justice in this country and to evaluate the efficacy of speech restrictions as a remedy. Why have hate speech controversies struck such a chord? To answer this, we must ask ourselves what we find today when we examine the legacy of the civil rights movement.

Forty years after *Brown v. Board of Education,* we are certainly not where we thought we would be by now. In the years following *Brown,* most of us believed that if we could get rid of Jim Crow laws everything would fall into place. We saw racial injustice as the major problem in our country, and we thought we knew how to fix it. Pass laws that strike down discrimination in employment. Pass laws that strike down discrimination in housing. Pass laws that strike down discrimination in public accommodations. Pass laws that end discrimination in voting. Keep appearing before the Supreme Court and persuade the Court to integrate the schools.

Those who were in the forefront of the movement in those days— Martin Luther King, Jr., and his colleagues, for example—caused what William Lloyd Garrison had a century earlier called a "tremendous excitement." That excitement flourished, grew, built throughout the late fifties and the sixties and by 1968, I think it is fair to say, all the legal barriers that supported segregation and that had seemed so impenetrable were struck down. Every legislative goal the civil rights movement had was achieved. As a matter of law, the Supreme Court had buried state-sanctioned discrimination. "Segregation now, segregation tomorrow, segregation forever," George Wallace's defiant cry of 1963, had been put to rest, at least as a matter of law. For the first time since Reconstruction, a broad range of federal antidiscrimination statutes was in place. A comprehensive legal framework for fighting discrimination existed.

But twenty-five years later, although all those laws are still in place and although significant numbers of African Americans enjoy equal citizenship and opportunity, severe racial stratification remains and seems in many ways much worse. The legal remedies in which we placed so much faith seem unable to address this stratification.

We thought that all we needed to do was decide whether or not segregation was right, whether it was legal, and once we had decided that correctly, and persuaded Congress and the courts, the problem would begin to fix itself. But it has not fixed itself. Legal barriers have been broken down. Jim Crow is long dead. But subjugation, subordination, and racial stratification remain. And we are still far from the time when where you live and how well you live, where you go to school and if you go to school, whether you are employed and what kind of a job you have, or whether you have access to medical care is not correlated with the color of your skin.

We thought back then that if we declared discrimination illegal, then the racial stratification of rights and benefits would disappear. But it hasn't. Whether you are in prison, whether you are in foster care, whether you are suspended from school, whether you have health insurance—all depend disproportionately on the color of your skin. Despite the substantial gains of the civil rights movement a generation ago, it turned out that American history was not so easily remedied. As Dante knew, full redemption is more painful and will certainly take longer than any of us imagined.

During the eighties, things got worse, not better. Inequality widened, and we endured a period of economic contraction. Poverty is not thought by many to be a civil rights problem, but poverty is not randomly distributed, and we need to ask ourselves why that is so.

In a city like New York, for example, 80 percent of the poor are black and Latino. Fifty percent of all black and Latino kids are born poor. Housing for the poor is often like a war zone. People stay inside because bullets are flying. And even that doesn't always help. When you look at the faces of the children who live under such conditions they look like the faces of children in war.

We see 50 to 70 percent failure rates among children of color in many of our urban schools. At a time and in an era when education is a prerequisite for economic mobility, this is an economic death sentence, a fatal barrier to equal opportunity. Fewer than 20 percent of black men between the ages of eighteen and twenty-four are in college; indeed, there are more young black men in prison than in college. And fully one in four are under the jurisdiction of the criminal justice system.

The unemployment rate for young blacks approached 40 percent at the dawn of the nineties. It was only 18 percent for the same age group of whites. We imprison 1,100 blacks per 100,000 population. This rate compares only with South Africa—and in fact is worse than South Africa. While we imprisoned 1,100 blacks per 100,000 population, the figure for whites was 164. The leading cause of death among young black men is homicide, while among young whites it is only the fourth. Half of all the homicide victims in this country are black.

Much of this situation is due to government policies and programs, or the lack of programs.

Consider our drug policies, for example. In many respects, drug trafficking is the predominant economic opportunity program we offer ghetto youth, with the possible exception of the military. How is this related to government policy? As increasing numbers of Americans have come to understand, the government's policy of prohibition establishes and maintains an illicit market that functions as a financial lure for young people, especially young people without other opportunities. It is an engine for crime and violence. Homicide rates are so high predominately because of our drug policies. Al Capone did not shoot people because he was drunk, and drug dealers do not shoot people because they are high on cocaine or heroin. Turf wars are a feature of ghetto life and the reason why housing is a war zone. Bystander shootings are an epidemic now. In one recent year, thirty-five children were killed in New York City, some in their beds, by bullets flying through the streets or bursting through windows and walls. When people are forced to settle commercial disputes with automatic weapons on the street, that's what happens. If Schenley's and Seagram have a price war or a jurisdictional dispute, they don't shoot each other, they hire advertising agencies or lawyers. But when cocaine dealers have a price war or a jurisdictional dispute, bullets fly and the innocent get shot. And the innocent are usually not white.

Imprisonment rates are also directly related to drug arrests. The predominant reason for the explosive rise in imprisonment are drug-related arrests. There are 1.2 million drug arrests now a year. When Richard Nixon started his war on drugs there were 200,000 arrests a year. Have those additional arrests made us safer or reduced the illicit trafficking in drugs? No. But they have decimated the population of young black males.

According to the FBI, only 12 percent of drug dealers and drug users are black, which is exactly their proportion in the population. But nearly 40 percent of all drug arrests are black. That's up from only 30 percent a few years ago. In one state recently, drug arrests in general doubled over the last five years but drug arrests for blacks tripled. How is it that if blacks constitute only 12 percent of users and dealers, they constitute such a high proportion of arrests? It is probably not because cops are looking to arrest blacks; rather it is because they arrest the people who are easy to arrest, the ones who are visible on the street. It is the same reason that street prostitutes get arrested while expensive call girls inside fancy townhouses do not. And the street prostitutes are predominately women of color, while the expensive call girls are predominately white. Similarly, street dealers are predominately people of color, and they get arrested at high rates (and sentenced to disproportionately long terms). But during the eighties not too many people were arrested in stock brokerage houses on Wall Street or in Hollywood or at universities, even though drug dealing was not uncommon in all these places. Disproportionate arrests were made in places like central Harlem and the mean streets of Bedford-Stuyvesant and the South Bronx, and people were rounded up on the street because they were easy to see and easy to bust. And those are the people who end up in prison.

Another consequence of our policy of prohibition has been to criminalize efforts to use or give out clean needles to drug users. A major way in which AIDS spreads today is through intravenous drug use. But in many American jurisdictions it is a crime to give out clean needles. In Amsterdam, where clean needles are given out by the government, the proportion of intravenous drug users who carry the AIDS virus is about 9 percent. In the United States, as of 1991, it was 26 percent, and in a city like New York it was over 60 percent. A disproportionate number of those are not white. When you look at who is being killed by our bans on clean needles; when you look at who's being disproportionately imprisoned; when you look at the faces of the victims of bystander shootings; when you understand the degree to which most of those results are functions of official government policies, you begin to grasp the evil that is abroad in this land. When people ask where are the young black men, when they want to know why they're not in college, the answers are dreadfully clear: it is because they're dead on the streets, it is because they're in prison cells, it is because they are dying of AIDS. And so much of this is the consequence of our social policies, a terrible web of state action and inaction. "Genocide" is not a word that should be used lightly, or as a metaphor, but when one looks at all these phenomena taken together, it becomes very hard to avoid the word.

Consider our health policies. There was an article in the *Washington Post* in 1991 that reviewed a series of diseases that nobody dies from anymore. Things like appendicitis, bronchitis, asthma, gallbladder disease, hypertension, hernias, normal pneumonias. Between 1980 and 1986 only 122,000 people died from those diseases. But 80 percent of them were black. That wasn't because of their genes. Dr. George Lumberg, the editor in chief of the *Journal of the American Medical Association*, wrote an editorial at that time in which he said that race was the predominant link in these kinds of statistics. He said that while over thirty million people in this country don't have health insurance, disproportionate numbers of them are not white. He said that because health insurance was the major means of access to health care in this country, and because the availability of health insurance is linked to employment, those who are disproportionately unemployed also disproportionately lack health insurance, and therefore don't have adequate access to medical care.

In that same year, the National Cancer Institute reported that poverty was the cause of the high cancer rate among blacks. The Institute concluded that it was a combination of bad nutrition, terrible living conditions, and lack of access to medical care that was causing more cancer to develop and less of it to be treated in time. Those conditions are also in substantial part functions of public policy.

We don't seem to have a national commitment to do anything about these problems. Fewer than 30 percent of the people in this country, according to a recent poll, think that there is any remaining inequality in our society that needs to be remedied by laws or public programs. The moral urgency, the sense of consensus that developed in the late fifties and sixties and that led to the passage of civil rights laws is gone. The sense of moral urgency is dissipated, as it was after Reconstruction. And as the dissipation then was heavily due to the nature of political leadership at the time, so the problem now has resulted heavily from the kind of leadership we have had. More than a dozen years of retrogressive national leadership convinced people that the playing field is level, and that if there is inequality it is the fault of those who are unequal. Now when we seek equal rights and remedies we are told that it is the blacks who have special privileges and the whites who are the victims. A whole generation of young people has grown up believing that. When we analyze the nature of racial bigotry among college students today, we must realize that they were four or five years old when Ronald Reagan took office, and they have come to political consciousness during a political time not unlike the late nineteenth century. They come to the campus with all this baggage, and if you ask them about affirmative action many will say that they and their parents worked hard for what they have and the black kids got here because of special privilege. And they believe it. A generation that believes this is not a generation prepared to recognize the problems I have described, much less deal effectively with them.

We do not lack money. We were prepared to spend a billion dollars a day to vanquish Saddam Hussein. We lack political will. But it is more than a lack of political will. It is an affirmative political backlash on the question of racial justice. We need something akin to a Marshall Plan. We need finally to recognize what was done to African slaves and their descendants in this country, and that the remedy is going to take far, far more than passing a few civil rights laws or formally ending Jim Crow.

But in order to recognize our obligations, we are going to have to create a constituency for change. We are going to have to create a constituency of morality. We are going to have to create a constituency that first comes to recognize these problems and then comes to find that they are intolerable. We are a long way from creating that constituency. We have to create what Garrison called a "tremendous excitement." And that means we have to act not only as lawyers and lobbyists but also as activists and missionaries. We have to get out there and send that message. Right now, it is a message few Americans believe. As long as that continues, our racial problems will remain unaddressed.

It is in the light of these daunting and urgent problems that one must evaluate the movement to restrict bigoted speech. The new advocates of speech restrictions are moved by the persistence of inequality and frustrated by the stamina of bigotry. But can they be serious when they suggest that if only we could repress college students and skinheads from *voicing* bigotry, we could reduce bigotry itself? Can they be serious about addressing the persistence of inequality when they devote so much energy and talent to drafting speech codes? Can anyone seriously believe that we can once again cause a tremendous moral excitement in this country, recapture a sense of moral urgency, create a constituency for change and actually do something about racially stratified social and economic inequities by focusing on racial epithets?

In the end, people do what they know how to do. The police respond to complex social problems with arrests, while the problems that generate crime remain largely unaddressed. I sometimes think that if architects were writing about racial inequalities, they would be telling us to build buildings. And so law professors are writing speech-restrictive laws, when so much more is needed.

The most damning critique of the new movement to restrict speech is finally not that it endangers the First Amendment, which it does, but that it diverts us all from meaningfully addressing the fundamental problems of racial injustice. Claiming to be motivated and energized by an intolerance for inequality, the new advocates for speech restrictions in fact have diverted themselves and others away from the central problems. Worried about being marginalized, they have chosen to fight on the outermost margins, focusing precious assets, media attention, and public awareness on an issue of little tangible relevance to the social realities of those whom they hope to help.

Professor Lively puts it bluntly when he says, "Given the broad contours and consequences of racism that await reckoning, attention to a relatively narrow slice of racist injury betrays a poor distribution of reformist resources." The agenda of those who seek to restrict racist speech, he charges, "seems framed largely from tenured faculty positions and academic halls where intellectual output may be more the grist for publishing mills than an engaged concern with real world disadvantages. Given its limited objectives and tortuous theory, the strategy seems better structured to impress and provoke colleagues than to effect real change. . . . [R]acist speech management," he concludes, "effectively conspires with the established order by demanding cosmetic change rather than a reshuffling of the cards of power."

And that, in the end, delivers the most telling blow to the new advocates of speech restrictions. They are certainly no friends of free speech; ironically, they aren't effective warriors for equality either.

1. War of Words: Critical Race Theory and the First Amendment

Henry Louis Gates, Jr.

As a thumbnail summary of the last two or three decades of speech issues in the Supreme Court, we may come to see the Negro as winning back for us the freedoms the Communists seemed to have lost for us.
—Harry Kalven, Jr., *The Negro and the First Amendment* (1965)

Writing in the heyday of the civil rights era, the great First Amendment scholar Harry Kalven, Jr., was confident that civil rights and civil liberties were marching in unison; that their mutual expansion represented, for a nation in a time of tumult, an intertwined destiny. He might have been surprised had he lived to witness the shifting nature of their relations. For today, the partnership named in the title of his classic study seems in hopeless disrepair: civil liberties are regarded by many as a chief obstacle to civil rights. To be sure, blacks are still on the front lines of First Amendment jurisprudence, only this time we soldier on the other side. The byword among many black activists and intellectuals is no longer the political imperative to protect free speech, but the moral imperative to suppress hate speech. And therein hangs a tale.

Like phrases such as "pro-choice" and "pro-life," the phrase "hate speech" is ideology in spansule form. It is the term-of-art of a movement—most active on college campuses and liberal municipalities—that has caused many civil rights activists to rethink their allegiance to the First Amendment, the amendment that licensed the protests, rallies, organization, and agitation that so galvanized the nation in a bygone era. Addressing the concerns of a very different era, the "hate speech" movement has enlisted the energies of some of our most engaged and interesting legal scholars. The result has been the proliferation of campus speech codes as well as municipal statutes enhancing penalties for bias crimes. Equally important, however, the movement has also provided an opportunity for those of us outside it to clarify and rethink the meaning of our commitment to freedom of expression.

It is an opportunity we have miserably bungled. Because we are content with soundbites and one-liners, our political deliberation on the subject has had all the heft of a Jay Leno monologue. Free speech? Perhaps you get what you pay for.

What makes this ironic is that if America has a civic religion today, the First Amendment may be its central credo. "It's a free country," we shrug, and what we usually mean is: you can say what you please. "Sticks and stones can break my bones," we are taught to chant as children, "but words can never hurt me." Americans "are taught this view by about the fourth grade, and continue to absorb it through osmosis from everything around them for the rest of their lives," Catharine MacKinnon writes with no little asperity in *Only Words,* her latest and most accessible book, "to the point that those who embrace it think it is their own personal faith, their own original view, and trot it out like something learned from their own personal lives every time a problem is denominated one of 'speech,' whether it really fits or not."

The strongest argument for regulating hate speech is the unreflective stupidity of most of the arguments you hear on the other side. I do not refer to the debate as it has proceeded in the law reviews: there you find a quality of caution, clarity, and tentativeness that has made few inroads into the larger public discourse. Regrettably enough, those law professors who offer the best analysis of public discourse exert very little influence *within* public discourse. And that leaves us with a now familiar stalemate. On the one hand are those who speak of "hate speech," a phrase that alludes to an argument without revealing anything much about it; to insist on probing further is to admit, fearsomely, that you just "don't get it." On the other hand are their opponents who invoke the First Amendment like a mantra and seem immediately to fall into a trance, so oblivious are they to further argumentation and evidence. A small number of anecdotes, either about racism on campus or about "politically correct" (PC) inquisitions on campus, are endlessly recycled: and a University of Pennsylvania undergraduate named Eden Jacobowitz—yes, he of "water buffalo" fame—becomes a Dreyfuss *de nos jours.*

There's a practical reason to worry about how impoverished the national discourse on free speech has become. For if we keep losing the arguments, in time we may lose our grip on the liberties they were meant to defend. We may come to think that our bad arguments are the only arguments to be made, and when someone finally disabuses us of them, we may switch sides without ever considering other and better arguments for staying put.

To get an appreciation of these arguments, though, we must be prepared to go beyond where the water buffalo roam. For all the pleasures of demonology, the burgeoning literature urging the regulation of racist speech has a serious claim on our attention. The time has come to accord these arguments the full consideration they deserve.

Conveniently enough, *Words That Wound: Critical Race Theory, Assaultive Speech, and the First Amendment* collects the three most widely cited and influential papers to make the case for the regulation of racist speech. (The collection also reprints a provocative essay by UCLA's Kimberlè Williams Crenshaw, though one whose principal concerns—about the conflicting allegiances posed by race and gender—place it beyond the ambit of this discussion.) Gathered together for the first time, these three papers—which originally appeared in law reviews over the past several years, only to circulate even more widely through the samizdat of the photocopier—complement each other surprisingly well. Though each makes larger arguments as well, one proposal focuses on criminal law, another focuses on civil law, and a third focuses on campus speech codes.

The authors of these proposals are "minority" law professors who teach at mainstream institutions—Mari J. Matsuda and Charles R. Lawrence III at Georgetown, Richard Delgado at the University of Colorado—and who write vigorous and accessible prose; their collected contributions cannot but elevate the level of discourse on the topic. They are, one can fairly say, the legal eagles of the crusade against racist hate speech.

But they are also, as the subtitle of the collections suggests, the principal architects of "critical race theory," one of the most widely discussed trends in the contemporary legal academy; and their jointly written introduction to the volume serves as the clearest manifesto it has yet received. Here the "social origins" of critical race theory are traced to a 1981 student boycott of a Harvard Law School course on "Race, Racism, and American Law." Organizing an informal alternative course, students invited lawyers and law professors of color to lecture weekly on the topic. Crenshaw was one of the student organizers of the alternative course, Matsuda one of its participants; Delgado and Lawrence were among its guest lecturers. And thus was formed the nucleus of "a small but growing group of scholars committed to finding new ways to think about and act in pursuit of racial justice."

The intellectual ancestry of the movement is complex, but its two main progenitors are, on the one hand, the particular brand of feminist theory associated with Catharine MacKinnon (like that of Marx, the name of MacKinnon designates a body of argument that can no longer be distinguished from a political movement) and, on the other, the radical skepticism toward traditional black-letter pieties associated with "critical legal studies." Almost invariably, the literature arguing for hate speech regulation cites MacKinnon as an authority and model; almost invariably, the literature takes on one or more of the traditional legal distinctions (such as that between "private" and "public") whose dismantling—though often pioneered by the legal realists—is a repertory staple in critical legal studies.

So it is no surprise that conservative pundits like George Will denounce these theorists of hate speech as faddish foes of freedom. In fact, we would more accurately describe their approach as neotraditional. And those conservatives who dream of turning the cultural clock back to the fifties should realize that the First Amendment law of those years is just what these supposedly faddish scholars wish to revive. That much should suggest something amiss about our rhetoric concerning our First Amendment "traditions." And therein hangs another tale.

The conventional defense of free speech absolutism—the kind your uncle bangs on about—rests upon three pillars, all pretty thoroughly rotted through. Dr. Johnson thought he could refute Bishop Berkeley by kicking a stone, and armchair absolutists, to begin with, often think they can win debates through the self-evident authority of the First Amendment itself. The invocation is generally folded together with a vague sort of historical argument. The First Amendment, we are told, has stood us in good stead through the more than two centuries of this great republic; quite possibly, our greatness depends on it. The framers knew what they were doing, and—this directed to those inclined to bog down in interpretative quibbles—at the end of the day, *the First Amendment means what it says.*

This is a dependable and well-rehearsed argument whose only flaw is that it happens to be entirely false and nobody ever believed it anyway. Indeed, the notion that the First Amendment has been a historical mainstay of American liberty is a paradigm instance of invented tradition. To begin with, the First Amendment, conceived as protecting the free speech of citizens, did not exist until 1931.[1] Before then, the Court took the amendment at its word: "*Congress* shall make no law..." Congress couldn't; but states and municipalities could do what they liked. Given this background, it shouldn't surprise us that even once the Supreme Court recognized freedom of expression as a right held by citizens, the interpretation of its scope remained quite narrow (notwithstanding such landmark cases as Learned Hand's opinion in *Masses Publishing* in 1917 and the Supreme Court's 1937 decision in *DeJonge v. Oregon*) until after World War II, when the Warren Court gradually ushered in a more generous vision of civil liberties. So the expansive First Amendment that people either celebrate or bemoan is really only a few decades old.

And even the Court's most expansive interpretation of First Amendment protection has always come with a list of exceptions, such as libel, invasion of privacy, and obscenity. "Categorization" is the legal buzzword for deciding whether expression is protected by determining which category the expression falls into—having first determined whether it qualifies as expression at all. While speech may be a species of conduct, much in case law still hangs on whether conduct (say, nude dancing in South Bend, Indiana, to allude to a case the Supreme Court decided a couple of years ago) will be allowed to count as expression for First Amendment purposes. Various refinements on the test have been proposed. To John Hart Ely, for example, the question for judicial scrutiny shouldn't be whether something is expression or conduct, for everything is both, but whether it is the expressive dimension of the speech-conduct amalgam that has provoked its prosecution. One may suspect that this refinement merely defers the difficulty of distinguishing. At the very least, Catharine MacKinnon's position—which extends no particular protection to "expression" over "conduct"—has the advantage of coherence. (More proof that in the real world, theoretical coherence is an overrated virtue.)

In their categorizing mode, the courts have also respected a general hierarchy of protected speech, such that political speech is deemed worthy of significant protection while commercial speech is highly subject to regulation. But even political speech is subject to the old clear-and-present danger exemption and a cluster of variants. To venture into murkier waters, the issue of speech management arises in the highly contested matter of "public forum": where may one exercise these supposedly valuable rights of free speech? How much (if any) access to these forums will we enjoy? And this isn't even to consider the unbounded array of criminal and civil offenses that are enacted through expression. As Frederick Schauer, Stanton Professor of the First Amendment at Harvard University, has observed, absolute protection would make unconstitutional "all of contract law, most of antitrust law, and much of criminal law." In view of this brambly legal landscape, to invoke the First Amendment as if it settled anything by itself can sound very much like know-nothingism.

When the myth of the self-justifying First Amendment is put aside, armchair absolutists are left with two fallback arguments. Dredging up childhood memories, they come up with that playground chant about sticks and stones. Offensive expression should be protected because it is costless, "only words." But if words really were inert, we wouldn't invest so much in their protection; it is a vacuous conception of expressive liberty that is predicated upon the innocuousness of its exercise. "Every idea is an incitement," Justice Holmes famously wrote, albeit in dissent. In his recent history of obscenity law, Edward de Grazia tells of an especially sad and instructive example of the power of words to cause harm. Evidently the heated rhetoric of Catharine MacKinnon's 1984 campaign for an anti-pornography ordinance in Minneapolis moved one young supporter to douse herself with gasoline and set herself afire. Porno for pyros indeed.

This leaves us with the armchair absolutists' Old Reliable: the slippery-slope argument. Perhaps racist speech is hurtful and without value, they will concede, but tolerating it is the price we must pay to ensure the protection of other, beneficial, and valuable speech. The picture here is that if we take one step down from the mountain peak of expressive freedom, we'll slide down to the valley of expressive tyranny. But a more accurate account of where we currently stand is somewhere halfway up the side of the mountain; we already are, and always were, on that

slippery slope. And its very slipperiness is why First Amendment jurisprudence is so strenuous, why the struggle for traction is so demanding.

I should be clear. Slippery-slopism isn't worthless as a consideration:
because the terrain is slippery we *ought* to step carefully. And there are
many example of "wedge" cases that have led to progressive restrictions
in civil liberties. (For example, *Bowers v. Hardwick,* the 1986 case
in which the Supreme Court affirmed the constitutionality of statutes
prohibiting private, consensual sex between men, has since been invoked
in over one hundred state and federal court decisions denying the right
to privacy.) Even so, slippery-slopism sounds better in the abstract than
in the particular. For one thing, courts often must balance conflicting
rights—as with "hostile environment" cases of work-place harassment.
For another, we do not always know immediately if the step taken will
ultimately lead us downhill or up—as with William Brennan's decision
in *Roth v. United States,* which affirmed Stanley Roth's conviction for
publishing an Aubrey Beardsley book and declared obscenity to be
utterly without redeeming value. The wording of that decision, however
unpromising at first glance, turned out to be a boon for the civil libertarian position.

But the hate speech movement hasn't been content with exposing the
sort of weaknesses I've just rehearsed. It has also aligned itself with
earlier traditions of jurisprudence—and it's here that the movement's
seeming atavism is most clearly displayed—by showing that the sort of
speech it wishes to restrict falls into two expressive categories that the
Supreme Court has previously held (and, they argue, correctly so) to be
undeserving of First Amendment protection. The categories are those of
fighting words and group defamation, as exemplified by two cases decided in 1942 and 1952.

It is out of respect for the prerogative of "categorization" that critical
race theorists root their model of assaultive speech in the Supreme Court
opinion of *Chaplinsky v. New Hampshire* (1942), which bequeathed us
the "fighting words" doctrine. Chaplinsky was a Jehovah's Witness who
was convicted for calling a city marshall a "God damned racketeer" and
"a damned Fascist." The statute he violated forbade one to address
"any offensive, derisive or annoying word to any other person" in a
public place.

Affirming the conviction, the Court held that "there are certain well-defined and narrowly limited classes of speech, the prevention and punishment of which have never been thought to raise any Constitutional problem." Among them were "the insulting or 'fighting' words—those which by their very utterance inflict injury or tend to incite an immediate breach of the peace." "Such utterances are no essential part of any exposition of ideas," Justice Murphy wrote for the majority, "and are of such slight social value as a step to truth that any benefit that may be derived from them is clearly outweighed by the social interest in order and morality."

The Court's reference to those words "which by their very utterance inflict injury" is especially cherished by the hate-speech movement, for it seems to presage its account of "assaultive speech," or words that wound. In accord with *Chaplinsky,* critical race theorists emphasize the immediate and visceral harms incurred by hate speech. "Many victims of hate propaganda have experienced physiological and emotional symptoms, such as rapid pulse rate and difficulty in breathing," Charles R. Lawrence writes. Mari J. Matsuda has even more alarming findings to report: "Victims of vicious hate propaganda experience physiological symptoms and emotional distress ranging from fear in the gut to rapid pulse rate and difficulty in breathing, nightmares, post-traumatic stress disorder, hypertension, psychosis, and suicide." And Richard Delgado further notes that the psychic injuries incurred by racist speech have additional costs down the road: "The person who is timid, withdrawn, bitter, hypertense, or psychotic will almost certainly fare poorly in employment settings." (As a member of the Harvard faculty, I would venture there are exceptions to this rule.)

But *Chaplinsky* has other useful elements, too. Thus the approach entailed by the Court's conclusion that such words as the Jehovah's Witness uttered "are no essential part of any exposition of ideas" has also been pressed into service. It shows up in the insistence that racist speech has no content, that it is more like a blunt instrument than a vehicle of thought. "The racial invective is experienced as a blow, not a proffered idea," Lawrence writes.

By contrast, the "fighting words" prong of the Chaplinsky test—specifying words likely to incite an immediate breach of the peace—has been widely condemned for bias: why should those persons (women, for example) who are less likely to strike back physically be less protected from abuse? For this reason, Lawrence in effect urges an expansion of the fighting words doctrine, arguing that racist speech (which may silence its victims, rather than provoking them to violence) should be understood as the "functional equivalent of fighting words," and thus equally unworthy of First Amendment protection.

The hate speech movement's deployment of *Chaplinsky* is certainly within the pale of standard legal argument; indeed, the carefully drafted speech code adopted by Stanford University explicitly extends only to "fighting words" or symbols, thus wearing its claim to constitutionality on its face. So if *Chaplinsky* can shoulder the legal and ethical burdens placed upon it, the regulationists have a powerful weapon on their side. Can it?

Probably not. To begin with, it's an open question whether *Chaplinsky* remains, as they say, "good law," given that in the fifty years since its promulgation the Supreme Court would never once affirm a conviction for uttering either "fighting words" or words that "by their very utterance inflict injury." Indeed, in part because of its functional desuetude, in part because of the male bias of the "breach of the peace" prong, the editors of the *Harvard Law Review* have recently issued a call for the doctrine's explicit interment. So much for the doctrine's judicial value.

But they also note, as others have, that statutes prohibiting "fighting words" have had discriminatory effects. An apparently not atypical conviction—upheld by the Louisiana state court—was occasioned by the following exchange between a white police officer and the black mother of a young suspect. He: "Get your black ass in the goddamned car." She: "You god damn mother fucking police—I am going to [the Superintendent of Police] about this." No prize for guessing which one was convicted for uttering "fighting words." As the legal scholar Kenneth Karst reports, "[S]tatues proscribing abusive words are applied to members of racial and political minorities more frequently than can be wholly explained by any special proclivity of those people to speak abusively." So much for the doctrine's political value.

Nor, finally, does the *Chaplinsky*-derived description of assaultive speech as being devoid of political or other ideational content—"experienced as a blow, not a proffered idea," in Lawrence's compelling formulation—survive closer inspection. Consider the incident that, Lawrence tells us, moved him to take up the hate speech cause in the first place. Two white Stanford freshmen had an argument with a black student about Beethoven's ancestry: he claimed, and they denied, that the Flemish-German composer was really of African descent. The next evening, apparently as a satirical commentary, the white students acquired a poster of Beethoven, colored it in with Sambo-like features, and posted it on the door of the student's dorm room at Ujamaa, Stanford's black theme house. Lawrence "experienced the defacement as representative of the university community's racism and not as an exceptional incident in a community in which the absence of racism is the rule"—and the rest is critical-race-theory history.

Now then, is Lawrence's paradigm example of racist hate speech in fact devoid of ideational or political content, as his analysis would suggest? Evidently not, for in their jointly written manifesto for critical race theory, the authors of *Words That Wound* spell out what they believe its message to have been: "The message said, 'This is you. This is you and all of your African-American brothers and sisters. You are all Sambos. It's a joke to think that you could ever be a Beethoven. It's ridiculous to believe that you could ever be anything other than a caricature of real genius.' " The defaced poster would also inspire a lengthy and passionate essay by the legal theorist Patricia J. Williams, an essay that extracts an even more elaborated account of its meaning. This was one picture, clearly, that really was worth a thousand words.

The same paradox surfaces in Richard Delgado's ground-breaking proposal for a tort action to redress racist speech. To define this tort, he must distinguish offensive racist speech from offensive political speech; for in *Cohen v. California* (1971), the Supreme Court decided that a jacket emblazoned with the words "Fuck the Draft" and worn in a courthouse would be protected as political speech, despite its patent offensiveness. Delgado argues that a racial insult, by contrast, "is not political speech; its perpetrator intends not to discover truth or advocate social action, but to injure the victim." It's a curious disjunction, this, between advocacy and injury. For if Delgado and his fellow contributors have a central message to impart, it's that racial insults are profoundly political, part of a larger mechanism of social subordination, and thus in contravention of the spirit of the "equal protection" clause of the Fourteenth Amendment. And the most harmful forms of racist speech are precisely those that combine injury with advocacy—those that are, in short, the most "political."

"Are racial insults ideas?" Lawrence asks. "Do they encourage wide-open debate?" He means the question to be rhetorical, but after reading his work and those of his fellow critical race theorists, who could possibly doubt it?

Even if we finally reject the picture of assaultive speech as empty of political content, along with the other tenets of the *Chaplinsky* doctrine, the hate-speech movement can still link itself to constitutional precedent through the alternative model of defamation. Indeed, I would argue that the defamation model is more central, more weight-bearing in these arguments than the assaultive one. And note that these *are* alternatives, not just different ways of describing the same thing. The "fighting words"/"assaultive speech" paradigm analogizes racist expression to physical assault: at its simplest, it characterizes an act of aggression between two individuals, victim and victimizer. By contrast, the defamation paradigm analogizes racist speech to libel, a dignitary affront. The harm is essentially social: to be defamed is to be defamed in the eyes of other people.

Here, the guiding precedent is Justice Frankfurter's majority opinion in the 1952 case of *Beauharnais v. Illinois,* in which the Court upheld a conviction under an Illinois group libel ordinance. The ordinance was clumsily written, but it essentially prohibited public expression that "portrays depravity, criminality, unchastity, or lack of virtue in a class of citizens of any race, color, creed, or religion," thereby exposing them to "contempt, derision, or obloquy." Mr. Beauharnais ran afoul of the ordinance when he circulated a leaflet that urged whites to unite against the menace posed by their black fellow citizens.

Preserve and Protect White Neighborhoods! from the constant and continuous invasion, harassment and encroachment by the Negroes. . . . The white people of Chicago must take advantage of the opportunity to be united. If persuasion and the need to prevent the white race from being mongrelized by the Negro will not unite us, then the aggressions, rapes, robberies, knives, guns, and marijuana of the Negro surely will.

So averred Mr. Beauharnais, and it was the last sentence, specifying the Negro's offenses, that was held to violate the law. In Justice Frankfurter's opinion: "If an utterance directed at an individual may be the object of criminal sanctions we cannot deny to a state power to punish the same utterance directed at a defined group," at least as long as the restriction is related to the peace and well-being of the state.

To be sure, *Beauharnais v. Illinois* has since fallen into judicial disrepute, having been reversed in its particulars by subsequent cases like the celebrated *Sullivan v. New York Times.* Indeed, more widely cited than Justice Frankfurter's opinion is Justice Hugo Black's dissent: "If there be minority groups who hail this holding as their victory, they might consider the possible relevancy of this ancient remark: 'Another such victory and I am undone.' " And yet Frankfurter's claim for the congruence of individual and group libel is not, on the face of it, implausible. One could argue (as MacKinnon does) that this precedent is deserving of revival—or, more elaborately (as Lawrence does), that it was never truly reversed, because the notion of group libel tacitly underlies and sponsors more prestigious Supreme Court precedents.

Thus MacKinnon, in *Only Words,* deplores the celebrated *Sullivan* case for undermining the vitality, and superior virtue, of *Beauharnais v. Illinois.* "This arrangement avoids the rather obvious reality that groups are made up of individuals," she writes. "In reality, libel of groups multiplies rather than avoids the very same damage through reputation which the law of individual libel recognizes when done one at a time, as well as inflicting some of its own. . . . The idea seems to be that injury to one person is legally actionable, but the same injury to thousands of people is protected speech." Where's the justice in that? MacKinnon would thus revive the state's winning argument in *Beauharnais:* "[P]etitioner cannot gain constitutional protection from the consequence of libel by multiplying victims and identifying them by a collective term." (A similar argument was elaborated in a classic defense of group defamation laws written by none other than David Riesman during his brief career as a law professor.)

And the plausibility of this simple but powerful idea is what has made it so attractive to theorists of hate speech. As Mari J. Matsuda writes movingly:

When the legal mind understands that reputational interests . . . must be balanced against first amendment interests, it recognizes the concrete reality of what happens to people who are defamed. Their lives are changed. Their standing in the community, their opportunities, their self-worth, their free enjoyment of life are limited. Their political capital—their ability to speak and be heard—is diminished. To see this, and yet to fail to see that the very same things happen to the victims of racist speech, is selective vision.

The defamation model plays an even more central role in Lawrence's analysis. He argues that *Brown v. Board of Education*, decided just two years after *Beauharnais*, is best interpreted as a "case about group defamation. The message of segregation was stigmatizing to Black children. . . . *Brown* reflects the understanding that racism is a form of subordination that achieves its purpose through group defamation." Indeed, Lawrence seems to move close to the position that *all* racism is essentially to be understood as defamation. And he protests that "there has not yet been a satisfactory retraction of the government-sponsored defamation in the slavery clauses, the Dred Scott decision, the Black codes, the segregation statutes, and countless *other group libels*" (italics are mine).

Let's leave aside for the moment Lawrence's intriguing reinterpretation of legal history. What's wrong with the basic claim here, one endorsed by judges and scholars across the ideological spectrum, that group libel is just individual libel multiplied?

As I say, we should grant that the claim has prima facie plausibility. And yet the very case of *Beauharnais* illustrates the attendant difficulties. For while Mr. Beauharnais's racism is everywhere in evidence, it's actually unclear what charge is being made in the one sentence of his leaflet that was found to be libelous. That is, the accusation about the "aggressions" and so forth of the Negro need not obtain about any particular Negro; and nobody claimed that *no* Negro was guilty of such misdeeds as he enumerated. Since the Sedition Act of 1798, truth has been allowed as a defense in American libel law. But the Illinois ordinance nowhere mentions the question of truth or falsity, and we might think it odd, even insulting, if it did. (At his trial, Mr. Beauharnais offered to prove the truth of his allegations by introducing evidence about the higher incidence of crime in black districts; his offer was declined.) And this points us toward the significant disanalogy between group and individual libel.

Start with the notion that individual libel involves the publication of information about someone that is both damaging and false. Charles Lawrence inadvertently directs us to the source of the problem. The racial epithet, he writes, "is invoked as an assault, not as a statement of fact that may be proven true or false." But that suggests that the evaluative judgments that are characteristic of racial invective do not lend themselves to factual verification, and here the comparison with individual libel breaks down. The same problem emerges when MacKinnon identifies pornography as group defamation whose message is (roughly) that it would be nice if women were available for sexual exploitation; for a proposition of that form may be right or wrong, but it cannot be true or false. The conclusion Lawrence draws is that racist speech is a form of defamation immune from the *Sullivan* rule protecting statements of fact that are later discovered to be erroneous. A more obvious conclusion to reach would be that racist invective isn't best understood as an extension of individual libel at all. You cannot libel someone by saying "I despise you," which seems to be the essential message common to most racial epithets.

Delgado himself, whose essay was published earliest, offers further reasons to reject the defamation model that colleagues like Lawrence, Matsuda, and MacKinnon find so attractive. As he notes: "A third party who learned that a person was the victim of a racial insult, but did not know the victim, would probably conclude that the victim is a member of a particular racial minority. But if this conclusion is true, the victim cannot recover [under defamation law] because no falsehood has occurred. And whether or not the conclusion is true, it is not desirable that the law view membership in a racial minority as damaging to a person's reputation, even if some members of society consider it so."

I think we may fairly conclude, then, that *Beauharnais* is best left undisturbed in its slumbers, and that the model of group libel founders on the flawed analogy to individual libel. "Nigger" (used in the vocative) is not helpfully treated as group libel for the same reason it is not helpfully treated as individual libel. On the categorization front, at least, civil libertarians need not cede critical race theory an inch.

Critical race theory is at its strongest, however, not when it seeks to establish a bridgehead with constitutional precedent but when it frontally contests what has recently emerged as a central aspect of Supreme Court First Amendment doctrine: the principle of content and viewpoint neutrality.

The principle of content and viewpoint neutrality is meant to serve as a guideline to how speech can permissibly be regulated, ensuring basic fairness by preventing the law from favoring one partisan interest over another. So, for example, a law forbidding the discussion of race would violate the principle of content neutrality, which is held to be a bad thing; a law that forbade the advocacy of black supremacy would violate the principle of viewpoint neutrality, which is held to be a worse thing. When the Minnesota Supreme Court affirmed the content-sensitive hate speech ordinance at issue in *R.A.V. v. St. Paul,* it cited Mari J. Matsuda's work in reaching its conclusions. When Justice Scalia reversed and invalidated the ordinance on the grounds of viewpoint discrimination, he was implicitly writing against Matsuda's argument. So what we saw was no merely academic conflict of vision; these are arguments with judicial consequences.

In my view, Matsuda's rejection of what she calls the "neutrality trap" is probably the most powerful element of her argument. Rather than trying to fashion neutral laws to further our social objectives, why not put our cards on the table and acknowledge what we know? As an example of where the neutrality trap leads, she cites the anti-mask statutes that many states passed "in a barely disguised effort to limit Ku Klux Klan activities."

These statutes purportedly cover the wearing of masks in general, with no specific mention of the intent to control the Klan. Neutral reasons, such as the need to prevent pickpockets from moving unidentified through crowds or the need to unmask burglars or bank robbers are proffered for such statutes. The result of forgetting—or pretending to forget—the real reason for antimask legislation is farcical. Masks are used in protest against terrorist regimes for reasons both of symbolism and personal safety. Iranian students wearing masks and opposing human rights violations by the Shah of Iran, for example, were prosecuted under a California antimask statute.

I call here for an end of such unknowing. We know why state legislatures—those quirkily populist institutions—have passed antimask statutes. It is more honest, and less cynically manipulative of legal doctrine, to legislate openly against the worst forms of racist speech, allowing ourselves to know what we know.

What makes her position particularly attractive is that she offers a pragmatic, pro-civil-liberties argument for such content specificity. "The alternative to recognizing racist speech as qualitatively different because of its content is to continue to stretch existing first amendment exceptions, such as the 'fighting words' doctrine and the 'content/conduct' distinction," she writes. "This stretching ultimately weakens the first amendment fabric, creating neutral holes that remove protection for many forms of speech. Setting aside the worst forms of racist speech for special treatment is a non-neutral, value-laden approach that will better preserve free speech."

Another cogent argument against the notion of neutral principles is the fact that facially neutral principles are often anything but in practice. "The law, in its infinite majesty, forbids rich and poor alike from sleeping under bridges," Anatole France famously observed. If neutrality is, in the end, a masquerade, why bother with it? Why not abandon neutral principles and permit what Matsuda calls "expanded relevance," allowing courts to take into account the experience of racism, the victim group's consciousness, in assessing the harm of racist speech? At the very least, this approach would promise a quick solution to the sorts of abuses of "fighting words" ordinances we saw. To see how, consider Matsuda's own approach to legal sanctions for racist speech.

By way of distinguishing "the worst, paradigm example of racist hate messages from other forms of racist and nonracist speech," she offers three identifying characteristics:

1. The message is of racial inferiority.
2. The message is directed against a historically oppressed group.
3. The message is persecutory, hateful, and degrading.

The third element, she says, is "related to the 'fighting words' idea"; and the first "is the primary identifier of racist speech"; but it is the second element that "attempts to further define racism by recognizing the connection of racism to power and subordination." And it is the second element that most radically departs from the current requirement that law be neutral as to content and viewpoint. Still, it would seem to forestall some of the abuses to which earlier speech ordinances have been put, simply by requiring the victim of the penalized speech to be a member of a "historically oppressed group." And there's something refreshingly straightforward about her call for "an end to unknowing." Is Matsuda on to something?

Curiously enough, what trips up the content-specific approach is that it can never be content-specific enough.

Take a second look at her three identifying characteristics of paradigm hate speech. First, recall, the message is of racial inferiority. Now,

Matsuda makes clear that she wants her definition to encompass, inter alia, anti-Semitic and anti-Asian prejudice: but anti-Semitism—as the (black, Jewish) philosopher Laurence Thomas observes—traditionally imputes to its target not inferiority but iniquity. And anti-Asian prejudice often more closely resembles anti-Semitic prejudice than it does anti-black prejudice. Surely anti-Asian prejudice that depicts Asians as menacingly superior, and therefore a threat to "us," is just as likely, perhaps more likely, to arouse the sort of violence that notoriously claimed the life of Vincent Chin ten years ago in Detroit. More obviously, the test of membership in a "historically oppressed" group is in danger of being either too narrow (just blacks?) or too broad (just about everybody). Are poor Appalachians—a group I knew well from growing up in a West Virginia mill town—"historically oppressed" or "dominant group members"?

Once we had adopted the "historically oppressed" proviso, I suspect it would just be a matter of time before a group of black women in Chicago are arraigned for calling a policeman a "dumb Polack." Evidence that Poles are a historically oppressed group in Chicago will be in plentiful supply; the policeman's grandmother will offer poignant firsthand testimony to that. Of course, we might—ever mindful that minority groups have been especially vulnerable to statutes forbidding abusive speech—amend the criminal code by exempting members of historically oppressed groups from its sanctions. This would circumvent the risk of authorities employing the rules, perversely, against the very minority groups they were designed to empower. But then the white male student facing disciplinary procedures for calling a black classmate a "nigger" will always have the option of declaring himself to be gay, raising what the military calls a rebuttable presumption. The disciplinary committee would have to decide if it will be satisfied with the defendant's sexual self-ascription, or, more rigorously, require evidence of actual conduct. Matsuda rightly observes that "the legal imagination is a fruitful one," but might we not wish to see it employed at more useful tasks?

My point is one that some recent pragmatists have been fond of making, since Matsuda wants to abandon not principles or rules but only "neutral" principles and rules; and the sort of complications she decries (the imperfect "fit" between a rule and the cases it must govern) is the sort those pragmatists find with all principles and rules, neutral or not. Rather than rescuing us from the legal game of Twister, her approach merely provides a differently colored mat. And that mars the practical appeal of her position. Why abandon the notion of content neutrality—which has a decent, if flawed, track record—if doing so just replaces one set of problems with another?

It's also important to distinguish between a position that advocates abandoning our adherence to general rules and principles and one that says there is nothing to abandon, for we never really had them in the first place: both are plausible positions, but to confuse them is like confusing Satanism and atheism. As we saw, Matsuda is no skeptic about rules: what worries her about neutral principles is that they detach themselves from original context and acquire a sometimes destructive measure of autonomy—as when the antimask statute was used against the Iranian protestor. From a pragmatist perspective, a more thorough-going skepticism about rule-based accounts of First Amendment law has been offered by my friend and colleague Stanley Fish, in a now notorious essay entitled "There's No Such Thing as Free Speech, and It's a Good Thing, Too." First, though, a caveat. Despite the arresting title (and some arresting turns of argument), Fish turns out to be no foe of free speech as it is conventionally understood. Indeed, he essentially endorses the balancing approach to First Amendment cases proposed by Judge Learned Hand (in *Dennis v. United States*), and in the scheme of history, Judge Learned Hand has come to be regarded as one of the best friends the First Amendment ever had. "My rule of thumb is, 'don't regulate unless you have to,' " Fish writes, though, as he recognizes, that simply defers the question about when you have to.

Fish's central claim is that there are no final principles that will adjudicate First Amendment disputes, and that there is no avoiding a somewhat ad hoc balancing of interests. This is so because, despite our disclaimers, free speech is always justified in reference to goals (the only alternative would be to refuse to justify it at all), and so we will end up deciding hard cases by an assessment as to how well the contested speech subserves those goals. Moreover, this is so even for those theorists, like Ronald Dworkin, who justify freedom of expression not by its possible long-term benefits (which Dworkin considers to be too much a matter of conjecture to support our firm commitment to expressive freedom), but by a view of these rights (along with, say, the subsuming ideal of moral autonomy) as a constitutive element of a liberal society. Even "deontological" theories like Dworkin's—in which conformity to rules or rights, not good consequences, is what justifies action—are consequentialist, too, Fish argues: so long as they make exceptions to their vaunted rights for familiar consequentialist reasons (as in the event of clear and present danger), they are as fallen as the rest of us.

You will notice that Fish's argument essentially has the same form as the old and undoubtedly sexist joke (a joke recently adapted into a film starring Demi Moore and Robert Redford) about the man who asks a woman if she would sleep with him for a million dollars. She allows that she probably would. In that case, the man presses, would you sleep with me for $10? "What kind of a woman do you think I am?" she asks, indignant. "We've already established what kind of a woman you are," the retort comes. "Now we're just negotiating over the price."

So, yes, if you up the stakes enough, it turns out that we are all whores—even the most chaste among us, even Demi Moore. And if you up the stakes enough, we are all consequentialists, too—even the most deontological among us, even Ronald Dworkin. Once Fish has exposed us, he won't allow us to keep our pretensions to chastity, or deontology, for pretensions are all they are. I am less demanding than he. I would allow that rights needn't be infinitely stringent, for they may conflict with other rights, and so in practice the whole affair will, as Fish does not miss, have an air of the ad hoc about it. But that doesn't mean that our principles and rules do no work, that they are merely subterfuge. Maybe there's a useful sense in which we are *not* all whores. Besides, isn't that all-or-nothing rhetoric at odds with the whatever-works eclecticism of pragmatism at its best? The fact that First Amendment jurisprudence represents a hodgepodge of approaches, some of them at odds with each other, isn't necessarily a weakness.

Fish quotes Frederick Schauer criticizing the First Amendment for being an "ideology." But what's wrong with, and what's the alternative to, ideology? Granted, "ideology" is a pejorative term, somebody else's politics, as another old joke has it; but it's precisely as an ideology, which is only to say as an ideal that commands our public loyalties, that it has the beneficial effect that Fish himself commends: the effect it has as a brake on the overregulation of speech, even if it cannot present a permanent obstacle to it.

Where legal pragmatists, mainstream scholars, and critical race theorists converge is in their affirmation of the balancing approach toward the First Amendment, and their corresponding skepticism toward what could be labeled the "Skokie school" of jurisprudence.

When the American Civil Liberties Union defended the right of neo-Nazis to march in Skokie, a predominantly Jewish suburb of Chicago where a number of Holocaust survivors lived, they did so to protect and fortify the constitutional right at issue. Indeed, they may have reasoned, if a civil liberty can be tested and upheld in so odious an exercise of it, the precedent will make it that much stronger in all the less obnoxious cases where it may be disputed in the future. Hard cases harden laws.

But the strategy of the "Skokie school" relies on a number of presuppositions that critical legal theorists and others regard as doubtful. Most importantly, it revolves around the neutral operation of principle in judicial decision-making. But what if judges really decided matters in a political, unprincipled way, and invoked principles only by way of window dressing? In cases close-run enough to require the Supreme Court to decide them, precedent and principle are elastic enough, or complex enough, that justices can often decide either way without brazenly contradicting themselves. And even if the justices want to make principled decisions, it may turn out that the facts of the case—in the real-world cases that come before them—are too various and complicated ever to be overdetermined by the rule of precedent, *stare decisis*. In either event, it could turn out that defending neo-Nazis was just . . . defending neo-Nazis.

Moreover, it may be that the sort of formal liberties vouchsafed by this process aren't the sort of liberties we need most. Maybe we've been overly impressed by the frisson of defending bad people for good causes, when the good consequences may be at best conjectural and the bad ones are real and immediate. Maybe, these critics conclude, it's time to give up the pursuit of abstract principles and defend victims against victimizers, achieving your results in the here-and-now, not the sweet hereafter.

Now, there's something to this position, but like the position it is meant to rebuff, it is overstated. Nadine Strossen, a general counsel to the American Civil Liberties Union, can show, for example, that the organization's winning First Amendment defense of the racist Father Terminiello in 1949 bore Fourteenth Amendment fruit when it was able to use the landmark *Terminiello* decision to defend the free speech rights of civil rights protestors in the sixties and seventies. Granted, this may not constitute proof, an elusive thing in historical argument, but such cases provide good prima facie reason to think that the "Skokie school" has pragmatic justification, not just blind faith, on its side.

Another problem with the abandonment of principled adjudication is what it leaves in its wake: which is the case-by-case balancing of interests. My point isn't that "normal" First Amendment jurisprudence can or should completely eschew balancing; but there's a difference between resorting to it *in extremis* and employing it as the first and only approach. Now, in the case of racist invective, a balancing approach may be especially tempting, because the class of expression to be restricted seems so confined, while the harms with which it is associated can be vividly evoked. As the Berkeley law professor Robert C. Post argues, however, this invitation to balance is best declined, because of what he terms "the fallacy of immaculate isolation."

The effect on public discourse is acceptable only if it is de minimis, and it is arguably de minimis only when a specific claim is evaluated in isolation from other, similar claims. But no claim is in practice immaculately isolated in this manner . . . there is no shortage of powerful groups contending that uncivil speech within public discourse ought to be 'minimally' regulated for highly pressing symbolic reasons . . . In a large heterogeneous country populated by assertive and conflicting groups, the logic of circumscribing public discourse to reduce political estrangement is virtually unstoppable.

But there are other reasons to be chary about the reign of balancing. For an unfettered regime of balancing simply admits too much to judicial inspection. What we miss when we dwell on the rarefied workings of high-court decision-making is the way in which laws exert their effects far lower down the legal food chain. It's been pointed out that when police arrest somebody for loitering or disorderly conduct, the experience of arrest—being hauled off to the station and fingerprinted before being released—very often *is* the punishment. "Fighting words" ordinances have lent themselves to similar abuse. Anthony D'Amato, a law professor at Northwestern, makes a crucial and often overlooked point when he argues: "In some areas of law we do not want judges to decide cases at all—not justly or any other way. In these areas, the mere possibility of judicial decisionmaking exerts a chilling effect that can undermine what we want the law to achieve."

But what if that chilling effect is precisely what the law is designed for? After all, one person's chill is another person's civility. In any event, it's clear that all manner of punitive speech regulations are meant to have effects far beyond the classic triad of deterrence, reform, and retribution.

In fact, the main appeal of speech codes usually turns out to be primarily expressive or symbolic rather than consequential in nature. That is, their advocates do not depend on the claim that the statute will spare victim groups some foreseeable amount of psychic trauma. They say, rather, that by adopting such a statute, the university *expresses* its opposition to hate speech and bigotry. More positively, the statute *symbolizes* our commitment to tolerance, to the creation of an educational environment where mutual colloquy and comity are preserved. (Of course, the symbolic dimension may be valued because of *its* consequences. Indeed, the conservative sociologist James Q. Wilson has made the parallel argument for the case of obscenity regulation when he writes of his "belief that human character is, in the long run, affected less by occasional furtive experiences than by whether society does or does not state that there is an important distinction between the loathsome and the decent.")

It is in this spirit that Matsuda writes, "[A] legal response to racist speech is a *statement* that victims of racism are valued members of our polity," and that "in a society that *expresses* its moral judgments through the law," the "absence of laws against racist speech is telling." It is in this spirit that Delgado suggests that a tort action for racist speech will have the effect of "*communicating* to the perpetrator and to society that such abuse will not be tolerated either by its victims or by the courts" (italics mine). And it is in this spirit that Thomas Grey, the Stanford law professor who helped draft the campus speech regulations, counsels: "Authorities make the most effective statement when they are honestly concerned to do something *beyond* making a statement," thus "putting their money where their mouth is." The punitive function of speech codes are thus enlisted to expressive means, as a means of bolstering the credibility of the anti-racist statement.

And yet once we have admitted that the regulation of racist speech is, in part or whole, a symbolic act, we must register the force of the other symbolic considerations that may come into play. So, even if you think that the notion of free speech contains logical inconsistencies, you need to register the symbolic force of its further abridgement. And it is this level of scrutiny that may tip the balance in the other direction. The controversy over flag burning is a good illustration of the two-edged nature of symbolic arguments. Perhaps safeguarding the flag symbolized something nice, but for many of us, safeguarding our freedom to burn the flag symbolized something nicer.

Note, too, the contradiction in the expressivist position I just reviewed: a university administration that merely condemns hate speech, without mobilizing punitive sanctions, is held to have done little, offering "mere words." Yet this skepticism about the potency of "mere words" comports oddly with the attempt to regulate "mere words" that, since they are spoken by those not in a position of authority, would seem to have even less symbolic force. Why is it "mere words" when a university condemns racist speech, but not when the student utters the abusive words in the first place? Whose words are "only words"? Why are racist words deeds, but anti-racist words just lip service?

Further, is the verbal situation as asymmetric as it first appears? Does the rebuke "racist" have no power to wound on a college campus? One of the cases that arose under the University of Michigan speech code involved a group discussion at the beginning of a dentistry class, in which the teacher, a black woman, sought to "identify concerns of students." A student reported that he had heard, from his roommate, who was a minority, that minority students had a hard time in the class and were not treated fairly. In response, the outraged teacher lodged a complaint against the student for having accused her (as she perceived it) of racism. For this black woman, at least, even an indirect accusation of racism apparently had the brunt of racial stigmatization.

Still, I would insist that there is nothing unusual about the movement's emphasis on the expressive aspect of the law. "To listen to something on the assumption of the speaker's right to say it is to legitimate it," the conservative legal philosopher Alexander Bickel told us. "Where nothing is unspeakable, nothing is undoable." And I think there's an important point of convergence there: Bickel's precept that to "listen to something on the assumption of the speaker's right to say it is to legitimate it" underlies much of the contemporary resistance to unregulated expression on campus and elsewhere. For the flip side of the view that hate speech ordinances are necessary to express sincere opposition to hate speech is the view—which recurs in much of the

literature on the subject—that to tolerate racist expression is effectively
to endorse it: the Bickel principle. Thus, "Government protection of the
right of the Klan to exist publicly and to spread a racist message promotes the role of the Klan as a legitimizer of racism," Matsuda writes.
For his part, Charles Lawrence seems to suggest that merely to defend
civil liberties on campus may be to "valorize bigotry."

Like many other positions identified with the hate speech movement,
the thesis that toleration equals endorsement is not as radical as first
appears. In fact, this is precisely the position elaborated by Lord Patrick
Devlin in 1965, in his famous attack on the Wolfenden Report's recom-
mendation to decriminalize homosexual behavior in Britain. "If society
has the right to make a judgment," he wrote, "then society may use the
law to preserve morality in the same way as it uses it to safeguard
anything else that is essential to its existence." On this basis, he argues,
"society has a prima facie right to legislate against immorality as such."
In Lord Devlin's account, as in Matsuda's, the law expresses the moral
judgment of society; to countenance things that affront public morality
is thus a betrayal of its purpose.

Of course, Matsuda's belief that the government that protects the
rights of the Klan has promoted its views would have many surprising
consequences. One might conclude that the government that provided
civic services to the March on Washington this past March was solidly
behind the cause of gay rights. Or that, in giving police protection to
several of the Reverend Al Sharpton's marches in New York, it was
lending its moral support to the cause of black resistance. Or that, in
providing services to the Wigstock festivities in Tompkins Square Park,
it was plumping for transvestitism. Or that, in policing both rallies in
favor of abortion and those opposed, it was somehow supporting both
positions. One might, but of course one wouldn't. And since, in the
scheme of things, policing Klan marches commands a tiny fraction of the
state's resources—less, I would surmise, than do such African-American
events as Caribbean Day parades—our worries on this score seem misplaced.

One final paradox fissures the hate speech movement. Because these
scholars wish to show that substantial restrictions on racist speech are
consistent with the Constitution, they must make the case that racist
speech is *sui generis* among offensive or injurious utterances; otherwise

the domain of unprotected speech would mushroom beyond the point of constitutional and political plausibility. The title of Delgado's trailblazing essay, and of the collection, *Words That Wound,* designates a category that includes but is scarcely exhausted by racist speech. Nor could we maintain that racist insults, which tend to be generic, are necessarily more wounding than an insult tailor-made to hurt someone: being jeered at for your acne, or obesity, may be far more hurtful than being jeered at for your race or religion.

So clearly the level of emotional distress associated with racist abuse cannot be its distinguishing characteristic; what must be distinguishing is its connection to systemic patterns of subordination. (Even so, there are other such patterns of subordination. "Racism is a breach of the ideal of egalitarianism, that 'all men are created equal' and each person is an equal moral agent, an ideal that is a cornerstone of the American moral and legal system," writes Richard Delgado. "A society in which some members regularly are subjected to degradation because of their race hardly exemplifies this ideal." But racism isn't the only reason people are subjected to degradation: what about shortcomings in appearance or intelligence, traits that, like race, we can do little about?)

Scholars like Mari Matsuda, Charles Lawrence, and Richard Delgado argue that racist speech is peculiarly deserving of curtailment precisely because it participates in (and is at least partly constitutive of) the larger structures of racism hegemonic in our society. "Black folks know that no racial incident is 'isolated' in the United States," writes Lawrence. "That is what makes the incidents so horrible, so scary. It is the knowledge that they are *not* the isolated unpopular speech of a dissident few that makes them so frightening. These incidents are manifestations of a ubiquitous and deeply ingrained cultural belief system, an American way of life."

What Matsuda annexes to this consideration is the further argument that what distinguishes racist speech from other forms of unpopular speech is "the universal acceptance of the wrongness of the doctrine of racial supremacy." Unlike Marxist speech, say, racist speech is "universally condemned." At first blush, this is a surprising claim. After all, if it *were* universally rejected, hate speech ordinances would be an exercise in antiquarianism.

And yet there is something in what Matsuda says: at the very least, it bespeaks a shared conviction about the weight of the anti-racist consensus, the conviction that at least overt racists are an unpopular minority, and that authority is likely to side with *us* against *them*. In truth, this conviction provides the hidden foundation for the hate speech movement. Why would you entrust authority with enlarged powers of regulating the speech of unpopular minorities unless you were confident the unpopular minorities would be racists, not blacks? Lawrence may know that racial incidents are never "isolated," but he must also believe them to be less than wholly systemic. You don't go to the teacher to complain about the school bully unless you know that the teacher is on your side.

Critical race theory's implicit confidence in the anti-racist consensus also enables its critique of neutral principles, as becomes clear when one considers the best arguments in favor of such principles. Thus, David Coles, a law professor at Georgetown University, suggests that "in a democratic society the only speech government is likely to succeed in regulating will be that of the politically marginalized. If an idea is sufficiently popular, a representative government will lack the political wherewithal to suppress it, irrespective of the First Amendment. But if an idea is unpopular, the only thing that may protect it from the majority is a strong constitutional norm of content neutrality." Reverse his assumptions about whose speech is marginalized and you can stand this argument on its head. If blatantly racist speech is unpopular and stigmatized, a strong constitutional norm of content neutrality may be its best hope for protection: and for critical race theory, that's a damning argument *against* content neutrality.

Here, then, is the political ambiguity that haunts the new academic activism. "Our colleagues of color, struggling to carry the multiple burdens of token representative, role model, and change agent in increasingly hostile environments, needed to know that the institutions in which they worked stood behind them," the critical race theory manifesto informs us. *Needed to know that the institutions in which they worked stood behind them:* I have difficulty imagining that this sentiment could have been expressed by their activist counterparts in the sixties, who defined themselves through their adversarial relation to authority and its institutions. And that is the crucial difference this time around. Today, the aim is not to resist power, but to enlist power.

"Critical race theory challenges ahistoricism and insists on a contextual/ historical analysis of the law," the critical race theory manifesto instructs us. It is not a bad principle. But what it suggests to me is that we get down to cases and consider, as they do not, the actual results of various regimes of hate speech regulation.

Matsuda, surveying United Nations conventions urging the criminalization of racist hate speech, bemoans the fact that the United States, out of First Amendment scruple, has declined fully to endorse such resolutions. By contrast, she commends to our attention states such as Canada and the United Kingdom. Canada's appeal to the hate speech movement is obvious. After all, the new Canadian Bill of Rights has not (as she observes) been allowed to interfere with its national statutes governing hate propaganda. What's more, Canada's Supreme Court has recently adopted MacKinnon's statutory definition of pornography as law of the land.

What you don't hear from the hate speech theorists is that the first casualty of the MacKinnonite anti-obscenity ruling was a gay and lesbian bookshop in Toronto, which was raided by the police because of a lesbian magazine it carried. (Homosexual literature is a frequent target of Canada's restrictions on free expression.) Nor are they likely to mention that as recently as June 1993, copies of a book widely assigned in women's studies courses, *Black Looks: Race and Representation* by the well-known black feminist scholar bell hooks, was confiscated by Canadian authorities as possible "hate literature." Is the Canadian system really our beacon of hope?

Even more perplexing—especially given the stated imperative to challenge ahistoricism and attend to context—is the nomination of Britain as an exemplar of a more enlightened free-speech jurisprudence. Does anyone believe that racism has subsided in Britain since the adoption of the 1965 Race Relations Act forbidding racial defamation? Or that the legal climate in that country is more conducive to searching political debate? Ask any British newspaperman about that. When Harry Evans, then editor of the London *Times,* famously proclaimed that the British press was, by comparison to ours, only "half-free," he was not exaggerating by much. The result of Britain's judicial climate is to make the country a net importer of libel suits launched by tycoons who are displeased with their biographers. By now, everyone knows that a British libel suit offers all the conveniences of a Reno divorce.

Is the British approach to the regulation and punishment of speech really an advance on ours? Ask the editors of the *New Statesman &*

Observer, whose continued existence was put in jeopardy after Prime Minister John Major sued the publication for mentioning, though not endorsing, the rumor that he was having an affair with a caterer. (Depending on how you interpret the facts in the case, it may be that I, in this publication, have just repeated the tortious offense.) Nor (in line with the Canadian example) has the British penchant for singling out gay publications for punishment escaped notice. Ask the editors of *Oz,* who discovered that the lesbian imagery on their cover represented a punishable offense. Ask the editors of the magazine *Gay News,* who were convicted for "blasphemous libel" when they published a poem involving a homosexual fantasy about Christ, and received jail sentences (later suspended). Ask the owner of Gay's the Word book shop in London, found guilty of "conspiring to import indecent and obscene material" in 1984. For that matter, ask Jenny White, who was prosecuted for privately purchasing lesbian videos from the United States in 1991.

The mordant irony is that American progressives should propose Britain, and its underdeveloped protection of expression, as a model to emulate at a time when many progressives in Britain are agitating for a bill of rights and broader First Amendment-style protections. To be sure, Britain has its attractions—scones, tea, cucumber sandwiches. But the jurisprudence of free speech isn't among them.

Nor is the record of U.K. student groups to be preferred. Nadine Strossen has pointed out the ironic history of a resolution adopted by the British National Union of Students in 1974, to the effect that representatives of "openly racist and fascist organizations" were to be kept from speaking on college campuses by "whatever means necessary (including disruption of the meeting)." It was a measure taken against groups like the National Front. But when, in the wake of the U.N. resolution, some British students designated Zionism a form of racism, the rule was invoked against Israelis, including Israel's ambassador to the United Kingdom—a turn of events that came much to the delight of the National Front.

To her credit, Mari Matsuda is up front about the sort of difficulties likely to arise in her regime of criminalization. In a section called "Hard Cases," she considers the hard case of Zionism and decides that some forms of Zionist expression—those expressed in "reaction to historical persecution"—is to receive protection, while other forms, which participate in the sort of "white supremacy" that some identify as intrinsic to the Middle East conflict, will not. She adds that "the various subordinated communities" are best equipped to identify such victimizing hate speech. In other words, the Palestinian is best equipped to decide whether and when the Zionist's speech should be criminalized. (It is unclear whether the Zionist can return the favor.)

And what of speech codes on American campuses? The record may surprise some advocates of hate speech regulations. "When the ACLU enters the debate by challenging the University of Michigan's efforts to provide a safe harbor for its Black, Latino, and Asian students," Lawrence writes, "we should not be surprised that nonwhite students feel abandoned." In light of the actual record of enforcement, you may view the situation differently.

During the year in which Michigan's speech code was enforced, more than twenty blacks were charged—by whites—with racist speech. As Nadine Strossen notes, not a single instance of racist speech by whites was punished. (Lawrence's talk of a "safe harbor" sounds more wishful than informed.) A full disciplinary hearing was conducted only in the case of a black social work student who was charged with saying, in a class discussion of research projects, that he believed that homosexuality was an illness, and that he was developing a social work approach to move homosexuals toward heterosexuality. ("These charges will haunt me for the rest of my life," the black student claimed in a court affidavit.)

By my lights, this is a good example of how speech codes kill critique. I think that the student's views about homosexuality (which may or may not have been well intentioned) are both widespread and unlikely to survive close intellectual scrutiny. Regrettably, we have not yet achieved a public consensus in this country on the moral legitimacy (or, more precisely, moral indifference) of homosexuality. Yet it may well be that a class on social work is not an inappropriate forum for a rational discussion of why the "disease" model of sexual difference has lost credibility among social scientists. (This isn't PC brainwashing, either; in a class on social work, this is simply education.) But you cannot begin to conduct this conversation when you outlaw the expression of the view you would critique.

Critical race theorists are fond of the ideal of conversation. "This chapter attempts to begin a conversation about the first amendment," Matsuda writes toward the end of her contribution. "Most important, we must continue this conversation," Lawrence writes toward the end of his. It is too easy to lose sight of the fact that the conversation to which they're devoted is aimed at limiting conversation; and that if there are costs to speech, there are costs, as well, to curtailing speech, often unpredictable ones.

Our homophobic social work student may have been one of its casualties. As the legal philosopher David A. J. Richards contends: "It is a vicious political fallacy of the right and the left to assume that our contempt for false evaluative opinions may justly be transferred to contempt for the persons who conscientiously hold and express such views. Such persons are not, as it were, beyond the civilizing community of humane discourse." Or as Samuel Johnson, who crafted an art out of words that wound, admonishes, "punishment is able only to silence, not to confute."

We should be clear that speech codes may be far more narrowly tailored, and the Stanford rules—carefully drafted by scholars, like the Stanford law professor Thomas Grey, with civil libertarian sympathies— have, justly, been taken as a model of such careful delimitation. For rather than following the arguments against racist speech to their natural conclusion, the Stanford rules prohibit only insulting expression that conveys "direct and visceral hatred or contempt" for people on the basis of their sex, race, color, handicap, religion, sexual orientation, or national and ethnic origin, and that is "addressed directly to the individual or individuals whom it insults or stigmatizes."

Chances are that the Stanford rule won't do much harm, if any. The chances are, too, that it won't do much good, if any. As long as the eminently reasonable Professor Grey is drafting and enforcing the restrictions, I won't lose much sleep over it either way. But we should also be clear how inadequate the code is as a response to the powerful arguments that were marshalled to support it.

Contrast the following two statements addressed to a black freshman at Stanford.

(A) LeVon, if you find yourself struggling in your classes here, you should realize it isn't your fault. It's simply that you're the beneficiary of a disruptive policy of affirmative action that places underqualified, underprepared, and often undertalented black students in demanding educational environments like this one. The policy's egalitarian aims may be well intentioned, but given the fact that aptitude tests place African-Americans almost a full standard deviation below the mean, even controlling for socioeconomic disparities, they are also profoundly misguided. The truth is, you probably don't belong here, and your college experience will be a long downhill slide.

(B) Out of my face, jungle bunny.

Surely there is no doubt which is likely to be more "wounding" and alienating to its intended audience. Under the Stanford speech regulations, however, the first is protected speech; the second may well not be: a result that makes a mockery of the words-that-wound rationale. If you really want to penalize such wounding words, it makes no sense to single out gutter epithets—which, on many college campuses, to be candid, are more likely to stigmatize the speaker than their intended victim—and leave the far more painful disquisition alone.

Taking the expressivist tack, Thomas Grey argues that punitive sanctions are useful because they shore up salutary symbolism: "When a university administration backs its anti-racist pronouncements with action, it puts its money where its mouth is." It's a punchy metaphor, and the implication is that by adopting these regulations his university has put itself on the line, taken measures that may extract real costs from it. In fact, this is a pretty costless trade. It's safe to say that Stanford's faculty and administration, however benighted or enlightened they may be on racial matters, manage nicely without the face-to-face deployment of naughty epithets. In adopting the regulations, therefore, they sacrifice nothing but the occasional drunken undergraduate. "Putting your money where your mouth is" may bolster your credibility; but whose money is it, really?

A rule of thumb: in American society today, the real power commanded by the racist is likely to vary inversely with the vulgarity with which it is expressed. Black professionals soon learn that it is the socially disenfranchised—the lower class, the homeless—who are most likely to hail them as "niggers." The circles of power have long since switched to a vocabulary of indirection. Unfortunately, those who pit the First Amendment against the Fourteenth invite us to spend more time worrying about speech codes than coded speech.

I suspect that many of those liberals who supported Stanford's restrictions on abusive language did so because they thought it was the civil thing to do. Few imagined that, say, the graduation rates or GPAs of Stanford's blacks (or Asians, gays, etc.) are likely to rise significantly as a result. Few imagined, that is, that the restrictions would lead to substantive rights or minority empowerment. They just believed that gutter epithets violate the sort of civility that ought to prevail on campus. In all likelihood, the considerations that prevailed owed more to Emily Post than to Robert Post. In spirit, then, the new regulations were little different from the rules about curfews, drinking, or the after-hours presence of women in male dormitories that once governed America's campuses and preoccupied their disciplinary committees.

Not that civility rules are without value. Charles Lawrence charges that civil libertarians who disagree with him about speech regulations may be "unconscious racists." I don't doubt this is so; I don't doubt that some of those who *support* speech codes are unconscious racists. What I doubt is whether the imputation of racism is the most effective way to advance the debate between civil rights and civil liberties.

"What is ultimately at stake in this debate is our vision for this society," write the authors of *Words That Wound,* and they are quite right. The risk, in parsing the reasoning of the hate speech movement, is of missing the civic forest for the legal trees. For beyond the wrangling over particular statutes and codes lies an encompassing vision of state and civil society. Moreover, it is one whose wellsprings are to be found not in legal scholarship or theory, but in the much more powerful cultural currents identified with the "recovery movement." At the vital center of the hate speech movement is the seductive vision of the therapeutic state.

We can see this vision clearly presaged in the critical race theory manifesto itself:

Too often victims of hate speech find themselves without the words to articulate what they see, feel, and know. In the absence of theory and analysis that give them a diagnosis and a name for the injury they have suffered, they internalize the injury done them and are rendered silent in the fact of continuing injury. Critical race theory names the injury and identifies its origins.

This sounds, of course, like a popular primer on how psychotherapy is supposed to work, and with a few changes, the passage might be from a book addressed to survivors of toxic parenting. Indeed, "alexathymia"—the inability to name and articulate one's feelings—is a faddish diagnosis within psychiatry these days. Nor is the affinity that critical race theory shares with the currently booming recovery industry a matter of fortuity: for at present, the recovery movement is perhaps the principal countertrend to an older, and now much-beleaguered American tradition of individualism.

"When the ideology is deconstructed and injury is named, subordinated victims find their voices," we are told in the manifesto. "They discover they are not alone in their subordination. They are empowered." Here the recovery/survivor-group paradigm does lead to a puzzling contradiction: we are told that victims of racist speech are cured—that is, empowered—when they learn they are "not alone" in their subordination, but subordinated as a group. Elsewhere we are told that what makes racist speech peculiarly wounding is that it conveys precisely that content, that you are a member of a subordinated group. How can the message of group subordination be both poison and antidote?

The therapeutic claims made for critical race theory cut against the hate speech offensive in more important ways. For if we took these claims at face value, critical race theory would not buttress speech regulations, but obviate the need for them. The problem Lawrence worries about—that racist speech "silenc[es] members of those groups who are its targets"—would naturally be addressed not through bureaucratic regulations, but through the sort of deconstruction and critique that critical race theory promises will enable victims to "find their voices." Another painful irony: this all sounds very much like Justice Brandeis's hoary and much-scorned prescription for redressing harmful speech: "more speech."

Yet while scholars like Delgado and Matsuda emphasize the adverse psychological effects of racial abuse, the proposed therapeutic regime is no mere talking cure. Richard Delgado writes: "Because they constantly hear racist messages, minority children, not surprisingly, come to question their competence, intelligence, and worth." But in the Republic of Self-Esteem, we are invited to conceive the lawsuit as therapy. "When victimized by racist language, victims must be able to threaten and institute legal action, thereby relieving the sense of helplessness that leads to psychological harm."

A similar therapeutic function could be played by criminal proceedings, in Matsuda's view. When the government does nothing about racist speech, she argues, it actually causes a second injury. "The second injury is the pain of knowing that the government provides no remedy and offers no recognition of the dehumanizing experience that victims of hate propaganda are subjected to." Indeed, "[T]he government's denial of personhood through its denial of legal recourse may even be more painful than the initial act of hatred." Of course, what this grievance presupposes is that the state is there, *in loco parentis,* to confer personhood in the first place.

What Matsuda has recourse to, finally, is not an instrumental conception of the state, but rather a conception of it as the "official embodiment of the society we live in," and as such rather remote and abstracted from the realities of our heterogeneous populace, with its conflicting norms and values. Perhaps that is only to say that psychotherapy cannot do the hard work of politics. But a similar therapeutic vision animates the more broad-gauged campus regulations, like those adopted in the late 1980s at the University of Connecticut. Its rules sought to proscribe such behavior as, inter alia:

Treating people differently solely because they are in some way different from the majority. . . .
Imitating stereotypes in speech or mannerisms. . . .
Attributing objections to any of the above actions to "hypersensitivity" of the targeted individual or group.

The last provision was especially cunning. It meant that even if you believed a complainant was overreacting to an innocuous remark, to try to defend yourself in this way would only serve as proof of your guilt. But the rationale of the university's rules was made explicit in its general prohibition on actions that undermined the "security or self-esteem" of persons or groups. (Would awarding low grades count?) Not surprisingly, the university's expressed objective was to provide "a positive environment in which everyone feels comfortable working or living." It was unclear whether any provisions were to be made for those who did not feel "comfortable" working or living under such restrictive regulations; in any event, they were later dropped under threat of legal action.

Still, perhaps the widespread skepticism about any real divide between public and private made it inevitable that the recovery movement would translate into a politics, and that this politics would center on a vocabulary of trauma and abuse, one in which their verbal and physical varieties are seen as equivalent. Perhaps it was inevitable that the Citizen at the center of classical Enlightenment political theory would be replaced by the Infant at the center of modern depth psychology and its popular therapeutic variants. The inner child may hurt and grieve, as we have been advised; is it also to vote?

But there are older ideas of civil society in conflict within the hate speech debate. To oversimplify, critical race theory sees a society composed of groups; moral primacy is conferred upon those collectivities whose equal treatment and protection ought to be guaranteed under law. The classic civil libertarian view, by contrast, sees a society composed of individuals who possess rights only as public citizens, whatever other collective allegiances they may entertain privately.

Individualism has its weaknesses, to be sure. Part of what we value most about ourselves as individuals often turns out to be a collective attribute—our religious or racial identity, say. And when we are discriminated against, it is as a member of a group. Nor does the implicit model of voluntarism work well for ethnic, sexual, racial, or religious identities, identities about which we may have little say. There is some thing unsatisfactory in a legal approach that treats being a black woman as analogous to being a stamp collector.

And yet the very importance of these social identities underscores one of the most potent arguments for an individualist approach toward the First Amendment. In a series of novella-length articles published over the past several year, Robert C. Post has examined just such issues as they relate to an emerging conception of public discourse. "One is not born a woman," Simone de Beauvoir famously avowed, and her point can be extended: the meaning of all our social identities is mutable and constantly evolving, the product of articulation, contestation, and negotiation.

Indeed, these are circumstances to which critical race theorists ought to be more attuned than most. Thus Lawrence approvingly quotes MacKinnon's observation that "to the extent that pornography succeeds in constructing social reality, it becomes invisible as harm." He concludes: "This truth about gender discrimination is equally true of racism." And yet to speak of the social construction of reality is already to give up the very idea of "getting it right." When Lawrence refers to "the continuing real-life struggle through which we define the community in which we live," he identifies a major function of unfettered debate, but does so, incongruously, by way of proposing to shrink its domain. To remove the very formation of our identities from the messy realm of contestation and debate is an elemental, not incidental, truncation of the ideal of public discourse. And so we must return to Catharine MacKinnon's correct insistence on "the rather obvious reality that groups are made up of individuals."

Now, as Post (citing the work of Charles Taylor) has observed, the neutrality of individualism is only relative. The autonomous moral agent of liberal society requires the entrenchment of a political culture conducive to that identity. Even though the strong tendency in legal culture is to overcriminalize and overregulate, the preservation of a broadly democratic polity entails that there will be, and must be, limits, and establishing them will involve political considerations. Thus Post writes, in a penetrating analysis of the Supreme Court decision in *Falwell v. Hustler:* "The ultimate fact of ideological regulation . . . cannot be blinked. In the end, therefore, there can be no final account of the boundaries of the domain of public discourse."

So perhaps the most powerful arguments of all for the regulation of hate speech come from those who maintain that such regulation will really enhance the diversity and range of public discourse. At their boldest, these argument pit free speech and hate speech as antagonists, such that public discourse is robbed and weakened by the silencing and exclusionary effects of racist speech. Restricting hate speech actually increases the circulation of speech, the argument runs, by defending the speech rights of victim-groups whom such abuse would otherwise silence. And so the purging of racist speech from the body politic is proposed as a curative technique akin to the suction cups and leeches of eighteenth-century medicine, which were meant to strengthen the patient by draining off excessive toxins.

Needless to say, the question of the safety and effectivity of the treatment is an open one. And, as Post points out, the "question of whether public discourse is irretrievably damaged by racist speech must itself ultimately be addressed through the medium of public discourse."

Because those participating in public discourse will not themselves have been silenced (almost by definition), a heavy, frustrating burden is de facto placed on those who would truncate public discourse in order to save it. They must represent themselves as "speaking for" those who have been deprived of their voice. But the negative space of that silence reigns inscrutable, neither confirming nor denying this claim. And the more eloquent the appeal, the less compelling the claim, for the more accessible public discourse will then appear to be to exactly the perspectives racist speech is said to repress.

The larger question—the political question—is how we came to decide that our energies were best directed not at strengthening our position in the field of public discourse, but at trying to move its boundary posts.

So I want to return to the puzzling disalignment with which I began. The struggle with racism has traditionally been waged through language, not against it; the tumult of the civil rights era was sponsored by an expansive vision of the First Amendment, a vision to which the struggle against racism in turn lent its moral prestige. And it is this concrete history and context that make it so perplexing that a new generation of activists— avowedly sensitive to history and context—should choose the First Amendment as a battlefield in their fight for Fourteenth Amendment guarantees.

I detect two motivations for the shift, one that relates to the academy, and one that relates to the world outside it.

In a trend we've already touched upon, there has been increased attention on the formative power of language in the creation of our social reality; on language as "performative," as itself constituting a "speech act." While these are phrases and ideas that the ordinary language philosopher J. L. Austin developed in the midcentury, Catharine MacKinnon adds them to her argumentative arsenal in her latest book. The notion of the speech act has new force when the act in question is rape.

Now, MacKinnon's emphasis on the realness, the actlike nature, of expression receives an interesting twist in the attempt by some hate speech theorists to "textualize" the Fourteenth Amendment. For if expression is act, than act must be expression. If the First Amendment is about speech, so, too, is the Fourteenth Amendment.

Following this reasoning, Charles Lawrence has proposed—in an influential and admired reinterpretation of legal history—that *Brown v. Board* and, on analogy, all subsequent civil rights decisions and legislation, are in fact prohibitions on expressive behavior, forbidding not racism in se but the expression of racism. In line with this argument, he tells us that "discriminatory conduct is not racist unless it also conveys the message of white supremacy," thus contributing to the social construction of racism.

This is a bold and unsettling claim, which commits Lawrence to the view that where discriminatory conduct is concerned, the only crime is to get caught. By this logic, racial redlining by bankers isn't racist unless people find out about it. And the crusading district attorney who uncovers previously hidden evidence of their discrimination isn't to be hailed as a friend of justice, after all: by bringing it to light, he was only activating the racist potential of those misdeeds.

Lawrence's analysis of segregation reaches the same surprising conclusion: "The nonspeech elements are by-products of the main message rather than the message being simply a by-product of unlawful conduct." By this logic, poverty is really about the *message* of class inequality, rather than material deprivation. We might conclude, then, that the problem of economic inequality would most naturally be redressed by promulgating a self-affirmative lower-class identity along the lines of Poverty Is Beautiful. Words may not be cheap, but they must be less costly than AFDC and job training programs.

Something, let us agree, has gone very wrong here. In arguments of this sort, the pendulum has swung from the absurd position that words don't matter to the equally absurd position that *only* words matter. Critical race theory, it appears, has fallen under the sway of a species of academic nominalism. Yes, speech is a species of action. Yes, there are some acts that only speech can perform. But there are some acts that speech alone cannot accomplish. You cannot heal the sick by pronouncing them well. You cannot uplift the poor by declaring them to be rich.

In their joint manifesto, the authors of *Words That Wound* identify theirs as "a fight for a constitutional community where 'freedom' does not implicate a right to degrade and humiliate another human being." These are heady words, but like much sweepingly utopian rhetoric, they would also signal a regime so heavily policed as to be incompatible with democracy. Once we are forbidden verbally to degrade and humiliate, will we retain the moral autonomy to elevate and affirm?

In the end, the preference for the substantive liberties supposedly vouchsafed by the Fourteenth Amendment to the exclusion of the formal ones enshrined in the First Amendment rehearses the classic disjunction that Sir Isaiah Berlin analyzed in his "Two Conceptions of Liberty" without having learned from it. His words have aged little since 1958. "Negative" liberty, the simple freedom from external coercion, seemed to him "a truer and more humane ideal than the goals of those who seek in the great, disciplined, authoritarian structures the ideal of 'positive' self-mastery by classes, or peoples, or the whole of mankind. It is truer, because it recognizes the fact that human goals are many, not all of them commensurable, and in perpetual rivalry with one another." More to the point, to suggest, as Lawrence and his fellow critical race theorists do, that equality must precede liberty is simply to jettison the latter without securing the former. The First Amendment will not, true enough, secure us substantive liberties, but neither will its abrogation. No one has come close to showing that First Amendment liberties are so costly that they significantly impede our chance of securing the equal protection guarantees of the Fourteenth Amendment. You cannot get the Fourteenth Amendment through the First, to be sure; but no one has persuaded me yet that you cannot have both. Still, it isn't hard to explain the disenchantment among minority critics with such liberal mainstays as the "marketplace of ideas" and the ideal of public discourse. In the end, I take it to be an extension of a larger crisis of faith. The civil rights era witnessed the development of a national consensus—something hammered out noisily, and against significant resistance, to be sure— that racism, at least overt racism, was wrong. Amazingly enough, things like reason, argumentation, and moral suasion *did* play a significant role in changing attitudes toward "race relations." But what have they done for us lately?

For all his robust good sense, Harry Kalven, Jr., was spectacularly wrong when he wrote: "One is tempted to say that it will be a sign that the Negro problem has basically been solved when the Negro begins to worry about group-libel protection." On the contrary, the disillusionment with liberal ideology rampant among many minority scholars and activists stems from the lack of progress in the struggle for racial equality over the past fifteen years. Liberalism's core principle of formal equity seems to have led us so far, but no farther. It "put the vampire back in its coffin but it was no silver stake," as Patricia J. Williams notes. The problem may be that the continuing economic and material inequality between black and white America—and, more pointedly, the continuing immiseration of large segments of black America—cannot be erased simply through better racial attitudes. The problem, further, may be that in some ways we intellectuals have not yet caught up to this changing reality. It isn't only generals who are prone to fight the last war.

As analysts on the left and the right alike have shown, poverty, white and black, can take on a life of its own, to the point that removing the conditions that caused it can do little to alleviate it. The eighties may have been the "Cosby Decade," as some declared, but you wouldn't know it from the South Bronx. What's become clear is that the political economy of race and poverty can no longer be reduced to a mirror of what whites think of blacks. But rather than responding by forging new and subtler modes of socioeconomic analysis, we have finessed the gap between rhetoric and reality by coming up with new and subtler definitions of the word "racism." Hence the new model of institutional racism—often just called racism—is one that can operate in the absence of actual racists. By progressively redefining our terms, we could always say of the economic gap between black and white America: the problem is still racism . . . and, by stipulation, it would be true.

But the grip of this vocabulary has tended to foreclose the more sophisticated and multivariate models of political economy we so desperately need. I cannot otherwise explain why some of our brightest legal minds believe that substantive liberties can be vouchsafed and substantive inequities redressed by punishing rude remarks. Or why their analysis of racism owes more to the totalizing theory of Catharine MacKinnon than to the work of scholar-investigators like Douglas Massey or William Julius Wilson or Gary Orfield: people who, whatever their disagreements, at least attempt to find out how things work in the real world, never confusing the empirical with the merely anecdotal.

Instead, critical theory is often allowed to serve as a labor-saving device. For if racism can be fully textualized, if its real existence is in its articulation, then racial inequity can be prized free from the moss and soil of political economy. "Gender is sexual," MacKinnon told us in *Toward a Feminist Theory of the State.* "Pornography constitutes the meaning of that sexuality." By extension, racist speech must prove to be the real content of racial subordination: banish it, and you banish subordination. The perverse result is a see-no-evil, hear-no-evil approach toward racial inequality. Alas, even if hate did disappear, aggregative patterns of segregation and segmentation in housing and employment would not. Conversely, in the absence of this material and economic gap, no one would much care about racist speech.

Beliefs cannot prosper that go untested and unchallenged. The critical race theorists must be credited with helping to reinvigorate the debate about freedom of expression; even if not ultimately persuaded to join them, the civil libertarian will be much further along for having listened to their arguments and examples. The intelligence, innovation, and thoughtfulness of their best work ask for and deserve a reasoned response: not, as so often happens, demonization and dismissal. And yet for all the passion and scholarship the critical race theorists have expended upon the hate speech movement, I cannot believe it will capture their attention for very much longer.

"It is strange how rapidly things change," Harry Kalven, Jr., wrote in 1965. "Just a little more than a decade ago we were all concerned with devising legal controls for the libeling of groups. . . . Ironically, once the victory was won, the momentum for such legal measures seemed to dissipate, and the problem has all but disappeared from view." It *is* strange how rapidly things change—and change back. Still, I suspect the results will be similar this time around: advocates of speech restrictions will grow disenchanted not with their failures, but their victories, and the movement will come to seem just another curious byway in the long history of our racial desperation.

And yet it will not have been without its political costs. I cannot put it better than Charles Lawrence himself, who writes: "I fear that by framing the debate as we have—as one in which the liberty of free speech is in conflict with the elimination of racism—we have advanced the cause of racial oppression and placed the bigot on the moral high ground, fanning the rising flames of racism." Though he does not intend it as such, I can only read this a harsh rebuke to the hate-speech movement itself. As the critical race theory manifesto acknowledges, "this debate has deeply divided the liberal civil rights/civil liberties community"; and so it has. It has created hostility between old and fast allies and fissured longtime coalitions.

Somewhere along the way, I fear, we have lost touch with the pragmatist's sturdily earthbound question: was it worth it? For while the
temporal benefits of its victories are at best conjectural, the political
damage to the already fragile liberal alliance is apparent in the here-and-
now. Meanwhile, Justice Black's words of dissent may return to us like
an unheeded tocsin: "Another such victory and I am undone."

Note

1. *Gitlow* in 1925 is often cited for this, although the comments are obiter
   dicta; and *Fisk* in 1927 is cited by others, although it does explicitly mention
   the First Amendment. *Near* in 1931 is, however, the first case to say explicitly
   that the First Amendment applies to the states.

2. Racial Myopia in the Age of Digital Compression

Donald E. Lively

Imagining a race-neutral society is not a difficult exercise. The vision of a culture ridded of discrimination, prejudice, and stereotyping on the basis of group status is, after all, what inspired and was nurtured by the challenge to official segregation and by the civil rights movement. Even recent affirmative action strategies criticized by some for their race-consciousness[1] are understood by many as a method of "getting beyond racism."[2] It is difficult to conceive of an argument, at least one offered in good faith, that questions the need for vigilance and dedication in undoing the nation's legacy of racial discrimination. Legal reform, although successful in defeating formal and overt methods of racial injustice,[3] has not erased values and attitudes that underlie group animus and prejudice.[4] Yet even as color-conscious judgment remains an embedded societal trait, manifested by such phenomena as "white flight" and the panoply of micro-segregative decisions[5] at work, education, and play, racial discrimination may be increasingly less determinative of racial disadvantage. As the social and economic order reconstitutes itself pursuant to technological, global, and competitive factors, it is possible to visualize a society that even if ridded of prejudice would be characterized by hardening of racial disadvantage.

The pursuit of racial equality and justice over the course of American history has been characterized by a redundant dialectic of powerful resistance, limited concession, and incremental progress. Slavery was defeated by civil war and the Thirteenth Amendment[6] which precipitated the Black Codes.[7] They in turn were undone by the Fourteenth Amendment,[8] which until the middle of this century was qualified by allowance for classifications and distinctions on the basis of race.[9] Desegregation and anti-discrimination[10] imperatives in the middle of the twentieth century evoked avoidance and procrastination and eventually were delimited as the law provided breathing room for subtle or unconscious discrimination. Against a backdrop of breakthrough, resistance, and consequent frustration, race-conscious remedial or diversification methods have been touted as a means of reckoning with the society's legacy of racism.[11] Whether cast in terms of racial preference in the distribution of opportunity, or special methods of accounting for minority sensitivity or dignity,[12] such strategies have yielded marginal returns upon reformist initiative.[13] As racial disadvantage has hardened, economic dislocation has disproportionately burdened traditionally excluded minorities, and the law itself has become a source of diminishing returns, it might seem logical to look to society's centers of knowledge and learning for meaningful debate and policy direction. Institutions of higher learning that were a key source of inspiration and energy in the past,[14] however, seem committed to a marginally relevant role in reckoning with modern problems of race. What pass as serious agendas on the contemporary academic landscape tend to be ideology and strategy concerned with cosmetics, and consequent exercises magnified by too little real debate or interest in transcendent issues of race. At a time when the causes and conditions of disadvantage are more complex and intimidating than ever, and real imperatives for progress are bridge building and empowerment, the need has never been greater for diverse, robust, and open dialogue. The academic community's contribution remains relatively underdeveloped, however, as output is dominated by attention to imagery and etiquette.

Measured against modern circumstances, recent agendas for racial progress have been seriously misconceived and generally disappointing. With the massive challenges of the abolitionist, desegregation, and civil rights movements as a backdrop, and landmark achievements already towering on the constitutional landscape, a comparatively diminished stature may be inevitable for even the grandest modern proposal for racial progress. Reformist initiative and strategy, however, must be measured not merely against the work of the past but the needs of the present. Pursuant to a legitimate sense that the desegregation process and civil rights laws have left much unfinished racially significant business, and even have been sources of underachievement, formal protocol has emerged as a popular method of racial reckoning. When assessed against past undertakings and modern imperatives, such strategy for change casts a lamentably small shadow.

As the intellectual godparents of hate speech codes and other racial management schemes, self-styled critical race theorists[15] have attained a significant role in delineating and developing modern issues of race at least in academic circles. "Critical race theory" has emerged in the nation's legal culture as the functional equivalent of a trade name. The term is claimed by "a small but growing group of scholars committed to finding new ways to think about and act in pursuit of racial justice."[16] Such a characterization is neither especially revealing nor exclusionary. A narrowing criterion is a focus shaped by personal and historical experience and premises that "embrace subjectivity of perspective and are avowedly political."[17] Critical race theory, even as so defined, technically seems capable of housing a broad spectrum of ideology. In practice, the term comprehends the work of academics whose primary impact has resulted from advocacy of hate speech codes. Pending a more developed identity or consequence, clarity and convenience may be better served by referring to critical race theorists (as this essay does) as "protocolists." The capacity of protocolists to command attention and define much of the contemporary debate on race is worrisome for at least two reasons that fuel pessimism about a serious reckoning with racial realities. One explanation for the protocolists' prominence may be that they trade in a void created by historical indifference to racial disadvantage and injustice. A second possibility is that potential critics, themselves relatively inexperienced in a real world of cultural diversity, are not confident enough of their own convictions to risk open discussion that might fail an ad hoc test of acceptability. As each side seeks shelter behind a wall of formalism, incentive to experience, learn, reflect, grow, seek common ground, and confront hard problems is diminished.

Multiple cycles of challenge to the established racial order, limited success in achieving reform, and persisting disadvantage despite change may illuminate a society that has mastered the art of formal capitulation without actual surrender or wholesale change. An unbroken pattern of legal progress—in the form of abolition, reconstruction, desegregation, and civil and political rights achievement—composes an impressive record of formal achievement. Such reform, however, exists within a broader context of a social order that historically has adapted to new legal imperatives in ways that preserve and even fortify racial advantage.

For all of the racially significant litigation, legislation and even amendment of fundamental law over the course of the nation's existence, personal decisions determining how most individuals live, work, play, worship, or are educated reflect a legacy of factoring race.

Taken at their best, systems of racial management are understandable as a response to realities that divided the nation at its outset and have vexed it ever since.[18] They reflect a sense that governing terms of neutrality and color-blindness[19] exceed actual moral development and are deceiving instrumentalities of the established order. Even if the future were to be less dynamic than what indications herald, such methods would be relatively inconsequential except for the rhetorical fireworks they engender.[20] A system of racial preferences, in a race-conscious order, may translate into a ceiling rather than a floor for opportunity. The long-term risks of such strategy are worth assuming for many who discern a reality of stalled progress and an immediate choice between limited or no achievement. Even that reed is too thin, however, when expressive management schemes are subject to risk analysis. The immediate benefits of racist speech regulation are negligible in a society that remains functionally segregated. Moreover, it is a strategy entirely unreferenced to a future, likely to condition racial progress upon lowered social barriers, enhanced multicultural experience, and a broader acquisition and sharing of knowhow. A danger of expressive management, unmitigated by any limited short-term gain, is that it provides no basis for and actually may deter cross-cultural engagement that is a necessary prelude for real progress.

The philosophy of racist speech management denotes a relatively insular, underdeveloped, and perilous effort to account for the harms it identifies and progress it envisions. Criticism of hate speech codes does not necessarily undervalue the harm that may be attributed to racially stigmatizing expression. Injury may be as real and profound as proponents of regulation maintain,[21] and the First Amendment itself has been compromised for less trenchant reasons.[22] Even factoring a discount for the charge that it is easier to oppose regulation in the abstract, when one has not borne the brunt of assaultive racist speech, the case for racist speech control is ultimately unpersuasive because it lacks general historical perspective, is underinclusive, and myopic. The case for hate speech control ignores a history of limited returns when legal change is uncoupled with coextensive moral development. It downplays the record of like methods that have been either unsuccessful or counterproductive. Bypassed also is the fact that in a functionally segregated society, points of interracial contact are relatively scarce, and beneficiaries of regulation constitute a relatively discrete subgroup. An awkward reality is that abasing intraracial expression represents a more common and profound source of harm. Given the broad contours and consequences of racism that await reckoning, and a growing peril that racial disadvantage may be hardened by nonracial dynamics, attention to a relatively discrete aspect of racist injury betrays a poor distribution of reformist resources.

The racist speech control agenda is formulated largely from tenured faculty positions in academic communities where intellectual output may be more the grist for publishing mills than an engaged concern with real-world disadvantage. Attention to the nature and decorum of cross-racial interaction is not new. A century ago, the Supreme Court ratified a comprehensive system of formal racial segregation that excluded non-whites from meaningful political, social, and economic opportunity.[23] Renewed interest in managing the conditions of cross-racial interaction arises less than four decades after the Court determined that prescriptive separation on the basis of race was inherently unequal.[24] In a post-desegregation society, where cross-racial contact still tends to be the exception rather than the norm, interest in speech control itself may be a function of integration shock.[25] Racial protocols have been in particular demand at academic institutions where cultural diversification is a fairly recent development, suggesting the possibility of a phenomenon that might give way to experience and education. For a society that in two centuries has not figured out how to make race irrelevant, however, a competing possibility is that the movement toward protocol represents the wave of the future. In neither event, given the forces at work redefining the national and world order, is such an agenda likely to have a meaningful effect upon the capacity of historically disadvantaged persons to seize opportunity and begin altering or undoing a compounding legacy of disadvantage. Nor does it reckon effectively with the "micro-aggressions"[26] that, for African Americans especially, represent continuing fallout from the stereotypes and inexperience that protocolism probably would not undo or help overcome.

With their lack of vision and breadth, and detachment from real world change, speech management agendas risk dismissal as a mere exercise in self-indulgence and political correctness.[27] Although summary rejection of the cause may not be a social disaster in its own right, a risk is that real racial imperatives may be trivialized by the pursuit of relatively marginal and highly debatable concerns. At a time when social and economic structures are being redefined with profound implications for American society, including its legacy of discrimination and disadvantage, attention to the "racial" factors of inequality and disadvantage is increasingly underinclusive.

As the employment market globalizes, fiscal realities induce pressure for downsizing public-sector bureaucracies that have been primary sources of minority employment, and information technology transforms cyclical layoffs into permanent work-force reductions, even the most vigorous accounting for discrimination and redistribution of opportunity may have but a marginal effect on the established racial order. As racial problems are influenced by forces that transcend racial ideology, the complexity of managing problems such as group disadvantage compounds. Eradication of discrimination "root and branch" at an earlier time may have facilitated achievement both of equality of opportunity and consequence. Racially targeted remedies focusing only upon racial injury, however, no longer are sufficient to account for racial disadvantage or injustice. A fundamental problem with the perspective and methods of protocolism is that they define an open-ended and evolving order in close-ended and unrelenting terms. Despite some valid observations by protocolists about racism's continuing vitality, the compounding causes of racial disadvantage leave them rather flatfooted in attempting to reckon with modern reality. For all of their acuity in "nam[ing] the injury,"[28] it is unfortunate that they are profoundly myopic at a time when a need exists for farsightedness.

As the world races into and through seemingly compressed eras, the nation's unfinished racial business presents increasingly difficult choices. It may be that society has not paid the economic or moral debt owed to those who were strategically and consciously outcast at the republic's commencement.[29] Continuing insistence that the society confront history and account for its consequences may be valid as an exercise in moral development. The overall utility of such a reckoning seems less certain, however, insofar as it focuses on action and policy that may be increasingly less determinative of access to opportunity or the ability to achieve. Civil rights laws that were effective in lowering barriers to the workplace, when industrial positions were abundant and well paying, have diminished relevance when demand for labor is exclusionary on the basis of geography, sophistication, or know-how. The case for formalistic strategies, moreover, must begin responding to indications that actual bigotry is a diminishing phenomenon and that the market itself increasingly is factoring imperatives of diversity.[30] Essential too is attention to a future in which those who have not overcome the burdens of historical disadvantage may fall farther behind even if race itself is a declining factor. As a method for progress, however, protocolism (1) seriously misreads history and disregards evolving social and economic conditions; (2) is an exercise in manipulating and avoiding racial reality; and (3) represents a serious misallocation of scarce reformist resources.

1. WOUNDING WORDS IN PERSPECTIVE

The case for protocol has been presented in terms that implicate a broad spectrum of law and its sources of inspiration. Racist speech management has been supported by reference to the law of torts,[31] of the Constitution,[32] and of nations.[33] A common regulatory premise is that racist expression constitutes a verbal assault that profoundly injures its victims.[34] As Charles Lawrence has described it, such speech represents an "instantaneous . . . slap in the face" that generates injury rather than dialogue.[35] Mari Matsuda characterizes hate speech as one of several "implements" of racism that "work in coordination, reinforcing existing conditions of domination."[36] From their perspective, the stigmatizing consequences of racist expression constitute a harm that implicates Fourteenth Amendment interests and necessitates penal sanction.[37]

Pursuant to arguments that the distinction between public and private action is false, and that hate speech codes derive from and logically extend the premises of *Brown v. Board of Education*, etiquette has emerged as a primary reformist method.[38] Enthusiasm for such strategy has not been diminished by historical reality or future need. Codes of cross-racial engagement revert to and reinvest in a sense of societal conditions "in the nature of things" — an understanding articulated initially when the Supreme Court upheld formal segregation in *Plessy v. Ferguson*.[39] The essence of *Plessy's* ideology was that distinctions and restrictions on the basis of race, even if instrumentalities for maintaining relative group advantage, were natural, essential, and indefeasible.[40] Reduced to its basics, renewed attention to racial protocol reflects a like sense of immutable conditions necessitating a formal code for governance of cross-cultural relations. Given the diverse and compounding sources of group disadvantage, attributable to historical and evolving realities, the construction of racial protocols is decidedly underwhelming as a strategy for progress. As the separate but equal era evidenced, such management schemes are valued primarily for their capacity to maintain and fortify the status quo.[41] In a society that remains functionally segregated, their utility seems, at best, dubious.

Much criticism of racist speech management has been driven by avowed concern for the First Amendment—a response that sometimes may be reflexive and overdone. The First Amendment is not an absolute[42] and, over the course of the past several decades, has been qualified by multiple exceptions to its general rule.[43] Deterrence of racially stigmatizing speech at least may be acknowledged as a substantial or compelling government interest. It also is possible to argue that the First Amendment has been affronted by less profound justifications. If George Carlin can be channeled from the nation's airwaves because of a complaint by one self-appointed decency vigilante,[44] or the publicity interests of human cannonballs can be prioritized over the First Amendment,[45] it seems legitimate to argue that racially stigmatizing or demeaning speech at least should be taken as seriously. Nor does it seem out of line to reason that if a term such as "indecency" can survive vagueness analysis,[46] "racially stigmatizing" speech should be able to pass a like test.

A typical critical reaction to modern racial protocols is the notion that they are a function of intolerance and overreaching, reflecting a failure to understand, as one newspaper editorial put it, that "after all, this is America."[47] Despite real deficiencies of such strategies, the suggestion that they are un-American is misplaced. Intolerance of ideological diversity or difference is well grounded in the nation's political culture, defining some of the nation's most historically respected agendas or movements. Animus toward competing viewpoints or beliefs was central to the nation's very creation, as American revolutionaries burned the offices and smashed the printing presses of Tory sympathizers.[48] Within a decade of the First Amendment's framing and ratification, criminal sanctions were imposed against critics of the Federalist order.[49] As the nation coursed toward disunion over the slavery issue, southern intolerance of abolitionists was rivaled by the mutual antagonisms of moderate and radical abolitionists.[50] Formal segregation was characterized, among other things, by a racial vision that could be challenged only at risk to life, limb, or property.[51] Anti-Communist crusades in the 1920s and 1950s imprisoned and ruined those who criticized the nation's political or economic system or its military involvements.[52] Given the historical record, thoughtful critics of racist speech management must transcend reflexive rhetoric and consider why it is inimical to both constitutional and regulatory objectives.

The harm attributed to racist expression is profound and real; the case for speech control is thus not frivolous on its face. First Amendment guarantees typically give way when either a compelling reason is established for regulation[53] or the speech at issue is generally bereft of value and unprotected.[54] Insofar as racist speech causes identifiable harm, it may be principled to maintain that it is without "significant social value" and, like obscenity or fighting words, should not be protected.[55] Or, it may be argued that regulatory interests at least should be balanced against First Amendment demands.[56] Even assuming that concerns with overbreadth and precision can be satisfied,[57] a speech control agenda represents a dubious exercise. Recent Fourteenth Amendment history discloses significant animus toward racial policy that singles out groups for special attention. First Amendment history illuminates a disturbing tendency to turn regimes for protecting minorities into schemes for persecuting them. The history of constitutional law, even when significant minority concerns are at stake, evidences a pattern of resistance and underachievement in accounting for them. Against that confluence of historical tendencies, the risk is not just that asking so little will result in achieving so little, but that real loss or regression will occur.

A century after *Plessy*, and two hundred years after the nation's founders prioritized their vision of a viable union over the interest of racial equality, protocol agendas may bear tidings that society is simply loath to accept. Despite questions concerning methodology or capacity to affect meaningful change, the movement's existence is a reminder that for all the legal reforms since Reconstruction, society is not as color-blind as its laws. Especially for a culture in which law increasingly reflects the sense that it cannot compel an "Emerald City in which persons of different races live side by side,"[58] protocolism has a hollow ring if offered as a serious method for progress. Protocolism, like any other reformist method, ultimately must be assessed upon its potential for responding meaningfully to the causes and conditions of racial injustice and disadvantage. A strategy for reckoning with speech, rather than thought, values, or understanding, is grand only in its minimalism. The appeal of protocol as a method for governing cross-racial experience nonetheless may depend in significant part on how reality is perceived. If functional segregation is understood as a final societal destination, the logic of formalized racial protocols is more compelling than if conditions are perceived as a temporary way station on the road toward racial progress. In neither event, however, is speech management an apt response to legal or social reality.

Even if the power to regulate racist speech is conceded, racial protocols are not necessarily validated as a meaningful or effective reform strategy. Measured against racially significant movements over the course of the nation's history, including abolitionism, the challenge to segregation, and the struggle for civil rights, attention to how people function in cross-cultural circumstances is dwarfed by the nature, risks, and achievements of past causes. The failure to measure up to such landmark initiatives is not attributable to a lack of challenging circumstances. If anything, the pervasiveness of racial prejudice and its consequences, glossed by compounding factors of disadvantage, presents more demanding tests of resources, commitment, and awareness. By promising a badge of multicultural sensitivity and maturity to persons who simply memorize and adopt an approved code of expression, protocol provides a remarkably accessible safe harbor that rewards disinterest and disengagement. Ultimate judgment becomes predicated upon projected appearance, mastery of a few critical moves, and avoidance of overt mistakes, while dialogue, achievement, and risk are neither encouraged nor rewarded. In significant ways, attention to protocol is indistinguishable from other racial scams that have accounted more for the illusion than the reality of achievement. Insofar as it is concerned primarily with cosmetics rather than underlying causes, a system of racial protocol indulges rather than challenges the nature and existence of the established order.

Given the diverse and compounding sources of group disadvantage, attention to racial protocol seems rather warped. In a society where integrated circumstances are neither well established nor extensive, the greatest possibility of stigmatizing encounters would seem to be for minorities who have edged into the mainstream.[59] Even then, group-referenced speech codes strike at least some intended beneficiaries as paternalistic methods that reinforce the imagery and reality of black dependence upon white kindness.[60] Although speech controls may be calculated to reduce the risk of degrading, insensitive, or stigmatizing experiences and processes,[61] they represent a method that has yet to prove its efficacy and even may be of significant disutility. Especially incongruous is a strategy focusing on legal change at a time when the limits of such reform as an agent of social progress have been exposed. Despite heralding new alternatives for reckoning with racial disadvantage and injustice,[62] protocolists primarily offer up recycled formalisms destined to reaffirm the law's limited capacity as a source of moral development. Having cast their lot with "(t)he analytical dexterity of legal thinkers,"[63] and pinned their hopes on their "legal imagination [being] a fruitful one,"[64] protocolists should not complain when their deconstruction of imagery results in the reconstruction of new symbols and tokens.

If not offered as a serious solution in the real world, protocolism might be valued for the academic exercise it provides on the meaning of *Brown* and its legacy. Apart from the problems of establishing protocol as a logical extension of the desegregation principle, a strategy that ties into *Brown* may assume too much about appearances and too little about achievements. The meaning and significance of *Brown* rest not just with the decision itself, but with its fate over the course of four decades. What began in 1954 as an epochal exercise in redefining the Constitution and recrafting the society it governs has yielded results that at best are uncertain and debatable and at worst delusionary and damaging. A generation of public school students experienced little if any benefit from desegregation, which begot widespread evasion, delay, and resistance. When the Court during the late 1960s finally demanded real compliance and achievement,[65] public recognition that change might be ordered on a national scale precipitated opposition and backlash—first in the political process and then in constitutional principle.[66] Thereafter, the potential for social engineering through the Fourteenth Amendment was curtailed by interpretive conditions of causation,[67] scope,[68] and duration of[69] relief. By the 1990s, insistence upon elimination of segregation "root and branch"[70] had been reduced to a demand for eradication of segregation "to the extent practicable."[71]

For all the powerful imagery that the *Brown* decision and its early progeny project, the record of achievement includes an educational sys-

tem "as separate and unequal ... in the future ... as in the past." [72]
Especially for advocates of formally managed progress through codes of
etiquette, the *Brown* experience should be a basis for second thoughts.
Striking down official segregation was an apt and belated exercise in
interpreting the Constitution. Beyond this accounting for formalism, and
given its ultimate unwinding by constitutional limiting principles, the
legacy of *Brown* is important for the insight it provides into the relative
value society has put on racial appearance and reality. The desegregation
decision generally is one of the most revered in the Court's history,
causing even conservative interpretivists to distort and gyrate in accom-
modating themselves to it. [73] The imagery it projects, however, has facilitated avoidance of persisting and unfinished racial business. Like the
touting of color-blindness, in an era of pervasive group-consciousness,
the largely cosmetic and formal achievements of the *Brown* era suggest
a real peril when imperatives of progress are staked to innovation or
redirection of the law. Regulation of racial wrong has proved vexingly
different from the sanctioning of almost any other civil or criminal
activity, given well-established habits of and easily identified opportunities for circumventing legal demands. Mere enactment of a law prohibiting offensive expression does not alter the likelihood of subsequent
equivocation toward and accommodation of the identified evil. By attempting to imitate the perceived success of *Brown,* racist speech management assumes the danger of achievement that is more illusory than
real.

For all of the noise and electricity generated by *Brown,* the Fourteenth
Amendment's annals disclose primarily a tradition of unresponsiveness
to or repudiation of group claims and concerns. Even conceding the
legitimacy of concern for the consequences of stigmatizing, degrading,
or hate-driven expression, the past also provides ample reason to pause
before investing in the process of speech control. Minorities historically
have borne a disproportionate brunt of fighting-words prosecutions. [74] A
like record characterizes experience with group defamation laws which,
when upheld by the Supreme Court, prompted Justice Black to warn
that "another such victory and I am undone." [75] As Black saw it, prohibition of expression that degraded or offended minorities was more
likely to imperil than protect them. [76] Subsequent experience bore out his
concern. Libel law a decade later was invoked in an effort to put the

civil rights movement out of business in the South,[77] much like abolition-ists were shut down prior to the Civil War.[78]

Evidence suggests that the resurrection of hate speech regulation will not reverse those historical trends.[79] To guard against misdirection and the transformation of protective into oppressive methodology, it has been suggested that racist speech regulation should cut only one way. As so conceived, hate speech laws would be enforced only when the victim of degrading expression is a minority.[80] The very urging of such a double standard, contemporaneous with clear constitutional trends against race-dependent attention or protection, suggests an exercise that not only is unattuned to recent trumpetings of constitutional color-blindness but is insular and disinterested in the lessons of history or considerations of practicality. The limited aims of group-referenced speech control arise at a time when, "after several hundred years of class-based discrimination, . . . the Court is unwilling to hold that a class-based remedy for that discrimination is permissible."[81] They are a focal point of forums and conferences, even as individuals confront the near impossible burden of proving they are specific "victims of discrimination" in a society where "racism . . . has been so pervasive that none . . . has managed to escape its impact."[82] From constitutional principle that "ignores the fact that for several hundred years Negroes have been discriminated against, not as individuals, but rather solely because of the color of their skins,"[83] a lesson exists that meaningful progress requires a significantly grander vision than the relatively discrete concern with racist speech. It is a message that should be reinforced by a view toward a future in which nonracial factors and accelerating rates of change magnify the task of reckoning with race. Stubborn touting of agendas that simply are not up to the real challenge suggest a commitment toward maintaining life support for a pet academic theory instead of contributing to the cause of resolution and progress.

Given the pertinent lessons of previous speech control experiments and the fresh evidence from their revival, it is mystifying that arguments for group protection still draw upon discredited or repudiated concepts. Like fighting words, racist expression has been characterized as speech that has no social value and constitutes a verbal assault preempting reasoned dialogue toward truth. The choice of fighting-words doctrine as a role model is especially mystifying. Since inventing the notion, the

Court consistently has found regulation of such speech to be vague and overbroad. Not surprisingly, when challenged under the First Amendment, adaptation of fighting-words doctrine to the management of racist speech has proved similarly defective.[84] For a formula that offers little meaningful protection but presents a high risk of harsh turnaround, racist speech management has commanded a degree of attention and even success that seems vastly disproportionate to its real utility. First and Fourteenth Amendment interests alike will be fortunate if the concept remains fodder primarily for academic warfare. Reformist needs and broad-spectrum progress will be worse off, however, to the extent that intellectual resources are tied up in relatively marginal pursuits.

2. MANIPULATING REALITY TO FIT THE CAUSE: CONSCIOUSNESS RAISING AS THE WORLD PASSES BY

The case for racist speech management is troubling not only for its deficient historical perspective but for its lack of acuity or honesty in describing the problem. For all of the attention that racist expression has elicited in current law and literature, it is a relatively marginal source of stigmatization and subordination. In a society that remains functionally segregated, groups tend to have limited if any direct contact across racial lines. The imagery and conditioning effects of television, in contrast, are experienced in virtually every household in the nation.[85] Contemporary prime-time programming now contains more series and shows featuring African-Americans than ever before.[86] The phenomenon is a function in part of the fact that black households watch considerably more television than white households.[87] The images communicated by television, however, tend "to reinforce social dominance and control with respect to preferred social relations between the races."[88] The institutionalization of demeaning stereotypes as a mainstream source of profit generates and indulges caricatures and misperceptions that are communicated and received in a voluntary but largely noninteractive process. In a context where defense mechanisms are less likely to be tripped, trade in stigmatization is compounded and perhaps validated by programming strategy and viewer choice.

The nation's heritage of racism includes the reality that most verbal racial blows are incidental to intragroup rather intergroup experience. Missing from modern concern with stigmatizing speech, however, is any attention to the subcultural usage of class-conscious terminology referenced to racial physiognomy. Racially demeaning speech within a group may be an especially effective means of stigmatizing and reinforcing pernicious stereotypes. The childhood experience of Justice Clarence Thomas has been referenced as a classic example in support of that point. As a child in a formally segregated society, he was taunted and demeaned by other blacks because of his thick lips, kinky hair, and dark skin.[89] Such intragroup differentiation, calculated to fortify an internal class and status hierarchy, discloses an especially perverse aspect of racism. The fact that the victimizers themselves are victims of racism makes the injury no less serious.[90] To the extent stigmatizing speech is an evil that must be controlled, constitutional principle affords no support for distinguishing on the basis of source.[91] Regulatory attention that is profoundly incremental and limited to cross-cultural incidents may respond to a legacy of easily recognized aspects and consequences of racism. Defining the problem of racist speech in cross-racial terms, when it far transcends rather than respects such limits, denotes a theory driven more by politics than principle.

In fortifying his argument for regulating stigmatizing interracial expression, Charles Lawrence adverts to an incident that affected his own family. He mentions the work of some white students who painted racist slogans and pictures on a large sign posted on a high school field. The drawing portrayed a black student identified by name with a gun pointed toward his head.[92] Also depicted were three Ku Klux Klansmen, "one of whom was saying that the student 'dies.' Next to the gun was a drawing of a burning cross under which was written 'Kill the Tarbaby.' "[93] Compounding the injury of the message was the lamentable but predictable response of many white parents who regarded the incident as a racially insignificant childish prank and dismissed or discounted its gravity or impact.[94]

While it is easy, or should be easy, to empathize and share the outrage generated by such an incident, a mere punitive response ensures a resolution of appearance rather than of the underlying problem. Especially given the reflexive and probably race-conditioned instincts of denial and minimization typified by reaction to the incident, the anticipation of meaningful enforcement seems wishful to the point that any enactment would be largely precatory. Reliance upon a community to enact and enforce protective regulation when the dominant culture itself has evidenced insensitivity toward the harm for which sanction is sought does not seem well placed. A mentality that trivializes incidents such as those that Lawrence relates is likely also to house the attitudes that historically have inspired the turning of racially significant regulation against minorities, especially because the dominant cultural group is less likely to temporize, discount offensive actions, or underuse power when its own interests are implicated. Strategies of education may be as difficult to implement as speech codes, especially where problems are habitually avoided or ignored. Such tactics are worth the effort, however, because unlike protocols they are an agent of enlightenment and change rather than holding.

Regulation of cross-racial incidents of racism discloses also a tendency to factor only a relatively small slice of racially harmful expression. Reality is, in a society that has progressed from formal to functional segregation, direct interracial contacts for members of any group are a limited or nonexistent phenomenon. Objectionable and even injurious as cross-racial verbal stigmatization may be, the frequency of interracial contacts and mathematical possibilities for any communication—harmful or otherwise—are slight compared to incidents of intraracial contact. Given the gross disparity in volumes of interaction, the potential for injurious expression is much higher in an intraracial than in an interracial context. Traditionally, the acceptability of racially referenced expression and the understanding of whether it demeans or not has been a function of source. Much expression considered stigmatizing or objectionable if uttered across racial lines has historically been traded in, indulged, and ratified to the extent it circulates within the same racial group. Awareness of that racial dividing line even has evidenced itself in constitutional jurisprudence, as Justice Brennan noted that "[w]ords generally considered obscene . . . are considered neither obscene nor derogatory in the [black] vernacular except in particular contextual situations and when used with certain intonations."[95]

The racially significant line between acceptability and unacceptability tends to be a function of folklore rather then science. At minimum, racial terminology is enmeshed in a racist legacy. Second thoughts about intragroup usage of race-sensitive terms such as "nigger" have edged into popular media even as protocolists remain fixed on a narrower piece of reality. A traditional view, to the effect that the term is acceptable and even a source of eloquence, subtlety, and pride when used intraracially, has been challenged by a perspective that sees a self-inflicted blow to image and esteem.[96] If such cause and effect exist, it may be that unregulated intragroup expression is even more injurious than cross-racial speech.[97] Not only are intraracial points of contact far more numerous than interracial encounters in a functionally segregated society; self-protective methods of processing information over a lifetime of race-conscious experience may be less operative in an intragroup setting. An initiative for offsetting the consequences of racially harmful speech that overlooks or factors out such a high-volume dimension of the problem is at least seriously underinclusive.

To the extent that personal and anecdotal evidence has been adduced to support regulation of intergroup racist speech, it seems fair to consider comparable data on the other side. The evidentiary supplement to the victimization that Lawrence described as occurring at the high school is the experience of many African Americans who, when encountering intraracial verbal degradation, sense confusion, uneasiness, shame, and a challenge to self-esteem. It is an experience that, contrasted with interracial disparagement or insult, is more subtle and may be more confounding and perhaps even more dangerous. My wife, while accustomed to the subtle or unconscious variants of cross-racial putdowns, recalls few personal experiences of overtly degrading or stigmatizing interracial expression. By contrast, she cannot begin to count the numerous times that she has been a victim of or bystander to demeaning intraracial speech. Being derided as a "skinny black bitch nigger," or similarly demeaned, for her has been more a function of intragroup than intergroup dynamics. Unlike academic theories focused upon and determined by concepts of relative power, reaction without the luxury of relatively detached intellectualization seems unlikely to draw precious doctrinal distinctions. A more likely response would be the sense of pain and confusion, experienced by my wife and others, over whether to risk feeling further betrayed if an effort to reeducate the offending person fails, or to dismiss the individual as an "ignorant fool."

Expressive management regardless of circumstance is unresponsive and largely irrelevant to real and multiplying problems of group disadvantage. Even if implemented, the most sophisticated and extensive program of speech management would not cause "[c]rack dealers . . . to run for cover" or induce "David Duke [to] change his ideology because we tightened our terminology."[98] Nor would it begin to reckon with the problems of health, housing, poverty, education, crime, criminal justice, alienation, and shortage of marketable know-how and basic coping skills that diminish not only esteem but opportunity. Finally, racial protocols speak not at all to the forces and consequences of economic change that are redefining opportunity and disadvantage independent of race.

In touting speech control, protocolists tend not only to manipulate but to avoid realities that may be inconvenient to their cause. If any single lesson permeates American racial history, it is that reliance upon the dominant culture's sense of responsibility or conviction for reform is destined to result in nonperformance or underachievement.[99] Such dependence has mostly begotten formalistic and cosmetic change. It also has reinforced relationships of dominance and subordination that need to be undone rather than fortified if real and lasting racial change is to eventuate. The most recent manifestation of futility in trading upon majoritarian duty or debt was the case for affirmative action. Whatever potential preferential methods had to break down stereotypes and ignorance largely has been shorted by insistence on comprehensive constitutional color-blindness. It is an especially unfortunate consequence that the general battle over preferences and the intramural conflict they engendered were over an increasingly obsolete cause. Even if preferential policies were upheld and racial injustice, discrimination, and stereotyping suddenly were to vanish, the distribution and contours of group disadvantage probably would not be significantly affected.

A multiplicity of factors, which by themselves have no racial significance, are becoming more pertinent to whether a legacy of racial disadvantage is maintained or consolidated. Possibly because past and present racial wrongs are so substantial, and deploring them is so habitual, attention to increasingly crucial determinants of opportunity and success has been deficient. Even as remedies have been structured pursuant to *Brown* and civil rights legislation over the past few decades, the performance of desegregative exercises where demographics allow no significant integration has previewed a future of declining remedial relevance or utility. Heightening the potential for limited or ineffective accounting methods are modern economic trends toward a higher-skilled economy and a globalized labor market. Although anti-discrimination methodology may represent a logical and useful means of reckoning with prejudice that impairs opportunity, its utility is limited to circumstances where race is the primary factor of impedance. To the extent racial disadvantage now is compounded by nonracial factors, it is illusory to tout anti-racist protocols as passkeys to meaningful change in status, condition, or even self-esteem. A focus upon protocol, in the context of political, economic, and social change that is racially neutral but of real racial significance, is profoundly Orwellian.

Modern and evolving influences that dramatically complicate the already vexing problem of racial disadvantage are especially confounding because they force serious reformists to move beyond traditional reflexes. Racially independent factors threatening to compound disadvantage to the point of indefeasibility, although interacting with a legacy of oppression and injustice, need to be reckoned with for what they are. Evidence exists that industrial layoffs in the United States are not simply a cyclical condition but a permanent structural response to evolving market imperatives. Fundamental change in the economic order is rooted in a global shift toward automated processes in both the public and private sectors that increase productivity with fewer workers. Competitive considerations meanwhile have induced the export of assembly and engineering functions to lower cost labor markets. As information technology eliminates the need for much middle management, preexisting demand for an extensive white-collar work force is being reduced.

Because racial barriers historically have impaired the quality of employment options available to African Americans, who as a group tend to have less education and a stronger presence in semiskilled and unskilled positions, they invariably are affected disproportionately by the imperatives and consequences of postindustrial society.[100] Movement toward a service and information-based economy is especially perilous to minorities who were excluded from the economic mainstream, at least until northern industrialization precipitated a massive recasting of racial demographics and opportunity. A second wave of racially significant economic progress, as minorities broke into the management ranks of corporate, government, and education structures, is a more recent phenomenon facilitated in significant part by civil rights legislation and affirmative action policies. Hard-earned racial reform that secured opportunity in an industrial economy and broke down some of the doors to positions of management and other responsibility now is at special risk insofar as progressive strategies fail to adapt to broader cultural dynamics.

As the private sector trims and redefines itself in response to competitive needs, it is conceivable that racial disparities will worsen regardless of how racially significant law is enforced or augmented. Such a possibility represents a real peril to the economic and social viability of groups that historically have been denied the opportunity to participate in the social mainstream. The danger is doubled insofar as government itself is profoundly affected by economic change and political expectation. Perhaps the safest harbor for minority opportunity in recent years has been public employment—especially in the military and in bureaucracies in those cities and counties where national minorities have a significant presence. Elimination of the draft in the early 1970s and consequent reliance upon an all-volunteer military induced significant changes in the armed forces. At a time when military service was systematically avoided, due to an unpopular war in Southeast Asia, military need generated opportunities that were seized by traditional victims of discrimination. Military and demographic imperatives eventually coalesced toward recognition of the need to establish an environment that was more responsive to and supportive of minority aspirations. The armed forces, committed to segregation a generation earlier, soon refashioned themselves and are now adverted to as a role model for melting-pot dynamics.[101] Despite extensive change in the racial aspects of military culture, and the skills training and educational benefits that have been a magnet for the disadvantaged, access to that avenue of opportunity is being narrowed by racially nonsignificant factors. The end of the Cold War and federal budget deficits in particular have generated substantial reductions in force sizes and diminished needs for new personnel.

Although demographic change has translated into enhanced political clout and status for minorities in many cities, economic benefits from that change also may prove relatively short-lived. In recent decades, dramatically expanded minority political presence has been an undeniable phenomenon of local government.[102] Enhanced involvement and influence may be attributed to the effects of federal voting-rights legislation and trends toward further residential segregation and polarization.[103] Demographic change in many instances has resulted in political empowerment as a function of white abandonment.[104] Political gain has occurred in many cities in the context of an eroding economic base. The effect of wealth and resource emigration from many urban centers, although facilitated by racially significant factors that accelerated white flight,[105] is being exacerbated by nonracial factors that include information systems and data bases that cut against the need for concentrated work forces and activities. Although densely populated communities were a logical and efficient structure when information, goods, and people were less mobile, private wealth, entrepreneurialism, and decision-making increasingly are being driven by considerations of decentralization, downsizing, and flexibility. The same factors that have diminished previously dominant private bureaucracies are at work too to redefine public organizations. What shareholder demands and competitive imperatives are achieving in the private sector may be duplicated as a function of limited fiscal resources and public resistance to taxation. Notwithstanding the demands or negotiating achievements of public sector unions, eroding revenue bases have generated pressure to cut costs, reduce work forces, and resort to technological and service innovation.

With significant and fundamental forces at work to heighten and consolidate racial disadvantage, as a function of incidental rather then intentional consequence, attention to protocol denotes an agenda that is not fully wired to reason or reality. For all the moral rectitude that may inspire anti-racist codes of etiquette, the peril is that whatever evolves in the way of formalistic change will prove irrelevant to the real problem. As public and private structures at the global and domestic levels reinvent and redefine themselves for the future, serious racial reformists will consider how their own aims and methods are affected by new realities. Those who subordinate achievement to cause, meanwhile, can be expected to spin more furiously an already convoluted and thin dogma.

Evidence of such egocentricity already is discernible in the case for racial protocol. At a time when a long legacy of massive sacrifice and incremental progress may be coalescing with market dynamics and irresistible forces of multiculturalism, protocolists indicate little if any interest in the possibilities of such historical change. Instead they propose a reinvented social order, constructed pursuant to their own sense of natural justice[106]—a vision unaccompanied by any method of achievement beyond the policies of "dialogue, debate, consciousness raising, and political struggle."[107] Factoring out ideology, the reliance upon narrative and storytelling seems essentially Reaganesque. Although the Reagan presidency perfected the usage of anecdote for political purposes, the technique must be viewed suspiciously as a means for understanding real-world norms. The methods match up against a culture driven primarily by self-interest in opportunity, achievement, and reward—social factors that historically have prevailed over far more concrete and compelling agendas. Protocolists claim that their program was inspired during the late 1970s by a perception that "[t]he civil rights movement of the 1960s had stalled, and many of its gains were being rolled back."[108] Such a sense of stoppage is supported by the work of the Supreme Court which, over the past two decades, has transformed the equal protection guarantee into a premise accounting primarily for claims by the dominant racial group.[109] As it turns out, protocolism touts a vision that is as arrested as the principles and structures it criticizes—even though posturing as an innovative and perhaps only authentic counterpoint "to visions of race, racism, and law dominant in [the] post-civil rights period."[110]

Racial protocolism is suffused with broad generalities and assertions that at best are debatable. Prioritizing the First Amendment over hate speech codes represents to protocolists a method of defending the status quo,[111] for instance, notwithstanding legitimate and well-reasoned arguments that speech regulation is inimical not only to constitutional but minority interests. A more fundamental overstatement and indulgence, largely left unchallenged in modern legal literature, is the portrayal of a monolithic white power structure in the academic community that has coopted "language of freedom struggles" in the course of "an emerging and increasingly virulent backlash against the extremely modest successes achieved by communities of color, women, and other subordinated groups in our efforts to integrate academic institutions run by and for white male elites."[112] Protocolists score a point for noting how First Amendment passion against racist speech sanctions often dissipates into passivity and disinterest in reckoning directly with racism or disadvantage.[113] They accurately identify an "emerging" response to the relatively recent influx of minority scholars who, until lately, have been rare or nonexistent at mainstream universities, colleges, and professional schools.[114] Diversification policies and practices in recent years have elicited not just "polite and polished"[115] but more traditional variants of racism.

Arguments that hostility is "increasing" to the point that change is impossible in the established order,[116] however, suggest a monolith that does not exist. Modern circumstances may not overflow with evidence of readiness to abandon a legacy of evading racial realities.[117] Nor are there widespread indicators of shared interest in honest dialogue on race. To be fair, if not flattering, the dominant culture's response to multiculturalism ranges across a broad spectrum from hostility to good faith. Between those extremes have been much fumbling, foolishness, and inexperience.[118] Hyperbole may not be unnatural when power and opportunity are at stake. Rhetorical overkill seems to be a particular stock in trade, however, of deconstructionist ideology. It is a technique that extends the methods of Catharine MacKinnon and others who distort reality to fit the cause rather than adapting their agenda to meet real needs. Calculated rhetoric that presumes an elite white male monolith or ideology,[119] or asserts that pornography is to women what lynching is to blacks,[120] seems indifferent to essential distinction or nuance. Nor is it above exploiting and cheapening historical suffering for its own purpose. Strategies that indulge stereotypes regardless of cause or ultimate objective should be regarded suspiciously. Buying into an agenda of comprehensive reconstruction requires more than a reference to historical tendencies and a leap of faith that any new structure will not simply prioritize a new power interest over an old one.

The tendency of protocolists to villainize those who share their ultimate concerns, but not their belief in what effectively reckons with racism or racial disadvantage, hardly builds trust in motive, judgment, sensitivity, or priorities. Nor do their anecdotal experiences, valid as they may be for the persons and institutions concerned, provide a basis for trumping competing stories—suggesting that the dominant culture is working through the early stages of its own learning curve in reckoning with multiculturalism. Neither set of narratives necessarily establishes an enduring truth. When protocolists claim that they "name[] the injury and identif[y] its origins,"[121] and that their revelation leads to "empowerment,"[122] they seem consumed by their own extravagance. Ordinarily, one does not receive much credit for discovering a well-known phenomenon. Recognizing what already is obvious even if denied or evaded, and touting it as the key to empowerment, transforms belated disclosure into false prophecy. Whatever empowerment follows from restatement of the truth hardly suffices for purposes of reckoning with a more complicated and changing world of racial disadvantage. Speaking volumes to manifest realities is not to be mistaken for responsiveness to the more complex and less categoric difficulties of the future.

What protocolists fail to factor, perhaps because more relevant to consequence than cause, is the possibility that market forces are pressuring a habitually insular and exclusive white world to interact with and adapt to multicultural realities. A fundamental assumption of protocolists is that "majoritarian self-interest [is] a critical factor in the ebb and flow of civil rights doctrine."[123] Although the observation is well supported by the record, an open and inquiring mind would consider how that persisting self-interest may translate into different results in a world driven by the imperatives of technology and multiculturalism. For the time being, it may be safe to assume that whites have the numbers, but it at least is open to debate whether they—and especially white males—will continue to have the dominance of power presently attributed to them.[124] By the middle of the next century, the total of non-Hispanic whites in the United States will have declined from three-quarters to one-half of the total population.[125] Such demographic trends may not ordain an impending redistribution of power driven by market factors. Insofar as power and opportunity are determined by higher education and specialized skills, and access to learning is characterized by racial disparity, it is conceivable that the established order will perpetuate itself. For the relevant one-quarter of the population—at least that segment which is fully qualified and credentialed for purposes of competing in the future, however—market forces at least are conspiring against exclusive domination of the political and economic order. Understanding the implications and potential of such a future, especially for those historically excluded from opportunity, seems a more logical focal point than managing an elusive and perhaps illusory status quo.

Ideology dedicated to the justification of protocol evinces a primary default in vision for a society that must still get beyond racism even as the factors contributing to racial disadvantage multiply and become more complex. Protocolists dress up their dogma as a synthesis of "liberalism, Marxism, the law and society movement, critical legal studies, feminism, postculturalism/postmodernism, and neopragmatism."[126] A penchant for intellectual name-dropping, however, suggests a limited relevance beyond academic circles—especially in those areas of life where racism and disadvantage are experienced as a function not of ignorant and insensitive words and deeds in newly and partially integrated contexts but of alienation, despair, and indifference. It may be legitimate to identify as a struggle the carriage of "multiple burdens of token representative, role model and change agent."[127] However, it is an exercise in overreaching and self-glorification to suggest that the experience of pioneering or playing the point in breaking down historical barriers establishes a nexus with or provides direct meaning to those who are entirely excluded from the social mainstream (or swimming with a different perspective).

Protocolists identify a worthy aspiration when they delineate their "vision of a society where the substance of freedom is freedom from degradation, humiliation, battering, starvation, homelessness, hopelessness, and other forms of violence to the person that deny one's full humanity."[128] It is a perspective that is shared by various orthodox political or social organizations, including significant factions of the Democratic party.[129] Protocolists fall out with traditional reformist achievers in their method of accomplishment or lack therefore. Unlike those who both inspired *and* facilitated the civil rights agenda, protocolists trade in the abstractions of "consciousness-raising" and "political struggle."[130] What they characterize as "the most important part of [their] work" is helping other victims who "discover they are not alone in their subordination," so that they can "find their voices" and become "empowered."[131] Self-awareness is a worthy goal, as is an understanding of one's context. Reality may be defined by many who disguise their real nature "in the rhetoric of shared values and neutral legal principles."[132] It also includes those, however, whose investment in different methods should not be taken as a sign of hollow commitment or disingenuous motive. A disinterest in factoring such distinctions may evidence more fidelity to cause and outcast maintenance than to achievement—a state of mind befitting a role as self-professed rather than real agent of change.

When concern with the disutility and mischief of speech management is pressed upon them, protocolists counter with a transcendent aim of formally registering government against racism.[133] Their overarching concern with having government weigh in officially on the "right" side discloses a fundamental anomaly and irony. A movement stressing resistance to tokenism as a primary animator of its existence[134] essentially offers to settle for the functional equivalent of recognizing February as Black History Month. Accepting so little when allegedly seeking so much makes it hard to avoid the suspicion that underlying theory and cause are staked more to personal than social concern. In crediting themselves with unmasking society's racist core,[135] protocolists suggest a means of empowerment that is illusory to great masses whose heritage of disadvantage is being accelerated and compounded by racially independent aggravating factors. The result is an agenda that not only is oblivious to evolving societal dynamics but, for all the rhetoric about social reinvention, is not about to deconstruct the privileges of insularity and irrelevance traditionally associated with academic culture. Given the indifferences, subtleties, evasions, denials, and standards of review that make it so hard to reckon with modern incarnations of racism, it is tempting to conclude that the annoyance and silliness of formal protocol are well deserved. Substantial evidence supports the proposition that if newly diversifying institutions demonstrated more concern and responsiveness to racism or racial indifference in their midst,[136] the inspiration and market for the authors' ideology of exasperation would be much slackened. Deferring to frustration and allowing the exponents of racial management to prevail, however, would compound blunder insofar as it allowed imagery to triumph over reality, fortified business as usual, and defaulted to a vision for the future that is profoundly myopic.

3. INTELLECTUAL MARGINALISM AND MISALLOCATED RESOURCES

Racial injustice has been an immutable aspect of American society. Although its contours and manifestations have varied over the course of time, racism has established a legacy that still awaits a final reckoning. For the most part, the dimensions of racism have elicited responses commensurate with the scope of the burdens they imposed and challenges they presented. Movements for African resettlement and gradual abolition during the early eighteenth century, for instance, were discrete strategies fostered in part by a sense that slavery was a limited and terminal institution. Such initiatives anticipated that slavery's awkward relationship to founding values could be resolved by pressure for gradual reform that eventually would result in slavery's disappearance. Although myopic, early abolition and colonization efforts at least responded coextensively with perceived dimensions of society's racial problem. So too did later abolitionist efforts, which reflected an awakening to the truth that slavery was not a dying institution but a phenomenon with an expansive capacity and demands that implicated the entire nation. The twentieth-century challenge to segregation likewise factored in broad-spectrum group interest. Although the desegregation agenda and its objectives were debated vigorously among African Americans,[137] no question existed that the legal challenge to the separate but equal doctrine was staked to groupwide interests.[138]

Measured against the backdrop of past challenges to racial disadvantage and injustice, not to mention the dimensions of modern problems, recent initiatives to reckon with the nation's legacy of racism fall short in vision and breadth. The push for racial preferences during the past few decades was vulnerable to objection that it was too narrow in both its conception and its potential for achievement. The case for affirmative action, however, at least attempted to reference itself to groupwide interests.[139] Even acknowledging the possibility that the benefits of racially preferential policies may accrue primarily to a discrete well-qualified subgroup, one commentator has offered the defense that a single policy choice should not exclude broader reformist responses and thus should not be condemned simply for limited focus or achievement.[140] The argument of nonexclusivity might be persuasive if the resources for change were unlimited. Fending off the underinclusiveness charge is more difficult, however, when higher groupwide needs exist and reformist resources are scarce. Unlike the case for racial preferences as a means of ensuring economic opportunity, an agenda of racial protocol has not managed to hinge itself to a clear groupwide interest. Inverted priorities, denoted by the limited aims and benefits of the racial protocol movement, may reflect a sense of being boxed in by slow change and arrested doctrine. Constitutional standards in recent years have limited substantially the capacity of the equal protection guarantee as an agent of change. Modern law and society reflect real animus toward remedial race factoring, whether effected through desegregation processes or through racially preferential policies. Constitutional case law, in addition to rejecting the group accounting methodologies of racial preferences and racist speech regulation, has established motive requirements that function as vexing impediments to progress beyond formalism. Social critics also have identified a sense of "race fatigue,"[141] which, as experienced by other generations that effected change but found race a still intractable problem,[142] has established an inertia of disinterest, resignation, or indifference. Even acknowledging that circumstances are not perfect for racial vision and change that more comprehensively account for group interests, the truth is that conditions for racial progress never have been ideal. If reformist energy historically had been harbored pending a welcoming embrace, official segregation might be absent from the record only because slavery never was defeated.

Despite legal, moral, and social barriers to progress beyond the present law's present accounting for formalism, significant responsibility for underachievement must be assigned to the quality of contemporary reformist ideas and strategy. A legitimate argument exists that historically outcast groups still face significant racism and discrimination. Even if formal discrimination is largely a relic, its modern subtler or unconscious incarnations and consequences endure. As Paul Brest has noted, "the injuries inflicted by [it] can place its victims at a disadvantage in a variety of future endeavors, and discrimination can also perpetuate itself by altering the social environment to harm new generations of victims."[143] Real and persisting harm notwithstanding, history has demonstrated that appeals for change cast basically in terms of victimization are not easy to market. Despite the raised consciousness of the Reconstruction era and the poignant case for former slaves, the nation's remedial interest abated swiftly. Progress was limited and actually undone, even when the gross injustice of slavery was fresh in the nation's mind.[144] More than a century later, when the achievements of *Brown* have been inflated to the point that imagery is indulged more than reality is understood, and even legal educators have lost touch with the abiding relevance of *Dred Scott v. Sandford*,[145] it should be evident that the touting of victim status by itself is a dead-end strategy for further progress.

Broad achievement under the law is dependent not just upon identifying historical wrong and disadvantaged status, as affirmative action strategy did, or the victimized circumstance of a subgroup, as speech management initiatives do. If serious reckoning with the nation's unfinished racial business is to occur as a real basis for further progress, it must be inspired by a grander vision and a sense of the increasing complexity of racial disadvantage. Essential too is an understanding that limited intellectual and material resources exist for pursuing racially significant change. The unwise and potentially counterproductive strategy of speech management, for all of its scholarly imagery, might not have been pressed so seriously if tested against some real-world sense and perspective. Had they performed a reality check first, protocolists

might have pondered the real priorities of the disadvantaged and isolated. Logic might have inspired the question of whether reformist energies should be dedicated toward primary impediments to development
and opportunity or to the relatively marginal phenomenon of interracial
speech. Assuming an obvious priority, the real challenge for protocolists
would seem to be to establish their relevance beyond a small corner of
the real world.

Poignant as narrative may be in defining personal context or perception, it is hard not to wonder how much intellectual energy is left to
illuminate conditions of racial disadvantage that are more prosaic but
less defeasible. If "experiential knowledge" is to be the basis for ideology
and policy, it seems fair to ask what range of experience is to be
referenced, what conditions are to be prioritized, and whether book
knowledge is a trump card. Are those whose interest in having the
established order work in some (but for them meaningful) way to be
taken seriously, or are they to be indulged by an understanding of their
"real needs"? Those whose struggle with racism's legacy is defined by a
repetition of debilitating challenges that for others are routinely or re-
flexively negotiated have no academic pulpit or power of position from
which to command an audience. Distanced as they are by class and
often by experience, and totally mystified by how formalized protocol is
relevant to them, it is their narrative that may be wrongly presumed
and undertold.

Instead of picking relatively small fights of their own convenience,
would-be agents of change might redirect their attention to obstacles
that more seriously impede further racial progress under the law. The
most crippling constitutional blow of the post-*Brown* era, largely fore-
closing interpretive progress beyond an accounting for formalism, has
been the installment of discriminatory intent requirements as a condition
for establishing an equal-protection violation. Such criteria arrest doctrinal development short of any capacity to account for subtle or unconscious racism. Motive-based criteria are to modern legal reckoning with
racial disadvantage and discrimination what the separate but equal doctrine was to constitutional progress from the late nineteenth through the
middle twentieth centuries.[146]

Like segregation before them, motive-based criteria are an apt and
ripe target for a tireless legal challenge. It took nearly four decades, in
a more intimidating social environment, for the challenge to official

segregation to express itself in a tactical fashion.[147] In half that amount of time, since the Court invested in motive-based inquiry,[148] protocolists have responded to the overarching equal-protection challenge of the time in generally unresponsive terms. Rather than conceiving strategies of litigation and education targeted toward the defeat of principles that indulge subtle and unconscious discrimination, reformist energy is being diverted into and dissipated by causes that generally are lost and would have limited significance even if successful. It may be an ominous sign for the future that as the process of framing strategic goals and development has progressed from circumstances of real human peril to the relative comfort of academic tenure, policy, vision, and strategy have become correspondingly uninspired and insular. The phenomenon of parochialism and interest stratification reflects John Hart Ely's concern, expressed as a critique of fundamental rights development, with "a bias in constitutional reason in favor of the values of the upper middle, professional class from which most lawyers . . . and for that matter most moral philosophers are drawn." [149]

A response to the inadequacies of modern anti-discrimination law, directed toward a broad market, is a useful albeit incomplete response to Charles Lawrence's plea "to think creatively as lawyers." [150] More significant strategies necessitate investing in interdisciplinary methods of problem-solving that will be essential to reckoning with race in a more complex social and economic order. Creative thought by itself, as recent reformist efforts demonstrate, does not ensure wise policy or useful results. Speech management, although creative, is distinguished by a lack of vision and historical perspective and a failed sense of marketability that risks tainting the historically profound movement for racial justice with the debatable and perhaps trendy agenda of political correctness. Unlike abolitionism, which managed to insinuate itself into mainstream politics, and the anti-segregation movement, which diligently cultivated legal and moral support, speech management theory has succeeded primarily in dividing traditional reformist allies.

Especially crucial to thinking that is both creative and productive may be the ability to transcend thinking like a lawyer. Creative thought, if it is to be bridled with real achievement, must factor in considerations other than legal theory and analytical prowess. Essential for real progress is an effective marketing strategy for selling change. Regardless of how aptly a strategy for change is conceived and developed, it may be largely for naught if sufficient attention also is not devoted to elevating levels of social awareness. Teaching a constitutional law class affords quick insight into the reality that the vast majority of law students, until exposed to modern equal protection doctrine, have no idea that vexing barriers to proving discrimination exist or that *Brown* and civil rights enactments did not solve the nation's racial problems. A safe inference would be that if a well-educated class of impendent professionals is largely oblivious to that reality, most persons have little if any clue that modern methods of discrimination are largely above the law. Like the evils of segregation before, the reality of contemporary legal circumstance is a tale that needs to be told well.

To the extent it begets little more than protocolism or doctrinal innovation, however, unbridled creativity seems reducible to intellectual tinsel. Storytelling that is a prelude to relevant strategy requires more than dogmatic revelation. Central to protocolist faith, for instance, is the tenet that principles of neutrality are a front for cultural powers that use them to rig and fortify the established order. Even acknowledging that regulatory radar is deficient for purposes of detecting modern racism, it is possible nonetheless that legal reform has reached the point of diminishing returns. Instead of building a case for more doctrinal exotica and achievement under the law, the ease of discriminating despite official dictate may support an argument against further formalistic regimens and for enhanced attention to educational and moral development. Effective narration of modern legal conditions may require some armchair advocates to enhance their exposure to and engagement in real world diversity, rather than define their pluralistic credentials on the basis of having jumped through a relatively unchallenging set of hoops. Real appreciation of, and accounting for, cultural pluralism in the end is denoted less by pushing the political cosmetology of protocolism than by a broader mix of actions, decisions, and involvement that more meaningfully confirms a person's or institution's values and commitments.

The legal culture's readiness to acknowledge "the sorry history of . . . discrimination,"[151] while still maintaining standards sheltering that legacy, should not beget merely cynicism, frustration or self-absorption. Consider the desegregation strategy, which provided a lesson not only in constitutional litigation but also in how to market an ideal. Racial reformists then, as now, faced the task of educating society and its governing institutions. Like the reckoning that ultimately must occur with subtle racism, the challenge to official segregation was vexed by much indifference toward and unawareness of how the law was responsible for disadvantage.[152] In its generation-long challenge to segregation, the NAACP pitched its case to the courts, politicians, academics, and the general public.[153] Such multidimensional groundwork fostered a legal and societal environment in which real change eventually became possible.

The model is especially apt for consideration at a time when strategy for progress has become so insular. While modern reformists may run a lesser risk of violence and peril than their predecessors, they face a daunting educational task insofar as much conventional wisdom assumes racial justice under the law has been achieved. Change is not likely to occur, however, when market priming consists of little more than exotic or esoteric academic theorizing. The interest of broad spectrum progress would be enhanced significantly, however, if the energies of a Charles Lawrence were redirected from promoting protocol to expanding access to his arresting insights into subtle and unconscious racism and how to move beyond motive-based equal protection standards.[154] Unlike the desegregation movement that succeeded against real intimidation and peril, modern reformists interested in wholesale change have the advantage of a broad media universe for disseminating their ideas and secure professional positions from which to frame and espouse them.

For any cause, selling change is a crucial prerequisite of change itself. History illustrates why social awakening is essential for any racially pertinent change that may be achieved by law. The latter half of this century has included two racially significant demands by the legal system for social and moral change. In *Brown,* the Court required dismantlement of formal segregation. Later, it prohibited racial preferences even for remedial purposes. Both decisions, despite their constitutional demands, have legacies demonstrating that the challenge of moral reform is at least as daunting as the task of legal change. A review of post-*Brown* litigation discloses the pervasiveness of resistance to the redefined imperatives of equal protection. Notwithstanding recent commands of constitutional color-blindness, one need look no farther than faculty hiring meetings at countless American law schools to witness an exercise in group prioritization[155] and effective repetition of *Brown*'s aftermath guided only by a different moral compass.

Creative thinking in its broadest sense also requires identifying and seizing advantage when opportunity presents itself. Trying to rework the magic of *Brown* by making its theory relevant to modern problems is an odd enterprise when the past two decades of relevant jurisprudence essentially have gutted it. In retrospect, *Brown* and its progeny represent a classic exercise in the treatment of symptoms rather than cause. Protocolism likewise inclines toward results that account more for the appearance than the actuality of social change. Peculiar too is the willingness to reinvest in a premise that indulges the imagery of achievement and reinforces habits of reliance on what history suggests will be unkept promises or inadequate results. Further appeals for special attention or protection miss a key lesson of the nation's racial legacy that the desegregation experience has reinforced. If the purpose of speech regulation is to safeguard against further victimization, it seems "somewhat self-defeating to appeal to the sense of the majority" as a strategy of accounting for minority rights.[156] Indications are that neither the present nor future of a society that rewards individual achievement and advantage will differ from the past, at least with respect to anyone's or any group's willingness to qualify or restrain self-interest as a condition for redistributing power, opportunity, and justice.[157]

The case for managing group interests, apart from reflecting an incompetent strategy, trades both in the imagery of patronization and the reality of false hope. What is missed by legal intellectuals, seduced by the allure of formalistic manipulation and discovery, is effectively articulated by grass-roots social critics who—having witnessed the underachievement of desegregation and broken promises of urban redevelopment—"don't expect whites to do anything for blacks."[158] Appeals for official management of group interest are viewed skeptically from a perspective that sees "[t]he only reason we could ever have to be a supplicant before another group [as being] our own lack of self-respect and belief in ourselves."[159] Even in a system burdened by the legacy of discrimination, strategy that prepares for emerging opportunities may prove more useful in the long run than trading in victimization or attempting to squeeze progress from *Brown* ever could be. Discrimination itself, like other well-established and seemingly immutable conditions, may yet prove vulnerable to the influence and fall-out of social and economic change.

To the extent African Americans traditionally were excluded from participation in the nation's political and economic mainstream, by systems of slavery and segregation, the opportunity to develop and market themselves was formally denied or limited. As the subtler aftermath of those methods evidences, habits of exclusion and discrimination have not vanished pursuant to change in the law. If evidence of diminishing prejudice and demographic change holds true, however, it ultimately will be programs of learning and empowerment that are most crucial to progress. Plotting a strategy that reckons effectively with the multiplying influences upon racial disadvantage necessitates enhanced attention to factors that themselves are independent of race. Despite society's failure to provide adequate satisfaction for historical pain and suffering, redistributive or protective methods have become inadequate, dated, and perhaps even deceitful. The record may show that a long and profound history of racial wrong never elicited extended policies of affirmative remediation. Reformist achievement for the most part has been limited to success in convincing society to give up certain formal racially pernicious practices. A broader spectrum approach to disadvantage, attentive both to racial and nonracial factors, might reflect absorption of an important history lesson. Because an adequate accounting for racial injustice never was achieved by reconstruction or desegregation, when serious wrongs were freshly impressed upon the nation's conscience, it seems unlikely to be forthcoming as they recede further from society's consciousness.

For purposes of its own relevance and efficacy, racial reform strategy must factor in the prospect of a future in which racism and discrimination will be nonexclusive factors in determining racial disadvantage. As the social and economic order evolves pursuant to potent forces unrelated to race, a one-dimensional focus upon past wrongs and injustices may prove to be as binding as racism itself. Single-minded attention to protocol and managed distribution of potentially obsolete opportunities trades in false hope and promise. Even as the reformist landscape is dominated by marginally relevant agendas, however, some models of change—reflecting frustration both with an abiding legacy of disempowerment and futile initiatives to reckon with it—have exhibited potential for higher productivity. Tactical planning to reckon with racial disparities in the distribution of environmental risks in particular has evidenced a shift away from exclusive rights-oriented strategies to more farsighted brokering, community participation, education, and practical politics.[160] Strategic redirection has been inspired by the same frustration with slow or nonexistent progress under the law that has begotten protocolism.[161] Instead of challenging an unremitting legal system with more novel theories, some reformists have invested in interdisciplinary methods impelled by self-determination and development rather than professional management.[162] Crucial to success has been rejection of "the macho law brain approach," [163] conceived and executed by disengaged theorists and engineers, in favor of a more participatory and self-reliant model.[164] The method represents an alternative of innovation, achievement, and ultimately empowerment.[165]

The long-term consequence of past reformist struggles ultimately will be determined by the choices made in reckoning with their aftermath. Continuing to focus on remnants of racial discrimination may succeed in eliminating all vestiges of racism. Although an exceptional achievement if it came to pass, actual eradication of racial discrimination would have less effect on accumulated disadvantage than it might have had in the past. Undoing the consequences of racism in the future requires attention to educational quality, so that special skills demanded by the future can be broadly accessed and learned; strategies for imparting basic know-how and generating confidence and motivation to seek, identify, and seize opportunity; a society that confirms a relationship between responsibility and reward and encourages new stakeholders; and institutions that will provide not only the technical support but the conditions necessary for personal development even under challenging circumstances. Looking to the future, however, does not justify becoming blind to the past. Broad-spectrum social progress and the ideal of an unbalkanized society driven by individual equality rather than group competition are contingent upon educational processes committed to facilitating multicultural appreciation and understanding.[166] Changing the law or underlying attitudes is a relatively easy task compared to the understanding, effort, and risk essential for adapting reform strategy to a rapidly changing social and economic order. Without the will to engage in such retrofitting, racial reform agendas are destined to count more as a cause than for achievement.

The work of protocolists may be understood as both a blessing and a curse. At minimum, their output reminds that serious problems of race remain untended to and unresolved. Even so, their focus and methods distract from real problems of disadvantage. They also may swim against the tide of history and even may overstate the modern power and influence of the dominant racial group. White people may have created the circumstances of disadvantage for blacks. But it increasingly is evident that, if the dominant culture were to become fully dedicated to a racial reckoning, its power to account for the multifold pathologies of racism's legacy would be limited. In a world where boundaries are being reduced by technological and economic change, and multiculturalism washes over political or structural barriers themselves weakened by a smaller and more interdependent world, the maintenance of insular and exclusive habits is becoming less affordable. Future competitiveness, if not advantage, in a social order defined by global markets, new economic alliances, and expanded information flow, will be determined by interactive rather than isolative skills and practices.

Attention to protocol is particularly unfortunate at a time of profound social and economic dynamism. Instead of considering the need for modern and innovative strategies necessitated by change, protocolists have opted for an armchair response. As Henry Louis Gates, Jr., has put it, their work represents "a species of academic nominalism" that functions "as a labor-saving device." [167] Rather than confronting new realities with "new and subtler modes of socioeconomic analysis, [they] have finessed the gap between rhetoric and reality by forging new and subtler definitions of the word racism." [168] A particularly egregious example of that pattern is Charles Lawrence's characterization of those who resist or question the merits of hate speech codes. Lawrence maintains that the response of many civil libertarians is reflexive and "barely notic[es]" the harm to "the assailed." [169] He at least seems to imply that a civil libertarian position is a significant indicator of the "side" one has taken on racism. [170] The premise is overinclusive as it relates to those who thoughtfully and rightly concern themselves with the limited reach and counterproductivity of protocol. Among those who can take legitimate offense are those whose personal decisions, actions, and existences denote more about their moral authenticity than a litmus test on a disputable issue ever could reveal.

Freedom of speech, which was the constitutional linchpin of a successful civil rights movement a generation ago, [171] remains a critical imperative for further progress. It is incongruous that those whose intellectual trade consists of b' ¬ring distinctions between private and public constructs,[172] and who .ress the paralyzing consequences of racist speech,[173] are using t' .ir own power to impair dialogue that is the essential prelude to r .ogress. Such political exercise reflects an unfortunate failure to lear.ı from recent history. Three decades ago, a government report sing!ing out fatherless homes as the primary cause of weakness in the black community[174] ignited a storm of controversy highlighted by criticism that the study and its author were blatantly racist.[175] As anger and intolerance deterred dialogue, reality was avoided. Today 62 percent of black families are headed by a single parent.[176] Only when the pattern had become well established, and a generation of children had actualized the risks associated with their upbringing,[177] did it become somewhat acceptable to discuss publicly the perils identified thirty years ago.

Protocolists maintain that their only interest is in punishing expression that stigmatizes and dehumanizes.[178] To assert as they do that speech restrictions can be drawn narrowly, so that legitimate expression concerning race is not deterred,[179] is naive or cocky. One of racism's most perverse legacies is the inducement of anxiety and reticence when the subject of race arises or a cross-racial encounter materializes[180] —a phenomenon that is not uncommon even among persons with positive instincts and intentions. Because communication is a merger of what is expressed and what is perceived, and unconscious racism by its very nature is a wild card in a person's makeup,[181] a strong incentive already exists to avoid risk and confine verbal interaction to safe subjects.[182] A further inducement to exaggerated risk aversion is extracted from the course of recent history, which demonstrates a strong cultural disposition for passing judgment as a function of ideologically driven projections when actual facts are inaccessible.[183] A system of speech penalties would seem destined to heighten a sense of jeopardy, enhance an already strong tendency to avoid judgment or embarrassment and fortify the resolve to avoid dialogue where it is most needed. The First Amendment, as viewed through the eyes of protocolists, must not be taken seriously when used as a refuge by racist scoundrels.[184] Racially significant history, however, suggests that promises not to squelch essential dialogue may be easier to make than to keep.

It may be that the most appealing pitch of protocolism is also its most hypocritical. The exponents of racist speech management stress the imperatives of dialogue. Mari Matsuda has described her work as an effort "to begin a conversation" that factors First Amendment interests and the liberty deprivations of hate speech victims.[185] Charles Lawrence makes the point that "we must continue this discussion."[186] Beyond such rhetoric, however, evidence suggests an interest in ending the conversation and declaring a winner, or perhaps in reconstructing the concept of dialogue. Recent experiences at least warn of the possibility that deconstructionist and reconstructionist agendas have little use for an open market of ideas,[187] and are driven less by an interest in "let's talk" than in "you listen." A reading of such specific action rather than calculated oratory suggests an overarching imperative of control—denominating an ideology interested more in power than in real equality.

The limited aims and underachieving methods of protocolists in their own way reflect a sense of race fatigue. Richard Posner has cautioned against believing that serious social problems are even solvable—a position that adapts well to those who are overwhelmed by the compounding pathology of racial disadvantage.[188] A similar but somewhat less pessimistic response is that the problems are so vexing and of such magnitude that it is impossible to know what to do or where to start.[189] Underdeveloped ideology and strategy, evidenced by attention to protocol instead of substance and by deterrence rather than facilitation of dialogue, provide a road map for nonachievement and ventilation of cynicism. With reconstructionist achievement being reducible to a new wave of formalism, protocolists paradoxically reinvent much of the methodology and consequence that they condemn. The primary beneficiaries of such an order are escapism and indifference, not to mention animus that becomes muted rather than exorcised.

Although modern problems of racial disadvantage are sufficiently mind numbing to induce mental paralysis, the problem remains as always not a matter of uncertainty about where to start. What has changed from the past is not the nature of the problem but its immensity and complexity. The bottom line for any "new way" or concept is whether it presents an alternative capable of outperforming the traditional models of progress that have relied heavily on dialogue and moral appeal.[190] Notwithstanding historical inattention to race, future achievement or maintenance of advantage requires adaptation to and accommodation of cultural diversity. Advocates of protocol urge deconstruction

of the existing order, ideology and means of change, and envision reconstruction of a new political and social regime that communicates by its
laws "freedom from racial oppression" as a primary value.[191] It is a
utopian vision, however, that overlooks the hard task of achieving it. By
relying on legal change to achieve their ends, protocolists disregard the
reality that so rattles them to begin with—that the law is largely tapped
out as a means of further racial progress.[192]

Given the choice between established models of reform and a society
with evolving incentives to account for multiculturalism, and a search
for new alternatives that has managed only to dredge up a social order
from an overtly pernicious and repudiated era, protocolists offer remarkably little inducement for investing in their agenda. Until the "new ways
of thinking about race" become relevant to a broader spectrum of
historical and future disadvantage, rather than the personal and often
different experiences of professional thinkers, the protocol manifesto
seems reducible to academic exhibitionism. Methods that trade upon
educating rather than silencing, and encouraging rather than chilling
dialogue, represent a real commitment to reform rather than an escape
from reality. Although necessitating much hard and unglamorous work
in exchange for vexingly slow progress, it is a more appealing option
than ideology that trades in uncertain utopias and draws more attention
to itself than to deeper and more challenging pathologies.

CONCLUSION

Four decades after *Brown,* at the terminus of the desegregation era, it is
time to begin framing and communicating a broader vision of racial
progress. With all deference to the *Brown* era, it is essentially over, and
further achievement rests not with revisiting its real or presumed glories
but learning from the multifaceted strategy that begot it. Legalistic creativity that trumpets the connection of a peripheral concern to a bygone
principle and era is a poor substitute for any vision of wholesale progress. Fundamental to any achievement in a morally competitive context
is an intelligent and informed analysis of and response to the market. A
strategy that lacks a full range of vision, ignores history, risks counterproductivity, and affects a relative few is an agenda for which champions
of the status quo might pay if their purported adversaries did not construct it for free. A more worthy successor to past struggle and achieve-

ment is an agenda framed as broadly as the problem it confronts, and calibrated toward change that makes a real difference.

Notes

1. The ultimate critic has been the Supreme Court, which has found racial preferences "suspect" and generally in violation of equal protection. City of Richmond v. J. A. Croson Co., 488 U.S. 469, 495 (1989); *id.* at 521–24 (Scalia, J., concurring).
2. E.g., Regents of the University of California v. Bakke, 438 U.S. 265, 407 (1978) (Blackmun, J., concurring and dissenting) (supporting a university medical school's preferential admissions program as a temporary but essential means "to get beyond racism").
3. Prime examples of major achievements as a function of legal reform include processes of desegregation, civil rights legislation, and abolition of slavery and accounting for civil and political rights by means of the Thirteenth, Fourteenth, and Fifteenth Amendments.
4. Equal protection standards actually have been constructed in a way that provides a safe harbor for prejudice that is not overtly manifested. See, e.g., Washington v. Davis, 426 U.S. 229, 240 (1976) (requiring proof of discriminatory motive in equal protection cases). Proof of discriminatory purpose, as an essential prerequisite for establishing an equal protection violation, places a litigant in the nearly impossible position of identifying what is in a person's head or heart. When discrimination is subtle or racism unconscious, as in the post-*Brown* era, existing standards of review are of minimal relevance. See Charles Lawrence III, "The Id, the Ego and Equal Protection: Reckoning with Unconscious Racism," 37 *Stan. L. Rev.* 317, 344–49 (1981). For criticism of the discriminatory purpose standard as a confounding criterion, see id.; Donald E. Lively, *The Constitution and Race,* 127–29, 170–72 (1992). Daniel R. Ortiz, *The Myth of Intent in Equal Protection,* 41 *Stan. L. Rev.* 1105, 1133–34 (1989).
5. Such tendencies are illuminated most brightly by private decision-making with respect to social affiliation, church membership, school selection where allowed, and residential choices that the Court, responding to circumstances of white flight, described as a "normal pattern of human migration." Pasadena City Board of Education v. Spangler, 427 U.S. 424, 436 (1976).
6. U.S. CONST. amend. XIII ("[n]either slavery nor involuntary servitude [except for a crime] . . . shall exist within the United States").
7. The Black Codes enacted throughout the defeated South immediately after the Thirteenth Amendment's ratification established comprehensive restrictions on the liberty of recently freed blacks and effectively introduced a

system of "slavery in fact after it has been abolished in theory." Lively, *Constitution and Race,* 43.

8. The Fourteenth Amendment thus was calculated to place the fledgling civil rights of the nation's new citizens "beyond normal politics . . . [and] fix them in the . . . Constitution." Cong. Globe, 39th Cong., 1st sess. 3462 (1866) (Rep. Garfield). A comprehensive account of the Fourteenth Amendment's background is provided in Charles Fairman, *History of the Supreme Court of the United States,* VII, pt. 1 (1987).

9. See, e.g., Plessy v. Ferguson, 163 U.S. 537, 550 (1896) (formal segregative classifications permissible so long as "reasonable," which they were found to be in accounting for public comfort, peace, and custom).

10. Following more then a decade of massive resistance to, evasion of, and delay in implementing the *Brown* mandate of desegregation, the Supreme Court eventually insisted upon remedies that promise to work "now." Green v. County School Board, 391 U.S. 430, 439 (1968) (emphasis in original). Within a few years, however, the Court began limiting the purview of *Brown* by restricting its reach to circumstances where segregative intent was demonstrated (Keyes v. School District No. 1, 413 U.S. 189, 208 [1973]), generally prohibiting interdistrict remedies that would have reckoned with the trend toward white suburbs and black urban centers (Milliken v. Bradley, 418 U.S. 717, 746–47 [1973]), and determining that resegregation was not constitutionally offensive so long as it did not result from purposeful official action (Pasadena City Board of Education v. Spangler, 427 U.S. 424, 436–37 [1976]). The demise of the desegregation era is denoted by a shift in aims from insisting upon "eliminat[ing] the vestiges of discrimination root and branch" (*Green,* 391 U.S. at 438), to eradicating it "to the extent practicable" and returning control of schools to local officials (Freeman v. Pitts, 112 S.Ct. 1430, 1446 [1992]).

11. Classic examples of redistributive policy are preferential hiring and layoff plans that the Court invalidated, among other reasons, because remediation of societal discrimination was too amorphous a goal, the methods would not necessarily achieve their aims, and they were sources of stigmatic harm and stereotype. City of Richmond v. J. A. Croson Co., 488 U.S. 469, 495 (1989) (striking down racial preferences in city public works programs); Wygant v. Jackson Board of Education, 476 U.S. 467, 475 (1986) (striking down preferential layoff policy for public school teachers).

12. Hate-speech codes adopted at various college campuses and in certain communities have attempted to account for stigmatizing or demeaning expression directed at designated groups. Variations of such regulation have been struck down in R.A.V. v. City of St. Paul, 112 S.Ct. 2538 (1992) (invalidating a city ordinance prohibiting display of symbols with knowledge or reason to know it will "arouse[ ] anger, alarm or resentment in others on the basis of race, color, creed, religion or gender"); Doe v. University of Michigan, 721 F.Supp. 852 (E.D. Mich. 1989).

13. Apart from being constitutionally vulnerable, they regulate cross-cultural interaction—a circumstance that is exceptional rather than normative in what remains a functionally segregated society.

14. The prime instigator of the NAACP's challenge to official segregation was Charles Houston, the dean of Howard University Law School. For a discussion of Houston's role in developing goals and strategy and attracting persons such as Thurgood Marshall as movement leaders, see Carl Rowan, *Dream Makers, Dream Breakers* (1993).

15. As described by the authors, critical race theory is reducible to the work of "a small but growing group of scholars committed to finding new ways to think about and act in pursuit of racial justice." Mari Matsuda et al., *Words That Wound,* 4 (1993). Their focus is shaped largely by personal and historical experience, and their premises "embrace subjectivity of perspective and are avowedly political." *Id.* at 3.

16. *Id.* Leading voices of critical race theory are anthologized in *Words That Wound.* Contributions to that book, cited in this essay, are Richard Delgado, "Words That Wound: A Tort Action for Racial Insults, Epithets and Name-Calling"; Charles R. Lawrence III, "If He Hollers Let Him Go: Regulating Racist Speech on Campus"; and Mari Matsuda, "Public Response to Racist Speech: Considering the Victim's Story." Citations hereafter are to the book and relevant essay (e.g., *Words That Wound* [Delgado]).

17. Mari Matsuda et al., *supra* note 15, at 4 (Introduction).

18. Given the historical dimensions of race, redistributive strategies respond to perceptions of an intractable problem and what the Court acknowledges as a "sorry legacy." City of Richmond v. J. A. Croson Co., 488 U.S. 469, 499 (1989).

19. The Court, in striking down racial preferences keyed to remediation of societal discrimination, asserted that the Fourteenth Amendment demands strict "race neutrality." *Id.* at 495. Principles of neutrality, from a protocolist perspective, represent methods for facilitating established hierarchies and power relationships. Mari Matsuda et al., *supra* note 15, at 14 (Introduction).

20. For a discussion of racial preferences as a low-impact method of accounting for discrimination and disadvantage, *see* Randall Kennedy, "Persuasion and Distrust: A Comment on the Affirmative Action Debate," 99 *Harv. L. Rev.* 1327, 1333–34 (1986).

21. See notes 34–37 and accompanying text.

22. Obscene expression is entirely unprotected under the First Amendment, for instance, so no constitutional demand exists for establishing harm from such expression as a condition for regulating it. Paris Adult Theatre I v. Slaton, 413 U.S. 60–62 (1973). Racially stigmatizing harm would seem a more consistently serious injury, moreover, than, say, the dubious economic harm of commercial appropriation when a broadcaster airs footage of an entertainer's performance that arguably may enhance economic value. See Zablocki v. Scripps Howard Broadcasting Co., 433 U.S. 562, 575 (1977);

id. at 580 n.2 (Powell, J., dissenting).

23. Plessy v. Ferguson, 163 U.S. 537, 550 (1896) (neither Thirteenth nor Four-teenth Amendments prohibited racial classifications reflecting reasonable exercises of state police power).

24. Brown v. Board of Educ., 347 U.S. 483, 495 (1954) (invalidating prescrip-tive segregation in public education).

25. The phenomenon of integration shock, characterized by anxiety, unfamiliar-ity, uncertainty, overreaction, and testing of traditional stereotype, is dis-cussed in Shelby Steele, *The Content of Our Character*, 24 (1991).

26. Such terminology comprehends the panoply of personal and subjective ac-tions that range from "snubs in restaurants, stores and social events" to being directed by a sales clerk "to the cheapest suits in the store." *Id.* Although the repetitive nature of such events establishes an undeniable racial cast, subtlety and easily constructed race-neutral alibis usually make it impossible to prove racial animus in a particular instance.

27. In concurring with the invalidation of a municipal anti-hate speech ordi-nance, Justice Blackmun expressed a "fear that the Court has been dis-tracted here from its proper mission by the temptation to decide the issue over 'politically correct speech' and 'cultural diversity.' " R.A.V. v. City of St. Paul, 112 S.Ct. 2538, 2561 (1992) (Blackmun, J., concurring). Black-mun's suspicions were aroused by the Court's extreme intellectual gymnas-tics that protected an otherwise unprotected form of expression—fighting words—from viewpoint discrimination. *Id.* at 2545. The net result is that regulation may not protect only the sensitivities of select groups from verbal assault. *Id.* In less contorted fashion, concurring justices found the ordi-nance invalid on grounds it was overbroad. *Id.* at 2550 (White, J., concur-ring); *id.* at 2561 (Stevens, J., concurring).

28. Mari Matsuda et al., *supra* note 15, at 13 (Introduction).

29. Slavery was accommodated by northern states as a cost of establishing a visible union. For a discussion of slavery as the paramount issue of division at the Constitutional Convention, see Lively, *supra* note 4, at 1–7.

30. See, e.g., Paul R. Sniderman and Thomas S. Piazza, *The Scar of Race* (1993) (presenting evidence that traditional bigotry is declining); Dirk Johnson, "White Communities: A Corporate Deterrent," the *New York Times,* Apr. 18, 1994, at A7 (noting reluctance of some corporations to relocate in racially homogeneous communities).

31. See, e.g., *id.* at 89–110 (Delgado).

32. See, e.g., *id.* at 59–66 (Lawrence).

33. See, e.g., *id.* at 26–31 (Matsuda).

34. See, e.g., *id.* at 67–69 (Lawrence). See generally *id.* at 49 (Matsuda).

35. *Id.* at 68.

36. *Id.* at 23–24 (Matsuda).

37. *Id.* at 58–69 (Lawrence); *id.* at 47–49 (Matsuda).

38. *Id.*

39. 163 U.S. 537, 544 (1896).

40. In addition to being perceived as a natural order, racial segregation also was tied to custom, decorum, and public order. *Id.* at 550.
41. Official segregation, as acknowledged by the Court, was calculated to normalize relations between races to maintain peace, order, and comfort. *Id.* It also was designed, as Justice Harlan noted, to fortify racial advantage. *Id.* at 560 (Harlan, J., dissenting). See also Leonard W. Levy, Plessy v. Ferguson, in *Civil Rights and Equality,* 174 (Kenneth Karst, ed., 1989).
42. Konigsberg v. State Bar of California, 366 U.S. 36, 49–51 (1961).
43. First Amendment protection, for instance, is categorically nonexistent for obscenity, Roth v. United States, 354 U.S. 476, 484 (1957), and fighting words, Chaplinsky v. New Hampshire, 315 U.S. 568, 572 (1941). Defamatory expression, also, is beyond the First Amendment's concern, except when an action is brought by a public official or public figure. Gertz v. Robert Welch, Inc. 418 U.S. 323, 334 (1973). State interests are balanced against constitutional concerns when privacy is implicated (the Florida Star v. B.J.F., 488 U.S. 524, 541 [1988]), speech is intended to incite violent action (Brandenburg v. Ohio, 395 U.S. 444, 447 [1969] [per curiam]), and when expression has a commercial purpose (Posadas de Puerto Rico v. Tourism Co. of Puerto Rico, 478 U.S. 328, 344 [1985]).
44. Primary case law on the subject of indecent broadcasting was generated by a single complaint lodged by "an official of Morality in Media." Nat Hentoff, "How the FCC Saves You from Indecency," *The Village Voice,* May 25, 1993, at 28, 29 (discussing origins of Federal Communications Commission v. Pacifica Foundation, 438 U.S. 726 [1978]).
45. Zacchini v. Scripps-Howard Broadcasting Co., 433 U.S. 562 (1977) (newsclip of performer being shot out of cannon at County Fair represented act of appropriation unprotected by First Amendment considerations of newsworthiness).
46. See Federal Communications Commission v. Pacific Foundation 438 U.S. at 742–43 (rejecting arguments that prohibition of "indecent" broadcasts was vague).
47. "Political Correctness," *Palm Beach Post,* June 8, 1993, at A8.
48. Intolerance toward competing ideology, manifesting itself in acts of violence against person and property is discussed in Leonard W. Levy, *Legacy of Suppression* (1960).
49. The Sedition Act, enacted in 1798, was designed to suppress criticism of a Federalist president and Congress by their Jeffersonian rivals. *Id.* at 258. When Jefferson and his followers took control of the federal political branches in 1801, the law was formally repealed. It eventually was overturned, as the Supreme Court has put it, by "the court of history." New York Times Co. v. Sullivan, 376 U.S. 254, 276 (1964). For purposes of understanding tradition, however, it is worth noting that the Jeffersonians were not above using similar tactics to suppress or deter political criticism. See Leonard W. Levy, *Jefferson and Civil Liberties: The Darker Side,* 56–65 (1963).

50. Expressive intolerance resulting in the banning of abolitionist speech in the antebellum South and frictions among abolitionists themselves is discussed in William M. Wiecek, *The Sources of Antislavery Constitutionalism in America, 1760–1848*, 172–82 (1977).

51. The extreme perils confronted by Thurgood Marshall, who became the chief legal strategist of the attack on segregation, are documented in Rowan, *Dream Makers, Dream Breakers*, 248.

52. For criticizing American participation in World War I, the prominent socialist Eugene V. Debs was sentenced to prison—where he still received 900,000 votes in the 1920 presidential election. Harry Kalven, "Ernst Freund and the First Amendment Tradition," 40 *U. Chi. L. Rev.* 235, 237 (1973).

53. Konigsberg v. State Bar of California, 366 U.S. 36, 51 (1961) (finding speech freedom defeasible by "subordinating valid governmental interests"). See Brandenburg v. Ohio, 395 U.S. 444, 447 (1969) (holding that a state may not regulate advocacy of force or lawlessness minus showing of intent to incite and likelihood of imminent and illegal action).

54. See, e.g., Roth v. United States, 354 U.S. 476, 484 (1957) (finding obscenity outside the protective scope of the First Amendment); Chaplinsky v. New Hampshire, 315 U.S. 568, 571–72 (1942) (finding fighting words outside protective scope of the First Amendment).

55. See, e.g., Mari Matsuda et al., *supra* note 15, at 66–71 (Lawrence).

56. See, e.g., *id.* at 71–72 (Lawrence); *id.* at 107–9 (Delgado).

57. A hate speech ordinance, to pass constitutional scrutiny, may not protect discrete groups even if they may be the most obvious targets of verbal attack. See R.A.V., 112 S.Ct. 2538, 2545 (1992) (holding that a group-referenced anti-hate speech law a function of unconstitutional viewpoint discrimination). As Justice White stressed, regulation that protects against "hurt feelings, offense, or resentment" or other "generalized reactions" is overbroad. *Id.* at 2559 (White, J., concurring).

58. Cleveland Board of Education v. Reed, 445 U.S. 938, 938 (1980) (Rehnquist, J., dissenting from denial of writ of certiorari).

59. See Ellis Cose, *The Rage of the Black Middle Class* (1993).

60. See Nadine Strossen, "Campus Speech Regulation: A Modest Proposal?," 1990 *Duke L.J.* 484, 487 & n.10 (1990).

61. Such an objective is described in Mari Matsuda et al., *supra* note 15, at 66–76 (Lawrence).

62. See *id.* at 3–5 (Introduction).

63. *Id.* at 50 (Matsuda).

64. *Id.*

65. See, e.g., Green v. County School Bd., 391 U.S. 430, 439 (1968) (insisting upon a desegregation "plan that promises realistically to work, and promises realistically to work *now*") (emphasis in original).

66. Richard Nixon was elected president in 1968 in part upon his criticism of and opposition to forceful application or extension of the desegregation

mandate through means such as busing. Lively, *supra* note at 118. Nixon won the election with a plurality of the total votes cast. *Id.* Critical to his triumph was the ardent segregationist campaign of George Wallace, who attracted enough votes to seal Nixon's victory. *Id.* Among other things, Nixon promised during his campaign to select Supreme Court nominees with a restrained vision of the Fourteenth Amendment. *Id.*

67. The duty to desegregate was conditioned upon proof of segregative intent. Keyes v. School District No. 1, 413 U.S. 189, 208 (1973). The resultant distinction between *de jure* and *de facto* segregation has been criticized as a false dichotomy, given the connection of modern functional segregation to official segregation. See, e.g., *id.* at 216 (Douglas, J., concurring); Paul Jacobs, *Prelude to Riot: A View of Urban America from the Bottom,* 140 (1967). As the precursor of the discriminatory intent requirement for proving an equal protection violation, insistence on proof of a *de jure* violation has proved a vexing demand.

68. Without proof of formal contributions to urban segregation by suburban communities, the Court has determined that metropolitan desegregation plans are unallowable. Milliken v. Bradley, 418 U.S. 717, 746–47 (1974). The decision created a ventilation opportunity for white flight and, as Justice Marshall observed, ensured "the same separate and inherently unequal education in the future as . . . in the past." *Id.* at 782 (Marshall, J., dissenting).

69. Once desegregation is achieved (even if only in a fleeting sense) and the community resegregated as a function of population resettlement, no constitutional responsibility exists for integration maintenance. Freeman v. Pitts, 112 S.Ct. 1430, 1439, 1447–48 (1992) (finding no enduring duty to desegregate even though there was a quick reversion to segregated status).

70. *Green* 391 U.S. at 438.

71. Board of Education v. Dowell, 111 S.Ct. 630, 638 (1991).

72. Milliken v. Bradley, 418 U.S. at 782 (Marshall, J., dissenting).

73. Robert H. Bork, for instance, has urged fidelity to original intent and neutrality in application of constitutional principles. Robert H. Bork, *The Tempting of America,* 144–51 (1990). The history of the Fourteenth Amendment suggests, however, that the framers contemplated segregation as a method not inconsistent with equality. See Lively, *supra* note 4, at 110. The Brown Court sidestepped the problem with the observation that it could not turn the clock back to 1868 when the amendment was adopted. Brown, 347 U.S. 483, 492 (1954). Bork, attempting to reconcile the result with his theory, suggests that the framer's intent had to give way if it meant vitiating the Fourteenth Amendment altogether. Bork, *Tempting,* at 82–83. The "either-or" choice is false, however, as the separate but equal doctrine represented not a total negation of, but limited understanding of, equality.

74. See, e.g., Lewis v. City of New Orleans, 416 U.S. 130 (1974); Gooding v. Wilson, 405 U.S. 518 (1972); Street v. New York, 394 U.S. 576 (1969); Edwards Co., v. South Carolina, 372 U.S. 229 (1963). Commentators have

noted that, although the Court consistently has struck down fighting-words convictions on grounds that the regulation was overbroad, it has left many cases unreviewed. See also Stephen W. Gard, "Fighting Words as Free Speech," 58 *Wash. U. L. Q.* 531, 564 (1980).

75. Beauharnais v. Illinois, 348 U.S. 250, 275 (1952) (Black, J., dissenting).

76. *Id.*

77. An Alabama jury awarded a $500,000 damage award in a libel action based on a newspaper advertisement by civil rights organizers that made minor mischaracterizations about the actions of police during a protest. See New York Times Co. v. Sullivan, 376 U.S. 254, 256 (1964). The verdict was overturned by the Supreme Court, which determined that a public official could not recover for defamation absent proof that a falsehood was disseminated with actual malice. *Id.* at 279–80.

78. Southern states, for instance, barred the distribution of abolitionist literature or the making of abolitionist speeches. See Lively, *supra* note 4, at 31–34. Because the First Amendment was not incorporated through the Fourteenth Amendment until the twentieth century (see Near v. Minnesota, 283 U.S. 697, 707 [1931]; Gitlow v. New York, 268 U.S. 652, 666 [1925]), such incidents did not at the time present a freedom of expression problem under the Constitution.

79. A University of Michigan speech code, before being struck down as vague and overbroad, was used to punish racist speech in two instances—including one against a black student's usage of the term "white trash" in a conversation with a white student. The incidents are discussed in Strossen, *supra* note 60, at 557 n.377.

80. Charles R. Lawrence III, "If He Hollers Let Him Go: Regulating Racist Speech on Campus," 1990 *Duke L.J.* 450 n.82 (1990) (proposing that regulation not cover "persons who were vilified on the basis of their membership in dominant majority groups").

81. Regents of the University of California v. Bakke, 438 U.S. 265, 400 (1978) (Marshall, J., dissenting).

82. *Id.*

83. *Id.*

84. See, e.g., Doe v. University of Michigan, 721 F. Supp. 852, 867 (E.D. Mich. 1989) (striking down hate speech policy, prohibiting stigmatizing or victimizing verbal or physical behavior, on grounds it was overbroad and vague).

85. Television penetrates 98.2 percent of the nation's households. U.S. Bureau of Census, Statistical Abstract of the United States: 1991, at 556 (11th ed.).

86. See Joshua Hammer, *"Must Blacks Be Buffoons?,"* *Newsweek,* Oct. 26, 1992, at 70.

87. *Id.* (citing 1990 A. C. Nielsen Survey showing black households average seventy hours of television viewing per week compared to forty-seven hours per week for white households).

88. The emphasis tends to be on comedic roles with limited dimensions that

indicate "fewer life opportunities, fewer resources, lower status, and a greater likelihood of victimization." Jannette L. Dates and William Barlow, *Split-Image African Americans in the Mass Media,* 261 (1991).

89. Frontline, Public Hearing, Private Pain (Public Broadcasting Service, Oct. 13, 1992).

90. See, generally, Kathy Russell, Midge Wilson, and Ronald Hall, *The Color Complex,* 2–3, 95–99 (1992).

91. It would follow that if a particular group cannot be singled out for protection (R.A.V. v. City of St. Paul, 112 S.Ct. 2538 [1992]), a distinction drawn on the basis of source represents an equally obvious case of viewpoint discrimination.

92. Mari Matsuda et al., at 73 (Lawrence).

93. *Id.*

94. *Id.* at 74.

95. Federal Communications Commission v. Pacifica Foundation, 438 U.S. 726, 776 (1978) (Brennan, J., dissenting) (quoting C. Bins, "Toward Ethnography of Contemporary African American Oral Poetry," *Language and Linguistics Working Papers,* no. 5, at 82 [1972]).

96. J. Clinton Brown, "In Defense of the *N* Word," *Essence,* June 1993, at 138.

97. Many racist speech control advocates urge regulation only when the offending expression is directed by a member of the dominant race at a person in a protected group. E.g., Lawrence, *supra* note 80, at 450 n.82 (1990). Such an asymmetrical strategy presents the vexing problem of determining which groups in a multicultural society receive protection and when. The maze of conflicting entitlement claims and confoundment even of asymmetry's exponents are illuminated in Strossen, *supra* note 60, at 559 n.387. For some persons, moreover, being singled out for protection is an especially "insidious" and "insulting" exercise in racism. *Id.*

98. Brown, *supra* note 97.

99. As one observer has put it, "whites are not going to feel guilty about racism . . . , haven't for the past 400 years [so] . . . [w]hy in the world does any educated man think they are going to start now." Charley Reese, "Black Americans Need to Think about Solving Their Own Problems," *Òrlando Sentinel,* Aug. 5, 1993, at A18. Even if somewhat hyperbolic, and at odds with the premise that white guilt has provided one of the few levees for extracting even limited concessions (see Steele, *supra* note 25, at 2–3), the argument can advert to historical returns of reliance upon the dominant culture for change.

100. Basic literacy in the past may have been less relevant to seizing opportunity and experiencing economic success in an unskilled or semiskilled position. It now is essential for even lower level positions in a service industry that runs on forms and technology. A recent federal study shows "that nearly half of adult Americans have such weak reading and math skills that they were unable to perform tasks any more difficult than filling out a bank

deposit slip or locating an intersection on a street map." "Report Offers More Evidence of Literacy Woes in Schools," *New York Times*, Sept. 16, 1993, at A9, cols. 5–6. On a national basis, the performance of African-Americans was lower than other groups (whites, Asians, and Hispanics) in the survey. *Id.*

101. Impressive as the progress has been, it did not come without significant turmoil and tension. Achievement was facilitated, moreover, as a function of an autocratic rather than democratic structure.

102. What some observers hail as progress has been minimized by others, insofar as blacks in many instances have achieved political power in certain venues pursuant to a white exodus and deteriorating economic and social base. E.g., Lani Guinier, "The Triumph of Tokenism: The Voting Rights Act and the Theory of Black Success," 89 *Mich. L. Rev.* 1077 (1991). Such circumstances suggest less achievement than inheritance of unwanted leftovers. Evidence exists that black candidates still cannot bargain effectively for white votes which, despite exceptions, tend to be disproportionately exercised in a race-conscious way. See *Detroit Free Press*, Oct. 22, 1989, §1, at 1, cols. 1–2. At the federal level, for purposes of contrast, minorities once elected have been able to broker deals and form multiracial coalitions that, among other things, produced the Civil Rights Act of 1991.

103. Electoral districting plans that overtly factor racial demographics, even to strengthen minority representation, have generated controversy and constitutional attention. E.g., Shaw v. Reno, 113 S.Ct. 2816 (1993) (remanding North Carolina congressional districting plan to lower court for purposes of determining whether weighing of race violated equal protection).

104. The exodus is documented in U.S. Bureau of the Census, *Reflections of America: Commemorating the Statistical Abstract Centennial*, 136–37, tables 1, 2 (1980).

105. A prime inducement of white flight in many cities was court-ordered busing to achieve desegregation. See Columbus Board of Education v. Penick, 443 U.S. 449, 483 (Powell, J., dissenting) (noting "process of resegregation stimulated by resentment against judicial coercion").

106. Although "insist[ing] on recognition of the experiential knowledge of people of color and our communities of origin in analyzing law and society" (Mari Matsuda et al., *supra* note 15, at 6 [Introduction]), protocolists seem to allow little room for variance in how racism is factored and responded to. As they put it, "[w]hat is ultimately at stake in this debate is *our* vision for this society" (*id.* at 15), a vision that regardless of its merits is not necessarily shared by all people of color. Even if common experience with racism and its effects may be acknowledged, perspective and response are subject to significant variances.

107. *Id.* at 11.

108. *Id.* at 3 (Introduction).

109. As the equal protection guarantee has become hinged to proof of overt

discriminatory purpose (*see supra* note 4), its primary utility over the past decade has been as a basis for invalidating race-conscious methods of accounting for the nation's legacy of discrimination. E.g., City of Richmond v. J. A. Croson, Co., 488 U.S. 469 (1989) (striking down municipal public works program because it intentionally stated a racial preference).

110. Mari Matsuda et al., *supra* note 15, at 3 (Introduction).

111. *Id.* at 14–15.

112. *Id.* at 14.

113. *Id.* at 82–83 (Lawrence). By failing to note the involvement of many "traditional civil libertarians" in challenging racism in other ways, however, the criticism is overbroad.

114. Charles R. Lawrence III, "Minority Hiring in AALS Law Schools: The Need for Voluntary Quotas," 20 *U.S.F. L. Rev.* 429, 441 (1986) (citing statistics showing approximately one minority faculty member per law school in 1981).

115. Mari Matsuda et al., *supra* note 15, at 14 (Introduction).

116. *Id.*

117. The phenomenon is exemplified by one law school's response to its low bar passage rate. As the school's associate dean put it, "(w)e are committed to our mission, which is one of serving diversity and allowing minorities access to the gateways of legal education, so we would expect a slightly lower Bar pass rate." *Miami Review*, Oct. 23, 1990, at A1. The explanation was not well received by black students in particular, who pointed out that no African American graduate had failed the exam in question.

118. Typical double standards within the author's range of observation have included requests for information not usually sought for white candidates, reference checks performed *sua sponte* by persons not charged with that responsibility, comments that a particular dialect denoted a lack of seriousness, and remarks that certain groups would not be happy in a particular community. "Turnabout" methods have included reranking candidates so that previously low-rated minorities could be prioritized over white candidates. Although both sides' methods technically are illegal, they are symmetrically indulged and frustrated by demanding standards of proof and impediments to accessing evidence.

119. Mari Matsuda et al., *supra* note 15, at 15 (Introduction).

120. Catharine MacKinnon, *Only Words*, 34–35 (1993).

121. Mari Matsuda et al., *supra* note 15, at 13 (Introduction).

122. *Id.*

123. *Id.* at 5.

124. *Id.* at 14.

125. Associated Press, "Changing Face of America," *Chicago Tribune*, Sept. 29, 1993, at A1.

126. Mari Matsuda et al., at 5 (Introduction).

127. *Id.* at 7.

128. *Id.* at 15.

129. See Peter B. Kovler, *Democrats and the American Idea,* 333 (1992).
130. Mari Matsuda et al., at 11 (Introduction).
131. *Id.* at 13.
132. *Id.* at 14.
133. *Id.* at 82 (Lawrence).
134. *Id.* at 7 (Introduction).
135. *Id.* at 13 ("[c]ritical race theory names the injury and identifies its origins").
136. At the author's university from the late 1980s into the early 1990s, for instance, the Office of Affirmative Action was headed by a director whose status was of an interim nature. Whatever reasons existed for the prolonged interim nature of the position, a general perception especially among minorities on campus was that the condition translated into institutional indifference or unconcern.
137. The desegregation concept and strategy competed against a rival sense that "Sympathy, Knowledge, and the Truth, outweigh all that the mixed school can offer." W. E. B. DuBois, "Does the Negro Need Separate Schools?," 4 *J. Negro Educ.* 328, 335 (1935).
138. The desegregation strategy thus was conceived as a means toward undoing "a caste system which is based on race and color." Richard Kluger, *Simple Justice* 259 (1976) (quoting Brief for Appellant, Sipuel v. Board of Regents, 322 U.S. 631 [1948]).
139. In the educational process, a preferential policy for hiring minority faculty was touted unsuccessfully as a means of establishing necessary "role models." Wygant v. Jackson Bd. of Educ., 267, 275–76 (1986) (finding that the role model theory does not necessarily reckon with harm caused by past discrimination). Also rejected was the argument that a preferential admissions program at a state medical school would improve the quality of health care in disadvantaged communities. Regents of the University of California v. Bakke, 438 U.S. 265, 310–11 (1978).
140. See Randall Kennedy, *supra* note 20, at 1327, 1333–34 (1986) (stressing that affirmative action does not operate to the exclusion of broader policies for remediating racial injustice and noting that the reaction is disproportionately vehement to relatively small impact).
141. Shelby Steele, *supra* note 25, at 23 (describing "race fatigue" as a "deep weariness with things racial").
142. Following ratification of the Thirteenth, Fourteenth, and Fifteenth Amendments and enactment of legislation intended to secure civil and political rights, see, for example, Enforcement Act of 1870, 16 Stat. 433 (1870) (making interference with the right to vote a criminal act); Ku Klux Klan Act of 1871, 17 Stat. 13 (1871) (prohibiting state interference with civil rights and private action denying equal protection), Reconstruction peaked with passage of the Civil Rights Act of 1875. The law prohibited discrimination in public transportation and various public venues. It was struck down on grounds it exceeded Congress's power to enforce the Thirteenth

and Fourteenth Amendments. Civil Rights Cases, 100 U.S. 3, 25 (1883). Evidencing the nation's weariness with race was the Court's observation that "[w]hen a man has emerged from slavery, and by the aid of beneficent legislation has shaken off the inseparable concomitants of that state, there must be some stage of his elevation when he takes the rank of mere citizen, and ceases to be the special favorite of the laws, and when his rights as a citizen or a man, are to be protected in the ordinary modes by which other men's rights are protected." *Id.* at 25. As Reconstruction interest wound down, the Fourteenth Amendment evolved over the next several decades as a source of doctrine that favored the established order through economic liberty concepts (see, e.g., Allgeyer v. Louisiana, 165 U.S. 578 [1897]), and resisted arguments for racially significant legal change. See, e.g., Plessy v. Ferguson, 163 U.S. at 550–51.

143. Paul Brest, "In Defense of the Antidiscrimination Principle," 90 *Harv. L. Rev.* 1, 31 (1976).

144. The Civil Rights Act of 1875, prohibiting racial discrimination in a variety of public venues, was invalidated in the Civil Rights Cases, 109 U.S. 3 (1883) (holding that the enactment exceeded Congress's power under the Thirteenth and Fourteenth Amendments). Congress itself, by the end of the nineteenth century, repealed Reconstruction laws that criminalized conspiracies to interfere with voting rights. See Lively, *supra* note 4, at 64.

145. 60 U.S. (19 How.) 393 (1857). Only one of the dominant modern constitutional law casebooks provides an edited version of the racially significant aspects of Dred Scott. See William Seidman et al., *Constitutional Law*, 477–80 (1991).

146. The Court's determination that legal distinctions on the basis of race did not translate into constitutional inequality or imprint a badge of inferiority precluded any reckoning with official segregation. See Plessy v. Ferguson, 163 U.S. at 543. Similarly, insistence on proof of discriminatory purpose defeats efforts to account for subtle or unconscious racism. See Lawrence, *supra* note 4, at 344–47.

147. The NAACP began to implement an antisegregation strategy in the 1930s. Its first triumph was in a state court, where Maryland was ordered to provide a separate legal education or admit a black student to its university law school. Pearson v. Murray, 182 A. 590, 594 (Md. 1936). Litigation against segregation in the South presented a high peril to the personal safety of NAACP attorneys. See Rowan, *supra* note 14, at 248.

148. The Court's investment in motive-based standards has been an analytical phenomenon of the past two decades. See Arlington Heights v. Metropolitan Housing Development Corp., 429 U.S. 252, 265 (1977) (finding failure to establish that exclusionary effect of zoning ordinance was racially motivated); Washington v. Davis, 426 U.S. 229, 246 (1976) (finding failure to establish that exclusionary effect of employment test was racially motivated). Such criteria were previewed by the *de jure–de facto* distinction in

the desegregation cases. See Keyes v. School District No. 1, 413 U.S. 189, 208 (1973).

149. John Hart Ely, "The Supreme Court, 1977 Term—Foreword: On Discovering Fundamental Values," 92 *Harv. L. Rev.* 5, 54 (1978).

150. Mari Matsuda et al., *supra* note 15, at 86 (Lawrence).

151. City of Richmond v. J. A. Croson Co., 488 U.S. 468, 499 (1989).

152. See Mark V. Tushnet, *The NAACP's Legal Strategy against Segregated Education, 1925–1950* (1987).

153. See *id.*; Richard Kluger, *Simple Justice*, 165–72, 203–5 (1976).

154. See Lawrence, *supra* note 4.

155. The author acknowledges having refused to vote in favor of any candidate who was not a minority, and in faculty recruiting has joined in various group-weighted selection processes. Such preference has not been uncommon based on conversations with colleagues at other law schools seeking to diversify their faculty. Such procedures at the same time establish race not just as a factor but the factor in recruiting and hiring.

156. Thomas Mayo, "Constitutionalizing the 'Right to Die,' " 49 *Md. L. Rev.* 103, 130 (1990) (citing John Hart Ely, *Democracy and Distrust*, 69 [1980]).

157. As Paul Brest has noted, "[i]f a society can be said to have an underlying political theory, ours has not been a theory of organic groups but of liberalism, focusing on the rights of individuals, including rights of distributive justice." Brest, *supra* note 143, at 49. Although the individualist premise may be contradicted by a history of racism that systematically has derogated on the basis of group status, the understanding does not seem significantly imperiled by the relatively narrow and unambitious reformist agendas of the day.

158. Tony Brown, "Affirmative Action—with a Twist," *Toledo Journal*, Feb. 3–9, 1993, at 35.

159. *Id.*

160. Challenges to the placement of waste disposal cites, for instance, have generated strategies not only of litigation but political pressure and public protest by affected citizens. See Marianne Lavelle and Marcia Coyle, "When Movements Coalesce," *Nat. L. J.*, Sept. 21, 1992, at 101. Attention to administrative responsibility and procedure compelled the Environmental Protection Agency to acknowledge the need for more attention to racial disparities in the distribution and remediation of environmental risks. See Marcia Coyle, "Lawyers Protection: The Racial Divide Try to Devise New Strategy," *Nat. L. J.*, Sept. 21, 1992, at 58.

161. See *id.*

162. See *id.*

163. *Id.*

164. *Id.*

165. *Id.*

166. For an extensive discussion of how multiculturally referenced processes of education and familiarization can be effective strategies in reckoning with racial prejudice and animus, see Charles Calleros, "Reconciliation of Civil Liberties After R.A.V. v. City of St. Paul: Free Speech, Antiharassment Policies, Multicultural Education, and Political Correctness at Arizona State University," 1992 *Utah L. Rev.* 1205 (1992).

167. Henry Louis Gates, Jr., "Let Them Talk," *New Republic,* Sept. 20 & 27, 1993, at 48.

168. *Id.*

169. Mari Matsuda et al., *supra* note 15, at 65 (Lawrence).

170. *Id.* at 82–83.

171. So critical was expressive freedom to the civil rights movement, in the face of southern suppressive and repressive tactics, that one prominent constitutional scholar credited "the Negro with reclaiming the First Amendment freedoms of all Americans." Harry Kalven, Jr., *The Negro and the First Amendment,* 4 (1965).

172. A favored thesis of the authors is that distinctions between public and private power are artificial. Mari Matsuda et al., *supra* note 15, at 62–66 (Lawrence). Under the existing order, the distinction is critical for purposes of establishing an institutional interest with respect to racial inequality. See, e.g., Burton v. Wilmington Parking Authority, 365 U.S. 715 (1961) (state action a prerequisite for Fourteenth Amendment violation).

173. Mari Matsuda et al., *supra* note 15, at 68–70 (Lawrence).

174. Daniel P. Moynihan, *The Moynihan Report and the Politics of Controversy* (1967).

175. See, e.g., William Ryan, *Blaming the Victim* (1976).

176. "Endangered Family," *Newsweek,* Aug. 30, 1993, at 18, col. 1.

177. See, e.g., James Tobin, "Births Soar since Abortion Funding Ban," *Detroit News and Free Press,* Sept. 26, 1993, at 16A (noting how cutoff in abortion funding and increase in births by single mothers has contributed to a generation of children with "physical, social and economic problems").

178. Mari Matsuda et al., *supra* note 15, at 17–27 (Matsuda).

179. *Id.* at 35–36.

180. The fragility and tensions of cross-racial socializing are illuminated in Steele, *The Content of Our Character,* 1–20 (1991).

181. For an incisive discussion of the phenomenon of unconscious racism, see Lawrence, *supra* note 4.

182. Evidence of how inexperience with diversity induces silence rather than dialogue is provided by debate in the executive branch over health care reform. Despite reservations over the cost of a health insurance plan advocated by predominantly female advocates, male economic advisers held back criticism pursuant to concerns that "a strong argument could come across as sexist and patronizing." Eleanor Clift, "The Gender Wars,"

Newsweek, Oct. 4, 1993, at 50. Even if the decision to hold back itself was patronizing, the point is that a cost of adjusting to new contextual realities is uncertainty, reticence, and sometimes foolishness. Such a condition is hardened rather than alleviated when formal sanctions diminish incentives for openness and risk-taking that are the price of learning and growth.

183. The social tendency has been evidenced in recent events ranging from the sexual harassment controversy in the Clarence Thomas confirmation hearings to a white student's use of the term "water buffalo" in telling five African American students making noise outside his window to "shut up." See Jacqueline Trescott, "Into the Bonfire of the Humanities," *Washington Post,* Sept. 29, 1993, at B1.

184. Mari Matsuda et al., *supra* note 15, at 14–15 (Introduction); *id.* at 35–38 (Delgado), *id.* at 82–87 (Lawrence).

185. *Id.* at 50 (Matsuda).

186. *Id.* at 87 (Lawrence).

187. The imperative of control has been noted as a possible factor in other contexts, where deconstructionist agendas are at work. Organizers of a judicial conference, who "had heard [Catharine MacKinnon] was not very receptive to be with women who disagree with her" concluded that she "would be less than pleased to be on the program with [Nadine] Strossen." David Margolick, "At the Bar," *New York Times,* Nov. 5, 1993, at B11. MacKinnon maintains that she would not have objected to Strossen's presence on the program, but organizers concluded that "we had a choice." *Id.* Strossen, who had agreed to address the conference, reports being told that "her services were no longer needed." *Id.* Responding to criticism that she will not debate those contesting her claim as an exclusive spokesperson for women's rights, MacKinnon has replied that "such debates played right into ... 'a pimp strategy to hide behind feminist women.' " *Id.*

188. Richard A. Posner, "Us v. Them," *New Republic,* Oct. 15, 1990, at 47, 50 (warning against "fool[ing] ourselves into thinking that profound social problems are actually solvable").

189. E.g., Robert J. Samuelson, "Should We Think the Unthinkable?," *Newsweek,* Sept. 13, 1993, at 43.

190. Classic examples of such strategies are the abolition, desegregation, and civil rights movements, each of which relied heavily upon appeals to commence and provided significant input for the nation's moral development.

191. Mari Matsuda et al., *supra* note 15, at 50 (Matsuda).

192. As the desegregation era has wound down, discrimination claims have been checked by the requirement of proving wrongful intent, state action remains a constitutional barrier, racial preferences largely have been fore-

closed, and hate-speech codes have been struck down, the law has stalled out at the point of sanctioning formal discriminatory practice. Further progress, barring a radical redirection of the law that is difficult to foresee, by necessity is dependent upon further moral progress, enlightened understanding of self-interest or divine intervention.

3. Racist Speech, Democracy, and the First Amendment

Robert C. Post

The curse of racism continues to haunt the nation. Everywhere we face its devastation, the bitter legacy of, in William Lloyd Garrison's prophetic words, our "covenant with death and . . . agreement with Hell."[1] This is the living consequence of the history that has produced us. We cannot overcome that history without changing ourselves and therefore also our legal order. Since *Brown v. Board of Education*[2] vast stretches of our law have passed through the flame of this challenge.[3] The question is always what to preserve, what to alter.

Now it is the turn of the First Amendment. Largely inspired by Richard Delgado's article "Words That Wound,"[4] the past few years have witnessed an extraordinary spate of articles analyzing the constitutionality of restrictions on racist speech.[5] This analysis is not merely academic. Motivated by an alarming increase in racist incidents,[6] universities throughout the nation have turned toward the task of restraining racist expression.[7] The justification of these restraints, and their relationship to First Amendment values, has become a matter of intense controversy.[8]

One approach has been to attempt to use legal regulation to eradicate all visible signs of that "racist sentiment" which, in the view of some, our history has caused to "pervade[ ] the life of virtually all white Americans."[9] The rules of the University of Connecticut, for example, plainly evince this remarkable ambition. These rules prohibit "[b]ehavior that denigrates others because of their race [or] ethnicity."[10] They provide that the "use of derogatory names, inappropriately directed laughter, inconsiderate jokes, anonymous notes or phone calls, and conspicuous exclusion from conversations and/or classroom discussions are examples of harassing behaviors that are prohibited."[11] The rules list the "signs" of proscribed "Harassment, Discrimination and Intolerance," some of which are the following:

Stereotyping the experiences, background, and skills of individuals

Treating people differently solely because they are in some way different from the majority

Responding to behaviors or situations negatively because of the background of the participants . . .

Imitating stereotypes in speech or mannerisms . . .

Attributing objections to any of the above actions to "hypersensitivity" of the targeted individual or group[12]

These rules do not appear to be designed to regulate specific forms of behavior or expression, but to encompass and to forbid all exterior "signs" of an interior frame of mind. One can readily understand the logic of this purpose. If our "common historical and cultural heritage" has made us "all racists,"[13] then racism must be seen as an unredeemed form of identity, whose every manifestation ought to be challenged and sanctioned. Punitive legal regulations are thus faced with the task of attempting to imagine and specify every possible indication of racism. But since the racist personality can express itself in an infinite variety of ways, the task is intrinsically elusive. The University of Connecticut rules are clearly caught up in the frustrating spiral of this logic, a logic that, when carried to its conclusion, can end only in the complete legal subjugation of the individual.[14]

The incompatibility of this logic with even the most elementary standards of freedom of speech is obvious. Any communication can potentially express the racist self, and thus no communication can ever be safe from legal sanction. It is therefore no surprise that the University of Connecticut was forced to withdraw its regulations, although apparently with reluctance and distress, because of a threatened lawsuit.[15] If the ambition of legal regulation is to suppress manifestations of racist personality, the necessary consequence will be the wholesale abandonment of all principles of freedom of expression.

To the extent that we care about First Amendment values, therefore, we must make do with more modest aspirations.[16] The possibility of effecting a reconciliation between principles of freedom of expression and restraints on racist speech depends upon deflecting our focus away from its spontaneous target, which is the racism of our cultural inheritance, and toward the redress of particular and distinct harms caused by racist expression. The specification of these harms will lead to the definition of discrete forms of speech, the legal regulation of which can then be assessed in light of relevant First Amendment values.

Such, in any event, will be the strategy of this essay. Its ambition is to be illustrative rather than comprehensive: the general issue of racist speech has simply too many facets to be encompassed by the small scope of this study. Although part 1 attempts to isolate and describe five specific kinds of harms said to be caused by racist speech, part 2 offers an account of only one of several possible relevant and important First Amendment values, that of democratic self-governance. In my view this value is primarily responsible for the constitutional safeguards that currently protect public discourse. The major part of this essay, part 3, addresses the narrow issue of the constitutionality of regulating public discourse to ameliorate specific harms caused by racist speech. Part 4 then briefly examines the quite different constitutional issues posed by the regulation of racist speech within public institutions of higher learning.

One significant drawback of this analytic structure is that it renders the term "racist speech" into something of a cipher. As the University of Connecticut regulations illustrate, the term is inherently labile and ambiguous. It probably has as many different definitions as there are commentators, and it would be pointless to pursue its endlessly variegated shades of meaning. I have decided, therefore, to focus instead on the constitutional implications of specific justifications for restraining racist expression, and to let the term "racist speech" absorb the content implied by these various justifications.

I should add that writing this essay has been difficult and painful. I am committed both to principles of freedom of expression and to the fight against racism. The topic under consideration has forced me to set one aspiration against the other, which I can only do with reluctance and a heavy heart.

1. THE HARMS OF RACIST SPEECH

Even a brief survey of the contemporary debate reveals it to be rich with textured and complex characterizations of the harms of racist expression. It would be impossible within the scope of this essay to disentangle and evaluate each of the many harms suggested in this literature. It will therefore be necessary to group these harms into five rough categories that represent the most prominent lines of analysis and that are at the same time convenient for First Amendment analysis.[17]

A. The Intrinsic Harm of Racist Speech

A recurring theme in the contemporary literature is that racist expression ought to be regulated because it creates what has been termed "deontic" harm.[18] The basic point is that there is an "elemental wrongness"[19] to racist expression, regardless of the presence or absence of particular empirical consequences such as "grievous, severe psychological injury."[20] It is argued that toleration for racist expression is inconsistent with "respect for the principle of equality"[21] that is at the heart of the Fourteenth Amendment.[22]

The thrust of this argument is that a society committed to ideals of social and political equality cannot remain passive: it must issue unequivocal expressions of solidarity with vulnerable minority groups and make positive statements affirming its commitment to those ideals. Laws prohibiting racist speech must be regarded as important components of such expressions and statements.[23]

If the basic harm of racist expression lies in its intrinsic and symbolic incompatibility with egalitarian ideals, then the distinct class of communications subject to legal regulation will be defined by reference to those ideals. For example, if the Fourteenth Amendment is thought to enshrine an antidiscrimination principle, then "any speech (in its widest sense) which supports racial prejudice or discrimination"[24] ought to be subject to regulation. But if the relevant ideals are thought to embody substantive racial equality, then the relevant class of communications would be defined as speech containing a "message . . . of racial inferiority."[25]

B. Harm to Identifiable Groups

A second theme in the current debate is that racist expression ought to be regulated because it harms those groups that are its target. There are two basic variations on this theme. One draws its inspiration from the tradition of group libel[26] and the decision of the Supreme Court in *Beauharnais v. Illinois*.[27] In this view, speech likely to cast contempt or ridicule on identifiable groups ought to be regulated to prevent injury to the status and prospects of the members of these groups. A second variation derives from the more contemporary understanding of racism as "the structural subordination of a group based on an idea of racial inferiority."[28] Racist expression is viewed as especially unacceptable because it locks in the oppression of already marginalized groups: "Racist speech is particularly harmful because it is a mechanism of subordination, reinforcing a historical vertical relationship."[29]

If the prevention of group harm is the basis for the regulation of communication, the definition of legally proscribed speech will depend on one's understanding of the nature of the group harm at issue and the way in which communication is seen as causing that harm. Regulation derived from a theory of group defamation, for example, would tend to safeguard all groups,[30] whereas regulation that derives from a theory of subordinate groups would sanction only speech "directed against a historically oppressed group."[31]

C. Harm to Individuals

A third prominent theme in the contemporary literature is that racist expression harms individuals. This theme essentially analogizes racist expression to forms of communication that are regulated by the dignitary torts of defamation, invasion of privacy, and intentional infliction of emotional distress. The law compensates persons for dignitary and emotional injuries caused by such communication, and it is argued that racist expression ought to be subject to regulation because it causes similar injuries. These injuries include "feelings of humiliation, isolation, and self-hatred,"[32] as well as "dignitary affront."[33] The injuries are particularly powerful because "racial insults . . . conjure up the entire history of racial discrimination in this country."[34] In Patricia Williams's striking phrase, racist expression is a form of "spirit-murder."[35]

Regulating racist expression because of its negative impact on particular persons would suggest that the class of communications subject to legal sanction be narrowed to those that are addressed to specific individuals, or that in some other way can be demonstrated to have adversely affected specific individuals. The nature of that class would vary, however, depending on the particular kind of harm sought to be redressed. If the focus is on preventing "dignitary harm,"[36] the injury might be understood to inhere in the very utterance of certain kinds of racist communications;[37] if the focus is instead on emotional damage, independent proof of distress might be required to sustain recovery.[38] There will also be variations in regulation depending on whether harm to individuals is understood to flow from the ideational content of racist expression, or instead from its abusive nature.[39]

D. Harm to the Marketplace of Ideas

A fourth theme in the current debate is that racist expression harms the very marketplace of ideas that the First Amendment is designed to foster. A variety of different arguments have been brought forward to support this position. It is argued that racist expression ought to be "proscribed . . . as a form of assault, as conduct" inconsistent with the conditions of respect and noncoercion prerequisite to rational deliberation.[40] It is argued that racist expression is inconsistent with the marketplace of ideas because it "is a disease which infects and skews or disables the operation of the market. . . . Racism is irrational and often unconscious."[41] Finally, it is argued that racism "systematically" silences "whole segments of the population,"[42] either through the "visceral" shock and "preemptive effect on further speech" of racist words,[43] or through the distortion of "the marketplace of ideas by muting or devaluing the speech of blacks and other nonwhites."[44]

The class of communication subject to legal sanction would depend upon which of these various arguments is accepted. Depending on exactly how racist expression is understood to damage the marketplace of ideas, the class might be confined to that communication experienced as coercive and shocking, or it might be expanded to include communication perceived as unconsciously and irrationally racist, or it might be expanded still further to encompass speech explicitly devaluing and stigmatizing victim groups.

E. Harm to Educational Environment

Each of the four categories of harm discussed so far can be caused by racist expression within public discourse. There is, however, yet a fifth kind of harm which is quite important to the contemporary controversy, but which is relevant only to the specific educational environment of institutions of higher learning. This is the harm that racist expression is understood to cause to the educational mission of universities or colleges. The prevention of this harm is central to the definition of a great number of campus regulations.

Universities and colleges characteristically seek to regulate racist communications that "directly create a substantial and immediate interference with the educational processes of the University," without articulating exactly how racist expression can cause that interference.[45] Sometimes campus regulations are more specific, focusing on the damage that racist expression is understood to cause individuals or groups. For example, some regulations only proscribe racist expression that "will interfere with the victim's ability to pursue effectively his or her education or otherwise to participate fully in University programs and activities."[46] Presumably this interference will occur for reasons similar to those that we have already canvassed.

In a number of instances, however, college or university regulations will enunciate special educational goals that are understood to be inherently incompatible with racist expression. For example, Mount Holyoke College seeks to inculcate the value of diversity, which it views as plainly inconsistent with racist expression. Accordingly Mount Holyoke's regulations provide:

To enter Mount Holyoke College is to become a member of a community. . . .
. . . Our community is committed to maintaining an environment in which diversity is not only tolerated, but is celebrated. Towards this end, each member of the Mount Holyoke community is expected to treat all individuals with a common standard of decency.[47]

Marquette University defines itself "as a Christian and Catholic institution . . . dedicated to the proposition that all human beings possess an inherent dignity in the eyes of their Creator and equality as children of God."[48] Accordingly Marquette's regulations seek to maintain "an environment in which the dignity and worth of each member of its community is respected" and in which "racial abuse or harassment . . . will not be tolerated."[49] Mary Washington College sets forth what appears to be a secular version of this same educational mission; its regulations provide that the "goal of the College is to help all students achieve academic success in an environment that nurtures, encourages growth, and develops sensitivity and appreciation for all people."[50] Accordingly "any activity or conduct that detracts from this goal—such as racial or sexual harassment—is inconsistent with the purposes of the College community."[51]

In such instances, racist expression interferes with education not merely because of general harms that it may inflict on groups or individuals or the marketplace of ideas,[52] but also, and more intrinsically, because racist expression exemplifies conduct that is contrary to the particular educational values that specific colleges or universities seek to instill.[53]

2. THE VALUES OF THE FIRST AMENDMENT

As any constitutional lawyer knows, First Amendment doctrine is neither clear nor logical. It is a vast Sargasso Sea of drifting and entangled values, theories, rules, exceptions, predilections. It requires determined interpretive effort to derive a useful set of constitutional principles by which to evaluate regulations of expression. In recent years there has been an unfortunate tendency, by no means limited to the controversy surrounding racist speech, to avoid this difficult work by relying instead on formulaic invocations of First Amendment "interests" that can be captured in such conclusory labels as "individual self-fulfillment," "truth," "democracy," and so forth.[54] These formulas cast an illusion of stability and order over First Amendment jurisprudence, an illusion that can turn dangerous when it substitutes for serious engagement with the question of why we really care about protecting freedom of expression.

What is most disappointing about the expanding literature proposing restrictions on racist speech is the palpable absence of that engagement. The most original and significant articles in the genre concentrate on uncovering and displaying the manifold harms of racist communications; the harms of regulating expression are on the whole perfunctorily dismissed. Of course this emphasis is readily understandable. It is a formidable task to attempt to carve out a new exception to the general protection of speech afforded by the armor of First Amendment doctrine. Even so staunch a defender of minority rights as Justice William Brennan might be taken to be unsympathetic, given his observation in *United States v. Eichman*[55] that "virulent ethnic and religious epithets"[56] ought to receive constitutional protection because of the " 'bedrock principle underlying the First Amendment . . . that the Government may not prohibit the expression of an idea simply because society finds the idea offensive or disagreeable.' "[57] In the face of such daunting obstacles, it is natural for proponents of restraints on racist speech to emphasize their affirmative case and to minimize countervailing considerations.

I agree, of course, that the question of regulating racist speech ought not to be settled simply by reference to present doctrine. But it is equally important that the question ought not to be settled without serious engagement with the values embodied in that doctrine. Regulations like those promulgated by the University of Connecticut and many other universities suggest that this lack of engagement is a real and practical problem.[58] Although earnest inquiry into the First Amendment values involved in the restraint of racist speech cannot by itself definitively solve the difficult constitutional issues we face, it can at least illuminate what is most deeply at stake for us in this controversy, and to that extent clarify the choices we must make.

A. Democracy, Public Discourse, and the First Amendment

This essay concentrates on the relevance for the regulation of racist speech of only one strand of First Amendment values. It is, however, an extraordinarily important strand, one that in my view accounts for a good deal of the shape of contemporary First Amendment doctrine. It concerns the relationship between freedom of expression and democratic self-governance. Its basic thrust is to provide certain kinds of protection to communication deemed necessary for the processes of democracy, communication that the Court has labeled "public discourse."[59]

In protecting public discourse, the First Amendment serves the purposes of democracy, and the question at hand is what we believe those purposes to be. This is not a simple question. Even so powerful a First Amendment theorist as Frederick Schauer can argue that "[a]ny distinct restraint on majority power, such as a principle of freedom of speech, is by its nature anti-democratic, anti-majoritarian."[60] If democracy means no more to us than that in each instance the majority ought to have its way, then of course Schauer is quite correct that speech comprising public discourse ought not for that reason to have any special exemption from majoritarian regulation.[61] But the underlying equation of democracy with the simple exercise of majority will is radically inadequate, not only as an explanation of contours of contemporary doctrine, but also as an account of the normative attraction of democracy.[62]

A far more persuasive account is one that begins with

the distinction between autonomy and heteronomy: democratic forms of government are those in which the laws are made by the same people to whom they apply (and for that reason they are autonomous norms), while in autocratic forms of government the law-makers are different from those to whom the laws are addressed (and are therefore heteronomous norms).[63]

This distinction between autonomy and heteronomy formed the basis of Hans Kelsen's definition of democracy, which he viewed as a form of government resting on "the principle of self-determination."[64] The distinction is manifestly at the root of the repudiation of seditious libel in *New York Times Co. v. Sullivan,*[65] which turned on Madison's differentiation of American and English forms of government: in England "the Crown was sovereign and the people were subjects," whereas in America " '[t]he people, not the government, possess absolute sovereignty.' "[66] For this reason in America " 'the censorial power is in the people over the Government, and not in the Government over the people.' "[67]

If democracy as a form of government is important to us because it embodies the value of self-determination, we must ask what it means for a collection of persons to decide governmental policy in a way that facilitates that value.[68] Kelsen answers the question in a way that begins with Rousseau's formulation in *The Social Contract,*[69] but that moves rapidly to a distinctively modern perspective:

A subject is politically free insofar as his individual will is in harmony with the "collective" (or "general") will expressed in the social order. Such harmony of the "collective" and the individual will is guaranteed only if the social order is created by the individuals whose behavior it regulates. Social order means determination of the will of the individual. Political freedom, that is, freedom under social order, is self-determination of the individual by participating in the creation of the social order.[70]

Because it is unconvincing to imagine that the will of individuals can be "in harmony" with the general will in all matters of political moment, Kelsen ultimately locates the value of self-determination in the ability of persons to participate in the process by which the social order is created. He conceives that process as preeminently one of communication:

The will of the community, in a democracy, is always created through a running discussion between majority and minority, through free consideration of arguments for and against a certain regulation of a subject matter. This discussion takes place not only in parliament, but also, and foremost, at political meetings, in newspapers, books, and other vehicles of public opinion. A democracy without public opinion is a contradiction in terms.[71]

For Kelsen, then, democracy serves the principle of self-determination because it subjects the political and social order to public opinion, which is the product of a dialogic communicative exchange open to all. The normative essence of democracy is thus located in the communicative processes necessary to instill a sense of self-determination,[72] and in the subordination of political decision-making to these processes.

This logic is widely shared. It leads Benjamin Barber, for example, to conclude that "there can be no strong democratic legitimacy without ongoing talk."[73] It leads John Dewey to remark that "[d]emocracy begins in conversation."[74] It leads Durkheim to observe that "[t]he more that deliberation and reflection and a critical spirit play a considerable part in the course of public affairs, the more democratic the nation."[75] It leads Claude Lefort to claim that "modern democracy invites us to replace the notion of a regime governed by laws, of a legitimate power, by the notion of a regime founded upon *the legitimacy of a debate as to what is legitimate and what is illegitimate*—a debate which is necessarily without any guarantor and without any end."[76]

In fact the notion that self-determination requires the maintenance of a structure of communication open to all commands a wide consensus. Jürgen Habermas characterizes that structure as determined by the effort to attain "a common will, communicatively shaped and discursively clarified in the political public sphere."[77] John Rawls views it as a process of "reconciliation through public reason."[78] Frank Michelman regards it as the practice of "jurisgenerative politics" through the "dialogic 'modulation' of participants' pre-political understandings."[79] For all three thinkers the goal of the structure is to facilitate the attainment of "agreement" that is "uncoerced, and reached by citizens in ways consistent with their being viewed as free and equal persons."[80]

Coercion is precluded from public debate because the very purpose of that debate is the practice of self-determination. The goal is "agreement" (or the attainment of "a common will") because in such circumstances the individual will is by hypothesis completely reconciled with the general will. It is important to understand, however, that this goal is purely aspirational. In fact, it is precisely because absolute agreement can never actually be reached that the debate which constitutes democracy is necessarily "without any end," and hence must be independently maintained as an ongoing structure of communication.

Without this structure, the simple kind of majoritarian rule Schauer equates with democracy loses its grounding in the principle of self-determination, and merely represents the heteronomous submission of a minority to the forceful command of a majority. With such a structure in place, on the other hand, both majority and minority can each be understood to have had the opportunity freely to participate within a "system"[81] of communication upon which the legitimacy of all political arrangements depends. Whether that opportunity will actually establish the value of autonomous self-determination for both majority and minority is a complex and contingent question, dependent on specific historical circumstances. But, in the absence of that opportunity, realization of the value of autonomous self-determination will be precluded under conditions characteristic of the modern state.[82]

The First Amendment principles that this essay considers are those that function to safeguard from majoritarian interference this structure of public discourse, so that our democracy will be able to serve the end of collective self-determination. Four aspects of that structure require emphasis, for they will be of importance when we subsequently examine in detail the regulation of racist speech.

First, the function of public discourse is to reconcile, to the extent possible, the will of individuals with the general will. Public discourse is thus ultimately grounded upon a respect for individuals seen as "free and equal persons."[83] In the words of Jean Piaget, "The essence of democracy resides in its attitude towards law as a product of collective will, and not as something emanating from a transcendent will or from the authority established by divine right. It is therefore the essence of democracy to replace the unilateral respect of authority by the mutual respect of autonomous wills."[84] The individualism so characteristic of First Amendment doctrine[85] flows directly from this central project of democracy.[86]

Second, some form of a public/private distinction is necessarily implied by democracy understood as a project of self-determination. This is because the state undermines the raison d'être of its own enterprise to the extent that it itself coercively forms the "autonomous wills" that democracy seeks to reconcile into public opinion.[87] If the adjective "private" is understood to designate that which is beyond the coercive formation of the state, public discourse must be conceptualized as a process through which "private" perspectives are transformed into public power.

Third, democracy is on this account inherently incomplete. This is because the "autonomous wills" postulated by democratic theory do not and cannot appear *ex nihilo*. The only reason that a person possesses a personality capable of autonomous choice is because the person has internalized "the institutions of [the] community into his own conduct."[88] This process of socialization, which is prerequisite for personal identity, is not itself a matter of independent election, but is rather attributable to accidents of birth and acculturation. Democracy thus necessarily presupposes important (not to say foundational) aspects of the social world organized along nondemocratic lines. For this reason public discourse must always exist in tension with other forms of communication ("nonpublic speech").

Fourth, democracy, like all forms of government, must ultimately be capable of accomplishing the tasks of governance. As Alexander Meiklejohn notes, "Self-government is nonsense unless the 'self' which governs is able and determined to make its will effective."[89] Democratic governments must therefore have the power to regulate behavior. But because public discourse is understood as the communicative medium through which the democratic "self" is itself constituted, public discourse must in important respects remain exempt from democratic regulation. We use the speech/action distinction to mark some of the boundaries of this exemption. Since all "words are deeds,"[90] this distinction is purely pragmatic. We designate the communicative processes necessary to sustain the principle of collective self-determination "speech" and thus insulate it from majoritarian interference.

B. Community, Civility Rules, and Public Discourse

Restraints on racist speech characteristically involve certain general First Amendment issues that I shall briefly review in this section in light of the functional concerns of public discourse. In so doing I shall confine myself to summarizing conclusions, the detailed arguments for which I have developed elsewhere.[91]

If democratic self-governance presupposes a social world in which "autonomous wills" are to be coordinated and reconciled, there is an important form of social organization, which I shall call "community," that rests on exactly the opposite presupposition. Building on the work of Michael Sandel,[92] I shall define a community as a social formation that inculcates norms into the very identities of its members. So far from being considered autonomous, persons within a community are understood to depend, for the very integrity and dignity of their personalities, upon the observance of these norms.

For hundreds of years an important function of the common law has been to safeguard the most important of these norms, which I shall call "civility rules." These rules apply to communication as well as to action, and their enforcement lies at the foundation of such communicative torts as defamation,[93] invasion of privacy,[94] and intentional infliction of emotional distress.[95] Through these torts the common law not only protects the integrity of the personality of individual community members, but it also serves authoritatively to articulate a community's identity.

There is an obvious tension between community and democracy. Public discourse within a democracy is legally conceived as the communicative medium through which individuals choose the forms of their communal life; public discourse within a community is legally conceived as a medium through which the values of a particular life are displayed and enacted.[96] Democracy seeks to open the space of public discourse for collective self-constitution; community seeks to bound that space through the enforcement of civility rules. In the inevitable negotiation between democracy and community, the First Amendment has, since the 1940s, generally served the purposes of democracy by suspending the enforcement of civility rules in such landmark cases as *Cantwell v. Connecticut*,[97] *New York Times Co. v. Sullivan*,[98] *Cohen v. California*,[99] and *Hustler Magazine v. Falwell*.[100]

There is, however, a complex and reciprocal tension between democracy and community. Democracy necessarily presupposes some form of social institution, like community, through which the concrete identity of the "autonomous" democratic citizen can be defined and instantiated. The paradigmatic examples of such institutions are the family and the elementary school. In these settings a child's identity is created in the first instance through decidedly undemocratic means; it "comes to be by way of the internalization of sanctions that are de facto threatened and carried out."[101]

This fact has important consequences for the practice of public discourse. The specific purpose of that discourse is the achievement of some form of "reconciliation through public reason,"[102] yet because the identity of democratic citizens will have been formed by reference to community norms, speech in violation of civility rules will characteristically be perceived as both irrational and coercive.[103] This creates what I have elsewhere termed the "paradox of public discourse": the First Amendment, in the name of democracy, suspends legal enforcement of the very civility rules that make rational deliberation possible.[104] The upshot of the paradox is that the separation of public discourse from community depends in some measure upon the spontaneous persistence of civility. In the absence of such persistence, the use of legal regulation to enforce community standards of civility may be required as an unfortunate but necessary option of last resort. A paradigmatic example of this use may be found in the "fighting words" doctrine of *Chaplinsky v. New Hampshire.*[105]

If community norms thus infiltrate and make possible the practice of democracy, so the ethical imperatives of democracy can be expected to reshape the terms of community life. A stable and successful democratic state will regulate the lives of its citizens in ways consistent with the underlying principle of "their being viewed as free and equal persons."[106] Such regulation will influence community institutions, moving them closer toward the realization of specifically democratic principles. The only intrinsic limitation on the ability of the democratic state to regulate community institutions in this manner is the public/private distinction, which requires that at some point the coercive formation of the identity of individuals remain beyond the purview of the state.

C. The Domain of Public Discourse

This essay primarily concerns the regulation of racist expression within public discourse. "Public discourse" may be defined as encompassing the communicative processes necessary for the formation of public opinion, whether or not that opinion is directed toward specific government personnel, decisions, or policies. Democratic self-governance requires that public opinion be broadly conceived as a process of "collective self-definition"[107] that will necessarily precede and inform any specific government action or inaction. Public discourse cannot encompass all communication within a democracy, however, because both the public/private distinction and the paradox of public discourse imply that the processes of democratic self-governance depend upon the persistence of other nondemocratic forms of social organization, such as community.

Because the First Amendment extends extraordinary protection to public discourse, it is important to demarcate the boundary between such discourse and other speech. I have discussed this issue in detail elsewhere,[108] and will not repeat that analysis here. Suffice it to say that the boundary is inherently uncertain and subject to perennial reevaluation. Factors which the Supreme Court has used to delineate the boundary include the content of speech and the manner of its dissemination.[109] Speech that can be said to be about a matter of "public concern" is ordinarily classified as public discourse,[110] as is speech that is widely distributed to the public at large through the mass media. There are exceptions, however, such as commercial speech, which flow from the influence of traditional conventions that define for us a recognizable "genre" of public speech.[111]

It is difficult to discuss profitably the abstract question of setting the boundaries of public discourse. At the most general level, these boundaries mark the point at which our commitment to the dialogue of autonomous self-governing citizens shifts to other values, as for example to that of the socially implicated self characteristic of community. Exactly where we wish our commitments to alter entails highly specific and contextual inquiries requiring case-by-case assessment.

I confine myself, therefore, to two preliminary observations. First, there are important differences between the constitutional protections extended to public discourse and those extended to nonpublic speech. Thus even if the First Amendment were to immunize from legal regulation the circulation of certain racist ideas in newspapers, it would not follow that the expression of those same ideas could not be restrained by the government within the workplace, where an image of dialogue among autonomous self-governing citizens would be patently out of place.[112] The First Amendment values at stake in the regulation of nonpublic speech are complex and diverse,[113] and I will not be able to review them within the limited span of this essay.

Second, the category of racist expression cannot be excluded as such from the domain of public discourse. The racist content of a particular communication is only one of many factors relevant to the determination of whether the communication lies within or without that domain. Thus the leaflet at issue in *Beauharnais v. Illinois*,[114] which was an effort "to petition the mayor and council of Chicago to pass laws for segregation,"[115] was plainly an effort to engage in public discourse, despite its overt and virulent racism. Similarly, the infamous Nazi march in Skokie was also an attempt to participate in public discourse, notwithstanding its repulsive political symbolism.[116] In both cases racists used well-recognized media for the communication of ideas in order to address and affect public opinion.[117]

3. RACIST SPEECH AND PUBLIC DISCOURSE

We are now in a position to assess the justifications for the regulation of racist expression in light of the First Amendment values associated with public discourse. In some cases this assessment will allow us to reach definite conclusions; in others it will simply help to clarify the issues raised by a particular form of regulation. In each case I shall use the term "racist speech" to encompass the class of communications that would have to be regulated in order to ameliorate the specific harm under consideration.

A. Public Discourse and the Intrinsic Harm of Racist Ideas

It is of course a commonplace of First Amendment jurisprudence "that the government must remain neutral in the marketplace of ideas."[118] The justification for this principle as applied to public discourse is straightforward. Democracy serves the value of self-determination by establishing a communicative structure within which the varying perspectives of individuals can be reconciled through reason. If the state were to forbid the expression of a particular idea, the government would become, with respect to individuals holding that idea, heteronomous and nondemocratic. This is incompatible with a form of government predicated upon citizens being treated "in ways consistent with their being viewed as free and equal persons."[119]

For this reason the value of self-determination requires that public discourse be open to the opinions of all. "[S]ilence coerced by law—the argument of force in its worst form"[120] is constitutionally forbidden. In a democracy, as Piaget notes, "there are no more crimes of opinion, but only breaches of procedure. All opinions are tolerated so long as their protagonists urge their acceptance by legal methods."[121] The notion that racist ideas ought to be forbidden within public discourse because of their "elemental wrongness"[122] is thus fundamentally irreconcilable with the rationale for First Amendment freedoms.

The contemporary debate nevertheless contains three distinct arguments that racist ideas ought to be proscribed because of their "deontic" harm. The first is that the idea of racism is "*sui generis*" because it is "universally condemned."[123] The same authors who make this claim, however, also stress "the structural reality of racism in America," a reality manifested not merely in an "epidemic of racist incidents," but also in the widespread racist beliefs characteristic of "upper-class whites" and important social "institutions."[124] In fact it is probably fair to characterize these authors as proponents of regulating racist speech precisely because of their urgent sense of the *prevalence* of racist practices. Although the nightmare of these practices ought to occasion strong public response, it substantially undermines the conclusion that racism is "universally condemned"[125] in any sense relevant for First Amendment analysis. Such practices can only be understood as manifestations of strongly held but otherwise unarticulated racist ideas.[126]

A second argument is that the failure to regulate racist ideas amounts to a symbolic endorsement of racist speech, which is intolerable in "a society committed to ideals of social and political equality."[127] In essence this argument repudiates the public/private distinction required by democratic self-governance.[128] But this repudiation strikes at the root of the project of self-determination. If the responsibility for ideas advanced by individuals in public discourse were to be attributed to the government, the government could not then also be deemed *responsive* to those ideas in the way required by the principle of self-governance. Just as a library could not function if it were understood as endorsing the views of the authors whose books it collects and displays, so also in a democracy the government could not serve the value of collective autonomy if it were understood as endorsing the ideas expressed by private persons in public discourse.[129]

A third argument is that the free expression of racist ideas is inconsistent with our commitment to the egalitarian ideals of the Fourteenth Amendment. At root this argument rejects collective autonomy as the principal value of democracy, and substitutes instead what Kenneth Karst has eloquently argued is "the substantive center of the fourteenth amendment: the principle of equal citizenship."[130] Although this position has been endorsed by some political theorists,[131] it runs against the overwhelming American commitment to the importance of "self-rule," to the fundamental belief "that the American people are politically free insomuch as they are governed by themselves collectively."[132]

Of course the principle of self-rule contains its own commitment to the value of equal citizenship, to the notion that, as a formal matter, citizens must be "viewed as free and equal persons."[133] But the meaning of this commitment is measured by the purpose of enabling the processes of self-determination. The appeal to the Fourteenth Amendment, on the other hand, is meant to signify commitment to a substantive value of equality that is not defined by reference to this purpose, so that the implementation of the value may adversely affect processes of self-determination.[134] The argument thus envisions the possibility of "balancing" Fourteenth Amendment values against First Amendment principles.

In balancing the value of equal citizenship against the principle of self-determination, however, we must ask who is empowered to interpret the meaning of the highly contestable value of equal citizenship. To the extent that the value of equal citizenship is used to justify limiting public discourse, the interpreter of the value cannot be the people, because the very function of the appeal to the Fourteenth Amendment is to truncate the communicative processes by which the people clarify their collective will.[135] In such circumstances the Ultimate Interpreter, whoever or whatever it may finally turn out to be, must impose its will without popular accountability. Our government currently contains no such Interpreter, not even the Supreme Court, whose constitutional decisions are always shadowed by the potential of constitutional amendment or political reconstruction through subsequent appointments. The impossibility of locating such an Interpreter suggests the difficulties that attend the argument from the Fourteenth Amendment.[136]

B. Public Discourse and Harm to Identifiable Groups

The purpose of public discourse is to reconcile through reason the differences occasioned by a collection of "autonomous wills." Groups neither reason nor have an autonomous will; only persons do. This is the source of the profound individualism that characterizes First Amendment doctrine. The question is whether that individualism is compatible with the regulation of public discourse in order to prevent harm to groups.

It is rather common for the laws of other countries to restrain speech deemed harmful to groups, speech that, in the words of the Illinois statute at issue in *Beauharnais,* casts "contempt, derision, or obloquy" on a particular group.[137] Such laws subordinate individual expression to the protection of group status and dignity, typically on the theory that group membership is an essential ingredient of personal identity. Hence, as Gary Jacobson notes in his description of Israeli law, groups are seen "as units whose corporate identity carries with it . . . claim[s] upon the state for specific entitlement."[138] Thus the law will in certain situations give "greater priority to fraternal and communal attachments over the subjective choices of individuals."[139]

In American law, by contrast, there is a tendency to view groups as mere "collections of individuals"[140] whose claims are no greater than those of their constituent members.[141] This tendency is virtually fixed by the individualist presuppositions of public discourse. Thus in *Cantwell v. Connecticut*[142] the Court extended First Amendment protection to an anti-Catholic diatribe so violent that it "would offend not only persons of that persuasion, but all others who respect the honestly held religious faith of their fellows."[143] The Court reasoned that such constitutional immunity was necessary so that "many types of life, character, opinion and belief can develop unmolested and unobstructed."[144] This reasoning presupposes that groups evolve through the informed choices of individuals.[145] The Court subordinated the sensibilities of members of established groups, such as Catholics, to the communicative structure necessary for these choices.[146] It thus refused to allow unattractive and highly offensive representations of the Church to be excluded from public discourse.

Cantwell makes special sense because American religious groups have since the nineteenth century been organized on the principle of "voluntarism,"[147] on the notion that "religion is . . . a matter of individual choice."[148] It might be argued, however, that race is quite another matter, one in which a certain kind of group identity is inescapably imposed upon a person by accident of birth. For this reason group identity might be seen as primary with respect to race, and the individualist foundations of public discourse—the assumption that racial groups are determined by processes of individual decision-making—repudiated as unrealistic.

This argument is powerful and requires close attention. In analyzing it, we can draw on the distinction that has emerged in feminist writings between "sex," which refers to biological facts, and "gender," which refers to socially constructed roles.[149] To confuse the two, to predicate the social content of gender upon the biological fact of sex, is to fall into "the determinist or essentialist trap."[150] The political point of the distinction is to keep perpetually open for discussion and analysis the social meaning of being born female and included within the group "women."[151] Even if one is not free to opt out of the group, the possibility ought nevertheless to be preserved that the identity of the group be ultimately determined, in the language of Nancy Fraser, "through dialogue and collective struggle."[152] Fraser writes that "[i]n a society as complex as ours, it does not seem to me wise or even possible to extrapolate" the outcome of that dialogue "from the current, prepoliticized experiences and idiolects of women, especially since it is likely, in my view, that these will turn out to be the current prepoliticized experiences and idiolects only of *some* women."[153]

Fraser's point is that regardless of the biological basis of sex, the social meaning of gender is a political issue whose outcome, like that of all political issues, must be regarded as indeterminate. She thus applies the structure of democratic self-determination to the constitution of group identity. The individualist assumptions of that structure create a form of communication in which political indeterminacy is preserved; they guarantee that the dialogue envisioned by Fraser will remain open to the perspectives of all women. If the identity of the group "women" were understood to have a content determinate enough to employ the force of law to silence dissenting views, the law would hegemonically impose the perspective of only *some* women.

The same logic, I believe, holds true for racial groups. We must distinguish race as a biological category from race as social category. Even if unfortunately "the attempt to establish a *biological* basis of race has not been swept into the dustbin of history," [154] it would nevertheless be deplorable to construct First Amendment principles on the basis of a biological view of race. What is most saliently at issue is rather "race as a social concept": "The effort must be made to understand race as *an unstable and 'decentered' complex of social meanings constantly being transformed by political struggle.*" [155] To the extent that the social meaning of race is thus profoundly controversial [156]—and it is controversial not merely for members of minority groups but also for the entire nation [157]—the individualist premises of public discourse will ensure that it remain open to democratic constitution.

This lack of closure may of course be threatening, for it casts the creation of group identity upon the uncertain currents of public discourse. The safe harbor of legal regulation may, by contrast, appear to promise members of minority groups more secure control over the meaning of their social experience. But that promise is illusory, for it is profoundly inconsistent with the analysis of racism prevalent in the contemporary literature. To the extent that racism is viewed as pervasive among whites, and to the extent that whites, as a dominant group, can be expected to hold the levers of legal power, there would seem little reason to trust the law to establish socially acceptable meanings for race. Such meanings cannot be determined by reference to easy or bright-line distinctions, as for example those between positive or negative ascriptions of group identity. The work of figures as diverse as William Julius Wilson, [158] Shelby Steele, [159] and Louis Farrakhan [160] illustrates how highly critical characterizations of racial groups can nevertheless serve constructive social purposes. To vest in an essentially white legal establishment the power to discriminate authoritatively among such characterizations and purposes would seem certain to be disempowering. [161]

The conclusion that group harm ought not to justify legal regulation is reflected in technical First Amendment doctrine in the fact that virtually all communications likely to provoke a claim of group harm will be privileged as assertions of evaluative opinion. [162] The following language, for example, gave rise to legal liability in *Beauharnais:* "If persuasion and the need to prevent the white race from becoming mongrelized by the negro will not unite us, then the aggressions . . . rapes, robberies, knives, guns and marijuana of the negro, SURELY WILL." [163] Justice Frankfurter interpreted this language as false factual assertion: "No one will gainsay that it is libelous falsely to charge another with being a rapist, robber, carrier of knives and guns, and user of marijuana." [164] This interpretation, however, seems plainly incorrect. To accuse an individual of using marijuana is to assert that she has committed certain specific acts. To accuse the group "African Americans" of using marijuana, however, is not to make an analogous assertion. Some African Americans will have used marijuana, and most will not have. The question is thus not the existence of certain specific acts, but rather whether those acts can appropriately be used to characterize the group. The fundamental issue is the nature of the group's identity, an issue that almost certainly ought to be characterized as one of evaluative opinion.

Because the social meaning of race is inherently controversial, most statements likely to give rise to actions for group harm will be negative assessments of the identity of racial groups, and hence statements of evaluative opinion. No serious commentator would advocate a trial to determine the truth or falsity of such statements; the point is rather that such statements should not be made at all because of the deep injury they cause. But in a context where group identity is a matter for determination through political struggle and disagreement, the hypostatized injury of a group cannot, consistent with the processes that instantiate the principle of self-determination, be grounds to legally silence characterizations of group identity within public discourse.

Commentators who stress the theme of group harm vigorously emphasize the fact that racist speech does not injure random groups; it damages precisely those groups who have historically suffered egregious oppression and subordination. [165] But although the tragedy of this fact is obvious, its constitutional implications are not. Our history certainly warrants the assumption that racist speech will inflict terrible injuries on victim groups. But the question is whether these injuries are so unspeakable as to justify suspending the democratic constitution of group identities. One approach might be to avoid this tension by characterizing the injuries of racist speech in such a way that their legal redress would actually be required by the principles of public discourse. Thus it can be argued that the stigmatizing and disabling effects of racist speech effectively exclude its victims from participation in public discourse. This approach suggests an important line of analysis, but I will defer consideration of it until part 3(D), where it can be placed in the context of other justifications for restraints on racist speech that turn on harms to the marketplace of ideas.

Another method of avoiding the tension between group harm and democratic principles would be to claim that racist speech ought to be characterized as a "mechanism of subordination" within a larger system of suppression, rather than as a form of communication.[166] This claim requires us to determine the criteria by which speech can be designated as action and hence excluded from public discourse. The standard implicitly advanced by the claim is that if communication is intimately connected to larger social relationships that are deeply undesirable, the communication can for that reason be characterized as action.

The difficulty with this standard is that all communication grows out of and embodies social relationships; for this reason all communication is both speech and action. The function of public discourse is to create a protected space within which communication, even if embodying social relationships, can be protected as speech if formulated and disseminated in ways relevant for democratic self-governance. Such a space opens up the possibility of subjecting social relationships to rational reflection, dialogue, and *self-control*. It thus enables "self-rule" to be reconciled with rule "by laws."[167] If communication could be excluded from this space because it embodies social relations of which we disapprove, public discourse could no longer perform this function. There is no difference between excluding speech from public discourse because we condemn the social relationships it embodies, and excluding speech from public discourse because we condemn the ideas by which those social relationships are embodied. In the end, therefore, the argument that racist speech is a form of action reduces to the claim, which we have already considered, that racist speech ought to be restrained because of its inconsistency with the egalitarian ideals of the Fourteenth Amendment.

C. Public Discourse and Harm to Individuals

There appear at first blush to be important differences between claims of group harm and claims of individual harm. To the extent group identity is understood to be a matter of political struggle (and hence dialogic interaction), speech containing negative ascriptions of that identity cannot be censored without undermining the democratic nature of that struggle. But individual identity does not seem to rest on political struggle and dialogue in this way. Indeed, one's spontaneous image is of fully formed individuals entering the realm of public discourse to reach agreement on issues that concern their collective, rather than personal life. Speech damaging personal life can thus be restricted without undercutting the very purposes of public discourse.

This perspective, however, rests on a rather sharp distinction between individual and collective identity, a distinction that simply cannot be maintained. The very reason that racist speech harms individual persons is because it so violently ruptures the forms of social respect that are necessary for the maintenance of individual personality. These forms of respect, when taken together, constitute a collective, community identity. Hence the state can prevent the individual harm caused by racist speech only by enforcing pertinent standards of community identity. The interdependence of individual and collective identity is thus presupposed in the very concept of individual harm.

This interdependence lies behind the well-established constitutional prohibition on restricting public discourse because it is "offensive" [168] or "outrageous," [169] or because it affronts "dignity" or is "insulting" or causes "public odium" or "public disrepute." [170] Such speech causes intense individual suffering because it violates community norms, yet the Court has required its toleration in order to prevent the state from using the authority of law to enforce particular conceptions of collective life. [171]

Questions of personal identity are in fact always at stake in discussions of collective self-definition. For this reason effective political dialogue requires that participants be constantly willing to be transformed. As Frank Michelman points out, public discourse is impossible so long as "the participants' pre-political self-understandings and social perspectives must axiomatically be regarded as completely impervious to the persuasion of the process itself." [172] As our collective aspirations change, so will our respective personal identities. Thus restrictions on public discourse designed to protect those identities from harm will necessarily also restrict self-determination as to our collective life. If group harm is an inevitable price of the political constitution of group identity, individual injury is an unavoidable cost of the political constitution of community identity.

It is important to emphasize the narrowness of this conclusion. In recent years an important theme of our national life has been the opposition to racism. We have enacted that opposition by legally regulating racist behavior such as discrimination. Because action both creates and manifests identity, this regulation inhibits the formation and expression of racist identities. So also does regulation prohibiting certain kinds of racist communication in nonpublic speech, as for example in the workplace.[173] In effect we have determined to use government force to reshape community institutions in order to combat racism. This is an appropriate and laudable use of democratic power.[174] But it is legitimate precisely because we have adopted it in a manner consistent with the principle of self-determination; it reflects a national identity that we have freely chosen.

This legitimacy is made possible by public discourse, which serves the value of self-determination because it is so structured that every call for national identity has the opportunity to make its case. There is a significant difference, therefore, between proscribing racial insults directed toward individuals in the workplace[175] and proscribing them in a political discussion or debate.[176] The harm to the individual victim may be the same, but for public discourse to enable self-government, racist speech within that discourse must be repudiated on the merits, rather than be silenced by force of law.

D. Public Discourse and Harm to the Marketplace of Ideas

The most effective arguments for regulating racist speech are those that double back on the concept of public discourse itself and contend that such regulation is necessary for public discourse truly to instantiate the principle of self-determination. On the surface there appear to be two distinct lines of analysis. The first stresses the irrational and coercive qualities of racist speech, the second the untoward effects of racist speech in silencing victim groups. In the end these lines of argumentation cross and depend upon each other.

Racist Speech as Irrational and Coercive. Public discourse must be more than simply a register of private preferences in order to serve as a medium for the enactment of collective autonomy. If persons communicated in public discourse merely through polling organizations to make known their "votes" on public issues, democracy would degenerate into the heteronomous system of majoritarian rule described by Schauer. The purposes of collective self-determination require instead that public action be founded upon a public opinion formed through open and interactive processes of rational deliberation. The argument that racist speech is irrational and coercive, that it is nothing more than a kind of "linguistic abuse (verbal abuse on an unwilling target),"[177] thus cuts to the very root of public discourse.

The argument, however, points to a more general problem, for all communication that violates civility rules is perceived as both irrational and coercive.[178] Because civility rules embody the norms of respect and reason we are accustomed to receive from members of our community, communication inconsistent with those rules is experienced as an instrument "of aggression and personal assault."[179] The argument from coercion and irrationality thus poses a generic dilemma for First Amendment doctrine. If the state were to be permitted to enforce civility rules, it would in effect exclude from public discourse those whose speech advocated and exemplified unfamiliar and marginalized forms of life. But if the state were to suspend the enforcement of civility rules, it would endanger the possibility of rational deliberation by permitting the dissemination of abusive and coercive speech. This tension between the requirement that self-government respect all of its citizens "as free and equal persons," and the requirement that self-government proceed through processes of rational deliberation, creates the paradox of public discourse.[180]

It might be thought that the specific case of racist speech dissolves this paradox, for such speech by hypothesis violates norms of both equality and civility and hence appears to be suppressible without harm to public discourse. But this conclusion is not accurate. The principle of equality at issue in the paradox of public discourse is formal; its extension to all persons is the fundamental precondition of the possibility of self-government. To the extent that the principle is circumscribed, so also is the reach of self-determination. The norm of equality violated by racist speech, on the other hand, is substantive; it reflects a particular understanding of how we ought to live. It is the kind of norm that ought to emerge from processes of public deliberation. Although the censorship of racist speech is consistent with this substantive norm of equality, it is inconsistent with the formal principle of equality, because such censorship would exclude from the medium of public discourse those who disagree with a particular substantive norm of equality. Such persons would thus be cut off from participation in the processes of collective self-determination.

First Amendment doctrine has tended to resolve the paradox of public discourse in favor of the principle of formal equality, largely because violations of that principle limit *pro tanto* the domain of self-government, whereas protecting uncivil speech does not automatically destroy the possibility of rational deliberation. The visceral shock of uncivil speech can sometimes actually serve constructive purposes, as when it causes individuals to question the community standards into which they have been socialized, and hence enables them, perhaps for the first time, to acknowledge the claims of others from radically different cultural backgrounds.[181] There is in fact a long tradition of oppressed and marginalized groups using uncivil speech to force recognition of the intensity and urgency of their needs.[182]

Tolerating uncivil speech, moreover, does not necessarily undermine the process of rational deliberation, so long as the extent of such speech is confined and does not infect the process as a whole. The judgment that rational deliberation can continue in spite of the presence of uncivil speech is exactly the point of Harlan's opinion in *Cohen v. California,*[183] in which the Court refused to permit the state to use the force of law "to maintain . . . a suitable level of discourse within the body politic":[184]

The constitutional right of free expression is powerful medicine in a society as diverse and populous as ours. It is designed and intended to remove governmental restraints from the arena of public discussion, putting the decision as to what views shall be voiced largely into the hands of each of us, in the hope that use of such freedom will ultimately produce a more capable citizenry and more perfect polity and in the belief that no other approach would comport with the premise of individual dignity and choice upon which our political system rests. . . .

To many, the immediate consequence of this freedom may often appear to be only verbal tumult, discord, and even offensive utterance. These are, however, within established limits, in truth necessary side effects of the broader enduring values which the process of open debate permits us to achieve. That the air may at times seem filled with verbal cacophony is, in this sense not a sign of weakness but of strength.[185]

It is of course a matter of judgment whether "open debate" within "the arena of public discussion" is indeed achieving "broader enduring values." How one makes that judgment will depend very much on one's circumstances. The call in recent literature to attend more carefully to "the victim's perspective"[186] is well taken in this regard. Members of dominant groups may be satisfied with the overall quality of public deliberation, but members of victim groups, at whom racist speech is systematically targeted, may feel quite otherwise.

It is at this point that the line of analysis stressing the irrational, coercive quality of racist speech crosses and depends upon the line of analysis stressing the silencing of victim groups. For when pressed the point is not that public discourse is pervasively disabled by racist speech, but rather that the concentrated effect of such speech on members of victim groups is to foreclose public discourse as an effective avenue of collective self-determination. In the contemporary debate this effect has been addressed under the rubric of "silencing."

Racist Speech as Silencing Minority Groups. The literature on "silencing" has burgeoned. So far as I can make out, the literature presents three distinct arguments to support the claim of silencing:[187] (1) Victim groups are silenced because their perspectives are systematically excluded from the dominant discourse;[188] (2) victim groups are silenced because the pervasive stigma of racism systematically undermines and devalues their speech; and (3) victim groups are silenced because the visceral "fear, rage, [and] shock" of racist speech systematically preempts response.[189] This section analyzes each of these arguments separately; the next section weaves them together into a more complex indictment of racist speech.

The first argument is that the language of public discourse, although seemingly neutral and objective, has a built-in bias that prevents the articulation of minority positions.[190] Thus racism in the dominant discourse is compressed into "the neutralized word 'discrimination,' " in which "the role of power, domination, and oppression as the source of the evil" is effaced, and "[m]uch of the political, historical, and moral content of 'equality' has been dropped."[191] Similarly, the understanding of whites that racism is an "intentional belief in white supremacy"—the perpetrators' perspective—has been folded into the very language of public debate, while the understanding of minorities that racism "refers *solely* to minority subordination"—the victims' perspective—is banished from the language.[192]

Although the premise of this argument seems to me true, it does not by itself support the conclusion that racist speech ought to be regulated. All communication rests on foundations of unarticulated assumptions. The very function of dialogue is often to move toward enlightenment by uncovering and exposing these assumptions. Enlightenment can be gradual and progressive, or it can result from the shock of intense political struggle. That our language always encompasses both more and less than our intentions is thus not an argument for the suppression of racist speech, but rather for the encouragement of further public debate.

The point might be made, however, that public debate fails to achieve such enlightenment because the pervasive racism of American society devalues and stigmatizes minority contributions to this debate. The voice of the victims goes unheard. There is thus a call for an "outsider jurisprudence"[193] which will legitimate that voice and enable "legal insiders ... [to] imagine a life disabled in a significant way by hate propaganda."[194]

Once again, the premise of this argument appears sound, but its conclusion does not. Audiences always evaluate communication on the basis of their understanding of its social context.[195] This is not a deformity of public discourse, but one of its generic characteristics.[196] It poses the question of how an audience's prepolitical understanding of social context may be altered, a question that confronts all participants in public dialogue. The urgency of the question does not justify restricting public discourse; it is rather a call for more articulate and persuasive speech, for more intense and effective political engagement.

Taken together, the argument from the inherent bias of accepted discourse and the argument from the stigmatic devaluation of minority speech fuse into a single indictment of public discourse as irrational. The systematic derogation of the specific perspectives of victim groups is said to be caused by the nation's particular history of racial oppression, rather than by concerns that should properly affect a legitimately rational public dialogue. Both arguments thus ultimately appeal to the concept of false consciousness,[197] to the notion that there is an ideal vantage from which the rationality of discourse can be "objectively" assessed.

It is one thing, however, to use the idea of false consciousness as a weapon *within* public discourse to convince others of the need to break with the prejudices of the past, and it is quite another to use the idea as a justification to limit public discourse itself. The first is a familiar rhetorical strategy. It is consistent with the processes of public discourse because its effectiveness ultimately depends on its persuasive power. But the second presupposes an intimacy with truth so vital as to foreclose opposing positions. The very point of using the idea of false consciousness to limit public discourse is to justify legally disregarding certain perspectives, on the grounds that they could not possibly be respected as true expressions of autonomous individuality. Circumscribing public discourse to ameliorate false consciousness thus does not protect public discourse from harm, but rather contradicts its very purpose of providing a medium for the reconciliation of autonomous wills.

The third argument for restraining racist speech does not turn on the characterization of public discourse as irrational, but rather as coercive. Recent literature contains searing documentation of the profound personal injury of racist speech, and this injury may in particular circumstances be so shocking as to literally preempt responsive speech. Although the analogous harm of uncivil speech is randomly scattered throughout the population, the disabilities attendant upon racist speech are concentrated upon members of victim groups. Hence where members of dominant groups perceive "isolated incidents,"[198] members of victim groups perceive instead a suffocating and inescapable "racism that is a persistent and constituent part of the social order, woven into the fabric of society and everyday life."[199]

Under such conditions it is to be expected that members of dominant and victim groups may well come to conflicting judgments about whether racist speech shocks significant segments of victim group populations into silence. The recent literature proposing restraints on racist speech is eloquent on the need to "listen[ ] to the real victims" of such speech, and to display "empathy or understanding for their injury."[200] And of course any fair and just determination about the regulation of public discourse would require exactly this kind of social sensitivity. But there is also a tendency in this literature to move from the proposition that a fair determination cannot be made unless "the victims of racist speech are heard,"[201] to the very different proposition that such a determination ought to use "the experience of victim-group members [as] a guide."[202] The latter proposition seems to me plainly false.

The issue on the table is whether irrationality and coercion have so tainted the medium of public discourse as to require shrinking the scope of self-government. That issue significantly affects every citizen, and its resolution therefore cannot be ceded to the control of any particular group. In fact I do not see how the issue can be adequately resolved at all unless some notion of civic membership is invoked that transcends mere group identification. If we cannot strive to deliberate together as citizens, distancing ourselves from (but not abandoning) our specific cultural backgrounds, the issue can be resolved only through the exercise of naked group power, a solution not at all advantageous to the marginalized and oppressed.[203]

Paradoxically, therefore, the question of whether public discourse is irretrievably damaged by racist speech must itself ultimately be addressed through the medium of public discourse. Because those participating in public discourse will not themselves have been silenced (almost by definition), a heavy, frustrating burden is de facto placed on those who would truncate public discourse in order to save it. They must represent themselves as "speaking for" those who have been deprived of their voice. But the negative space of that silence reigns inscrutable, neither confirming nor denying this claim. And the more eloquent the appeal, the less compelling the claim, for the more accessible public discourse will then appear to exactly the perspectives racist speech is said to repress.

Even if this burden is lifted, however, and it is simply accepted that members of victim groups are intimidated into silence, it would still not follow that restraints on racist speech within public discourse are justified. One might believe, for example, that such silencing occurs chiefly through the structural conditions of racism, rather than specifically through the shock of racist speech. "The problem," as the controversial chair of the black studies department of New York's City College once remarked in response to the racist comments of an academic colleague, does not lie with specific communicative acts, but rather with "racism" itself, "insidious in our society and built into our culture."[204] If the chair's diagnosis were true, restraints on racist speech would impair public discourse without at the same time repairing the silence of victim groups.

Alternatively, one might believe that racist speech silences victim groups primarily because of its "ideas," because of its messages of racial inferiority, rather than because of its incivility. The distinction is important for the following reason: although it is consistent with the internal logic of public discourse to excise in extreme circumstances certain kinds of uncivil speech that are experienced as coercive,[205] it is fundamentally incompatible with public discourse to excise specific ideas because they are "analogously" deemed to be coercive. Public discourse is the medium within which our society assesses the democratic acceptability of ideas; to exclude certain ideas as prima facie "coercive" and hence destructive of public discourse is to contradict precisely this function. Therefore "harm" to public discourse cannot justify restraints on racist ideas on the grounds that such ideas are perceived to be threatening or coercive.[206]

There are also other possibilities. One might believe, for example, that because it is difficult to distinguish ideas from incivility, and because it is essential to collective self-determination to protect all ideas, the law will as a practical matter be able to restrain only a small category of blatant racist epithets, which, although deeply offensive and lacking in ideational content, have relatively little to do with the more widespread phenomenon of silencing. Or one might believe that racist speech silences primarily when shocking racist epithets are used in the face-to-face confrontations characteristic of the "fighting words" doctrine of *Chaplinsky*,[207] so that the essential insight of the argument from silencing is already reflected within First Amendment doctrine.

My own conclusion, in light of these alternative considerations, is that the case has not yet been made for circumscribing public discourse to prevent the kind of preemptive silencing that occurs when members of victim groups experience "fear, rage, [and] shock." I say this with some hesitation, and with considerable diffidence. But even if the empirical claim of systematic preemptive silencing were accepted (and I am not sure that I do accept it), it is in my view most directly the result of the social and structural conditions of racism, rather than specifically of racist speech. Because the logic of the argument from preemptive silencing does not impeach the necessity of preserving the free expression of ideas,[208] public discourse could at most be regulated in a largely symbolic manner so as to purge it of outrageous racist epithets and names. It seems to me highly implausible to claim that such symbolic regulation will eliminate the preemptive silencing that is said to justify restraints on public discourse.

Racist Speech as Symbolic Cultural Oppression. When distinguished and parsed in this analytic manner, therefore, the various arguments for restraining racist speech in order to preserve the integrity of public discourse do not in my judgment support their desired conclusion. But the arguments can be braided together to fund an accusation more powerful than its separate strands.

In ordinary life members of victim groups do not experience a string of distinct disadvantages. Rather, if representations in the current literature are accepted as true, they confront in public discourse an undifferentiated complex of circumstances in which they are systematically demeaned, stigmatized, ignored; in which the very language of debate resists the articulation of their claims; in which they are harassed, abused, intimidated, and systematically and egregiously injured both individually and collectively. The question is not whether these liabilities, when taken individually and singly, justify restraining racist speech within public discourse, but rather whether, when taken together as a complex whole, they render public discourse unfit as an instrument of collective self-determination for members of victim groups, and whether this unacceptable situation would be cured by restraints on racist speech.

What makes this question so very formidable is that it turns on the nexus between public discourse and the value of collective self-determination. Although the formal preconditions of that nexus can be described, its actual substantive realization must remain contingent upon conditions of history, culture, and social structure. Thus when members of victim groups claim that public discourse no longer serves for them the value of self-government, it is no answer to reply that they have been embraced within its formal preconditions. If members of victim groups in fact perceive themselves to be systematically excluded from public dialogue, that dialogue can scarcely achieve for them those "broader enduring values" that are its democratic justification. The very legitimacy of democratic self-governance is thus called into question.

The dependence of the value of public discourse upon matters of social perception poses complex and delicate questions, but the difficulty of these questions is profoundly magnified in the context of the controversy over racist speech. First, the truth of the claim that members of victim groups are cut off from meaningful participation within public discourse cannot be directly experienced and hence evaluated by members of dominant groups. Its resolution must therefore depend, to one degree or another, upon the acceptance of representations by members of victim groups. As a practical political matter, therefore, what is called into question is not merely the truth of these representations, but also the trust and respect with which they are received by members of dominant groups.[209] Second, the focus on trust and respect is reinforced by the remedial claim that racist speech ought to be censored so as to open up public discourse to victim groups. Essentially this claim requires self-determination to be denied to some so that it may be made available to others. Society's willingness to circumscribe public discourse is thus transformed into a touchstone of the esteem with which it regards victim groups.

In fact it is this transformation that most precisely supports the argument. The argument turns on the interpretive meaning which members of victim groups ascribe to their place in American life; the contention is that this meaning is one of exclusion. Such an interpretation cannot be reduced to any specific empirical claims or conditions. Instead the need of those who feel alienated is most exactly met by a gesture of social esteem. By conveying in the strongest possible terms messages of respect and welcome, the censorship of racist speech might go a long way toward allowing members of victim groups to reinterpret their experience as one of inclusion within the dialogue of public discourse. The objections we noted earlier, that the regulation of racist speech within public discourse could at most restrict the publication of highly offensive racist epithets and names and that such regulation could only serve symbolic purposes, is thus no longer to the point. For the argument now turns squarely on the politics of cultural symbolism.

The most salient characteristic of such politics is that the particular content of government regulation is less important than its perceived meaning. We have already noted how claims like those of individual injury or preemptive silencing define concrete classes of communications that are said empirically to cause a particular harm. But the claim of cultural exclusion is fundamentally different, for it implies no such specific referent. The claim, when pressed, is not that any specific class of communications actually causes members of victim groups to feel excluded, but rather that a particular regulatory gesture will be the occasion for members of victim groups to feel included.[210]

This suggests, however, that restraints on public discourse are only one of a wide variety of strategies that government can pursue to ameliorate the sense of cultural exclusion experienced by victim groups. Alternatives might include antidiscrimination laws, affirmative action programs, redistribution of economic resources, restraints on racist forms of nonpublic speech, and so forth. All these modifications of community life could be interpreted as significant gestures of respect and inclusion. It is a matter of political choice and characterization to reject these alternatives as insufficient and to deem the limitation of public discourse as necessary to overcome the alienation of victim groups.

At root, therefore, the argument from cultural exclusion seeks to subordinate public discourse, whose very purpose is to serve as the framework for all possible forms of politics, to a particular political perspective. The argument begins with the sound premise that a cultural sense of participation is necessary for public discourse to serve the value of collective self-determination. But instead of conceiving public discourse as a means of rousing the nation's political will to actions designed to facilitate that sense of participation, the argument instead turns on public discourse itself, and, as a matter of political perception and assertion, deems the limitation of that discourse to be prerequisite for the elimination of disabling alienation. The argument therefore does not ultimately rest on the importance of protecting public discourse from harm, but rather on the need to sacrifice public discourse in order to recuperate profound social dislocations.

Bluntly expressed, the argument requires us to balance the integrity of public discourse as a general structure of communication against the importance of enhancing the experience of political participation by members of victim groups. The argument thus reiterates the position that public discourse ought to be subordinated to the egalitarian ideals of the Fourteenth Amendment. It adopts a sophisticated version of that position, however, for it is able to contend that public discourse need be impaired in only slight and symbolic ways. Even so minimal a gesture as purging outrageous and shocking racist epithets could be sufficient to make members of victim groups feel welcome within the arena of public discourse, and thus to enable public discourse to serve for them the value of self-determination.[211] In this form, the argument is analogous to that advanced in the controversy over prohibiting flag burning, in which it is also urged that public discourse ought to be minimally impaired for highly important symbolic reasons.[212] Just as it has been contended that any idea can be expressed without burning a flag,[213] so it can be asserted that any idea can be expressed without recourse to vile racist epithets.[214] In both cases, therefore, it can be argued that the de minimis effects on public discourse are outweighed by the significance of the interests at stake.[215]

I believe, however, that this invitation to balance ought to be declined. This is not because balancing can be ruled out in advance by some "absolutist" algorithm; the attraction of a purely formal democracy may itself in certain circumstances no longer command limitless conviction. It is rather because, in the American context, the temptation to balance rests on what might be termed the fallacy of immaculate isolation.[216] The effect on public discourse is acceptable only if it is de minimis, and it is arguably de minimis only when a specific claim is evaluated in isolation from other, similar claims. But no claim is in practice immaculately isolated in this manner. As the flag-burning example suggests, there is no shortage of powerful groups contending that uncivil speech within public discourse ought to be "minimally" regulated for highly pressing symbolic reasons.[217]

This is evident even if the focus of analysis is narrowly limited to the structure of the claim at issue in the debate over racist speech. In a large heterogeneous country populated by assertive and conflicting groups, the logic of circumscribing public discourse to reduce political estrangement is virtually unstoppable. The nation is filled with those who feel displaced and who would feel less so if given the chance symbolically to truncate public discourse. This is already plain in the regulations that have proliferated on college campuses, which commonly proscribe not merely speech that degrades persons on the basis of their race, but also, to pick a typical list, speech that demeans persons on the basis of their "color, national origin, religion, sex, sexual orientation, age, handicap, or veteran's status."[218] The claim of de minimis impact loses credibility as the list of claimants to special protection grows longer.

The point I want to press does not depend on the intellectual difficulty of drawing lines to separate similar claims. It is rather that the remedial and political logic of equal participation applies with analogous force to a broad and growing spectrum of group claims. One might, of course, devise arguments, perhaps based on the specific history of the Fourteenth Amendment, to distinguish racial epithets from blasphemous imprecations, or from degrading and pornographic characterizations of women, or from vicious antigay slurs, or from gross ethnic insults. But the question is whether such arguments can withstand the compelling egalitarian logic that unites these various situations. My strong intuition is that they cannot, and hence that the claim of de minimis impact on public discourse is implausible.[219]

In the specific context of the argument from cultural exclusion, moreover, a refusal to balance is far less harsh than it might superficially appear. The fundamental challenge is to enable members of victim groups to reinterpret their experience within the American political and cultural order as one of genuine participation. There are a host of ways to address this challenge short of truncating public discourse. The most obvious and potentially effective strategy would be to dismantle systematically and forcefully the structural conditions of racism. If we were so blessed as to be able to accomplish that feat—if we were truly able to eliminate such conditions as chronic unemployment, inadequate health care, segregated housing, or disproportionately low incomes—then we would no doubt also have succeeded in ameliorating the experience of cultural exclusion.

4. THE FIRST AMENDMENT AND HARM TO THE EDUCATIONAL ENVIRONMENT

If public discourse is bounded on one side by the necessary structures of community life, it is bounded on the other by the need of the state to create organizations to achieve explicit public objectives. These organizations, which are nonpublic forums, regulate speech in ways that are fundamentally incompatible with the requirements of public discourse.[220] Public discourse is the medium through which our democracy determines its purposes, and for this reason the legal structure of public discourse requires that all such purposes be kept open to question and reevaluation. Within nonpublic forums, on the other hand, government objectives are taken as established, and communication is regulated as necessary to achieve those objectives.

Although the Supreme Court has often held that "the First Amendment rights of speech and association extend to the campuses of state universities," and even that "the campus of a pubic university, at least for its students, possesses many of the characteristics of a public forum,"[221] in fact state institutions of higher learning are public organizations established for the express purpose of education. The Court has always held that "a university's mission is education," and it has never construed the First Amendment to deny a university's "authority to impose reasonable regulations compatible with that mission upon the use of its campus and facilities."[222] The Court has explicitly recognized "a university's right to exclude . . . First Amendment activities that . . . substantially interfere with the opportunity of other students to obtain an education."[223] Thus student speech incompatible with classroom processes may be censored; faculty publications inconsistent with academic standards may be evaluated and judged; and so forth.

The regulation of racist speech within public institutions of higher learning, therefore, does not turn on the value of democratic self-governance and its realization in public discourse. Instead the constitutionality of such regulation depends on the logic of instrumental rationality, and specifically on three factors: (1) the nature of the educational mission of the university; (2) the instrumental connection of the regulation to the attainment of that mission; and (3) the deference that courts ought to display toward the instrumental judgment of institutional authorities.[224] The current controversy regarding the constitutionality of regulating racist speech on university and college campuses may most helpfully be interpreted as a debate about the first of these factors, the constitutionally permissible educational objectives of public institutions of higher learning.[225]

Courts have advanced at least three different concepts of those objectives. The most traditional concept, which I refer to as "civic education," views public education as an instrument of community life, and holds "that respect for constituted authority and obedience thereto is an essential lesson to qualify one for the duties of citizenship, and that the schoolroom is an appropriate place to teach that lesson."[226] Civic education conceptualizes instruction as a process of cultural reproduction, in which community values are authoritatively handed down to the young. The validity of those values is largely taken for granted, and there is a strong tendency to use them as a basis for the regulation of speech in the manner of the traditional common law.

The concept of civic education held sway in the years before the Warren Court and has recently been forcefully resurrected with regard to the regulation of speech within high schools. Thus in *Bethel School District No. 403 v. Fraser*[227] the Court upheld the punishment of a high school student for having delivered an "offensive" and "indecent" student-government speech.[228] The Court reasoned that "the objectives of public education" included "the 'inculcat[ion of] fundamental values necessary to the maintenance of a democratic political system.' "[229] Among these values were "the habits and manners of civility as . . . indispensable to the practice of self-government."[230]

The undoubted freedom to advocate unpopular and controversial views in schools and classrooms must be balanced against the society's countervailing interest in teaching students the boundaries of socially appropriate behavior. . . .

. . .

. . . [S]chools must teach by example the shared values of a civilized social order. . . . The schools, as instruments of the state, may determine that the essential lessons of civil, mature conduct cannot be conveyed in a school that tolerates lewd, indecent, or offensive speech and conduct such as that indulged in by this confused boy.[231]

That the concept of civic education would lead to similar conclusions if applied to institutions of higher learning is evidenced by Chief Justice Burger's 1973 dissent in *Papish v. University of Missouri Curators*.[232]

In theory, at least, a university is not merely an arena for the discussion of ideas by students and faculty; it is also an institution where individuals learn to express themselves in acceptable, civil terms. We provide that environment to the end that students may learn the self-restraint necessary to the functioning of a civilized society and understand the need for those external restraints to which we must all submit if group existence is to be tolerable.[233]

Because racist speech is both deeply uncivil and contrary to "the shared values of [our] civilized social order,[234] its restraint would be relatively unproblematic if civic education were understood to constitute a constitutionally acceptable purpose of public institutions of higher learning.[235] A number of public universities have fashioned their regulations on exactly this understanding. For example, the Policy Against Racism of the Board of Regents of Higher Education of the Commonwealth of Massachusetts argues that "institutions must vigorously strive to achieve diversity in race, ethnicity, and culture sufficiently reflective of our society. However, diversity alone will not suffice":

There must be a unity and cohesion in the diversity which we seek to achieve, thereby creating an environment of pluralism. Racism in any form, expressed or implied, intentional or inadvertent, individual or institutional, constitutes an egregious offense to the tenets of human dignity and to the accords of civility guaranteed by law. Consequently, racism undermines the establishment of a social and academic environment of genuine racial pluralism.[236]

The policy clearly postulates the fundamental task of the university to be the inculcation of the value of "genuine racial pluralism," and it proscribes racist speech because of its incompatibility with that value.

A second concept of the mission of public education, which I refer to as "democratic education," begins with the very different premise that the "public school" is "in most respects the cradle of our democracy,"[237] and it therefore understands the purpose of public education to be the creation of autonomous citizens, capable of fully participating in the rough and tumble world of public discourse.[238] Democratic education strives to introduce that world into the generically more sheltered environment of the school.

The concept of democratic education was most fully expressed during the era of the Warren Court in *Tinker v. Des Moines School District*,[239] in which the Court held that the purpose of public education is to prepare students for the "sort of hazardous freedom . . . that is the basis of our national strength and of the independence and vigor of Americans who grow up and live in this relatively permissive, often disputatious, society."[240] The majority in *Tinker* explicitly rejected the premise of civic education that the purpose of public schooling is the transmission of canonical values. It concluded instead that "[i]n our system, state-operated schools may not be enclaves of totalitarianism. . . . [S]tudents may not be regarded as closed-circuit recipients of only that which the [s]tate chooses to communicate. They may not be confined to the expression of those sentiments that are officially approved."[241] According to *Tinker* the objective of public education is to lead students to think for themselves.

The chief characteristic of democratic education is its tendency to assimilate speech within public educational institutions to a model of public discourse. Recognizing that this ambition is "not without its costs in terms of the risk to the maintenance of civility and an ordered society," the Court nevertheless strongly advanced the concept of democratic education during the late 1960s and early 1970s, in part because it believed the concept essential to the maintenance of "our vigorous and free society."[242] If, as I have argued, racist speech is and ought to be immune from regulation within public discourse, we can expect courts guided by the concept of democratic education to be quite hostile to the regulation of racist speech within universities, preferring instead to see students realistically prepared for participation in the harsh but inevitable world of public discourse.

There is yet a third concept of public education, one most often specifically associated with institutions of higher learning. This concept, which I refer to as "critical education," views the university as an institution whose distinctive "primary function" is "to discover and disseminate knowledge by means of research and teaching." [243] Critical education locates the principal prerequisite for university life in "the need for unfettered freedom, the right to think the unthinkable, discuss the unmentionable, and challenge the unchallengeable." [244]

[I]f a university is a place for knowledge, it is also a special kind of small society. Yet it is not primarily a fellowship, a club, a circle of friends, a replica of the civil society outside it. Without sacrificing its central purpose, it cannot make its primary and dominant value the fostering of friendship, solidarity, harmony, civility, or mutual respect. To be sure, these are important values; other institutions may properly assign them the highest, and not merely a subordinate priority; and a good university will seek and in some significant measure attain these ends. But it will never let these values, important as they are, override its central purpose. We value freedom of expression precisely because it provides a forum for the new, the provocative, the disturbing, and the unorthodox. Free speech is a barrier to the tyranny of authoritarian or even majority opinion as to the rightness or wrongness of particular doctrines or thoughts.[245]

The university as the purveyor of critical education serves important social purposes. These include not only the disciplined pursuit of truth, but also the exemplary enactment of a "model of expression that is meaningful as well as free, coherent yet diverse, critical and inspirational." [246] The concept of critical education has strong affinities to the traditional "marketplace of ideas" theory of the First Amendment, and it is not uncommon for courts who use the concept to speak of the "classroom" as "peculiarly the 'marketplace of ideas,' " deserving of protection because the "Nation's future depends upon leaders trained through wide exposure to that robust exchange of ideas which discovers truth 'out of a multitude of tongues, [rather] than through any kind of authoritative selection.' " [247]

The concept of critical education differs significantly from both civic and democratic education. In contrast to civic education, it rejects the notion of canonical values that are to be reproduced in the young. Public universities committed to critical education are not free to posit certain values (apart from the value of critical education itself) and to punish those who disagree. The logic of critical education would constitutionally require that a public university "not restrict speech ... simply because it finds the views expressed by any group to be abhorrent."[248] This stands in stark contrast to the educational project of institutions like the University of Massachusetts, Mount Holyoke, Marquette, or Mary Washington,[249] which are committed to the mission of civic education.

The concept of critical education would also sharply limit the ability of universities to censor uncivil speech. Speech can be uncivil for many reasons, including the assertion of ideas that are perceived to be offensive, revolting, demeaning, or stigmatizing. Critical education, however, would require the toleration of all ideas, however uncivil.[250] This toleration would be consistent with the Court's 1973 holding that "the mere dissemination of ideas—no matter how offensive to good taste—on a state university campus may not be shut off in the name alone of 'conventions of decency.' "[251]

Critical education also differs in important respects from democratic education. The telos of critical education lies in pursuit of truth, rather than in the instantiation of the responsible autonomy of the citizen. The pursuit of truth requires not only an unfettered freedom of ideas, but also honesty, fidelity to reason, and respect for method and procedures. Reason, as we have seen, carries its own special requirements of civility, which preclude coercion and abuse.[252] Although enforcement of these requirements and values would be inconsistent with democratic education, it may well be required by critical education. Moreover, critical education requires freedom of ideas only with respect to that speech which forms part of the truth-seeking dialogue of the university. Thus, for example, nothing in the concept of critical education would prevent a university from penalizing malicious racist speech communicated *solely for the purpose* of harassing, humiliating, or degrading a victim.[253] The trick, of course, would be to distinguish such speech in a manner that does not chill communication intended to form part of a truth-seeking exchange.[254] This represents a formidable technical challenge, for it is all too easy to permit revulsion with the content of speech to infect regulation ostensibly justified by other reasons.[255]

Although there is insufficient space in this short essay to engage in a full-scale exploration of the purposes of higher education, some conclusions are clear enough. The Constitution would not permit a public university, in the name of civic education, to prohibit the teaching of communism because of its conflict with community values. Nor would the Constitution, in the name of democratic education, preclude a public university from enforcing regulations against highly offensive racial epithets within a classroom.

Examples like these incline me toward the concept of critical education, yet the extent to which state universities ought constitutionally to be *required* to pursue one or the other of these educational missions does not seem to me without difficulties.[256] The analysis is further complicated by the possibility that public universities may have various educational functions with constitutionally distinct characteristics. Thus it is conceivable that public universities may be permitted to pursue the mission of civic education within their dormitories, but be required to follow the requirements of democratic education with regard to their open spaces.[257] These are matters that require extended and careful consideration.

I conclude, therefore, by stressing two brief points. First, the constitutionality of restraints on racist speech within public universities does not depend on the constitutionality of such regulation within public discourse. Second, the constitutionality of restraints on racist speech within public universities will depend to a very great extent on the educational purposes that we constitutionally attribute to public institutions of higher learning, and on the various modalities through which such institutions are understood to pursue those purposes. We ought to see debate turn toward the achievement of a fuller and more reflective comprehension of these questions.

5. CONCLUSION: THE QUESTION OF FORMAL DEMOCRACY

This account of the constitutionality of university restrictions on racist speech suggests that a principal flaw of the contemporary debate has been its pervasive assumption that the relationship of racist speech to the First Amendment can be assessed independently of social context. Communication, however, does not form a constitutionally undifferentiated terrain. The standards of First Amendment protection afforded to public discourse will not be the same as those applied to nonpublic speech, and these in turn will differ from those that govern the regulation of speech within governmental institutions like universities. The concrete circumstances of racist speech thus figure prominently in the constitutional equation.

Public discourse is the realm of communication we deem necessary to facilitate the process of self-determination. As that process is open-ended, reflecting the boundless possibility of social self-constitution, so we fashion public discourse to be as free from legal constraint as is feasible to sustain. But as self-determination requires the antecedent formation of a "self" through socialization into the particularity of a given community life, so public discourse must at some point be bounded by nonpublic speech, in which community values are embodied and enforced. And as the decisions of a self-determining democracy require actual implementation, so public discourse must at some other point be bounded by the instrumentally regulated speech of the nonpublic forum.

I have attempted to explain the unique protections that American First Amendment jurisprudence affords to public discourse through a self-consciously formal analysis; that is, I have attempted to uncover the formal prerequisites for the instantiation of the value of democracy as self-determination. Although this kind of formal analysis has the advantage of forcing us to clearly articulate the values in whose name we purport to act, it has the disadvantage of obscuring the messy complications of the world. Formal analysis is always subject to the critique that actual, substantive conditions have undermined its very point and meaning.

From a formal perspective, democracy fulfills the purposes of autonomous self-government because we accept an image of independent citizens deliberating together to form public opinion. We therefore structure constitutional policy according to the requirements of that image. But it is an image blatantly vulnerable to the most forceful empirical attack.[258] Citizens are not autonomous; they are manipulated by the media, coerced by private corporations, immured in the toils of racism. Citizens do not communicate together; they are passive, irrational, and voiceless.

Deliberation is impossible because of the technical and economic structure of the mass media; public opinion is therefore imposed upon citizens rather than spontaneously arising from them. The very aspiration to self-determination reinforces preexisting inequalities by empowering those with the resources and competence to take advantage of democratic processes; it systematically handicaps socially marginalized groups who lack this easy and familiar access to the media of democratic deliberation. And so forth: the litany is by now depressingly familiar.

Of course these criticisms, and others like them, contain important elements of truth. They therefore force us to choose: either we decide to retain the ideal of democracy as deliberative self-determination and work to minimize the debilitating consequences of these criticisms, or we decide that these criticisms have so undermined the ideal of deliberative self-determination that it must be abandoned and a different value for democracy embraced. If we choose the second alternative, we have the responsibility of articulating and defending a new vision of democracy. But if we choose the first, we have the responsibility of working to foster the constitutional values upon which we rely. We have the obligation of doing so, however, in ways that do not themselves contravene the necessary preconditions of the ideal of deliberative self-determination.[259] The function of formal analysis is to make clear the content of that obligation.

The strict implication of this essay, then, is not that racist speech ought not to be regulated in public discourse, but rather that those who advocate its regulations in ways incompatible with the value of deliberative self-governance carry the burden of moving us to a different and more attractive vision of democracy. Or, in the alterative, they carry the burden of justifying suspensions of our fundamental democratic commitments. Neither burden is light.

Notes

I am deeply indebted to the many friends and colleagues who read the manuscript of this essay: Alexander Aleinikoff, Richard Delgado, Melvin Eisenberg, Cynthia Fuchs Epstein, Byran Ford, Angela Harris, Sanford Kadish, Kenneth Karst, Mari Matsuda, Frank Michelman, Martha Minow, Paul Mishkin, Rachel Moran, John Powell, Terrance Sandalow, Joseph Sax,

Philip Selznick, Reva Siegel, Jerome Skolnick, Jan Vetter, James Weinstein, and Franklin Zimring.

1. D. Dumond, *Antislavery: The Crusade for Freedom in America,* 273 (1961) (quoting William Lloyd Garrison).
2. 346 U.S. 483 (1954).
3. For a representative discussion, see Fiss, "Foreword: The Forms of Justice," 93 *Harv. L. Rev.* 1 (1979).
4. Delgado, "Words That Wound: A Tort Action for Racial Insults, Epithets, and Name-Calling," 17 *Harv. C.R.-C.L. L. Rev.* 133 (1982) (hereafter Delgado, "Words That Wound"); see Heins, "Banning Words: A Comment on 'Words That Wound,' " 18 *Harv. C.R.-C.L. L. Rev.* 583 (1983); Delgado, "Professor Delgado Replies," 18 *Harv. C.R.-C.L. L. Rev.* 593 (1983).
5. Delgado, "Campus Antiracism Rules: Constitutional Narratives in Collision," 85 *Nw. U. L. Rev.* 343 (1990); Gale, "On Curbing Racial Speech," *Responsive Community,* Winter 1990–91, at 47; Glass, "Anti-Racism and Unlimited Freedom of Speech: An Untenable Dualism," 8 *Can. J. Phil.* 559 (1978); Grano, "Free Speech v. the University of Michigan," *Academic Questions,* Spring 1990, at 7; Greenawalt, "Insults and Epithets: Are They Protected Speech?," 42 *Rut. L. Rev.* 287 (1991); Grey, "Civil Rights vs. Civil Liberties: The Case of Discriminatory Verbal Harassment," *Soc. Phil. & Policy,* Spring 1991, at 81; Hughes, "Prohibiting Incitement to Racial Discrimination," 16 *U. Tor. L. J.* 361 (1966); Jones, "Article 4 of the International Convention on the Elimination of All Forms of Racial Discrimination and the First Amendment," 23 *How. L. J.* 429 (1980); Kretzmer, "Freedom of Speech and Racism," 8 *Cardozo L. Rev.* 445 (1987); "Language as Violence v. Freedom of Expression: Canadian and American Perspectives on Group Defamation," 37 *Buffalo L. Rev.* 337 (1989) (hereafter "Language as Violence"); Lasson, "Racial Defamation as Free Speech: Abusing the First Amendment," 17 *Colum. Hum. Rts. L. Rev.* 11 (1985) (hereafter Lasson, "Racial Defamation"); Lasson, "Group Libel Versus Free Speech: When Big Brother Should Butt In," 23 *Duq. L. Rev.* 77 (1984) (hereafter Lasson, "Group Libel"); Lawrence, "If He Hollers Let Him Go: Regulating Racist Speech on Campus," 1990 *Duke L.J.* 431; Love, "Discriminatory Speech and the Tort of Intentional Infliction of Emotional Distress," 47 *Wash. & Lee L. Rev.* 123 (1990); Matsuda, "Public Response to Racist Speech: Considering the Victim's Story," 87 *Mich. L. Rev.* 2320 (1989); Minow, "On Neutrality, Equality, & Tolerance: New Norms for a Decade of Distinction," *Change,* Jan.–Feb. 1990, at 17; Partlett, "From Red Lion Square to Skokie to the Fatal Shore: Racial Defamation and Freedom of Speech," 22 *Vand. J. Trans. L.* 431 (1989); Richardson, "Racism: A Tort of Outrage," 61 *Ore. L. Rev.* 267 (1982); Smolla, "Rethinking First Amendment Assumptions about Racist and Sexist Speech," 46 *Wash. & Lee L. Rev.* 171 (1990); Strossen, "Regulating Racist Speech on Campus: A Modest Proposal," 1990 *Duke L.J.* 484; Wedgwood, "Freedom of Expression and Racial Speech," 8 *Tel Aviv U. Stud. L.* 325 (1988); Wright,

"Racist Speech and the First Amendment," 9 *Miss. C. L. Rev.* 1 (1988); Note, "A Communitarian Defense of Group Libel Laws," 101 *Harv. L. Rev.* 682 (1988); Note, "The University of California Hate Speech Policy: A Good Heart in Ill-Fitting Garb," 12 *J. Comm. & Ent. L.* 593 (1990); Comment, "Freedom from Fear," 15 *Lincoln L. Rev.* 45 (1984) (authored by Kammy Au); Edelman, "Punishing Perpetrators of Racist Speech," *Legal Times*, May 15, 1989, at 20.

6. See, e.g., H. Ehrlich, *Campus Ethnoviolence and the Policy Options*, 41–72 (1990); Gibbs, "Bigots in the Ivory Tower: An Alarming Rise in Hatred Roils U.S. Campuses," *Time*, May 7, 1990, at 104.

7. David Rieff writes that 137 American universities "have in the past two years passed proscriptions on hate speech." Rieff, "The Case Against Sensitivity," 114 *Esquire* 120, 124 (1990). See "Lessons from Bigotry 101," *Newsweek*, Sept. 25, 1989, at 48; Wilson, "Colleges' Anti-Harassment Polices Bring Controversy over Free Speech Issues," *Chronicle of Higher Education*, Oct. 4, 1989, at A1; Fields, "Colleges Advised to Develop Strong Procedures to Deal with Incidents of Racial Harassment," *Chronicle of Higher Education*, July 20, 1988, at A11.

8. For a chronicle of the effect of this controversy on the American Civil Liberties Union (ACLU), see Hentoff, "The Colleges: Fear, Loathing, and Suppression," *Village Voice*, May 8, 1990, at 20; Hentoff, "What's Happening to the ACLU?," *Village Voice*, May 15, 1990, at 20; Hentoff, "Putting the First Amendment on Trial," *Village Voice*, May 22, 1990, at 24; Hentoff, "A Dissonant First Amendment Fugue," *Village Voice*, June 5, 1990, at 16; Hentoff, "An Endangered Species: A First Amendment Absolutist," *Village Voice*, June 12, 1990, at 24; Hentoff, "The Civil Liberties Shootout," *Village Voice*, June 19, 1990, at 26; "Policy Concerning Racist and Other Group-Based Harassment on College Campuses," *ACLU Newsletter*, Aug.–Sept. 1990, at 2.

9. J. Kovel, *White Racism: A Psycho-History*, 34 (1970). See Lawrence, "The Id, the Ego, and Equal Protection: Reckoning with Unconscious Racism," 39 *Stan. L. Rev.* 317, 321–26 (1987).

10. Department of Student Affairs, University of Connecticut, "Protect Campus Pluralism" (available from the Dean of Students Office, University of Connecticut). The regulations provide that "[e]very member of the University is obligated to refrain from actions that intimidate, humiliate, or demean persons or groups or that undermine their security or self-esteem." They define "harassment" as "abusive behavior directed toward an individual or group because of race, ethnicity, ancestry, national origin, religion, gender, sexual preference, age, physical or mental disabilities," and they prohibit "harassment that has the effect of interfering with an individual's performance or creating an intimidating, hostile or offensive environment." *Id.*

11. *Id.* The regulations continue: "All members of the University community are responsible for the maintenance of a positive environment in which everyone feels comfortable working and learning." *Id.*

12. *Id.* The regulations instruct a student to inform the Discrimination and Intolerance Response Network if "[y]ou have experienced or witnessed any of the signs" and to "[k]now that the University will not tolerate such behavior." *Id.*

13. Lawrence, *supra* note 9, at 322.

14. One is reminded of the escalating efforts of the Inquisition in sixteenth-century Spain to discover and punish all external signs of inward backsliding on the part of Moors and Jews who had outwardly converted to Catholicism in order to avoid expulsion. These efforts eventually led the Inquisition to conclude that eating couscous or disliking pork were themselves punishable as heresy. See Root, "Speaking Christian: Orthodoxy and Difference in Sixteenth-Century Spain," *Representations,* no. 23 (Summer 1988), at 118, 126, 129.

15. Ravo, "Campus Slur Alters a Code against Bias," *New York Times,* Dec. 11, 1989, at B1, B3.

16. Modest aspirations, however, will not be easy in the highly charged atmosphere of many universities. See Detlefsen, "White Like Me," *New Republic,* Apr. 10, 1989, at 18. The University of Connecticut is hardly unique in its use of punitive legal regulation to block all manifestations of racism. The Board of Regents of Higher Education of the Commonwealth of Massachusetts, for example, adopted on June 13, 1989, a "Policy against Racism" that "prohibits all forms of racism." Board of Regents of Higher Education, Commonwealth of Massachusetts, "Policy against Racism and Guidelines for Campus Policies against Racism" 1 (June 13, 1989). This prohibition includes:

> [A]ll conditions and all actions or omissions including all acts or verbal harassment or abuse which deny or have the effect of denying to anyone his or her rights to equality, dignity, and security on the basis of his or her race, color, ethnicity, culture, or religion. . . . Racism in any form, expressed or implied, intentional or inadvertent, individual or institutional, constitutes an egregious offense to the tenets of human dignity and to the accords of civility guaranteed by law.

Id. at 2.

17. These categories by no means exhaust the field. In the European literature, for example, there is a well-developed jurisprudence of regulating racist speech based on the harm of potential violence. See Cotterrell, "Prosecuting Incitement to Racial Hatred," 1982 *Pub. L.* 378; Kretzmer, *supra* note 5, at 456; Leopold, "Incitement to Hatred—The History of a Controversial Criminal Offense," 1977 *Pub. L.* 389, 391–93. I do not discuss this category of harm because it is relatively unimportant in the American setting. I suspect that this is largely because of the accepted dominion of the *Brandenburg* version of the clear and present danger test. See Brandenburg v. Ohio, 395 U.S. 444, 447–49 (1969).

18. Wright, *supra* note 5, at 14–22.

19. *Id.* at 10.

20. *Id.* at 9.
21. Hughes, *supra* note 5, at 364.
22. Lawrence, *supra* note 5, at 438–49.
23. Kretzmer, *supra* note 5, at 456.
24. *Id.* at 454.
25. Matsuda, *supra* note 5, at 2357.
26. Riesman, "Democracy and Defamation: Control of Group Libel," 42 *Col. L. Rev.* 727 (1942).
27. 343 U.S. 250 (1952). For work in this vein, see Lasson, *supra* note 5; Note, "Group Vilification Reconsidered," 89 *Yale L.J.* 308 (1979).
28. Matsuda, *supra* note 5, at 2358.
29. *Id.*
30. See, e.g., Lasson, "Racial Defamation," *supra* note 5, at 48.
31. Matsuda, *supra* note 5, at 2357.
32. Delgado, "Words That Wound," *supra* note 4, at 137.
33. *Id.* at 143.
34. *Id.* at 157.
35. Williams, "Spirit-Murdering the Messenger: The Discourse of Fingerpointing as the Law's Response to Racism," 42 *U. Miami L. Rev.* 127, 151 (1987).
36. Love, *supra* note 5, at 158.
37. Richard Delgado, for example, proposes that courts create a tort for racial insult whenever a plaintiff can prove that "[l]anguage was addressed to him or her by the defendant that was intended to demean through reference to race; that the plaintiff understood as intended to demean through reference to race; and that a reasonable person would recognize as a racial insult." Delgado, "Words That Wound," *supra* note 4, at 179.
38. *See,* for example, the proposed regulation of the University of Texas at Austin, which prohibits racial harassment and which defines racial harassment as "extreme or outrageous acts or communications that are intended to harass, intimidate or humiliate a student or students on account of race, color, or national origin and that reasonably cause them to suffer severe emotional distress." President's Ad Hoc Committee on Racial Harassment, the University of Texas at Austin, "Report of President's Ad Hoc Committee on Racial Harassment" 4–5 (Nov. 27, 1989). The drafters of the proposed regulation state that it is "much preferable for a racial harassment policy to focus on the real injury of severe emotional distress." *Id.* at 20.
39. Compare, for example, the former regulations of the University of Wisconsin, which reach "racist or discriminatory comments, epithets or other expressive behavior directed at an individual," Board of Regents of the University of Wisconsin System, Wis. Admin. Code UWS § 17.06(2)(a) (Aug. 1989) (struck down as a violation of the First Amendment in UWM Post, Inc. v. Board of the Univ. of Wis. Sys., 774 F.Supp. 1163 [E.D. Wis. 1991]), with those of Stanford University, which reach only racist speech that is "addressed directly to the individual or individuals whom it insults

or stigmatizes" and that consists of "insulting or 'fighting' words." Stanford University, "Fundamental Standard Interpretation: Free Expression and Discriminatory Harassment" 2 (draft, Mar. 15, 1990).

40. Lasson, "Group Libel," *supra* note 5, at 123. "The speech clause protects the marketplace of ideas, not the battleground." *Id.*
41. Lawrence, *supra* note 5, at 468.
42. *Id.* at 447 n.66 (quoting MacKinnon, "Not a Moral Issue," 2 *Yale L. & Pol. Rev.* 321, 340 [1984]).
43. *Id.* at 452.
44. *Id.* at 470.
45. Office of Student Life Policy and Service, Rutgers University at New Brunswick, "University Student Life Policy Against Insult, Defamation, and Harassment" 1 (May 31, 1989) (revised); see also Doe v. University of Mich., 721 F.Supp. 852, 856 (E.D. Mich. 1989); Oberlin College, "Policy on Race Relations and Informal Procedures for Racial Grievances"; Office of the Dean for Student Affairs and the Special Assistants to the President, Massachusetts Institute of Technology, "Information on Harassment," Sept. 1989; State University of New York College at Brockport, "Discriminatory Harassment," § 285.02; University of Pennsylvania, "Harassment Policy" (*Almanac Supp.*, Sept. 29, 1987) (as published originally in the *Almanac* of June 2, 1987).
46. University of California, "Universitywide Student Conduct: Harassment Policy" (Sept. 21, 1989) (available from the Office of the President). For an example of a regulation based on group harm, see Clark University's Code of General Conduct: "Harassment includes any verbal or physical conduct which has the intent or effect of unreasonably interfering with any individual's or group's work or study, or creating an intimidating, hostile, or offensive environment." Clark University, "Code of General Conduct and University Judicial Procedures" 1 (Fall Semester, 1988). For other examples of similar kinds of regulations, see Emory University, "Policy Statement on Discriminatory Harassment"; Marquette University, "Racial Abuse and Harassment Policy" (May 5, 1989); Office of University News and Information of Kent State University, "Policy to Combat Harassment," *For the Record* (Feb. 6, 1989).
47. Mount Holyoke College, "The Honor Code: Academic and Community Responsibility § III, Community Responsibility, Introduction" (reprinted from the *Student Handbook*).
48. Marquette University, "Racial Abuse and Harassment Policy" 1 (May 5, 1989).
49. *Id.*
50. Mary Washington College, *Mary Washington College Student Handbook* 20 (1990–91) (available from Office of the Dean of Students).
51. *Id.*
52. "If the university stands for anything, it stands for freedom in the search for truth. . . . [But] can truth have its day in court when the courtroom is made

into a mud-wrestling pit where vicious epithets are flung?" Laney, "Why Tolerate Campus Bigots?," *New York Times,* Apr. 6, 1990, at A35.

53. Thus James T. Laney, the president of Emory University: "Educators are by definition professors of value. Through education we pass on to the next generation not merely information but the habits and manners of our civil society. The university differs from society at large in its insistence on not only free expression but also an environment conducive to mutual engagement." *Id.*

54. See, e.g., Delgado, "Words That Wound," *supra* note 4, at 175–79; Note, "A First Amendment Justification for Regulating Racist Speech on Campus," 40 *Case W. Res.* 733 (1989–90).

55. 496 U.S. 310 (1990).

56. *Id.* at 318.

57. *Id.* at 319 (quoting Texas v. Johnson, 491 U.S. 397, 414 [1989]). See Brennan's remark in Texas v. Johnson to the same effect: "The First Amendment does not guarantee that . . . concepts virtually sacred to our Nation as a whole—such as the principle that discrimination on the basis of race is odious and destructive—will go unquestioned in the marketplace of ideas." 491 U.S. 397, 418 (1989). In Johnson Brennan cites Brandenburg v. Ohio, 395 U.S. 444 (1969), in support of his conclusion. In Brandenburg, First Amendment protection was extended to a Ku Klux Klan rally, which featured such revolting comments as: "Bury the n___s." "A dirty n_____r." "Send the Jews back to Israel." *Id.* at 446 n.1

58. Charles Lawrence, for example, writes that the University of Michigan regulations invalidated by a federal court (see *supra* note 45) were so patently unconstitutional that "it is difficult to believe that anyone at the University of Michigan Law School was consulted" in their drafting. Lawrence, *supra* note 5, at 477 n.161. "It is almost as if the university purposefully wrote an unconstitutional regulation so that they could say to the black students, 'We tried to help but the courts just won't let us do it.' " *Id.* A great many contemporary university regulations are similar to those of the University of Michigan.

59. Hustler Magazine v. Falwell, 485 U.S. 46, 54 (1988).

60. F. Schauer, *Free Speech: A Philosophical Enquiry,* 40 (1982). On the equation of democracy with majoritarianism, see A. De Tocqueville, *Democracy in America,* vol. 1, 264 (F. Bowen, trans., 1945): "The very essence of democratic government consists in the absolute sovereignty of the majority."

61. Schauer writes: "The more we accept the premise of the argument from democracy, the less can we impinge on the right of self-government by restricting the power of the majority. If the argument from democracy would allow to be said things that the 'people' do not want to hear, it is not so much an argument based on popular will as it is an argument against it." Schauer, *supra* note 60, at 41.

62. The equation is nevertheless quite commonplace. See, e.g., Partlett, *supra*

note 5, at 458 (footnote omitted) ("I take it that a central tenet of democracy is majority rule. If the majority decides to suppress free speech, how can it be defended upon democratic lines?").

63. N. Bobbio, *Democracy and Dictatorship*, 137 (P. Kennealy, trans., 1989).
64. H. Kelsen, *General Theory of Law and State*, 284–86 (A. Wedberg, trans., 1961).
65. 376 U.S. 254 (1964).
66. *Id.* at 274 (quoting 4 *Elliot's Debates* 569 [1876]) (citation omitted in original).
67. *Id.* at 275 (quoting 4 *Annals of Congress* [1794]).
68. This is the central problematic of Alexander Meiklejohn's work. A. Meiklejohn, *Political Freedom: The Constitutional Powers of the People*, 11 (1948). Meiklejohn was concerned to analyze "the difference between a political system in which men do govern themselves and a political system in which men, without their consent, are governed by others."
69. J. Rousseau, *The Social Contract* (C. Frankel, trans., 1947).
70. H. Kelsen, *supra* note 64, at 285.
71. *Id.* at 287–88.
72. For a good discussion of this point, see Freeman, "Reason and Agreement in Social Contract Views," 19 *Phil. & Pub. Aff.* 122, 154–57 (1990).
73. B. Barber, *Strong Democracy: Participatory Politics for a New Age*, 136 (1984). See Pitkin and Shumer, "On Participation," *Democracy* (Fall 1982), 43–54.
74. *Dialogue on John Dewey*, 58 (C. Lamont, ed., 1959).
75. E. Durkheim, *Professional Ethics and Civic Morals*, 89 (C. Brookfield, trans., 1958).
76. C. Lefort, *Democracy and Political Theory*, 39 (D. Macey, trans., 1988).
77. J. Habermas, *The Theory of Communicative Action*, vol. 2, 81 (T. McCarthy, trans., 1987).
78. Rawls, "Justice as Fairness: Political not Metaphysical," 14 *Phil. & Pub. Aff.* 223, 230 (1985).
79. Michelman, "Law's Republic," 97 *Yale L. J.* 1493, 1526–27 (1988).
80. Rawls, *supra* note 78, at 229–30; see J. Habermas, *The Theory of Communicative Action*, vol. 1, 25–26 (T. McCarthy, trans., 1984); Michelman, *supra* note 79, at 1526–27.
81. Fiss, *supra* note 3, at 38.
82. I do not mean to foreclose the possibility that, under special conditions of charismatic leadership or identification with traditional authority, the value of self-determination can be achieved in the absence of a communicative structure of public discourse. I mean only to imply that such conditions will not ordinarily obtain in the modern rational and bureaucratic state.
83. Rawls, *supra* note 78, at 230.
84. J. Piaget, *The Moral Judgment of the Child*, 366 (M. Gabain, trans., 1948).
85. See Post, "Cultural Heterogeneity and Law: Pornography, Blasphemy, and the First Amendment," 76 *Calif. L. Rev.* 297, 314–24 (1988).

86. See, for example, Kateb, "Democratic Individuality and the Claims of Politics," 12 *Pol. Theory* 331, 332 (1984): "To speak, therefore, of individualism is to speak of the most characteristically democratic political and moral commitment. It would be a sign of defection from modern democracy to posit some other entity as the necessary or desirable center of life. There is therefore nothing special (much less, arbitrary) in assuming that the doctrine of the individual has the preeminent place in the theory of democracy."

87. See, e.g., Bowers v. Hardwick, 478 U.S. 186, 203–6 (1986) (Blackmun, J., dissenting). Such a public/private distinction must, of course, be understood as inherently unstable and problematic, for all government regulation influences, to one degree or another, the formation of individual identity. See, e.g., Sunstein, "Legal Interference with Private Preferences," 53 *U. Chi. L. Rev.* 1129, 1138–39 (1986). For this reason the distinction should be regarded as a pragmatic instrument for distinguishing those aspects of the self considered indispensable for the exercise of political and moral autonomy, and hence as beyond the coercive formation of the state.

88. G. Mead, *Mind, Self and Society,* 162 (C. Morris, ed., 1937).

89. A. Meiklejohn, *supra* note 68, at 14.

90. L. Wittgenstein, *Culture and Value,* 46e (P. Winch, trans., 1980).

91. See, generally, Post, "The Constitutional Concept of Public Discourse: Outrageous Opinion, Democratic Deliberation, and Hustler Magazine v. Falwell," 103 *Harv. L. Rev.* 601 (1990) (hereafter Post, "The Constitutional Concept"); Post, "The Social Foundations of Defamation Law: Reputation and the Constitution," 74 *Calif. L. Rev.* 691 (1986) (hereafter Post, "Defamation Law"); Post, "The Social Foundations of Privacy: Community and Self in the Common Law Tort," 77 *Calif. L. Rev.* 957 (1989) (hereafter Post, "Privacy").

92. See M. Sandel, *Liberalism and the Limits of Justice* (1982).

93. See Post, "Defamation Law," *supra* note 91, at 699–719.

94. See Post, "Privacy," *supra* note 91, at 959–87.

95. See Post, "The Constitutional Concept," *supra* note 91, at 616–46.

96. See, e.g., *id.* at 627–33.

97. 310 U.S. 296 (1940).

98. 376 U.S. 254 (1964).

99. 403 U.S. 15 (1971).

100. 485 U.S. 46 (1988). The American First Amendment is unique in thus separating democracy from community. I suspect that the origins of this separation lie both in our tradition of individualism and in the fact of our cultural diversity. For instructive contrasts, see Jacobson, "Alternative Pluralisms: Israeli and American Constitutionalism in Comparative Perspective," *The Review of Politics,* Spring 1989, 159–89; Kommers, "The Jurisprudence of Free Speech in the United States and the Federal Republic of Germany," 53 *S. Calif. L. Rev.* 657 (1980).

101. J. Habermas, *supra* note 77, at 38.

102. Rawls, *supra* note 78, at 230.
103. Post, "The Constitutional Concept," *supra* note 91, at 641–44.
104. *Id.*
105. 315 U.S. 568 (1942).
106. Rawls, *supra* note 78, at 230.
107. Pitkin, "Justice: On Relating Private and Public," 9 *Pol. Theory* 327, 346 (1981).
108. See Post, "The Constitutional Concept," *supra* note 91, at 667–84.
109. *Id.* at 667.
110. *Id.*
111. *Id.* at 680.
112. See, e.g., Rogers v. EEOC, 454 F.2d 234, 237–38 (5th Cir. 1971); *cert. denied,* 406 U.S. 957 (1972); EEOC v. Murphy Motor Freight, 488 F.Supp. 381, 385 (D. Minn. 1980); cf. Meritor Sav. Bank v. Vinson, 477 U.S. 57, 65–66 (1986) (holding that speech that constitutes sexual harassment may be regulated). I do not mean to imply, however, that *all* speech within the workplace is excluded from public discourse. See, e.g., Connick v. Myers, 461 U.S. 138, 149 (1983); Givhan v. Western Line Consol. School Dist., 439 U.S. 410, 415–16 (1979).
113. It should be emphasized that I am in text using the adjective "public" in a discrete and stipulative sense to refer to that speech necessary for democratic self-governance. Thus I do not mean to imply that speech within the workplace is "nonpublic" in the sense that it is unimportant, or that it is "private" in the sense of being intrinsically insulated from governmental control or regulation. See Karst, "Private Discrimination and Public Responsibility: Patterson in Context," 1989 *Sup. Ct. Rev.* 1, 10–11; *supra* text accompanying notes 106–11. My point is instead that if the regulation of such speech is in fact protected by the First Amendment, it will be on the basis of constitutional values other than democratic self-governance.
114. 343 U.S. 250 (1952). The leaflet is reproduced in Justice Black's dissenting opinion. *Id.* at 276 (Black, J., dissenting).
115. *Id.* at 267 (Black, J., dissenting).
116. See Collin v. Smith, 447 F.Supp. 676 (N.D., Ill.), *aff'd,* 578 F.2d 1197 (7th Cir.), *cert. denied,* 439 U.S. 916 (1978).
117. To exclude from public discourse the category of racist speech as such would be equivalent to establishing a per se exclusion of racist ideas from public discourse, a form of regulation whose constitutionality is assessed in section 3(A) *infra*.
118. Hustler Magazine v. Falwell, 485 U.S. 46, 56 (1988) (quoting FCC v. Pacifica Found., 438 U.S. 726, 745–46 [1978]).
119. Rawls, *supra* note 78, at 230.
120. Whitney v. California, 274 U.S. 357, 375–76 (1927) (Brandeis, J., concurring).
121. J. Piaget, *supra* note 84, at 57. See *id.* at 63.
122. Wright, *supra* note 5, at 10.

123. Matsuda, *supra* note 5, at 2359. See Kretzmer, *supra* note 5, at 458.
124. Matsuda, *supra* note 5, at 2332–34. "Racist hate messages are rapidly increasing and are widely distributed in this country using a variety of low and high technologies." *Id.* at 2336. Kretzmer is also concerned with the potential spread of racist ideas. See Kretzmer, supra note 5, at 464–65.
125. See *supra* note 123 and accompanying text.
126. I thus do not reach the theoretically more fundamental question of why it should make a constitutional difference that racist ideas are "universally condemned." See, for example, the Court's rejection in United States v. Eichman, 496 U.S. 310 (1990), of the Solicitor General's invitation to overrule Texas v. Johnson, 491 U.S. 397 (1989), on the grounds of "Congress' recent recognition of a purported 'national consensus' favoring a prohibition on flag-burning. . . . Even assuming such a consensus exists, any suggestion that the Government's interest in suppressing speech becomes more weighty as popular opposition to that speech grows is foreign to the First Amendment." *Eichman*, 496 U.S. at 318.
127. Kretzmer, *supra* note 5, at 456. See Matsuda, *supra* note 5, at 2338:

    However irrational racist speech may be, it hits right at the emotional place where we feel the most pain. The aloneness comes not only from the hate message itself, but also from the government response of tolerance. When hundreds of police officers are called out to protect racist marchers, when the courts refuse redress for racial insult, . . . the victim becomes a stateless person. Target-group members can either identify with a community that promotes racist speech, or they can admit that the community does not include them.

128. Matsuda, *supra* note 5, at 2378.
129. See Greenawalt, *supra* note 5, at 304–5.
130. Karst, "Citizenship, Race, and Marginality," 30 *Wm. & Mary L. Rev.* 1, 1 (1988).
131. See, e.g., N. Bobbio, *supra* note 63, at 157–58; C. Gould, *Rethinking Democracy: Freedom and Cooperation in Politics, Economy, and Society,* 90 (1988); J. Pennock, *Democratic Political Theory,* 3–161 (1979).
132. Michelman, *supra* note 79, at 1500–1501. Michelman notes that "no earnest, non-disruptive participant in American constitutional debate is quite free to reject" this "belief." *Id.* at 1500.
133. Rawls, *supra* note 78, at 230.
134. See, for example, "Language as Violence," *supra* note 5, at 360 (remarks of Mari Matsuda): "I use the principle of equality as a starting point. . . . [I]f I were to give primacy to any one right, and if I were to create a hierarchy, I would put equality first, because the right of speech is meaningless to people who do not have equality. I mean substantive as well as procedural equality."
135. That members of minority groups are now embraced within the circle of the people and afforded the formal equality required by First Amendment processes of self-determination is not, of course, due to any principle of

the First Amendment, but rather to the principle of equal citizenship embodied in the Fourteenth. In this fundamental sense, therefore, no hierarchical relationship between the First and Fourteenth Amendments can exist.

136. For a fuller consideration of a sophisticated form of "balancing" the values of the Fourteenth Amendment against those of the First, see *infra* text accompanying notes 210–19.

137. Beauharnais v. Illinois, 343 U.S. 250, 251 (1952) (citing Ill. Rev. Stat. ch. 38 ¶ 471 [1949]). Anti-blasphemy regulations are a common example of such laws. See Post, *supra* 85, at 305–17; *The Law Commission, Offenses against Religion and Public Worship*, 39–53 (Working Paper No. 79, 1981). Many countries also have laws prohibiting group defamation. See, e.g., E. Barendt, *Freedom of Speech*, 161–67 (1985); Lasson, "Group Libel," *supra* note 5, at 88–89; Matsuda, *supra* note 5, at 2341–48.

138. Jacobson, *supra* note 100, at 175.

139. *Id.* at 170.

140. *Id.* at 175.

141. See, e.g., City of Richmond v. J. A. Croson Co., 488 U.S. (1989).

142. 310 U.S. 296 (1940).

143. *Id.* at 309.

144. *Id.* at 310.

145. For an excellent study of the efforts of contemporary Americans to forge new communities, like the Castro district in San Francisco, and hence to "reinvent themselves" by constructing "new lives, new families, even new societies," see F. Fitzgerald, *Cities on a Hill: A Journal through Contemporary American Cultures*, 23 (1986). Fitzgerald views such efforts as "quintessentially American"; try to imagine, she suggests, "Parisians creating a gay colony or a town for grandparents." *Id.* If in Europe or Canada group identity precedes the attempt to ask "the essential questions of who we . . . are, and how we ought to live" (*id.* at 20, 389–90), Fitzgerald's work illustrates the extent to which group identity in America tends to follow on that attempt, and hence ultimately to rest on individualist premises.

146. For a more detailed discussion, see Post, *supra* note 85, at 319–35.

147. See P. Miller, *The Life of the Mind in America*, 40–43 (1965).

148. R. Bellah, M. Madsen, W. Sullivan, A. Swidler, and S. Tipton, *Habits of the Heart: Individualism and Commitment in American Life*, 225 (1985).

149. See, e.g., D. Rhode, *Justice and Gender*, 5 (1989); Marcus, "Reflections on the Significance of the Sex/Gender System: Divorce Law Reform in New York," 42 U. Miami L. Rev. 55, 55–63 (1987).

150. Marcus, *supra* note 149, at 61. See Harris, "Race and Essentialism in Feminist Legal Theory," 42 *Stan. L. Rev.* 581 (1990).

151. See Harris, *supra* note 150, at 615–16.

152. Fraser, "Toward a Discourse Ethic of Solidarity," 5 *Praxis Int'l* 425, 429 (1986).

153. *Id.*

154. M. Omi and H. Winant, *Racial Formation in the United States: From the 1960s to the 1980s,* 59 (1986). For an example of the persistence of a biological model of race, see, e.g., Herrnstein, "Still an American Dilemma," *The Public Interest,* no. 98 (Winter 1990), 3–17.

155. M. Omi and H. Winant, *supra* note 154, at 60, 68. Omi and Winant write of the "continuous temptation to think of race as an essence, as something fixed, concrete and objective." *Id.* at 68. See Appiah, "The Uncompleted Argument: Du Bois and the Illusion of Race," in H. L. Gates, *"Race," Writing, and Difference,* 36 (1986): "Talk of 'race' is particularly distressing for those of us who take culture seriously. . . . What exists 'out there' in the world—communities of meaning, shading variously into each other in the rich structure of the social world—is the province not of biology but of hermeneutic understanding."

156. For a good example, see Scales-Trent, "Black Women and the Constitution: Finding Our Place, Asserting Our Rights," 24 *Harv. C.R.-C.L. L. Rev.* 9 (1989).

157. For a brief history of the interdependence of understandings of national identity and understandings of race, see Gleason, "American Identity and Americanization," in W. Petersen, M. Novak, and P. Gleason, *Concepts of Ethnicity,* 57–143 (1982). A small but I suspect paradigmatic example of this interdependence may be found in the following passage from a student letter to *The Daily Californian:*

> Advertising, television, schools and government are areas of society where racism is largely promoted. Its existence is not easily eradicated. Phrases like "blackmail," "black ball" and "black mood" are common ways "blackness" is communicated in negative terms. . . . One of my professors frequently employs terms like "black lie" to mean the worst of all lies. It takes a conscious effort to disregard these statements and prevent such negative influence on one's psyche. But we must understand that daily use of this terminology reinforces the attack on African-American identity and value.

Broughton, "Promote Afro-American Culture," *The Daily Californian,* Tuesday, Sept. 12, 1989, at 4. The writer's point is relevant to the perspectives of members of both minority and majority groups; in fact, the point effectively demonstrates the essential reciprocity of these perspectives.

158. Wilson, "Social Research and the Underclass Debate," *Bulletin of the American Academy of Arts and Sciences,* vol. 43, no. 2 (Nov. 1989), 30–44.

159. S. Steele, *The Content of Our Character: A New Vision of Race in America* (1990).

160. See "Black Power, Foul and Fragrant," *Economist,* Oct. 12, 1985, at 25, for a summary of Farrakhan's critical assessment of the condition of many African Americans.

161. Note, in this regard, Nadine Strossen's evidence that regulations of racist speech have historically proved to be "particularly threatening to the

speech of racial and political minorities." Strossen, *supra* note 5, at 556–59.

162. Or, in the language that the Court proposed in Milkovich v. Lorain Journal Co., 497 U.S. 1 (1990), claims of group harm will most likely be privileged as nonfactual assertions of "ideas." For a discussion of the First Amendment distinction between fact and ideas, see Post, "The Constitutional Concept," *supra* note 91, at 649–61. For a discussion of the close relationship between group defamation and nonfactual ideas, see D. Richards, *Toleration and the Constitution*, 190–93 (1986); Greenawalt, *supra* note 5, at 305–6.

163. Beauharnais v. Illinois, 343 U.S. 250, 276 (1952) (ellipses in the original).

164. *Id.* at 257–58.

165. See, e.g., Matsuda, *supra* note 5, at 2358.

166. *Id.*

167. Michelman, *supra* note 79, at 1501.

168. Cohen v. California, 403 U.S. 15, 16 (1971).

169. Hustler Magazine v. Falwell, 485 U.S. 46, 52 (1988).

170. Boos v. Barry, 485 U.S. 312, 316, 322 (1988). "[I]n public debate our own citizens must tolerate insulting, and even outrageous, speech in order to provide 'adequate "breathing space" to the freedoms protected by the First Amendment.' " *Id.* at 322 (quoting *Hustler* magazine, 485 U.S. at 56); see Texas v. Johnson, 491 U.S. 397 413–18 (1989).

171. I elaborate on this argument in Post, "The Constitutional Concept," *supra* note 91, at 626–46. The cases cited in notes 168–70 *supra* thus stand foursquare against the application to public discourse of the tort of racial insult as proposed by Delgado, *supra* note 4, Love, *supra* note 5, and Wright, *supra* note 5.

172. Michelman, *supra* note 79, at 1526. See F. Cunningham, *Democratic Theory and Socialism*, 188–91 (1987).

173. *See supra* notes 112–13 and accompanying text.

174. It should be noted, however, that the public/private distinction necessary for democratic governance will require that at some point limitations be placed on the ability of the state coercively to form citizens with nonracist identities. See note 87, *supra*.

175. See, e.g., Contreras v. Crown Zellerbach Corp., 88 Wash. 2d 735, 565 P.2d 1173 (1977); Alcorn v. Anbro Engineering, Inc., 2 Cal. 3d 493, 468 P.2d 216, 86 Cal. Rptr. 88 (1970); Love, *supra* note 5, at 128–33.

176. Cf. Dominguez v. Stone, 97 N.M. 211, 638 P.2d 423 (1981) (penalizing racist insults in political speech).

177. Lasson, "Group Libel," *supra* note 5, at 122.

178. Thus "fighting words" are understood to be those which "by their very utterance inflict injury." Chaplinsky v. New Hampshire, 315 U.S. 568, 572 (1942). Outrageous words intentionally inflicting emotional distress are "nothing more than a surrogate" for a "punch or kick." Wright, "Hustler Magazine v. Falwell and the Role of the First Amendment," 19

Cumb. L. Rev. 19, 23 (1988). "Ridicule" is experienced as a form of "intimidation." Dewey, "Creative Democracy—The Task before Us," in *Classic American Philosophers,* 389, 393 (M. Fisch, ed., 1951). Pornography is received not as "expression depicting the subordination of women, but [as] the practice of subordination itself." Brest and Vandenberg, "Politics, Feminism, and the Constitution: The Anti-Pornography Movement in Minneapolis," 39 *Stan. L. Rev.* 607, 659 (1987). And blasphemous communications are nothing more than a form of "brawls." F. Holt, *The Law of Libel,* 70–71 (1816).

179. Time, Inc. v. Hill, 385 U.S. 374, 412 (1967) (Fortas, J., dissenting). Alexander Bickel once remarked that such communication "amounts to almost physical aggression." A. Bickel, *The Morality of Consent,* 72 (1975); see also Cohen v. California, 403 U.S. 15, 27 (1971) (Blackmun, J., dissenting).

180. See *supra* text and accompanying notes 91–105.

181. Thus Terminiello v. Chicago:

> [A] function of free speech under our system of government is to invite dispute. It may indeed best serve its high purpose when it induces a condition of unrest, creates dissatisfaction with conditions as they are, or even stirs people to anger. Speech is often provocative and challenging. It may strike at prejudices and preconceptions and have profound unsettling effects as it presses for acceptance of an idea. That is why freedom of speech, though not absolute . . . is nevertheless protected against censorship or punishment, unless shown likely to produce a clear and present danger of a serious substantive evil that rises far above public inconvenience, annoyance, or unrest. . . . There is no room under our Constitution for a more restrictive view. For the alternative would lead to standardization of ideas either by legislatures, courts, or dominant political or community groups.

337 U.S. 1, 4–5 (1949) (citations omitted).

182. For an excellent discussion, see Karst, "Boundaries and Reasons: Freedom of Expression and the Subordination of Groups," 1990 *U. Ill. L. Rev.* 95.

183. 403 U.S. 15.

184. *Id.* at 23.

185. *Id.* at 24–25.

186. Matsuda, *supra* note 5, at 2340; Lawrence, *supra* note 5, at 436.

187. I omit discussion of speech that silences through outright intimidation and threats. The regulation of such speech is not problematic under any theory.

188. For a good introduction to the concept of "discourse," see Bove, "Discourse," in *Critical Terms for Literary Study,* 50 (F. Lentricchia and T. McLaughlin, eds., 1990).

189. Lawrence, *supra* note 5, at 452.

190. *Id.* at 474–75. See Crenshaw, "Race, Reform, and Retrenchment: Transformation and Legitimation in Antidiscrimination Law," 101 *Harv. L. Rev.* 1331, 1370–81 (1988).

191. Finley, "Breaking Women's Silence in Law: The Dilemma of the Gendered Nature of Legal Reasoning," 64 *Notre Dame L. Rev.* 886, 889 (1989).

192. Note, "Racism and Race Relations in the University," 76 *Va. L. Rev.* 295, 304 N.32 (1990) (quoting Brooks, "Anti-Minority Mindset in the Law School Personnel Process: Toward an Understanding of Racial Mindsets," 5 *J.L. & INEQUALITY* 1, 8–11 [1987]).
193. Matsuda, *supra* note 5, at 2323–26.
194. *Id.* at 2375. See Lawrence, *supra* note 5, at 458–61.
195. Riesman, "Democracy and Defamation: Fair Game and Fair Comment II," 42 *Colum. L. Rev.* 1282, 1306–7 (1942).
196. See P. Chevigny, *More Speech: Dialogue Rights and Modern Liberty,* 53–72 (1988); Michelman, "Conceptions of Democracy in American Constitutional Argument: The Case of Pornography Regulation," 56 *Tenn. L. Rev.* 291, 313 (1989).
197. For a general discussion of the concept of false consciousness, see R. Geuss, *The Ideal of a Critical Theory: Habermas and the Frankfurt School* (1981).
198. Matsuda, *supra* note 5, at 2331.
199. Note, *supra* note 192, at 295.
200. Lawrence, *supra* note 5, at 436.
201. *Id.* at 481.
202. Matsuda, *supra* note 5, at 2369. This tendency is explicitly thematized in Iris Marion Young's artless proposal that "a democratic public" will necessarily cede to "constituent groups that are oppressed or disadvantaged" a "veto power regarding specific policies that affect a group directly." Young, "Polity and Group Difference," 99 *Ethics* 250, 261–62 (1989).
203. The "grand tradition" of republican participation, the notion that "we can lift our public realm above the fallen and compromised realm of factional politics," thus does not appear to me so easily abandoned as would appear from recent literature stressing fidelity to the particular cultural "tradition" of minority groups. See Lopez, "The Idea of a Constitution in the Chicano Tradition," 37 *J. Leg. Educ.* 162, 164–65 (1987). Even Young notes that a "heterogeneous public . . . is a *public,* where participants discuss together the issues before them and are supposed to come to a decision that they determine as best or most just." Young, supra note 202, at 267.

> It is possible for persons to maintain their group identity and to be influenced by their perceptions of social events derived from their group-specific experience, and at the same time to be public spirited, in the sense of being open to listening to the claims of others and not being concerned for their own gain alone. It is possible and necessary for people to take a critical distance from their own immediate desires and gut reactions in order to discuss public proposals. Doing so, however, cannot require that citizens abandon their particular affiliations, experiences, and social location.

Id. at 257–58.
204. Berger, "Professors' Race Ideas Stir Turmoil at College," *New York Times,* Apr. 20, 1990, at B1, col. 2.

205. *See supra* text accompanying notes 178–80.
206. Note that the argument in text does not hold against the contention that certain ideas should be excluded from public discourse because they cause extensive harm to individuals or victim groups. Such harm is extrinsic to the function of public discourse. To evaluate the contention that public discourse ought to be limited because of harm to individuals or groups, therefore, we must assess the importance of democratic self-governance in light of our commitment to protecting stable personal and group identities. See *supra,* part 3(B)&(C).

The argument that certain ideas ought to be excluded from public discourse because they are intrinsically "coercive," on the other hand, turns upon harm to the function of public discourse itself. The argument is unsatisfactory because the concept of "coercion" must itself be defined by reference to a "moral baseline" determined by the practice in question. See A. Wertheimer, *Coercion* (1987). Within the practice of public discourse no idea can be deemed intrinsically "coercive" because the very function of public discourse presupposes a formal equality of persons and hence of ideas.
207. Chaplinsky v. New Hampshire, 315 U.S. 568 (1942).
208. See *supra* note 206.
209. See Lawrence, *supra* note 5, at 474–75. That this is a general characteristic of group claims can be seen by the development of an analogous dynamic among those who support the regulation of pornography. See, e.g., C. MacKinnon, "On Collaboration," in *Feminism Unmodified: Discourses of Life and Law,* 198 (1987).
210. The success or failure of the gesture will depend entirely on the perception of members of victim groups. There is thus no guarantee that any particular regulatory scheme will in fact actually cause members of victim groups to reinterpret their position within public discourse. This inherent gap between regulatory design and the achievement of regulatory purpose, coupled with the fact that only members of victim groups can experience and evaluate the claim of cultural exclusion, creates disturbing possibilities for strategic manipulation.
211. Of course so minimal a gesture might not be sufficient to achieve this purpose. The intrinsically speculative quality of the argument must be taken into account in its evaluation.
212. According to the solicitor general, the state's interest in prohibiting flag burning turns on the importance of "safeguard[ing] the flag's identity 'as the unique and unalloyed symbol of the Nation.' " United States v. Eichman, 496 U.S. 310, 315 (1990) (quoting Brief for United States at 28, 29).
213. Texas v. Johnson, 491 U.S. 397, 430–32 (1989) (Rehnquist, C.J., dissenting).
214. I should be plain that I myself reject the premise of this argument and do not believe that the meaning of speech can be disentangled from the manner of its presentation. Style and substance are always interdependent,

for, in the words of Georg Lukacs, "[c]ontent determines form." G. Lukacs, *Realism in Our Time: Literature and the Class Struggle,* 19 (J. and N. Mander, trans., 1962). For a discussion, see Post, "The Constitutional Concept," *supra* note 91, at 663 n.314. I therefore do not think that the impact on public discourse of prohibiting certain kinds of words can ever properly be said to be de minimis. I nevertheless want to evaluate the case for balancing on the strong assumption of this kind of de minimis impact.

215. For a discussion of this argument in the context of flag burning, see Eichman, 496 U.S. at 320–23 (Stevens, J., dissenting).

216. In evaluating this balance, I do not mean to call into question the holding of Chaplinsky, which in my view attempts to distinguish private fracases from political debate. See Post, "The Constitutional Concept," *supra* note 91, at 679–81. It is clear enough that racial epithets, when uttered in certain face-to-face situations, would constitute "fighting words" and hence not form part of public discourse. See Greenawalt, *supra* note 5, at 306. The point of the argument in text, however, is to evaluate restraints on racist epithets in what would otherwise clearly be deemed public discourse, as for example in political debates, newspapers, pamphlets, magazines, novels, movies, records, and so forth.

217. Anyone inclined to doubt this proposition should review again the controversy over funding for the National Endowment for the Arts, or the prosecutions occasioned by the Mapplethorpe exhibition or the recordings of 2 Live Crew. See "Rap Band Members Found Not Guilty in Obscenity Trial," *New York Times,* Oct. 21, 1990, § 1, at 1, col. 1; "Cincinnati Jury Acquits Museum in Mapplethorpe Obscenity Case," *New York Times,* Oct. 6, 1990, § 1, at 1, col. 1; "Reverend Wildman's War on the Arts," *New York Times,* Sept. 2, 1990, § 6 (Magazine), at 22, col. 1.

218. Emory University, "Policy Statement on Discriminatory Harassment" (1988); see Doe v. University of Mich., 721 F.Supp. 852, 856 (E.D. Mich. 1989) (concerning sanctions for speech victimizing an individual "on the basis of race, ethnicity, religion, sex, sexual orientation, creed, national origin, ancestry, age, martial status, handicap, or Vietnam-era veteran status"). The regulations of Michigan State University include the prohibited category of "political persuasion." Michigan State University, *Your Ticket to an Adventure in Understanding* (1988) (available from University Housing Program). The regulations of West Chester University include the category of "lifestyle." West Chester University, *Ram's Eye View: Every Student's Guide to West Chester University,* 61 (1990) (available from Student Development Office). The regulations of Hampshire College include that of "socioeconomic class." Hampshire College, *College Policies: Updates and Revisions* (1988–89).

219. This claim is also implausible, as I noted earlier, because of its vulnerable assumption that style can be sharply distinguished from substance. See *supra* note 214.

220. The argument in this and the following two paragraphs is developed in

detail in Post, "Between Governance and Management: The History and Theory of the Public Forum," 34 *UCLA L. Rev.* 1713 (1987) (hereafter Post, "Between Governance"). See also Post, "The Constitutional Concept," *supra* note 91, at 684–85.

221. Widmar v. Vincent, 454 U.S. 263, 267 n.5, 268–69 (1981).
222. *Id.* at 268 n.5.
223. *Id.* at 277 (citing Healy v. James, 408 U.S. 169, 189 [1972]).
224. Judicial application of these factors in nonpublic forums like universities is discussed in greater detail in Post, "Between Governance," *supra* note 220, at 1765–1824.
225. This short discussion considers only issues pertaining to the *constitutionality* of the regulation of racist speech. It does not consider the *educational* issues raised by such regulation. These issues are, however, profound and revolve around the question of whether legal restraint is the heuristically most effective response to racist speech.
226. Pugsley v. Sellmeyer, 158 Ark. 247, 253, 250 S.W. 538, 539 (1923).
227. 478 U.S. 675 (1986).
228. *Id.* at 678.
229. *Id.* at 681 (quoting Ambach v. Norwick, 441 U.S. 68, 77 [1979]).
230. *Id.* (quoting C. Beard and M. Beard, *New Basic History of the United States,* 228 [1968]).
231. *Id.* at 681, 683. For another example of the same kind of reasoning, see Hazelwood School Dist. v. Kuhlmeier, 484 U.S. 260, 271–72 (1988).
232. 410 U.S. 667 (1973).
233. *Id.* at 672 (Burger, C.J., dissenting).
234. Bethel v. School Dist. No. 403 v. Frazer, 478 U.S. 675, 681 (1986).
235. For the development of this logic at the pre-university level, see, for example, Clarke v. Board of Educ., 215 Neb. 250, 338 N.W. 2d 272 (1983).
236. Commonwealth of Massachusetts Board of Regents of Higher Education, "Policy against Racism and Guidelines for Campus Policies against Racism," 2 (June 13, 1989).
237. Alder v. Board of Educ., 342 U.S. 485, 508 (1952) (Douglas, J., dissenting). For a fully developed statement of this position, see Abington School Dist. v. Schempp, 374 U.S. 203, 241–42 (1963) (Brennan, J., concurring).
238. The tension between the concepts of democratic and civic education closely recapitulates the informative debate between Piaget and Durkheim over the question of how to teach moral values. Durkheim stressed the importance of discipline, authority, and constraint, whereas Piaget emphasized cooperation, agreement, and autonomy. See J. Piaget, *supra* note 84, at 341–71.
239. 393 U.S. 503 (1969).
240. *Id.* at 508–9.
241. *Id.* at 511.
242. Healy v. James, 408 U.S. 169, 194 (1972).

243. "Report of the Committee on Freedom of Expression at Yale," 4 *Hum. Rts.* 357, 357 (1975) (hereafter "Report of the Committee"). This function is not one that we ordinarily attribute to high schools, much less elementary schools.
244. *Id.*
245. *Id.* at 357–58; see Schmidt, "Freedom of Thought: A Principle in Peril?," *Yale Alumni Mag.*, Oct. 1989, at 65, 65–66.
246. Byrne, "Academic Freedom: A 'Special Concern of the First Amendment,' " 99 *Yale L.J.* 251, 261 (1989). The presence of such a model "contributes profoundly to society at large. We employ the expositors of academic speech to train nearly everyone who exercises leadership within our society. Beyond whatever specialized learning our graduates assimilate, they ought to be persuaded that careful, honest expression demands an answer in kind. The experience of academic freedom helps secure broader, positive liberties of expression." *Id.*
247. Keyishian v. Board of Regents, 385 U.S. 589, 603 (1967) (quoting United States v. Associated Press, 52 F.Supp. 362, 372 [S.D.N.Y. 1943]); see Healy v. James, 408 U.S. 169, 180–81 (1972).
248. Healy, 408 U.S. at 186–88.
249. See *supra* notes 47–51 and accompanying text.
250. "If the university's overriding commitment to free expression is to be sustained, secondary social and ethical responsibilities must be left to the informal processes of suasion, example, and argument." "Report of the Committee," *supra* note 243, at 360.
251. Papish v. University of Mo. Curators, 410 U.S. 667, 670 (1973).
252. See *supra* part 3(D).
253. As a matter of policy, however, it is always dangerous to make the legality of speech depend primarily upon an assessment of a speaker's intent, for there is a powerful tendency to attribute bad motives to those with whom we fundamentally disagree.
254. The inability to make this distinction contributed to a court's decision to strike down as unconstitutional the regulations of the University of Michigan. See Doe v. University of Mich., 721 F.Supp. 852 (E.D. Mich. 1989); Grano, *supra* note 5, at 7.
255. For an admirable attempt to meet this challenge, see Grey, *supra* note 5, and the regulations that Professor Grey drafted for Stanford University.
256. Cases like Tinker and Healy make clear, however, that the Supreme Court's First Amendment jurisprudence has rested on the assumption that there are constitutional limits to the freedom of public educational institutions to define their own educational mission.
257. Some universities have regulated racist speech in ways that turn on such functional and geographic considerations. See Doe, 721 F.Supp. at 856; "Tufts Restores Free Speech after T-Shirt Confrontation," *San Francisco Chronicle*, Dec. 9, 1989, at B6, col. 1; Wilson, "Colleges Take 2 Basic Approaches in Adopting Anti-Harassment Plans," *Chronicle of Higher*

Education, Oct. 4, 1989, at A38, col. 1; Russo, "Free Speech at Tufts: Zoned Out," *New York Times,* Sept. 27, 1989, at A29.

258. See, e.g., E. Purcell, *The Crisis of Democratic Theory: Scientific Naturalism and the Problem of Value* (1973).

259. For a striking illustration of the untoward (and in retrospect horrifying) consequences of repudiating that obligation, see Marcuse, "Repressive Tolerance," in R. Wolff, B. Moore, and H. Marcuse, *A Critique of Pure Tolerance,* 81 (1965).

4. Regulating Racist Speech on Campus: A Modest Proposal?

Nadine Strossen

Freedom of speech is indivisible; unless we protect it for all, we will have it for none.

—Harry Kalven, Jr.

If there be minority groups who hail this holding [rejecting a First Amendment challenge to a group libel statute] as their victory, they might consider the possible relevancy of this ancient remark: "Another such victory and I am undone."

—Hugo Black, Jr.

The civil rights movement would have been vastly different without the shield and spear of the First Amendment. The Bill of Rights . . . is of particular importance to those who have been the victims of oppression.

—Benjamin L. Hooks

It is technically impossible to write an anti-speech code that cannot be twisted against speech nobody means to bar. It has been tried and tried and tried.

—Eleanor Holmes Norton

The basic problem with all these regimes to protect various people is that the protection incapacitates. . . . To think that I [as a black man] will . . . be told that white folks have the moral character to shrug off insults, and I do not. . . . That is the most insidious, the most insulting, the most racist statement of all!

—Alan Keyes

Whom will we trust to censor communications and decide which ones are "too offensive" or "too inflammatory" or too devoid of intellectual content? . . . As a former president of the University of California once said: "The University is not engaged in making ideas safe for students. It is engaged in making students safe for ideas."

—Derek Bok

[R]estrictive codes . . . may be expedient, even grounded in conviction, but the university cannot submit the two cherished ideals of freedom and equality to the legal system and expect both to be returned intact.
　　　　　　　—Carnegie Foundation for the Advancement of Teaching

In the political climate that surrounds [racial] issues on campus, principle often yields to expediency and clarity turns into ambiguity, and this is no less true for some of our finest scholars.
　　　　　　　—Joseph Grano

When language wounds, the natural and immediate impulse is to take steps to shut up those who utter the wounding words. When, as here, that impulse is likely to be felt by those who are normally the first amendment's staunchest defenders, free expression faces its greatest threat. At such times, it is important for those committed to principles of free expression to remind each other of what they have always known regarding the long term costs of short term victories bought through compromising first amendment principles.
　　　　　　　—Civil Liberties Union of Massachusetts

As a former student activist, and as a current black militant, [I] believe[ ] that free speech is the minority's strongest weapon. . . . [P]aternalism [and] censorship offer the college student a tranquilizer as the antidote to campus and societal racism. What we need is an alarm clock. . . . What we need is free speech . . . and more free speech.
　　　　　　　—Michael Meyers

Charles Lawrence, Mari Matsuda, Richard Delgado, and other "critical race theorists" recently have made provocative contributions to the perennial debate concerning the extent to which courts and civil libertarians[1] should continue to construe the Constitution as protecting some forms of racist expression. This recurring issue has resurfaced most recently in connection with the distressing increase of racial incidents at colleges and universities around the country. In response, many of these institutions have adopted, or are considering, regulations that curb "hate speech"—that is, speech that expresses hatred or bias toward members of racial, religious, or other groups.

Several recent judicial rulings, issued since the initial publication of the writings by Lawrence and his colleagues advocating hate speech regulations, have cast grave doubt on the constitutionality of any such regulations. In the only three legal challenges to campus hate speech codes that have led to judicial rulings all three courts held that the codes violated the First Amendment.[2] Moreover, although the U.S. Supreme Court has not ruled on campus hate-speech codes, in 1992 the Court unanimously struck down a city's hate speech law, invoking rationales that appear to doom campus speech codes too.[3] In these rulings, the courts concluded that restrictions on hate speech inevitably violate the cardinal free speech principle that speech may not be punished on the basis of its content or viewpoint, and also are inescapably vague and overbroad, thus punishing and chilling much expression that is constitutionally protected.

Notwithstanding the courts' continuing view that hate speech must be protected, in accordance with time-honored free speech principles, it is nevertheless important to respond to the calls that Lawrence and others have made for a reexamination of those principles. It is also important to respond to the intriguing new arguments that they have made for limiting hate speech, at least in the campus context. In particular, they forcefully urge that the Constitution's equality guarantee compels the restriction of hate speech, because such speech fosters discrimination and undermines equality.

Because civil libertarians are fully committed to securing constitutional values of equality, as well as those of free speech, it is especially imperative for us thoughtfully to consider, and respond to, the arguments made by Lawrence and other contemporary advocates of restricting hate speech. This article constitutes such a consideration and response. Although it uses Lawrence's writings as a focal point, it also addresses the issues that have been raised by the many other recent proposals to regulate hate speech, including those advanced by Delgado and Matsuda.

Civil libertarians are committed to the eradication of racial discrimination and the promotion of free speech throughout society. We have worked especially hard to combat both discrimination and free speech restrictions in educational institutions, which should be bastions of equal opportunity and unrestricted exchange. Therefore, we find the upsurge of both campus racism and regulation of campus speech particularly disturbing, and we have undertaken efforts to counter both.

Because civil libertarians have learned that free speech is an indispensable instrument for the promotion of other rights and freedoms—including racial equality—we fear that the movement to regulate campus expression will undermine equality as well as free speech. Combating racial discrimination and protecting free speech should be viewed as mutually reinforcing rather than antagonistic goals. A diminution in society's commitment to racial equality is neither a necessary nor an appropriate price for protecting free speech. Those who frame the debate in terms of this false dichotomy simply drive artificial wedges between would-be allies in what should be a common effort to promote civil rights and civil liberties.

Lawrence urges civil libertarians to "abandon[ ] . . . overstated rhetorical and legal attacks on individuals who conscientiously seek to frame a public response to racism while preserving our first amendment liberties."[4] I join in this invitation, and I extend a corresponding one: Those individuals who espouse "new perspectives" on the First Amendment in an effort to justify hate speech regulations should avoid overstated attacks on those who conscientiously seek to preserve our First Amendment liberties while responding to racism.

In important respects, Lawrence inaccurately describes and unfairly criticizes both traditional civil libertarians in general and the American Civil Liberties Union (ACLU) in particular. His argument depends on a "straw civil libertarian" who can be easily knocked down, but who does not correspond to the flesh and blood reality.[5] For example, contrary to Lawrence's assumption, traditional civil libertarians do not categorically reject every effort to regulate racist speech. The ACLU has never argued that harassing, intimidating, or assaultive conduct should be immunized simply because it is in part based on words. Accordingly, traditional civil libertarians would agree with Lawrence that some examples of racially harassing speech should be subject to regulation consistent with First Amendment principles—for example, the often-cited incident of a group of white male students pursuing a black female student across campus shouting, "I've never tried a nigger."

Of course, traditional civil libertarians have urged that any restrictions on expressive activity must be drawn narrowly, and carefully applied, to avoid chilling protected speech. But, to a substantial extent, Lawrence appears to endorse a similarly cautious approach. He stresses that he supports only limited regulations and invokes as a model the relatively limited code that Stanford University adopted in 1990.[6]

Insofar as Lawrence advocates relatively narrow rules that apply traditionally accepted limitations on expressive conduct to the campus setting, his position should not be alarming (although it is certainly debatable). In portions of his article, Lawrence seems to agree with traditional civil libertarians that only a small subset of the racist rhetoric that abounds in our society should be regulated. Although we may disagree about the contours of such concepts as "captive audience," "fighting words," or "intentional infliction of emotional distress," these differences should not obscure strong common goals. Surely our twin aims of civil rights and civil liberties would be advanced more effectively by fighting together against the common enemy of racism than by fighting against each other over which narrow subset of one symptom of racism—namely, verbal and symbolic expressions—should be regulated.

What is most disquieting about Lawrence's article is not the relatively limited Stanford code he defends, but rather his simultaneous defense of additional, substantially more sweeping speech prohibitions. The rationales that Lawrence advances for the regulations that he endorses are so open-ended that, if accepted, they would appear to warrant the prohibition of *all* racist speech, and thereby would cut to the core of our system of free expression.

Although Lawrence's specific proposed code appears relatively modest, his supporting rationales depend on nothing less immodest than the abrogation of the traditional distinctions between speech and conduct and between state action and private action. He equates *private* racist *speech* with *governmental* racist *conduct*.[7] This approach offers no principled way to confine racist speech regulations to the particular contours of the Stanford code, or indeed to any particular contours at all. Lawrence apparently acknowledges that, if accepted, his theories could warrant the prohibition of *all* private racist speech.[8] Moreover, although he stresses the particular evils of racism, he also says that "much of my analysis applies to violent pornography and homophobic hate speech."[9] Thus, Lawrence himself demonstrates that any specific, seemingly modest proposal to regulate speech may in fact represent the proverbial "thin edge of the wedge" for initiating broader regulations.

As just explained, the relatively narrow Stanford code that Lawrence endorses is incongruous with his broad theoretical rationale. The Stanford code also is at odds with Lawrence's pragmatic rationale. The harms of racist speech that he seeks to redress largely remain untouched by the rule. For example, Lawrence movingly recounts the pain suffered by his sister's family as a result of racist expression, as well as the anxiety he endured as a boy even from the *possibility* of racist expression. Yet the Stanford code clearly would not apply to any of the unspoken racist expressions that may well lurk beneath the surface of much parlance in American life. Moreover, the regulation also would not apply unless the speech was directly targeted at a specific victim. Therefore, it would not have relieved Lawrence or his family of the traumas they experienced. Furthermore, the Stanford code would not address the racist incident at Stanford that led to its adoption.[10] Likewise, many additional campus racist incidents catalogued by Lawrence and others would be beyond the scope of the Stanford code.

Two problems arise from the disharmony between the breadth of the racist speech regulations endorsed by Lawrence and the harm that inspires them. First, this disparity underscores the rules' ineffectiveness. The regulations do not even address much of the racist speech, let alone the innumerable other manifestations of racism which—as Lawrence himself stresses—pervade our society. Second, this disharmony encourages the proponents of hate speech regulations to seek to narrow the gap between the underlying problem and their favored solution by recommending broader regulations. For example, Mari Matsuda has proposed a substantially more restrictive hate speech regulation, and Lawrence has indicated his approval of Matsuda's approach. So the wedge widens.

In this chapter I attempt to bridge some of the gaps that Lawrence believes separate advocates of equality from advocates of free speech. I show that, insofar as proponents of hate speech regulations endorse relatively narrow rules that encompass only a limited category of racist expression, these gaps are not so significant in practical effect. I also demonstrate that the First and Fourteenth Amendments are allies rather than antagonists. Most importantly, in this chapter I maintain that equality will be served most effectively by continuing to apply traditional, speech-protective precepts to racist speech, because a robust freedom of speech ultimately is necessary to combat racial discrimination. Lawrence points out that free speech values as well as equality values may be promoted by regulating certain verbal harassment and retarded by not regulating it. But we must also recognize that equality values may be promoted most effectively by not regulating certain hate speech and retarded by regulating it.

Part 1 of this chapter demonstrates that traditional civil libertarians agree with Lawrence's point that some speech amounts to verbal assault or harassment and may be subject to government regulation. Part 2 shows that Lawrence's conception of regulable racist speech is broader than that permitted by established constitutional doctrine and would endanger fundamental free speech values. Part 3 explores the even greater danger to free speech values posed by Lawrence's expansive rationales. Of primary importance, part 3 exposes the flaws in Lawrence's major argument—that *Brown v. Board of Education* and other decisions that invalidate *governmental* racist *conduct* somehow legitimize regulation of *nongovernmental* racist *speech.*

Notwithstanding my differences with Lawrence about the boundaries of regulable racist expression, it is important to place these differences in proper perspective. Even the racist speech that he would regulate constitutes only a small fraction of all racist speech. Thus, most racist expression would remain untouched under both Lawrence's approach and the approach traditionally endorsed by civil libertarians and the Supreme Court. More importantly, as is discussed in part 4, Lawrence's proposal would not effectively address the underlying problem of racism itself, of which racist speech is a symptom. Part 4 shows that suppressing racist speech could even aggravate racially discriminatory attitudes. Thus, the goals of free speech and of eradicating racism are not incompatible, as Lawrence sometimes suggests. Rather, as he also recognizes, these goals are mutually reinforcing. Although my discussion focuses on Lawrence's specific proposal, it applies as well to all other proposals to censor hate speech.

Finally, part 5 maintains that we should channel our efforts toward devising means to combat racism that are consistent with the First Amendment. This strategy ultimately will be more effective than censorship in promoting both equality and free speech. The resurgence of racist expression on American campuses has sparked a revitalized national dedication to promoting racial equality on college campuses and throughout our society and the forging of creative strategies for doing so. In order to counter racist speech, Lawrence urges us to "think creatively as lawyers."[11] But if we are to understand and eradicate the complex root causes of racial discrimination, then we must think creatively as *more* than just lawyers.[12] We must draw upon the insights and skills of educators, sociologists, and psychologists. To draft legal rules that address only one manifestation of these deeper problems of racial inequality is at best ineffective, and at worst counterproductive.

1. SOME LIMITED FORMS OF CAMPUS HATE SPEECH MAY BE REGULABLE UNDER CURRENT CONSTITUTIONAL DOCTRINE

A. General Constitutional Principles Applicable to Regulating Campus Hate Speech

To put in proper perspective the points of disagreement between Lawrence's analysis and traditional civil-libertarian views, the points of agreement first should be noted. Lawrence usefully rehearses the many shared understandings between advocates of traditional First Amendment doctrine, which protects much racist speech, and advocates of various hate speech regulations. Lawrence acknowledges that there are strong reasons for sheltering even racist speech, in terms of reinforcing society's commitment to tolerance and mobilizing its opposition to intolerance. Consequently, he recognizes that to frame the debate in terms of a conflict between freedom of speech and the elimination of racism poses a false dichotomy. Accordingly, he urges civil libertarians to examine not just the substance of our position on racist speech, but also the way in which we enter the debate, to ensure that we condemn racist ideas at the same time as we defend the right to utter them.

There may be even more common ground between Lawrence and the traditional civil libertarian position than he expressly acknowledges. In presenting the civil libertarian position as absolute and uni-focused, he oversimplifies and thereby distorts it. For example, as previously noted, Lawrence sets up a "straw civil libertarian" who purportedly would afford *absolute* protection to *all* racist speech—or at least "all racist speech that stops short of physical violence." [13] In fact, as evidenced by ACLU policies, traditional civil libertarians do not take such an extreme position. Moreover, as a matter of both policy and practice, the ACLU already condemns the ideas expressed by racist and other anti-civil libertarian speakers at the same time that it defends their right to utter them. Thus, contrary to Lawrence's implication, such condemnation would not constitute an innovation.

Lawrence also mischaracterizes traditional civil libertarians when he asserts that we tolerate the regulation of "garden variety" fighting words, but not racist fighting words. Some civil libertarians might agree with the Supreme Court's formerly stated view that a narrowly defined category of "fighting words" might not be constitutionally protected.[14] Other civil libertarians maintain, consistent with the Court's apparent repudiation of its earlier view, that "fighting words" should not be excluded from First Amendment protection.[15] All agree, however, that racist fighting words should receive the same degree of protection (or nonprotection) as other fighting words.

Consistent with Lawrence's free speech concerns, the category of racist speech he seeks to regulate under the Stanford code is relatively narrow compared to other campus hate speech rules.[16] In important respects, this proposal overlaps with the traditional civil libertarian position.

On the end of the spectrum where speech is constitutionally protected, Lawrence agrees with courts and traditional civil libertarians that the First Amendment should protect racist speech in a *Skokie*-type context.[17] The essentials of a *Skokie*-type setting are that the offensive speech occurs in a public place and the event is announced in advance. Hence, the offensive speech can be either avoided or countered by opposing speech. Traditional civil libertarians recognize that this speech causes psychic pain. We nonetheless agree with the decision of the U.S. Seventh Circuit Court of Appeals in *Skokie* that this pain is a necessary price for a system of free expression, which ultimately redounds to the benefit of racial and other minorities.[18] Lawrence apparently shares this view.

On the other end of the spectrum, where expression may be prohibited, traditional civil libertarians agree with Lawrence that the First Amendment should not necessarily protect targeted individual harassment just because it happens to use the vehicle of speech. The ACLU maintains this nonabsolutist position with regard to both racist harassment on campus and sexual harassment in the workplace. For example, the ACLU's "Policy Statement on Free Speech and Bias on College Campuses," which its National Board of Directors adopted without dissent in 1990 (see Appendix for its full text), while opposing all regulations that "interfere with the freedom . . . to teach, learn, discuss and debate or . . . express ideas, opinions or feelings in classroom, public or private discourse," also recognizes that colleges and universities may restrict "acts of harassment, intimidation and invasion of privacy," because "[t]he fact that words may be used in connection with otherwise actionable conduct does not immunize such conduct from appropriate regulation."

As the ACLU policy on campus hate speech acknowledges, terms such as " 'harassment,' 'intimidation,' and 'invasion of privacy' are imprecise" and hence "susceptible of impermissibly overbroad application." Nevertheless, each term "defines a type of conduct which is legally proscribed in many jurisdictions when directed at a specific individual or individuals and when intended to frighten, coerce, or unreasonably harry or intrude upon its target." The policy cites as an example of expressive conduct that would be appropriately sanctionable "[t]hreatening telephone calls to a minority student's dormitory room," but stresses that, in contrast, "[e]xpressive behavior which has no other effect than to create an unpleasant learning environment . . . would not be the proper subject of regulation."

Because there is no clear boundary between expression that constitutes proscribable harassment and expression that constitutes protected free speech, even civil libertarians who agree that this is the appropriate line to draw still would be expected to disagree about whether particular expressive conduct fell on one side of the boundary or the other. However, the essential underlying point still stands: traditional civil libertarians share what Lawrence describes as a "moderate" perspective with regard to harassing speech on campus—that is, that such speech should be neither absolutely protected nor absolutely prohibited.[19]

In other situations involving racist speech, the ACLU also has recognized that otherwise punishable conduct should not be shielded simply because it relies in part on words. Some examples were provided by ACLU president Norman Dorsen: "During the Skokie episode, the ACLU refused to defend a Nazi who was prosecuted for offering a cash bounty for killing a Jew. The reward linked the speech to action in an impermissible way. Nor would we defend a Nazi (or anyone else) whose speech interfered with a Jewish religious service, or who said, 'There's a Jew; let's get him.' "[20]

The foregoing ACLU positions are informed by established principles that govern the protectability of speech. Under these principles, speech may be regulated if it is an essential element of violent or unlawful conduct, if it is likely to cause an immediate injury by its very utterance, and if it is addressed to a "captive audience" unable to avoid assaultive messages. It should be stressed that each of these criteria is ambiguous and may be difficult to apply in particular situations. Accordingly, the ACLU insists that these exceptions to free speech must be strictly construed and would probably find them to be satisfied only in rare factual circumstances. Nevertheless, ACLU policies expressly recognize that if certain speech fits within these narrow parameters, then it could be regulable.[21]

The captive audience concept in particular is an elusive and challenging one to apply. As Laurence Tribe has cautioned, this concept "is dangerously encompassing, and the Court has properly been reluctant to accept its implications whenever a regulation is not content-neutral."[22] Noting that we are "often 'captives' outside the sanctuary of the home and subject to objectionable speech,"[23] the Court has ruled that, in public places, we bear the burden of averting our attention from expression we find offensive.[24] Otherwise, the Court explained, "a majority [could] silence dissidents simply as a matter of personal predilections."[25] The Court has been less reluctant to apply the captive audience concept to private homes.[26] However, the Court has held that even in the home, free speech values may outweigh privacy concerns, requiring individuals to receive certain unwanted communications.[27]

The Court's application of the captive audience doctrine illustrates the general notion that an important factor in determining the protection granted to speech is the place where it occurs. At one extreme, certain public places—such as public parks—have been deemed "public forums," where freedom of expression should be especially protected. At the other extreme, some private domains—such as residential buildings—have been deemed places where freedom of expression should be subject to restriction in order to guard the occupants' privacy and tranquility. In between these two poles, certain public areas might be held not to be public forums because the people who occupy them might be viewed as "captive." Thus, the question whether any particular racist speech should be subject to regulation is a fact-specific inquiry. We cannot define particular words as inherently off limits, but rather we must examine every word in the overall context in which it is uttered.

The foregoing principles that govern the permissibility of speech regulations in general should guide our analysis of the permissibility of particular speech regulations in the academic setting. The Supreme

Court has declared that within the academic environment freedom of expression should receive heightened protection[28] and that a "university campus . . . possesses many of the characteristics of a traditional public forum."[29] These considerations would suggest that hate speech should receive special protection within the university community. Conversely, Mari Matsuda argues that equality guarantees and other principles that might weigh in favor of prohibiting racist speech also are particularly important in the academic context.

The appropriate analysis is more complex than either set of generalizations assumes. In weighing the constitutional concerns of free speech, equality, and privacy that hate speech regulations implicate, decision makers must take into account the particular context within the university in which the speech occurs. For example, the Court's generalizations about the heightened protection due free speech in the academic world certainly are applicable to some campus areas, such as parks, malls, or other traditional gathering places. The generalizations, however, may not be applicable to other areas, such as students' dormitory rooms. These rooms constitute the students' homes. Accordingly, under established free speech and privacy tenets, students should have some rights to avoid being exposed to others' expression by seeking refuge in their rooms.

Some areas on campus present difficult problems concerning the appropriate level of speech protection because they share characteristics of both private homes and public forums. For example, one could argue that hallways, common rooms, and other common areas in dormitory buildings constitute extensions of the individual students' rooms. On the other hand, one could argue that these common areas constitute traditional gathering places and should be regarded as public forums, open to expressive activities at least by all dormitory residents if not by the broader community. The latter argument would derive general support from the Supreme Court decisions that uphold the free speech rights of demonstrators in residential neighborhoods on the theory that individual residents' rights of stopping "the flow of information into [their] household[s]" does not allow them to impede the flow of this same information to their neighbors.[30] The Supreme Court, however, recently declined to resolve the specific issue of whether university dormitories constitute public forums for free speech purposes.[31]

Even in the areas of the university reserved for academic activities, such as classrooms, the calculus to determine the level of speech protection is complex. On the one hand, the classroom is the quintessential "marketplace of ideas,"[32] which should be open to the vigorous and robust exchange even of insulting or offensive words, on the theory that such an exchange ultimately will benefit not only the academic community but also the larger community in its pursuit of knowledge and understanding.[33]

On the other hand, advocates of campus hate speech codes contend that in the long run, the academic dialogue might be stultified rather than stimulated by the inclusion of racist speech. They maintain that such speech not only interferes with equal educational opportunities, but also deters the exercise of other freedoms, including those secured by the First Amendment. Lawrence argues that, as a consequence of hate speech, minority students are deprived of the opportunity to participate in the academic interchange, and that the exchange is impoverished by their exclusion. It must be emphasized, though, that expression subject to regulation on this rationale would have to be narrowly defined in order to protect the free flow of ideas that is vital to the academic community; thus, much expression would remain unregulated—expression that could be sufficiently upsetting to interfere with students' educational opportunities.[34]

Another factor that might weigh in favor of imposing some regulations on speech in class is that students arguably constitute a captive audience. This characterization is especially apt when the course is required and class attendance is mandatory. Likewise, the case for regulation becomes more compelling the more power the racist speaker wields over the audience.[35] For example, the law should afford students special protection from racist insults directed at them by their professors.

Even if various areas of a university are not classified as public forums, and even if occupants of such areas are designated captive audiences, any speech regulations in these areas still would be invalid if they discriminated on the basis of a speaker's viewpoint. Viewpoint-based discrimination constitutes the most egregious form of censorship[36] and almost always violates the First Amendment. Accordingly, viewpoint discrimination is proscribed even in regulations that govern non-public forum government property and regulations that protect captive audiences.[37]

Because most hate speech regulations are viewpoint discriminatory, targeting only expression that conveys derogatory ideas, they could not be justified even to protect captive audiences. The Stanford policy, for example, proscribes only expression that "is intended to insult or stigmatize" on the basis of race and other prohibited categories. The variation on the Stanford code that Lawrence endorsed would have compounded this viewpoint discrimination by expressly excluding insulting speech directed at "dominant majority groups."[38] Moreover, although the code that Stanford adopted does not expressly reflect this particularly egregious form of viewpoint discrimination, the chair of the committee that propounded the rule indicated that it would be enforced as if it did incorporate an exception for speech that is insulting to "dominant majority groups."[39]

B. Particular Speech Limiting Doctrines Potentially Applicable to Campus Hate Speech

In addition to the foregoing general principles, Lawrence and other proponents of campus hate speech regulations invoke three specific doctrines in an attempt to justify such rules: the fighting words doctrine; the tort of intentional infliction of emotional distress; and the tort of group defamation.[40] As the following discussion shows, the Supreme Court has recognized that each of these doctrines may well be inconsistent with free speech principles. Therefore these doctrines may not support any campus hate speech restrictions whatsoever. In any event, they at most would support only restrictions that are both narrowly drawn and narrowly applied.

1. Fighting Words. The fighting words doctrine is the principal model for the Stanford code, which Lawrence supports. However, this doctrine provides a constitutionally shaky foundation for many reasons: it has been substantially limited in scope and is probably no longer good law; even if the Supreme Court were to apply a narrowed version of the doctrine, such application would threaten free speech principles; and, as actually implemented, the fighting words doctrine suppresses protectible speech and entails the inherent danger of discriminatory application to speech by members of minority groups and dissidents.

In addition to the foregoing, independently sufficient bases for rejecting campus hate speech regulations modeled on the fighting words doctrine, in 1992 the Supreme Court dealt such regulations yet another devastating blow. In *R.A.V. v. City of St. Paul,*[41] the Court unanimously invalidated a city ordinance that criminalized hate speech, and which the state supreme court had construed to apply only to fighting words. Although the U.S. Supreme Court expressly declined to consider the ongoing validity of the fighting words exception to the First Amendment, it ruled that even if some such speech could constitutionally be restricted, it could never be restricted on the basis of its content or subject matter, or on the basis of its viewpoint. Because campus hate speech regulations, like the city ordinance at issue in *R.A.V.,* focus only on fighting words that address certain subjects—namely, race, religion, gender, and other prohibited bases of discrimination—they are content based. Moreover, because they condemn only derogatory statements about those subjects, they suffer the additional constitutional defect of being viewpoint based. Accordingly, the Court's explanation for striking down the St. Paul hate speech law would apply fully to campus hate speech regulations as well:

[T]he ordinance applies only to "fighting words" that insult, or provoke violence, "on the basis of race, color, creed, religion or gender." [Expressions] containing abusive invective, no matter how vicious or severe, are permissible unless they are addressed to one of the specified disfavored topics. Those who wish to use "fighting words" in connection with other ideas—to express hostility, for example, on the basis of political affiliation, union membership, or homosexuality—are not covered. The First Amendment does not permit St. Paul to impose special prohibitions on those speakers who express views on disfavored subjects. . . .

In its practical operation, moreover, the ordinance goes even beyond mere content discrimination, to actual viewpoint discrimination. [Expressions] containing some words—odious racial epithets, for example—would be prohibited to proponents of all views. But "fighting words" that do not themselves invoke race, color, creed, religion, or gender—aspersions upon a person's mother, for example—would seemingly be usable ad libitum in the placards of those arguing in favor of racial, color, etc. tolerance and equality, but could not be used by that speaker's opponents. . . . St. Paul has no such authority to license one side of a debate to fight freestyle, while requiring the other to follow Marquis of Queensbury Rules.[42]

While the Court in *R.A.V.* did not reach the issue of the ongoing constitutional validity of any fighting words exception to the First Amendment, analysis reveals that the fighting words concept that the

Court initially formulated in 1942 has since been substantially limited, essentially to the point of nonexistence, because the initial formulation contravenes fundamental free speech principles.

Although the Court originally defined constitutionally regulable fighting words in fairly broad terms in its 1942 ruling in *Chaplinsky v. New Hampshire*,[43] subsequent decisions have narrowed the definition to such a point that the doctrine probably would not apply to any of the instances of campus racist speech that Lawrence and others seek to regulate. As originally formulated in *Chaplinsky*, the fighting words doctrine excluded from First Amendment protection "insulting or 'fighting' words, those which by their very utterance inflict injury or tend to incite an immediate breach of peace."

In light of subsequent developments, it is significant to note that the first prong of *Chaplinsky's* fighting words definition, words "which by their very utterance inflict injury," was dictum. The Court's actual holding was that the state statute at issue was justified by the state's interest in preserving the public peace by prohibiting "words likely to cause an average addressee to fight." The Court stressed that "no words were forbidden except such as have a direct tendency to cause acts of violence by the person to whom, individually, [they are] addressed." The Court also held that the statute had been applied appropriately to Mr. Chaplinsky, who had called a city marshal "a God damned racketeer" and "a damned Fascist." It explained that these "epithets [are] likely to provoke the average person to retaliation, and thereby cause a breach of the peace."

In 1972, in *Gooding v. Wilson*,[44] the Court substantially narrowed *Chaplinsky's* definition of fighting words by bringing that definition into line with *Chaplinsky's* actual holding. In *Gooding*, as well as in every subsequent fighting words case, the Court disregarded the dictum in which the first prong of *Chaplinsky's* definition was set forth and treated only those words that "tend to incite an immediate breach of peace" as fighting words. Consistent with this narrowed definition, the Court has invalidated regulations that hold certain words to be per se proscribable and has insisted that each challenged utterance be evaluated contextually.[45] Thus, under the Court's current view, even facially valid laws that restrict fighting words may be applied constitutionally only in circumstances where their utterance almost certainly will lead to immediate violence.[46] Laurence Tribe described this doctrinal development as, in effect, incorporating the so-called clear and present danger test into the fighting words doctrine; in other words, speech may be limited only if necessary to avert an imminent, tangible harm.

In accordance with its narrow construction of constitutionally permissible prohibitions upon "fighting words," the Court has overturned every single fighting words conviction that it has reviewed since *Chaplinsky*. Moreover, in one post-*Chaplinsky* decision, the Court overturned an injunction that had been based on the very word that had led to the conviction in *Chaplinsky* itself (fascist).[47]

For the foregoing reasons, Supreme Court justices and constitutional scholars persuasively maintain that *Chaplinsky's* fighting words doctrine is no longer good law.[48] Even more fundamentally, constitutional scholars have convincingly argued that this doctrine should no longer be good law, for reasons that are particularly weighty in the context of racist slurs. First, as Stephen Gard concluded in a comprehensive review of both Supreme Court and lower court decisions that apply the fighting words doctrine, the asserted governmental interest in preventing a breach of the peace is not logically furthered by this doctrine. He explained:

[I]t is fallacious to believe that personally abusive epithets, even if addressed face-to-face to the object of the speaker's criticism, are likely to arouse the ordinary law abiding person beyond mere anger to uncontrollable reflexive violence. Further, even if one unrealistically assumes that reflexive violence will result, it is unlikely that the fighting words doctrine can successfully deter such lawless conduct.[49]

Second, just as the alleged peace-preserving purpose does not rationally justify the fighting words doctrine in general, that rationale also fails to justify the fighting words doctrine when applied to racial slurs in particular. As Harry Kalven noted, "outbursts of violence are not the necessary consequence of such speech and, more important, such violence when it does occur is not the serious evil of the speech."[50] Rather, as Lawrence stresses, the serious evil of racial slurs consists of the ugliness of the ideas they express and the psychic injury they cause to their addressees. Therefore, the fighting words doctrine does not address and will not prevent the injuries caused by campus racist speech.

Even if there were a real danger that racist or other fighting words would cause reflexive violence, and even if that danger would be reduced by the threat of legal sanction, the fighting words doctrine still would be problematic in terms of free speech principles. As Zechariah Chafee observed, this doctrine "makes a man a criminal simply because his neighbors have no self-control and cannot refrain from violence." [51] In other contexts, the Court appropriately has refused to allow the address-ees of speech to exercise such a "heckler's veto." [52]

The fighting words doctrine is constitutionally flawed for the additional reasons that it suppresses much protectible speech and that the protectible speech of minority group members is particularly vulnerable. Notwithstanding the Supreme Court's limitation of the doctrine's scope, Gard's survey reveals that the lower courts apply it much more broadly. Since the Supreme Court reviews only a fraction of such cases, the doctrine's actual impact on free speech must be assessed in terms of these speech-restrictive lower court rulings. Gard concluded that, in the lower courts, the fighting words doctrine "is almost uniformly invoked in a selective and discriminatory manner by law enforcement officials to punish trivial violations of a constitutionally impermissible interest in preventing criticism of official conduct." [53] Indeed, Gard reported, "it is virtually impossible to find fighting words cases that do not involve either the expression of opinion on issues of public policy or words directed toward a government official, usually a police officer." [54] Even more disturbing is that the reported cases indicate that blacks are often prosecuted and convicted for the use of fighting words, including in situations where they are advocating civil rights. [55] Thus, the record of the actual implementation of the fighting words doctrine demonstrates that—as is the case with all speech restrictions—it endangers principles of equality as well as free speech. That record substantiates the risk that such a speech restriction will be applied discriminatorily against the very minority group members whom it is intended to protect.

Lawrence himself notes that many Supreme Court decisions that overruled fighting words convictions involved a "potentially offended party [who] was in a position of relative power when compared with the speaker." [56] As Gard demonstrated, for each such conviction that was reviewed and overturned by the Supreme Court, many others were not. [57] Thus, Lawrence and other proponents of university speech codes that are based on the fighting words model must believe that university officials will enforce them in a manner that differs from the general enforcement pattern of similar regulations. They must have faith that university officials, as opposed to other officials, are unusually sensitive to free speech rights in general, and to the free speech rights of minority group members and dissidents in particular.

Based on his analysis of the actual application of the fighting words doctrine, Gard adheres to no such faith in the discretion of enforcing officials. In response to another legal academic's suggestion that the fighting words doctrine could be invoked to protect the aged and infirm from "the vilest personal verbal abuse," Gard said that this was "a romantic vision that exists only in the imagination of a law professor." [58] Even assuming that university officials might be unusually attentive to free speech values when implementing the fighting words doctrine, the use of that doctrine by universities could fuel an increased use by other officials, who might well fail to implement it in a speech-sensitive fashion. [59]

2. Intentional Infliction of Emotional Distress. A committee report that was considered by the University of Texas recommended regulating campus hate speech in accordance with the common law tort of intentional infliction of emotional distress. This doctrinal approach has a logical appeal because it focuses on the type of harm potentially caused by racist speech that universities are most concerned with alleviating — namely, emotional or psychological harm that interferes with studies. In contrast, the harm at which the fighting words doctrine aims — potential violence by the addressee against the speaker — is of less concern to most universities.

Traditional civil libertarians caution that the intentional infliction of emotional distress theory should almost never apply to verbal harassment. A major problem is that, as Gard notes, "the innate vagueness of the interest in preventing emotional injury to listeners suggests that any attempt at judicial enforcement will inevitably result in the imposition of judges' subjective linguistic preferences on society, *discrimination against ethnic and racial minorities,* and ultimately the misuse of the rationale to justify the censorship of the ideological content of the speaker's message." [60] Again, as was true for the fighting words doctrine, there is a particular danger that the intentional infliction of emotional distress doctrine also will be enforced to the detriment of the very minority groups whom the hate speech code advocates hope to protect.

The significant general problems with the intentional infliction of emotional distress theory counsel against its application in the campus context specifically. Citing these reasons, Stanford University declined to base its hate speech regulation on this tort model. Moreover, even though the University of Texas committee report concluded that the emotional distress approach was less problematical than the fighting words approach, it cautioned: "[T]here can be no guarantee as to the constitutionality of any university rule bearing on racial harassment and sensitive matters of freedom of expression."

The position that the intentional infliction of emotional distress tort should virtually never apply to words received substantial support in the Supreme Court's 1988 decision in *Hustler Magazine v. Falwell*.[61] Writing for a unanimous Court, Chief Justice Rehnquist reversed a jury verdict that had awarded damages to the nationally known minister, Jerry Falwell, for the intentional infliction of emotional distress. The Court held that a public figure such as Falwell may not "recover damages for emotional harm caused by the publication of an ad parody offensive to him, and doubtless gross and repugnant in the eyes of most." The Court further ruled that public figures and public officials may not recover for this tort unless they could show that the publication contained a false statement of fact that was made with "actual malice," that is, with knowledge that the statement was false or with reckless disregard as to whether or not it was false. In other words, the Court required public officials or public figures who claim intentional infliction of emotional distress to satisfy the same heavy burden of proof it imposes upon such individuals who bring defamation claims.

Although the specific *Falwell* holding focused on public-figure plaintiffs, much of the Court's language indicated that, because of First Amendment concerns, it would strictly construe the intentional infliction of emotional distress tort in general, even when pursued by nonpublic plaintiffs. For example, the Court said, to require a statement to be "outrageous" as a prerequisite for imposing liability did not sufficiently protect First Amendment values. Because the "outrageousness" of the challenged statement is a typical element of the tort (it is included in the *Restatement of Torts* definition) the Court's indication that it is constitutionally suspect has ramifications beyond the sphere of public-figure actions. The Court warned:

"Outrageousness" in the area of political and social discourse has an inherent subjectiveness about it which would allow a jury to impose liability on the basis of the jurors' tastes or views, or perhaps on the basis of their dislike of a particular expression. An "outrageousness" standard thus runs afoul of our longstanding refusal to allow damages to be awarded because the speech in question may have an adverse emotional impact on the audience.[62]

For the reasons signaled by the unanimous Supreme Court in *Falwell,* any cause of action for intentional infliction of emotional distress that arises from words must be narrowly framed and strictly applied in order to satisfy First Amendment dictates.

3. Group Defamation. Lawrence does not elaborate on either the constitutionality or efficacy of the group defamation concept, yet he approvingly notes others' alleged support for it. The group defamation concept, however, has been thoroughly discredited by judges and scholars.[63]

First, group defamation regulations are unconstitutional in terms of both Supreme Court doctrine and free speech principles. To be sure, the Supreme Court's only decision that expressly reviewed the issue, *Beauharnais v. Illinois,*[64] upheld a group libel statute against a First Amendment challenge. However, that 5–4 decision was issued more than forty years ago, in 1952, at a relatively early point in the Court's developing free speech jurisprudence. *Beauharnais* is widely assumed no longer to be good law in light of the Court's subsequent speech-protective decisions on related issues, notably its holdings that strictly limit individual defamation actions so as not to chill free speech. In particular, as Laurence Tribe has noted, the Court's landmark ruling in *New York Times v. Sullivan*[65] "seemed . . . to eclipse *Beauharnais'* sensitivity to . . . group defamation claims . . . because *New York Times* required public officials bringing libel suits to prove that a defamatory statement was directed at the official personally, and not simply at a unit of government."

Statements that defame groups convey opinions or ideas on matters of public concern, and therefore should be protected even if those statements also injure reputations or feelings. The Supreme Court recently reaffirmed this principle in a 1990 decision involving an individual defamation action, *Milkovich v. Lorain Journal Co.*[66]

In addition to flouting constitutional doctrine and free speech principles, rules sanctioning group defamation are ineffective in curbing the specific class of hate speech that Lawrence advocates restraining. Even Justice Frankfurter's opinion for the narrow *Beauharnais* majority repeatedly expressed doubt about the wisdom or efficacy of group libel laws. Justice Frankfurter stressed that the Court upheld the Illinois law in question only because of judicial deference to the state legislature's judgments on these points. Ironically, though, the Illinois legislature apparently did not consider its group libel law to be particularly wise or effective, because it repealed that law in its first revision of the state criminal code following the Supreme Court's decision, only nine years after the decision.

The concept of defamation encompasses only false statements of fact that are made without good-faith belief in their truth. Therefore, any disparaging or insulting statement would be immune from this doctrine, unless it were factual in nature, demonstrably false in content, and made in bad faith. Members of minority groups that are disparaged by an allegedly libelous statement would hardly have their reputations or psyches enhanced by a process in which the maker of the statement sought to prove his good-faith belief in its truth, and they were required to demonstrate the absence thereof.

One additional problem with group defamation statutes as a model for rules sanctioning campus hate speech should be noted. As with the other speech-restrictive doctrines asserted to justify such rules, group defamation laws introduce the risk that rules will be enforced at the expense of the very minority groups sought to be protected. The Illinois statute[67] upheld in *Beauharnais* is illustrative. According to a leading article on group libel laws, during the 1940s the Illinois statute was "a weapon for harassment of the Jehovah's Witnesses," who were then "a minority . . . very much more in need of protection than most."[68]

C. Even a Narrow Regulation Could Have a Negative Symbolic Impact on Constitutional Values

Taking into account the constraints imposed by free speech principles and doctrines potentially applicable to the regulation of campus hate speech, it might be possible—although difficult—to frame a sufficiently narrow rule to withstand a facial First Amendment challenge. However, it bears reemphasizing that, as the University of Texas committee report stressed, "[T]here can be no guarantee as to the constitutionality of any university rule bearing on racial harassment and sensitive matters of freedom of expression."

Even assuming that a regulation could be crafted with sufficient precision to survive a facial constitutional challenge, several further problems would remain, which should give any university pause in evaluating whether to adopt such a rule. Although these inherent problems with any hate speech regulation are discussed in greater detail below, in the context of analyzing Lawrence's specific proposal, they are summarized here. First, because of the discretion entailed in enforcing any such rule, they all involve an inevitable danger of arbitrary or discriminatory enforcement.[69] Therefore, the rule's implementation would have to be monitored to ensure that it did not exceed the bounds of the regulation's terms or threaten content-and viewpoint-neutrality principles.[70] This danger is graphically illustrated by the experience with the only campus hate speech rules for which a full enforcement record is available (because they were subject to litigation, and hence, disclosure): those at the Universities of Michigan and Wisconsin.

Second, there is an inescapable risk that any hate speech regulation, no matter how narrowly drawn, will chill speech beyond its literal scope. Members of the university community may well err on the side of caution to avoid being charged with a violation. For example, there is evidence that the hate speech policy adopted by the University of Wisconsin in 1989 had this effect, even before it was directly enforced. A third problem inherent in any campus hate speech policy, as Lawrence concedes, is that such rules constitute a precedent that can be used to restrict other types of speech. As the Supreme Court has recognized, the long-range precedential impact of any challenged governmental action should be a factor in evaluating its lawfulness.[71]

Further, in light of constitutional constraints, any campus hate speech policy inevitably would apply to only a tiny fraction of all racist expression, and accordingly it would have only a symbolic impact. Therefore, in deciding whether to adopt such a rule, universities must ask whether that symbolic impact is, on balance, positive or negative in terms of constitutional values. On the one hand, some advocates of hate speech regulations maintain that the regulations might play a valuable symbolic role in reaffirming our societal commitment to racial equality (although this is debatable). On the other hand, we must beware of even symbolic or perceived diminution of our impartial commitment to free speech. Even a limitation that has a direct impact upon only a discrete category of speech may have a much more pervasive indirect impact, by undermining the First Amendment's moral legitimacy.[72] Recently, the Supreme Court ringingly reaffirmed the core principle that a neutral commitment to free speech should trump competing symbolic concerns. In *United States v. Eichman,* which invalidated the Flag Protection Act of 1989, the Court declared:

Government may create national symbols, promote them, and encourage their respectful treatment. But the Flag Protection Act goes well beyond this by criminally proscribing expressive conduct because of its likely communicative impact.

We are aware that desecration of the flag is deeply offensive to many. But the same might be said, for example, of virulent ethnic and religious epithets, vulgar repudiations of the draft, and scurrilous caricatures. "If there is a bedrock principle underlying the First Amendment, it is that the Government may not prohibit the expression of an idea simply because it finds the idea itself offensive or disagreeable." Punishing desecration of the flag dilutes the very freedom that makes this emblem so revered, and worth revering.[73]

2. LAWRENCE'S CONCEPTION OF REGULABLE RACIST SPEECH ENDANGERS FREE SPEECH PRINCIPLES

The preceding discussion of relevant constitutional doctrine points to several problems with the Stanford regulations, as well as other regulations adopted or considered by other universities. As previously explained, the Stanford regulations violate the cardinal principles that speech restrictions must be content- and viewpoint-neutral. Moreover, although these regulations purportedly incorporate the fighting words doctrine, they in fact go well beyond the narrow bounds that the Court has imposed on that doctrine, and they chill protected speech.

A. The Proposed Regulations Would Not Pass Constitutional Muster

1. The Regulations Exceed the Bounds of the Fighting Words Doctrine. As discussed above, the fighting words doctrine is fraught with constitutional problems.[74] As a result, it has been abrogated *sub silentio* and should be expressly invalidated (except to the very limited extent that it simply reflects the "clear and present danger" doctrine). In any event, even assuming that the doctrine is still good law, it has been severely circumscribed by Supreme Court rulings. Because those limits are necessitated by free speech principles, they must be strictly enforced.

Most recently and most pointedly, as previously discussed, in it 1992 decision in *R.A.V. v. City of St. Paul,* the Court held that, to survive constitutional scrutiny, at the very least, fighting words regulations must be neutral in terms of the subject matter and the viewpoint of the targeted expression. For this reason alone, the First Amendment is violated by the Stanford policy, along with all other campus speech codes that prohibit only expression that conveys discriminatory ideas about race and other specified societal groupings.

Additionally, even before its *R.A.V.* decision, the Court had prescribed other limitations on the fighting words doctrine, which are also violated by campus speech codes of the type adopted by Stanford. Stephen Gard's thorough study of the law in this area summarizes these pre-1992 limitations on the fighting words doctrine:

The offending language (1) must constitute a personally abusive epithet, (2) must be addressed in a face-to-face manner, (3) must be directed to a specific individual and be descriptive of that individual, and (4) must be uttered under such circumstances that the words have a direct tendency to cause an immediate violent response by the average recipient. If any of these four elements is absent, the doctrine may not justifiably be invoked as a rationale for the suppression of the expression.[75]

The operative language of the Stanford code provides:

Speech or other expression constitutes harassment by personal vilification if it:

 a) is intended to insult or stigmatize an individual or small number of individuals on the basis of their sex, race, color, handicap, religion, sexual orientation, or national and ethnic origin; and

 b) is addressed directly to the individual or individuals whom it insults or stigmatizes; and

 c) makes use of insulting or "fighting" words or non-verbal symbols. In the context of discriminatory harassment by personal vilification, insulting or "fighting" words or non-verbal symbols are those "which by their very utterance inflict injury or tend to incite to an immediate breach of the peace," and which are commonly understood to convey direct and visceral hatred or contempt for human beings on the basis of their sex, race, color, handicap, religion, sexual orientation, or national and ethnic origin.

A comparison of the Stanford code to the Supreme Court's four pre-1992 criteria for constitutional fighting words restrictions, as summarized by Gard, reveals that the code clearly does not satisfy one of the Court's criteria, and it may not satisfy the other three either. Most importantly, as previously explained, since its 1972 decision in *Gooding v. Wilson,* the Court consistently has invalidated fighting words definitions that refer only to the nature of the words. Instead, it has insisted that these words must be evaluated contextually, to assess whether they are likely to cause an imminent breach of the peace under the circumstances in which they are uttered. (This requirement is set forth in Gard's fourth criterion.) Yet the Stanford code punishes words "which are commonly understood to convey" group-based hatred. By categorically proscribing certain words, without considering their context, the Stanford code falls afoul of the First Amendment.[76]

2. The Regulations Will Chill Protected Speech. Beyond its facial problems of violating content and viewpoint neutrality principles and fighting words limitations, the Stanford code also will dampen academic discourse. This inevitable outcome is indicated by the experience under the University of Michigan hate speech regulation.[77]

Even though the Michigan regulation was in some respects broader than its Stanford counterpart, the latter rule also suffers from facial overbreadth and ambiguity. One of the key terms in the Stanford regulation, the term "stigmatize," also was contained in the Michigan policy and specifically was ruled unconstitutionally vague. Accordingly, the Stanford code appears to be as constitutionally suspect as the Michigan rule, contrary to Lawrence's assumption.

In *Doe v. University of Michigan,*[78] the United States District Court for the Eastern District of Michigan held that the University of Michigan's anti-hate speech policy violated the First Amendment because, as applied, it was overbroad and impermissibly vague. The court concluded that during the year when the policy was in effect, the University "consistently applied" it "to reach protected speech."[79] Moreover, because of the policy's vagueness, the court concluded that it did not give adequate notice of which particular expressions would be prohibited and which protected. Consequently, the policy deterred members of the university community from engaging in protected expression for fear it might be sanctioned. This "chilling effect" of any hate speech regulation is particularly problematic in the academic environment, given the special importance of a free and robust exchange of ideas there.

The judge who ultimately found the Michigan rule unconstitutional did not share Lawrence's opinion that it was "poorly drafted and obviously overbroad."[80] To the contrary, his opinion expressly noted that he would not have found the rule unconstitutionally overbroad merely based on its language. Rather, he found it unconstitutional in light of the enforcement record. These findings show the relevance of the Michigan case not only to the Stanford situation, but also to all other campus hate speech regulations. Regardless of how carefully these rules are drafted, they inevitably are vague and unavoidably invest officials with substantial discretion in the enforcement process; thus, such regulations exert a chilling effect on speech beyond their literal bounds. Accordingly, even though the University of Wisconsin's hate speech policy was somewhat narrower than the University of Michigan's policy, it too was ruled to be substantially overbroad and unduly vague, thus violating the First Amendment.[81] As Eleanor Holmes Norton has cautioned, "It is technically impossible to write an anti-speech code that cannot be twisted against speech nobody means to bar."[82]

In the recent wave of college crackdowns on racist and other forms of hate speech, examples abound of attempts to censor speech conveying ideas that clearly play a legitimate role in academic discourse, although some of us might find them wrongheaded or even odious. For example, the University of Michigan's anti-hate speech policy could justify attacks on author Salman Rushdie's book, *The Satanic Verses,* on the ground that it was offensive to Muslims.[83]

Such incidents are not aberrational. Any anti-hate speech rule inescapably entails some vagueness, due to the inherent imprecision of key words and concepts common to all such proposed rules. For example, most regulations employ one or more of the following ambiguous terms: "demeaning," "disparaging," "hostile," "insulting," and "stigmatizing." Therefore, there is real danger that even a narrowly crafted rule will deter some expression that should be protected, especially in the university environment.[84] In particular, such a rule probably will add to the silence on "gut issues" about racism, sexism, and other forms of bias that already impede interracial and other intergroup dialogues.

Additionally, it must be recognized that silencing certain expressions may be tantamount to silencing certain ideas.[85] As the plaintiff in *Doe v. Michigan* argued:

[T]he policy . . . is an official statement that at the University of Michigan, some arguments will no longer be tolerated. Rather than encourage her maturing students to question each other's beliefs on such diverse and controversial issues as the proper role of women in society, the merits of particular religions, or the moral propriety of homosexuality, the University has decided that it must protect its students from what it considers to be "unenlightened" ideas. In so doing, the University has established a secular orthodoxy by implying, among other things, that homosexuality is morally acceptable, [and] that . . . feminism [is] superior to the traditional view of women.[86]

The Michigan plaintiff was victimized directly by the "pall of ortho-doxy"[87] that the university's anti-hate speech policy cast over the campus. As a graduate student specializing in behavioral psychology, he felt that the rule deterred him from classroom discussion of theories that some psychological differences among racial groups and between the sexes are related to biological differences, for fear of being charged with racial or sexual harassment.

In addition to their chilling effect on the ideas and expressions of university community members, policies that bar hate speech could also engender broader forms of censorship. As noted by William Cohen of Stanford Law School, an anti-hate speech rule such as the one adopted by his university "purports to create a personal right to be free from involuntary exposure to any form of expression that gives certain kinds of offense." Therefore, he explains, such a rule "could become a sword to challenge assigned readings in courses, the showing of films on campus, or the message of certain speakers."[88]

B. The Proposed Regulations Would Endanger Fundamental Free Speech Principles

The various proposed campus hate speech regulations, including the Stanford code that Lawrence endorses, are not only inconsistent with current Supreme Court doctrine prescribing permissible limits on speech. Even more problematic is the fact that they jeopardize basic free speech principles. Whereas certain conduct may be regulable, speech that advocates such conduct is not, and speech may not be regulated on the basis of its content or viewpoint, even if many of us strongly disagree with—or, worse yet, are repelled by—that content or viewpoint.

1. Protection of Speech Advocating Regulable Conduct. Civil libertarians, scholars, and judges consistently have distinguished between speech advocating unlawful conduct and the unlawful conduct itself. Although this distinction has been drawn in numerous different factual settings, the fundamental underlying issues always are the same. For example, within recent years, some pro-choice activists have urged civil libertarians and courts to make an exception to free speech principles in order to restrain the expressive conduct of anti-abortion activists. Instead, civil libertarians have persuaded courts to prohibit assaults, blockages of clinic entrances, trespasses, and other illegal conduct by anti-choice activists. Similarly, civil libertarians and courts have rejected pleas by some feminists to condone an exception to free speech guarantees for sexually explicit materials that reflect sexist attitudes. Instead, civil libertarians have renewed their efforts to persuade courts and legislatures to invalidate sexist actions. A decade ago, civil libertarians and several courts—including the Supreme Court—rejected the plea of Holocaust survivors in Skokie, Illinois, to prohibit neo-Nazis from peacefully demonstrating. Instead, civil libertarians successfully have lobbied for the enactment and enforcement of laws against anti-Semitic vandalism and other hate-inspired conduct.

A pervasive weakness in Lawrence's analysis is his elision of the distinction between racist speech, on the one hand, and racist conduct, on the other.[89] It is certainly true that racist speech, like other speech, may have some causal connection to conduct. As Justice Holmes observed, "[e]very idea is an incitement" to action.[90] However, as Justice Holmes also noted, to protect speech that advocates conduct you oppose does not "indicate that you think the speech impotent, . . . or that you do not care wholeheartedly for the result."[91] Rather, this protection is based on the critical distinction between speech that has a direct and immediate link to unlawful conduct and all other speech, which has less direct and immediate links. In Holmes's immortal words:

[W]e should be eternally vigilant against attempts to check the expression of opinions that we loathe and believe to be fraught with death, unless they so imminently threaten immediate interference with the lawful and pressing purposes of the law that an immediate check is required to save the country. . . . Only the emergency that makes it immediately dangerous to leave the correction of evil counsels to time warrants making any exception to the sweeping command, "Congress shall make no law . . . abridging the freedom of speech."[92]

Justice Holmes's stirring phrases were penned in dissenting opinions. However, the Court enshrined his view as the law of the land in 1969, in *Brandenburg v. Ohio*.[93] In a unanimous opinion overturning the conviction of a Ku Klux Klansman for an anti-black and anti-Semitic speech, the Court said that the First Amendment does "not permit a state to forbid . . . advocacy of the use of force or of law violation except where such advocacy is directed to inciting or producing imminent lawless action and is likely to incite or produce such action."[94]

2. Proscription on Content-Based Speech Regulations.

a. The indivisibility of free speech. It is important to place the current debate about campus racist speech in the context of efforts to censor other forms of hate speech. Such a broadened perspective suggests that consistent principles should be applied each time the issue resurfaces in any guise. Every person may find one particular type of speech especially odious, and one message may most sorely test his or her dedication to free speech values. But for each person who would exclude racist speech from the general proscription against content- or viewpoint-based speech regulations, recent experience shows that there is another who would make such an exception only for anti-choice speech, another who would make it only for sexist speech, another who would make it only for anti-Semitic speech, another who would make it only for flag desecration, another who would make it only for speech at odds with traditional religious or moral values, and so on.

The recognition that there is no principled basis for curbing speech that expresses some particular ideas is reflected in the time-honored prohibition on any content- or viewpoint-based regulations. As stated by Laurence Tribe, "If the Constitution forces government to allow people to march, speak, and write in favor of peace, brotherhood, and justice, then it must also require government to allow them to advocate hatred, racism, and even genocide."[95]

The position stated by Tribe is not just the traditional civil libertarian view, but it also is the law of the land. The courts consistently have agreed with civil libertarian claims that the First Amendment protects the right to engage in racist and other forms of hate speech. Why is this so, and should it be so? Lawrence rightly urges us to take a fresh look at this issue, no matter how well settled it is as a matter of law. I have taken that invitation seriously and reflected long and hard upon his thought-provoking analysis and the questions it presents. Having done so, however, I conclude that the courts and traditional civil libertarians are correct in steadfastly rejecting laws that create additional new exceptions to free speech protections for racist expression.

One longstanding rationale for the view that speech must be protected, regardless of its content or views, is the belief that we need a free marketplace of ideas, open even to the most odious and offensive ideas and expressions, because truth ultimately will triumph in an unrestricted marketplace.[96] The marketplace metaphor is subject to some criticism, as Lawrence notes. Nevertheless, the marketplace of ideas does sometimes work to improve society: this has been particularly true with regard to the promotion of racial equality. Moreover, there are other, independently sufficient rationales for the content- and viewpoint-neutral protection even of hate speech. Another important, more recently articulated rationale is that freedom of expression promotes individual autonomy and dignity.[97] Lawrence himself endorses an additional theory for the protection of racist speech, a view that has been advanced by Lee Bollinger: free speech reinforces our society's commitment to tolerance and to combating racist ideas.[98]

Although the foregoing theories may be acceptable in general, one might ask why they do not permit exceptions for racist speech. Racism in America is unique in important respects. For most of our country's history, racism was enshrined legally through slavery or de jure discrimination. The post-Civil War constitutional amendments guaranteed racial equality. More recently, all branches and levels of the government have sought to implement these constitutional guarantees by outlawing any vestiges of state-sponsored, as well as many forms of private, racial discrimination. Given our nation's special obligation to eradicate the "badges and incidents" of the formerly government-sanctioned institutions of racism, is it not appropriate to make broader exceptions than usual to free speech doctrines for racist speech? As Rodney Smolla has noted, "Racist speech is arguably different in kind from other offensive speech, because the elimination of racism is *itself* enshrined in our Constitution as a public value of the highest order."[99]

The American commitment to eradicate racial discrimination is reinforced by a parallel international commitment, as expressed in such documents as the United Nations Charter, the Universal Declaration of Human Rights, and the International Convention on the Elimination of All Forms of Racial Discrimination. Moreover, the United States is apparently alone in the world community in sheltering racist speech. Both under international agreements and under the domestic law of many other countries, racist speech is outlawed.

In light of the universal condemnation of racial discrimination and the worldwide regulation of racist speech, it certainly is tempting to consider excepting racist speech from First Amendment protection. Episodes of racist speech, such as those cited by Lawrence and others, make a full commitment to free speech at times seem painful and difficult. Civil libertarians certainly find such speech abhorrent, given our dedication to eradicating racial discrimination and other forms of bigotry. But experience has confirmed the truth of the indivisibility principle articulated above: history demonstrates that if the freedom of speech is weakened for one person, group, or message, then it is no longer there for others. The free speech victories that civil libertarians have won in the context of defending the right to express racist and other anti-civil libertarian messages have been used to protect speech proclaiming antiracist and pro-civil libertarian messages. For example, in 1949, the ACLU defended the right of Father Terminiello, a suspended Catholic priest, to give a racist speech in Chicago. The Supreme Court agreed with that position in a decision that became a landmark in free speech history.[100] Time and again during the 1960s and 1970s, the ACLU and other civil rights groups were able to defend free speech rights for civil rights demonstrators by relying on the *Terminiello* decision.

b. The slippery slope dangers of banning racist speech. To attempt to craft free speech exceptions only for racist speech would create a significant risk of a slide down the proverbial "slippery slope." To be sure, lawyers and judges are capable of—indeed, especially trained in—drawing distinctions between similar situations. Therefore, I agree with Lawrence and other critics of the absolutist position that slippery slope dangers should not be exaggerated. It is probably hyperbole to contend that if we ever stepped off the mountaintop where all speech is protected regardless of its content, we would inevitably end up in the abyss where the government controls all our words. On the other hand, critics of absolutism should not minimize the real danger: we would have an extremely difficult time limiting our descent to a single downward step by attempting to prohibit only racist expression on campus. It would be very hard to craft applicable rules and supporting rationales that would meaningfully distinguish this type of speech from others.

First, hard questions would be presented about the groups that should be protected. Should we regulate speech aimed only at racial and ethnic groups, as the University of Texas considered? Or should we also bar insults of religious groups, women, gay men and lesbians, individuals with disabilities, Vietnam War veterans, and so on, as do the rules adopted by Stanford and the University of Michigan?

Second, it would be highly challenging to define proscribable harassing speech without encompassing important expression that should be protected. Censorial consequences would likely result from all proposed or adopted university policies, including the Stanford code, which sanction speech intended to "insult or stigmatize" on the basis of race or other prohibited grounds. For example, certain feminists suggest that all heterosexual sex is tantamount to rape because heterosexual men are aggressors who operate in a cultural climate of pervasive sexism and violence against women. Aren't these feminists insulting or stigmatizing heterosexual men on the basis of their sex and sexual orientation? And how about a Holocaust survivor who blames all ("Aryan") Germans for their collaboration during World War II? Doesn't this insult or stigmatize on the basis of national and ethnic origin? And surely we can think of numerous other examples that would have to give us pause.

The difficulty of formulating limited, clear definitions of prohibited hate speech, which do not encompass valuable contributions to societal discourse, is underscored by the seemingly intractable ambiguities in various campus rules. Even proponents of campus hate speech regulations recognize their inevitable ambiguities and necessarily contextualized applications, with the result that the individuals who enforce them must have substantial discretion to draw distinctions based upon the particular facts and circumstances involved in any given case. Richard Delgado, an early advocate of rules proscribing hate speech, acknowledged that the offensiveness of even such a traditionally insulting epithet as "nigger" would depend on the context in which it was uttered, since it could be a term of affection when exchanged between friends.[101] The imprecise nature of racist speech regulations is underscored further by the fact that even their proponents are unsure or disagree as to their applicability in particular situations.[102]

Once we acknowledge the substantial discretion that anti-hate speech rules will vest in those who enforce them, then we are ceding to the government the power to pick and choose whose words to protect and whose to punish. Such discretionary governmental power is fundamentally antithetical to the free speech guarantee. As soon as the government is allowed to punish any speech based upon its content, free expression exists only for those with power.

   c. The content- and viewpoint-neutrality principles reflect sensitivity to hate speech's hurtful power. Contrary to Lawrence's apparent assumption, the conclusion that free speech protections must remain indivisible, even for racist speech, has nothing to do with insensitivity to the feelings of minority group members who are vilified by hate speech and suffer acutely from it. Traditional civil libertarians recognize the power of words to inflict psychic and even physiological harm. For example, precisely because the ACLU both acknowledges the power of speech and defends the exercise of that power even by those who express anti-civil libertarian ideas, the ACLU expressly dissociates itself from such ideas and makes it a priority to combat them through counterspeech and action. Nor are traditional civil libertarians unconcerned with the rights of hate speech victims, as Lawrence implies. To the contrary, civil libertarians champion the rights of all individuals to live in a society untainted by racism and other forms of bias; since its founding in 1920, the ACLU has directed considerable resources and efforts toward securing these rights.

   I was appalled by Lawrence's account of the vicious racist vilification to which his sister's family recently was subjected.[103] This account powerfully demonstrates that the old nursery rhyme is wrong: maybe words are different from sticks and stones insofar as they cannot literally break our bones, but words can and do hurt—brutally.

   Two prominent defenders of content-neutral protection for hate speech have described painful personal experiences as victims of such speech. I refer to Stanford law professor Gerald Gunther, who was a leading opponent of the proposed Stanford code that Lawrence advocates,[104] and Aryeh Neier, who as executive director of the ACLU during the Skokie episode vigorously championed the free speech rights of racists and anti-Semites.[105] Far from opposing censorship *despite* the suffering they personally experienced as a result of hate speech, Gunther[106] and Neier[107] oppose censorship precisely *because* of these personal experiences. The justification for not outlawing "words that wound" is not based on a failure to recognize the injurious potential of words. The refusal to ban words is due precisely to our understanding both of how very powerful they are and of the critical role they play in our democratic society.

3. LAWRENCE'S RATIONALES FOR REGULATING RACIST SPEECH WOULD JUSTIFY SWEEPING PROHIBITIONS, CONTRARY TO FREE SPEECH PRINCIPLES

Although Lawrence actually advocates regulating only a relatively narrow category of racist speech, his rationales could be asserted to justify broader rules. Indeed, he himself appears to recognize that, if accepted, his approach could lead to outlawing all racist speech, as well as other forms of hate speech. Since many universities and individuals have advocated broader-ranging regulations—and since Lawrence also endorses restrictions that have a "considerably broader reach" than the Stanford code[108]—it is important to consider the problems with Lawrence's more expansive rationales. His general theories about racist speech entail substantial departures from traditional civil libertarian and constitutional law positions.

A. *Brown* and Other Cases Invalidating Governmental Racist Conduct Do Not Justify Regulating Nongovernmental Racist Speech

Lawrence intriguingly posits that *Brown v. Board of Education,*[109] Bob Jones University v. United States,[110] and other civil rights cases justify regulation of private racist speech.[111] The problem with drawing an analogy between all of these cases and the subject at hand is that the cases involved either *government* speech, as opposed to speech by private individuals, or *conduct,* as opposed to speech. Indeed, *Brown* itself is distinguishable on both grounds.

1. The Speech/Conduct Distinction. First, the governmental defendant in *Brown*—the Topeka, Kansas, Board of Education—was not simply *saying* that blacks are inferior. Rather, it was *treating* them as inferior through pervasive patterns of conduct, by maintaining systems and structures of segregated public schools. To be sure, a by-product of the challenged conduct was a message, but that message was only incidental. Saying that black children are unfit to attend school with whites is materially distinguishable from legally prohibiting them from doing so, despite the fact that the legal prohibition may convey the former message.

Lawrence's point proves too much. If incidental messages could transform conduct into speech, then the distinction between speech and conduct would disappear completely, because *all* conduct conveys a message. To take an extreme example, a racially motivated lynching expresses the murderer's hatred or contempt for his victim. But the clearly unlawful act is not protected from punishment by virtue of the incidental message it conveys. And the converse also is true. Just because the government may in effect suppress particular hate messages that are the by-product of unlawful conduct that it directly prohibits, it does not follow that the government may directly suppress all hate messages. Those messages not tightly linked to conduct that is independently unlawful must still be protected.

The Supreme Court has recognized these critical distinctions by subjecting to more demanding First Amendment scrutiny governmental measures that directly target the expressive element of expressive conduct. When a governmental measure seeks to regulate the communicative aspect of expressive conduct, the measure is presumptively unconstitutional. In contrast, when a governmental measure seeks to regulate the noncommunicative aspect of expressive conduct, the measure is presumptively constitutional. For example, in *United States v. O'Brien*,[112] the Court upheld a statute that criminalized the destruction of draft cards, because it concluded that the government's interest was limited to the nonexpressive aspect of this conduct. Conversely, in two later decisions, the Court struck down laws criminalizing the burning of the American flag,[113] because it concluded that these laws aimed at the expressive aspect of the forbidden conduct.

Brown v. Board of Education does not constitute a precedent for regulating racist hate speech precisely because of these critical distinctions. The *Brown* Court's invalidation of laws mandating racially segregated schools was not aimed at the expressive aspect of those laws.[114] In stark contrast, anti-hate speech rules are aimed squarely at the communicative aspect of any expressive conduct.

2. The Private Action/State Action Distinction. Even if *Brown* had involved only a governmental message of racism, without any attendant conduct, that case still would be distinguishable in a crucial way from a private individual's conveyance of the same message. Under the post-Civil War constitutional amendments, the government is committed to eradicating all badges and incidents of slavery, including racial discrimination. Consistent with the paramount importance of this obligation, the Supreme Court has held that the equal protection clause bars the government from lending textbooks to racially discriminatory private schools,[115] even though the Court had held previously that the establishment clause does *not* bar the government from lending textbooks to private religious schools.[116] In this respect, the government's constitutional duty to dissociate itself from racism is even greater than its constitutional duty to dissociate itself from religion. The government's supreme obligation to counter racism clearly is incompatible with racist speech promulgated by the government itself. Private individuals, though, have no comparable duty.

Mari Matsuda has argued that the government's failure to punish private hate speech could be viewed as state action insofar as this failure conveys a message that the state tolerates such speech. Because the Court construes the First Amendment's establishment clause as prohibiting government action that conveys a message of state support for religion,[117] establishment clause cases constitute instructive precedents for evaluating Matsuda's argument. In the analogous establishment clause context, the Court repeatedly has held that the government's neutral tolerance and protection of private religious expression, along with all other expression, does not convey a message that the government endorses religion. In its 1990 decision in *Board of Education of Westside Community Schools v. Mergens,*[118] the Court expressly reaffirmed the crucial distinction between government and private speech, in the establishment clause context, in terms fully applicable to the racist speech controversy. The Court declared, "[T]here is a crucial difference between *government* speech endorsing religion, which the Establishment Clause forbids, and *private* speech endorsing religion, which the Free Speech and Free Exercise Clauses protect."[119] Paraphrasing this language and applying it to the hate speech context, one could say, "There is a crucial difference between *government* speech endorsing racism, which the Equal Protection Clause forbids, and *private* speech endorsing racism, which the Free Speech Clause protects."

In light of the government's special duty to dissociate itself from racism, one might try to distinguish private religious speech from private racist speech—much as the Court distinguished textbook loans to racially discriminatory private religious schools from the same kind of loans to private religious schools. However, the direct, tangible, explicit government support of racially discriminatory schools through textbook lending programs is critically different from the indirect, intangible, implicit government support allegedly lent to racist conduct by the government's failure to outlaw private racist speech.

Lawrence makes a telling point when he says that our government never has repudiated the group libels it perpetrated for years against blacks and that it is insufficient for the government simply to cease uttering those libels. Accordingly, one strategy for promoting racial equality, which is consistent with free speech, is to urge the government to proclaim anti-racist messages. The ACLU policy on campus hate speech (which is set out in the appendix to this chapter) expressly endorses this strategy.

Lawrence also makes the persuasive point that there is no absolute distinction between state and private action in the racist sphere, insofar as private acts of discrimination (as well as government acts) also are unlawful. This point, however, raises the other distinction discussed above—the distinction between words and conduct. Civil libertarians vigorously support the civil rights laws that make private discriminatory acts illegal, but that is a far cry from making private *speech* illegal. The *Bob Jones* case,[120] upon which Lawrence seeks to rely, illustrates this critical distinction. What was objectionable there was the government conduct that supported and endorsed the private racist conduct—namely, the government's financial contributions, through the tax system, to racially discriminatory private educational institutions. Moreover, even if a private university could be prohibited from *undertaking* discriminatory actions—in the case of Bob Jones University, barring interracial marriage and dating—it still could not be prohibited from *advocating* such actions. The ACLU amicus brief in the *Bob Jones* case made precisely these points in countering the university's claim that withdrawing its tax benefits would violate its First Amendment rights. The ACLU argued, and the Court agreed, that the university was still free to urge its students not to engage in interracial marriage or dating, and that this was as far as its First Amendment rights extended. Prohibited racist acts are no different from other prohibited acts. The government may punish the acts, but it may not punish words that advocate or endorse them.

The other cases upon which Lawrence premises his argument also do not authorize the regulation of private racist speech. For example, he draws a false analogy between private racist speech and a local government's financing of allegedly "private" segregated (all-white) schools, after the government had closed down public schools in defiance of desegregation orders. Lawrence misreads these cases, which invalidated tangible government support for segregated schools, as standing for the proposition "that the defamatory message of segregation would not be insulated from constitutional proscription simply because the speaker was a non-government entity." [121] For example, in *Griffin v. Prince Edward County School Board*,[122] the Supreme Court held that the governmental financing of segregated schools constituted prohibited state action. In contrast, had individual school district residents urged their government to undertake such action, or expressed their support for such action to black residents, that would have constituted protected private speech.[123]

B. The Nonintellectual Content of Some Racist Speech Does Not Justify Its Prohibition

In addition to his principal argument that private racist speech may be regulated because it is indistinguishable from governmental racist conduct, Lawrence offers a second purported justification for restricting racist speech. He contends that "[a] defining attribute of speech is that it appeals first to the mind of the hearer who can evaluate its truth or persuasiveness," [124] and that because certain racist speech lacks this attribute, it should not be viewed as speech. This position is inconsistent with fundamental free speech values.

Lawrence's argument overlooks the teachings of such landmark Supreme Court decisions as *Terminiello v. Chicago* [125] and *Cohen v. California*,[126] which recognize that protectible speech often appeals to the emotions as well as the mind. As early as 1948, the Court recognized that First Amendment protection is not restricted to the "exposition of ideas." [127] As Justice Douglas declared in a celebrated passage in *Terminiello*:

[A] function of free speech under our system of government is to invite dispute. It may indeed best serve its high purpose when it induces a condition of unrest, creates dissatisfaction with conditions as they are, or even stirs people to anger. Speech is often provocative and challenging. It may strike at prejudices and preconceptions and have profound unsettling effects as it presses for acceptance of an idea. That is why freedom of speech, though not absolute, is nevertheless protected against censorship or punishment, unless shown likely to produce a clear and present danger of a serious substantive evil that rises far above public inconvenience, annoyance, or unrest. There is no room under our Constitution for a more restrictive view. For the alternative would lead to standardization of ideas either by legislatures, courts, or dominant political or community groups.[128]

Justice Harlan[129] echoed this theme in *Cohen* when he explained that protectible expression

conveys not only ideas capable of relatively precise, detached explication, but otherwise inexpressible emotions as well. In fact, words are often chosen as much for their emotive as their cognitive force. We cannot sanction the view that the Constitution, while solicitous of the cognitive content of individual speech, has little or no regard for that emotive function which, practically speaking, may often be the more important element of the overall message sought to be communicated.[130]

Together, *Terminiello* and *Cohen* recognize that speech often expresses the speaker's emotions and appeals to the audience's emotions. This generalization applies not only to the ugly words of racist vituperation, but also to the beautiful words of poetry. Indeed, much indisputably valuable language, as well as expressive conduct, has the intention and effect of appealing not directly or not only to the mind. Such language also seeks to and does engage the audience's emotions. If emotion-provoking discourse were denied protected status, then much political speech—which is usually viewed as being at the apex of First Amendment protection—would fall outside the protected realm. The Court in *Terminiello* and *Cohen* rejected the restricted First Amendment paradigm of "a sedate assembly of speakers who calmly discussed the issues of the day and became ultimately persuaded by the logic of one of the competing positions."[131]

Lawrence reveals his narrower view when he asks, "[A]re racial insults ideas? Do they encourage wide-open debate?"[132] In light of the *Terminiello-Cohen* line of cases, Lawrence wrongly implies that a negative response to these questions should remove racial insults from the domain of protected speech. Lawrence also incorrectly implies that the response to these questions should be negative. Racial insults convey ideas of racial supremacy and inferiority. Objectionable and discredited as these ideas may be, they are ideas nonetheless.

4. PROHIBITING RACIST SPEECH WOULD NOT EFFECTIVELY COUNTER, AND COULD EVEN AGGRAVATE, THE UNDERLYING PROBLEM OF RACISM

A. Civil Libertarians Should Continue to Make Combating Racism a Priority

Despite Lawrence's proffered justifications for regulating a broader spectrum of racist speech, he in fact advocates regulating only a quite limited category of such speech. Thus, even Lawrence's views of regulable speech, although broader than those of the Supreme Court or traditional civil libertarians, would allow most racist speech on campus.

I do not think it is worth spending a great deal of time debating the fine points of specific rules or their particular applications to achieve what necessarily will be only marginal differences in the amount of racist insults that can be sanctioned. The larger problems of racist attitudes and conduct—of which all these words are symptoms—would remain. Those who share the dual goals of promoting racial equality and protecting free speech must concentrate on countering racial discrimination, rather than on defining the particular narrow subset of racist slurs that constitutionally might be regulable.

I welcome Lawrence's encouragement to civil libertarians to "engage actively in speech and action that resists and counters the racist ideas the first amendment protects." [133] But Lawrence need not urge traditional civil libertarians to "put[ ] at least as much effort and as many resources into fighting for the victims of racism as we put into protecting the rights of racists." [134] The ACLU, for example, always has put far more effort and resources into assisting the victims of racism than into defending the rights of racists.

Although ACLU cases involving the Ku Klux Klan and other racist speakers often generate a disproportionate amount of publicity, they constitute only a tiny fraction (approximately one-tenth of one percent) of the ACLU's caseload. In the recent past, the ACLU has handled about six cases a year advocating the free speech rights of white supremacists, out of a total of more than six thousand cases, and these white supremacist cases rarely consume significant resources. Moreover, the resources the ACLU does expend to protect hatemongers' First Amendment rights are well invested. They ultimately preserve not only civil liberties, but also our democratic system, for the benefit of all. Aryeh Neier persuasively drew this conclusion, for example, with respect to the ACLU's defense of the American Nazi party's right to demonstrate in Skokie:

[W]hen it was all over no one had been persuaded to join [the Nazis]. They had disseminated their message and it had been rejected.

Why did the Nazi message fall on such deaf ears? Revolutionaries and advocates of destruction attract followers readily when the society they wish to overturn loses legitimacy. Understanding this process, revolutionaries try to provoke the government into using repressive measures. They rejoice, as the American Nazis did, when their rights are denied to them; they count on repression to win them sympathizers.

In confronting the Nazis, however, American democracy did not lose, but preserved its legitimacy. . . .

The judges who devoted so much attention to the Nazis, the police departments that paid so much overtime, and the American Civil Liberties Union, which lost a half-million dollars in membership income as a consequence of its defense, used their time and money well. They defeated the Nazis by preserving the legitimacy of American democracy.[135]

In contrast with its small, albeit important, investment in protecting the free speech rights of racists, the ACLU has throughout its history devoted substantial resources to the struggle against racism. The ACLU backed the civil rights movement in its early years, working with lawyers from the National Association for the Advancement of Colored People to plan the attack on segregation. In 1931, the ACLU published *Black Justice,* a comprehensive report on legalized racism. The ACLU also played an important role in the infamous Scottsboro cases, in which seven young black men were convicted of raping two white women after sham trials before an all-white jury; an ACLU attorney argued and won the first of these cases to reach the Supreme Court.

During World War II, the ACLU sponsored a challenge to the segregated draft and organized the Committee Against Racial Discrimination. In the 1950s, the ACLU successfully challenged state laws that made it a crime for a white woman to bear a child she had conceived with a black father. In the 1960s, the ACLU provided funds and lawyers to defend civil rights activists, and since then it has lobbied extensively for civil rights legislation.

The ACLU's Voting Rights Project has helped to empower black voters throughout the southern United States, facilitating the election of hundreds of black officials. The ACLU also maintains several other special "Projects" whose constituents or clients are (alas) predominantly black—for example, the Capital Punishment Project, the Children's Rights Project, and the National Prison Project. Since the late 1980s, the ACLU's national legal department has focused on civil liberties issues related to race and poverty, and has won pathbreaking victories in cases involving racial discrimination in education and housing. In addition, state and local-level branches of the ACLU consistently allocate substantial resources to civil rights cases.

As indicated by both policy and action, the ACLU is committed to eradicating racial discrimination on campus as an essential step toward its larger goal of eliminating racial discrimination from society at large. For example, ACLU leaders have corresponded and met with university officials to recommend measures that they could implement to combat campus racism, consistent with both equality and free speech values. In the same vein, ACLU officials have worked for the implementation of educational programs designed to counter racist attitudes among college students, as well as younger students. Additionally, ACLU representatives have participated in universities' deliberations about whether to adopt anti-hate speech rules, and if so, how to frame them. Representatives of the ACLU have also organized investigations of racist incidents at specific campuses, for purposes of advising university officials about how to respond to and prevent such problems. Furthermore, ACLU officials have organized and participated in protests of racist incidents, both on campus and more generally.

In light of these efforts, Lawrence's suggestion that "the call for fighting racist attitudes and practices rather than speech [is] 'just a lot of cheap talk' "[136] is a cheap shot. In particular, it is noteworthy that the ACLU affiliates that have brought lawsuits challenging campus hate speech regulations also have undertaken specific efforts to counter campus and societal racism.[137] Moreover, the charge of "cheap talk" more appropriately might be leveled at those who focus their attention on hate speech regulations. Such regulations may appear to provide a relatively inexpensive "quick fix," but racist speech is only one symptom of the pervasive problem of racism, and this underlying problem will not be solved by banning one of its symptoms.

B. Punishing Racist Speech Would Not Effectively Counter Racism

Parts 2 and 3 of this chapter emphasized the principled reasons, arising from First Amendment theory, for concluding that racist speech should receive the same protection as other offensive speech. This conclusion is also supported by pragmatic or strategic considerations concerning the efficacious pursuit of equality goals. Not only would rules censoring racist speech fail to reduce racial bias, but they might well even undermine that goal.

First, there is no persuasive psychological evidence that punishment for name-calling changes deeply held attitudes. To the contrary, historical experience and psychological studies show that censored speech becomes more appealing and persuasive to many listeners merely by virtue of the censorship.

Nor is there any empirical evidence, from the countries that do outlaw racist speech, that censorship is an effective means to counter racism. For example, Great Britain began to prohibit racist defamation in 1965. Almost three decades later, this law has had no discernible adverse impact on the National Front and other neo-Nazi groups active in Britain. As discussed above, it is impossible to draw narrow regulations that precisely specify the particular words and contexts that should lead to sanctions. Fact-bound determinations are required. For this reason, authorities have great discretion in determining precisely which speakers and which words to punish. Consequently, even vicious racist epithets have gone unpunished under British law.[138] Moreover, even if actual or threatened enforcement of the law has deterred some overt racist insults, that enforcement has had no effect on more subtle, but nevertheless clear signals of racism. Some observers believe that racism is even more pervasive in Britain than in the United States.[139]

C. Banning Racist Speech Could Aggravate Racism

For several reasons, banning the symptom of racist speech may compound the underlying problem of racism. Lawrence sets up a false dichotomy when he urges us to balance equality goals against free speech goals. Just as he observes that free speech concerns should be weighed on the pro-regulation as well as the anti-regulation side of the balance, he should recognize that equality concerns weigh on the anti-regulation as well as the pro-regulation side.

The first reason that laws censoring racist speech may undermine the goal of combating racism flows from the discretion such laws inevitably vest in the prosecutors, judges, and other individuals who implement them. One ironic, even tragic, result of this discretion is that members of minority groups themselves—the very people whom the law is intended to protect—are likely targets of punishment. For example, among the first individuals prosecuted under the British Race Relations Act of 1965, which criminalized the incitement of racial hatred, were black-power leaders. Their overtly racist messages undoubtedly expressed legitimate anger at real discrimination, yet the statute drew no such fine lines, nor could any similar statute possibly do so. Rather than curbing speech offensive to minorities, this British law instead has been regularly used to curb the speech of blacks, trade unionists, and anti-nuclear activists. In perhaps the ultimate irony, this statute, which was intended to restrain the neo-Nazi National Front, instead has barred expression by the Anti-Nazi League.

The British experience is not unique. History teaches us that anti-hate speech laws regularly have been used to oppress racial and other minorities. For example, none of the anti-Semites who were responsible for arousing France against Captain Alfred Dreyfus were ever prosecuted for group libel. But Emile Zola was prosecuted for libeling the French clergy and military in his famous "J'accuse," and he had to flee to England to escape punishment.[140] Additionally, closer to home, the very doctrines that Lawrence invokes to justify regulating campus hate speech—for example, the fighting words doctrine, upon which he chiefly relies—have always been particularly threatening to the speech of racial and political minorities.

That the foregoing examples simply illustrate a longstanding global pattern was documented in a 1992 book published by Article XIX, the London-based International Centre Against Censorship (which takes its name from the provision in the Universal Declaration of Human Rights that guarantees free speech), and the Human Rights Centre at the University of Essex in Great Britain. Drawing upon contemporary analyses of the experience in fourteen different countries, with various laws punishing racist and other hate speech, the book shows that such laws consistently have been used to suppress expression by members of racial and other minority groups. Article XIX's legal director described this pattern:

The flagrant abuse of laws which restrict hate speech by the authorities . . . provides the most troubling indictment of such laws. Thus, the laws in Sri Lanka and South Africa have been used almost exclusively against the oppressed and politically weakest communities. . . . Selective or lax enforcement by the authorities, including in the UK, Israel, and the former Soviet Union, allows governments to compromise the right of dissent and inevitably leads to disaffection and feelings of alienation among minority groups.[141]

The general lesson that anti-hate speech laws will be used to punish members of groups that are relatively politically powerless and targets of discrimination has also proven true in the specific context of campus hate speech regulations. In 1974, in a move aimed at the National Front, the British National Union of Students (NUS) adopted a resolution that representatives of "openly racist and fascist organizations" were to be prevented from speaking on college campuses "by whatever means necessary (including disruption of the meeting)." A substantial motivation for the rule had been to stem an increase in campus anti-Semitism. Ironically, however, following the United Nations' cue, some British students deemed Zionism a form of racism beyond the bounds of permitted discussion. Accordingly, in 1975 British students invoked the NUS resolution to disrupt speeches by Israelis and Zionists, including the Israeli ambassador to England. The intended target of the NUS resolution, the National Front, applauded this result. However, the NUS itself became disenchanted by this and other unintended consequences of its resolution and repealed it in 1977.

The British experience under its campus anti-hate speech rule parallels the experience in the United States under the first such rule that led to a judicial decision. During the year-and-a-half that the University of Michigan rule was in effect, there were more than twenty cases of whites charging blacks with racist speech. More importantly, the only two instances in which the rule was invoked to sanction racist speech (as opposed to sexist and other forms of hate speech) involved the punishment of speech by or on behalf of black students.[142] Additionally, the only student who was subjected to a full-fledged disciplinary hearing under the Michigan rule was a black student accused of homophobic and sexist expression. In seeking clemency from the sanctions imposed following this hearing, the student asserted that he had been singled out because of his race and his political views. Others who were punished for hate speech under the Michigan rule included several Jewish students accused of engaging in anti-Semitic expression[143] and an Asian-American student accused of making an anti-black comment.[144] Likewise, the student who brought a lawsuit (which was ultimately settled when the university agreed to abandon its policy in favor of a narrow one) challenging the University of Connecticut's hate speech policy, under which she had been penalized for an allegedly homophobic remark, was Asian American. She claimed that, among the other students who had engaged in similar expression, she had been singled out for punishment because of her ethnic background.

Lawrence himself recognizes that rules regulating racist speech might backfire and be invoked disproportionately against blacks and other traditionally oppressed groups. Indeed, he charges that other university rules already are used to silence anti-racist, but not racist, speakers.[145] Lawrence proposes to avoid this danger by excluding from the rule's protection "persons who were vilified on the basis of their membership in dominant majority groups."[146] Even putting aside the fatal First Amendment flaws in such a radical departure from content- and viewpoint-neutrality principles, the proposed exception would create far more problems of equality and enforceability than it would solve.[147]

A second reason why censorship of racist speech actually may subvert rather than promote the goal of eradicating racism is that such censorship measures often have the effect of glorifying racist speakers. Efforts at suppression result in racist speakers' receiving attention and publicity that they otherwise would not have garnered. As previously noted, psychological studies reveal that whenever the government attempts to censor speech, the censored speech—for that very reason—becomes more appealing to many people. Still worse, when pitted against the government, racist speakers may appear as martyrs or even heroes.

Advocates of hate speech regulations do not seem to realize that their own attempts to *suppress* speech increase public interest in the ideas they are trying to stamp out. Thus, Lawrence wrongly suggests that the ACLU's defense of hatemongers' free speech rights "makes heroes out of bigots"; in actuality, experience demonstrates that it is the attempt to *suppress* racist speech that has this effect, not the attempt to *protect* such speech.[148]

There is a third reason why laws that proscribe racist speech could well undermine goals of reducing bigotry. As Lawrence recognizes, given the overriding importance of free speech in our society, any speech regulation must be narrowly drafted. Therefore, it can affect only the most blatant, crudest forms of racism. The more subtle, and hence potentially more invidious, racist expressions will survive. Virtually all would agree that no law could possibly eliminate all racist speech, let alone racism itself. If the marketplace of ideas cannot be trusted to winnow out the hateful, then there is no reason to believe that censorship will do so. The most it could possibly achieve would be to drive some racist thought and expression underground, where it would be more difficult to respond to such speech and the underlying attitudes it expresses. The British experience confirms this prediction.

The positive effect of racist speech—in terms of making society aware of and mobilizing its opposition to the evils of racism—are illustrated by the wave of campus racist incidents now under discussion. Ugly and abominable as these expressions are, they undoubtedly have had the beneficial result of raising public consciousness about the underlying societal problem of racism. If these expressions had been chilled by virtue of university sanctions, then it is doubtful that there would be such widespread discussion on campuses, let alone more generally, about the real problem of racism. Consequently, society would be less mobilized to attack this problem. Past experience confirms that the public airing of racist and other forms of hate speech catalyzes communal efforts to redress the bigotry that underlies such expression and to stave off any discriminatory conduct that might follow from it.[149]

Banning racist speech could well undermine the goal of combating racism for additional reasons. Some black scholars and activists maintain that an anti-racist speech policy may perpetuate a paternalistic view of minority groups, suggesting that they are incapable of defending themselves against biased expressions. Additionally, hate speech restrictions stultify the candid intergroup dialogue that is an essential precondition for reducing discrimination. Education, free discussion, and the airing of misunderstandings and failures of sensitivity are more likely to promote positive intergroup relations than are legal battles. The rules barring hate speech will continue to generate litigation and other forms of controversy that will exacerbate intergroup tensions. Moreover, hate speech rules could well fuel resentment against the minority group mem-

bers who are likely to be perceived as the proponents or intended beneficiaries of such rules. Finally, the censorship approach is diversionary.
It makes it easier for communities to avoid coming to grips with less
convenient and more expensive, but ultimately more meaningful, approaches for combating discrimination.

5. MEANS CONSISTENT WITH THE FIRST AMENDMENT
CAN PROMOTE RACIAL EQUALITY MORE EFFECTIVELY
THAN CAN CENSORSHIP

The Supreme Court recently reaffirmed the time-honored principle that
the appropriate response to speech conveying ideas that we reject or find
offensive is not to censor such speech, but rather to exercise our own
speech rights. In *Texas v. Johnson,*[150] the Court urged this counterspeech strategy upon the many Americans who are deeply offended by
the burning of their country's flag: "The way to preserve the flag's
special role is not to punish those who feel differently about these
matters. It is to persuade them that they are wrong."[151] In addition to
persuasion, the types of private expressive conduct that could be invoked
in response to racist speech include censure and boycotts.

In the context of countering racism on campus, the strategy of increasing speech—rather than decreasing it—not only would be consistent with First Amendment principles, but also would be more effective
in advancing equality goals. All government agencies and officers, including state university officials, should condemn slavery, de jure segregation, and other racist institutions and policies that the government
formerly supported. State university and other government officials also
should affirmatively endorse equality principles. Furthermore, these government representatives should condemn racist ideas expressed by private speakers.[152] In the same vein, private individuals and groups should
exercise their First Amendment rights by speaking out against racism.
Traditional civil libertarians have exercised their own speech rights in
this fashion and also have defended the First Amendment freedoms of
others who have done so.[153]

In addition to the preceding measures, which could be implemented
on a society-wide basis, other measures would be especially suited to
the academic setting. (The ACLU policy on campus hate speech urges
universities to take various suggested steps to counter racism and other

forms of discrimination, consistent with free speech and equality values. See Appendix.) First, universities should encourage members of their communities voluntarily to restrain the *form* (but not the *substance*) of their expression in light of the feelings and concerns of various minority groups. Universities could facilitate voluntary self-restraint by providing training in communications, information about diverse cultural perspectives, and other education designed to promote intergroup understanding. Members of both minority and majority groups should be encouraged to be mutually respectful. Individuals who violate these norms of civility should not be subject to any disciplinary or mandatory action, but instead should be offered education, information, and advice on a voluntary basis. Of course, universities must vigilantly ensure that even voluntary limits on the *manner* of academic discourse do not chill its *content*.

In addition to the foregoing measures, universities also should create forums in which controversial race-related issues and ideas could be discussed in a candid but constructive way. Further, universities could encourage students to receive education in the history of racism and the civil rights movement in the United States and be exposed to the culture and traditions of racial and ethnic groups other than their own. Consistent with free speech tenets, these courses must allow all faculty and students to express their own views and must not degenerate into "reeducation camps."

The proposed measures for eliminating racism on campus are consistent not only with American constitutional norms of free speech and equality, but also with internationally recognized human rights. For example, the Universal Declaration of Human Rights provides, in Article 26(2), that individuals have a right to receive, and states have an obligation to provide, education which "promote[s] understanding, tolerance and friendship among all nations, racial or religious groups."

Many universities appear to be responding constructively to the recent upsurge in campus hate speech incidents by adopting some of the measures suggested here. This development demonstrates the positive impact of racist speech, in terms of galvanizing community efforts to counter the underlying attitudes it expresses.

It is particularly important to devise anti-racism strategies consistent with the First Amendment because racial and other minority groups ultimately have far more to lose than to gain through a weakened free speech guarantee. History has demonstrated that minorities have been among the chief beneficiaries of a vigorous free speech safeguard. In his 1994 book, *Hate Speech: The History of an American Controversy*, Samuel Walker shows that, throughout the twentieth century, the equality rights of African Americans and other minority groups were dependent on a robust free speech concept. He further shows that, realizing the importance of protecting even speech viewed as hateful or dangerous— because their own speech certainly was so viewed in many Southern and other communities—the major civil rights organizations consistently opposed efforts to restrict hate speech. As Walker concluded, "the 'lessons' of the civil rights movement were that the interests of racial minorities and powerless groups were best protected through the broadest, most content-neutral protection of speech." [154]

Lawrence offers two rebuttals to the proposition that blacks are (on balance) benefited rather than hurt by a strong free speech guarantee. First, he notes that "[t]he first amendment coexisted with slavery." [155] It is undeniable that, until the Union won the Civil War, not only the First Amendment, but also all of the Constitution's provisions guaranteeing liberty, coexisted with the total negation of liberty through the institution of slavery. It is also true, however, that the free speech guarantees of the federal Constitution and some state constitutions allowed abolitionists to advocate the end of slavery. Moreover, it must be recalled that until the 1930s, the First Amendment provided no protection whatsoever against speech or press restrictions enacted by state or local governments. Further, although the First Amendment from its adoption provided theoretical protection against actions by the national government, in practice it was not enforced judicially until the latter half of the twentieth century. Not until 1965 did the Supreme Court initially exercise its power to invalidate unconstitutional congressional statutes, which it had recognized 162 years earlier, in the First Amendment context. [156] Thus, under the Espionage Act of 1918 and similar state statutes, numerous individuals were punished for expressing unpopular political opinions. During World War I and its aftermath, the First Amendment did not prevent these laws from contributing to "the gravest period of political repression in American history." [157]

In short, although slavery coexisted with the theoretical guarantees enunciated in the First Amendment, slavery did not coexist with the judicially enforceable version of those guarantees that emerged only after World War I. We never can know how much more quickly and peacefully the anti-slavery forces might have prevailed if free speech and press, as well as other rights, had been judicially protected against violations by all levels of government earlier in our history. That robust freedoms of speech and press ultimately might have threatened slavery is suggested by southern states' passage of laws limiting these freedoms in an effort to undermine the abolitionist cause.

The second basis for Lawrence's lack of "faith in free speech as the most important vehicle for liberation"[158] is the notion that "equality [is] a precondition to free speech."[159] Lawrence maintains that racism devalues the ideas of non-whites and of anti-racism in the marketplace of ideas. Like the economic market, the ideological market sometimes works to improve society, but not always.[160] Odious ideas, such as the idea of black inferiority, will not necessarily be driven from the marketplace. Therefore, the marketplace rationale alone might not justify free speech for racist thoughts. But that rationale does not stand alone.

The civil libertarian and judicial defense of racist speech also is based on the knowledge that censors have stifled the voices of oppressed persons and groups far more often than those of their oppressors. Censorship traditionally has been the tool of people who seek to subordinate minorities, not those who seek to liberate them. As Harry Kalven has shown, the civil rights movement of the 1960s depended on free speech principles.[161] These principles allowed protestors to carry their messages to audiences who found such messages highly offensive and threatening to their most deeply cherished views of themselves and their way of life. Equating civil rights activists with Communists, subversives, and criminals, government officials mounted inquisitions against the NAACP, seeking compulsory disclosure of its membership lists and endangering the members' jobs and lives. Only strong principles of free speech and association could—and did—protect the drive for desegregation. Martin Luther King, Jr., wrote his historic letter from a Birmingham jail,[162] but the Birmingham parade ordinance that King and other demonstrators had violated eventually was declared an unconstitutional invasion of their free speech rights.[163] Moreover, the Civil Rights Act of 1964, which these demonstrators championed, did become law.

The more disruptive forms of protest, which Lawrence credits with having been more effective—such as marches, sit-ins, and kneel-ins—

were especially dependent on generous judicial constructions of the free speech guarantee.[164] Notably, many of these protective interpretations initially had been formulated in cases brought on behalf of anti-civil rights demonstrators. Similarly, the insulting and often racist language that more militant black activists hurled at police officers and other government officials also was protected under the same principles and precedents.[165]

The foregoing history does not prove conclusively that free speech is an essential precondition for equality, as some respected political philosophers have argued. But it does belie Lawrence's theory that equality is an essential precondition for free speech. Moreover, this history demonstrates the symbiotic interrelationship between free speech and equality, which parallels the relationship between civil liberties and civil rights more generally. Both sets of aims must be pursued simultaneously because the pursuit of each aids the realization of the other. The mutual interdependence of equality and liberty was forcefully described by Kenneth Karst:

[T]he constitutional values of equality and liberty are fundamentally linked by the notion that equal access to certain institutions and services is a prime component of any meaningful liberty. This link is reflected in the language of egalitarian movements. The civil rights movement of the 1960s, for example, marched under the banner of "Freedom" even though its chief objective was equal access—to the vote, to education, to housing, even to lunch counters. "Liberation" is today a theme of more than rhetorical significance in egalitarian causes such as the women's movement.[166]

CONCLUSION

Some traditional civil libertarians may agree with Lawrence that a university rule banning a narrowly defined class of assaultive, harassing racist expression might comport with First Amendment principles and make a symbolic contribution to the racial equality mandated by the Fourteenth Amendment. However, Lawrence and other members of the academic community who advocate such steps must recognize that educators have a special responsibility to avoid the danger posed by focusing on symbols that obscure the real underlying issues.

The recent exploitation of the American flag as a symbol of patriotism, to distort the true nature of that concept, serves as a sobering reminder of this risk. Joseph S. Murphy, chancellor of The City University of New York, recently offered lessons for educators from the flag-related controversies. His cautionary words apply even more powerfully to the campus hate speech controversy, since the general responsibility of academics to call for an honest and direct discourse about compelling societal problems is especially great within our own communities:

> As educators, we should be somewhat concerned [about the manipulation of such symbols as the flag for partisan political purposes]. At our best, we convey ideas in their full complexity, with ample appreciation of the ambiguity that attaches to most important concepts. We use symbols, but we do so to illuminate, not to obscure. . . . The real question is how we use our position in the university and in society to steer national discourse away from an obsessive fixation on the trivial representation of ideas, and toward a proper focus on the underlying conflicts that define our era.[167]

An exaggerated concern with racist speech creates a risk of elevating symbols over substance in two problematic respects. First, it may well divert our attention from the causes of racism to its symptoms. Second, a focus on the hateful message conveyed by particular speech could likely distort our view of fundamental neutral principles applicable to our system of free expression generally. We should not let the racist veneer in which expression is cloaked obscure our recognition of how important free expression is and of how effectively it has advanced racial equality.

Appendix
ACLU Policy Statement: Free Speech and Bias on College Campuses (adopted by the ACLU National Board of Directors, without dissent, on October 13, 1990)

PREAMBLE

The significant increase in reported incidents of racism and other forms of bias at colleges and universities is a matter of profound concern to the ACLU. Some have proposed that racism, sexism, homophobia and other such biases on campus must be addressed in whole or in part by restrictions on speech. The alternative to such restrictions, it is said, is to permit such bias to go unremedied and to subject the targets of such bias to a loss of equal educational opportunity. The ACLU rejects both these alternatives and reaffirms its traditional and unequivocal commitment both to free speech and to equal opportunity.

POLICY

1. Freedom of thought and expression are indispensable to the pursuit of knowledge and the dialogue and dispute that characterize meaningful education. All members of the academic community have the right to hold and to express views that others may find repugnant, offensive, or emotionally distressing. The ACLU opposes all campus regulations which interfere with the freedom of professors, students and administrators to teach, learn, discuss and debate or to express ideas, opinions or feelings in classroom, public or private discourse.

2. The ACLU has opposed and will continue to oppose and challenge disciplinary codes that reach beyond permissible boundaries into the realm of protected speech, even when those codes are directed at the problem of bias on campus.

3. This policy does not prohibit colleges and universities from enacting disciplinary codes aimed at restricting acts of harassment, intimidation and invasion of privacy. Although "harassment," "intimidation," and "invasion of privacy" are imprecise terms susceptible of impermissibly overbroad application, each term defines a type of conduct which is legally proscribed in many jurisdictions when directed at a specific individual or individuals and when intended to frighten, coerce, or unreasonably harry or intrude upon its target. Threatening telephone calls to a minority student's dormitory room, for example, would be proscribable conduct under the terms of this policy. Expressive behavior which has no other effect than to create an unpleasant learning environment, however, would not be the proper subject of regulation. The fact that words may be used in connection with otherwise actionable conduct does not immunize such conduct from appropriate regulation. For example, intimidating phone calls, threats of attack, extortion and blackmail are unprotected forms of conduct which include an element of verbal or written expression. As always, however, great care must be taken to avoid applying such provisions [that proscribe harassment and similar conduct] overbroadly to protected expression. The ACLU will continue to review such college codes and their application in specific situations

on a case-by-case basis. . . . In determining whether a university disciplinary code impermissibly restricts protected speech, there must be a searching analysis both of the language of the code and the manner in which it is applied. Many factors, which are heavily fact-oriented, must be considered, including time, place, pattern of conduct and, where relevant, the existence of an authority relationship between speaker and target.

4. All students have the right to participate fully in the educational process on a nondiscriminatory basis. Colleges and universities have an affirmative obligation to combat racism, sexism, homophobia, and other forms of bias, and a responsibility to provide equal opportunities through education. To address these responsibilities and obligations, the ACLU advocates the following actions by colleges and universities:

(a) to utilize every opportunity to communicate through its administrators, faculty, and students its commitment to the elimination of all forms of bigotry on campus;

(b) to develop comprehensive plans aimed at reducing prejudice, responding promptly to incidents of bigotry and discriminatory harassment, and protecting students from any such further incidents;

(c) to pursue vigorously efforts to attract enough minorities, women and members of other historically disadvantaged groups as students, faculty members and administrators to alleviate isolation and to ensure real integration and diversity in academic life;

(d) to offer and consider whether to require all students to take courses in the history and meaning of prejudice, including racism, sexism, and other forms of invidious discrimination (see ACLU Policy #60, which states: "In the classroom, a teacher should promote an atmosphere of free inquiry. This should include discussion of controversial issues without the assumption that they are settled in advance or that there is only one 'right' answer in matters of dispute. Such discussion should include presentation of divergent opinions and doctrines, past and present, on a given subject.");

(e) to establish new-student orientation programs and continuing counseling programs that enable students of different races, sexes, religions, and sexual orientations to learn to live with each other outside the classroom;

(f) to review and, where appropriate, revise course offerings as well as extracurricular programs in order to recognize the contributions of those whose art, music, literature and learning have been insufficiently reflected in the curriculum of many American colleges and universities;

(g) to address the question of de facto segregation in dormitories and other university facilities; and

(h) to take such other steps as are consistent with the goal of ensuring that all students have an equal opportunity to do their best work and to participate fully in campus life.

Notes

The title of this chapter is drawn from Jonathan Swift's essay "A Modest Proposal for preventing the Children of poor People from being a Burden to their Parents or the Country, and for Making them Beneficial to the Public" (Dublin 1729), in *Jonathan Swift*, 492 (A. Ross and D. Woolley, eds., 1984). This chapter not only responds to the specific points made in Lawrence, "If He Hollers Let Him Go: Regulating Racist Speech on Campus," 1990 *Duke L.J.* 431, reprinted in Mari Matsuda et al., *Words that Wound*, 1993 (hereafter Lawrence), but also addresses the general issues raised by the many other recent proposals to regulate racist and other forms of hate speech on campus. Strossen's and Lawrence's pieces are expanded versions of oral presentations they made at the Biennial Conference of the American Civil Liberties Union in Madison, Wisconsin, on June 16, 1989.

I thank Charles Baron, Jean Bond, Ava Chamberlain, Elsa Cole, Donald Downs, Eunice Edgar, Stephen France, Mary Ellen Gale, Ira Glasser, David Goldberger, Thomas Grey, Gerald Gunther, Nat Hentoff, Mary Heston, Martin Margulies, Mari Matsuda, Michael Meyers, Gretchen Miller, Colleen O'Connor, Taggarty Patrick, john powell, John Roberts, Alan M. Schwartz, Judge Harvey Schwartz, Robert Sedler, Norman Siegel, Peter Siegel, William Van Alstyne, and Jane Whicher for information and insights they shared regarding the subject of this chapter. For comments on earlier versions of the chapter, I thank Ralph Brown, Edward Chen, Norman Dorsen, Bernie Dushman, Stanley Engelstein, Eric Goldstein, Martin Goldstein, Franklyn Haiman, Morton Halperin, Alon Harel, Leanne Katz, Martin Margulies, Maimon Schwarzschild, and Samuel Walker. For their research assistance, special thanks go to Jennifer Colyer, Thomas Hilbink, and Marie Newman, who provided the most help. For additional research assistance, I thank Marie Costello, Jayni Edelstein, William Mills, Ramyar Moghadassi, Tony Ross, and Julia Swanson.

1. There is no single "civil libertarian" or ACLU position on many of the issues discussed in this article. For example, both Lawrence and Strossen are avowed civil libertarians and ACLU supporters, although they disagree on certain civil liberties issues.

On October 13, 1990, the ACLU's National Board of Directors adopted a policy opposing campus disciplinary codes against hate speech. For the text of this policy, which was adopted without dissent, see the Appendix.

In addition to the national organization, the ACLU includes fifty-one statewide or regional "affiliates," all of which may adopt their own policies. Although an affiliate's policies must be "in accordance" with those of the national organization, this requirement is designed "to obtain general unity, rather than absolute uniformity." See *Policy Guide of the American Civil Liberties Union,* at Policy No. 501 (rev. ed. 1990) (hereafter *ACLU Policy Guide*). Accordingly, some ACLU affiliates may adopt policies concerning the regulation of campus hate speech that are to some extent divergent from each other, and from the national ACLU policy.

To reflect the fact that civil libertarians may differ about some specific issues discussed in this chapter, the term "traditional civil libertarian" is used only to describe the general view that much hate speech is entitled to First Amendment protection. All other, more specific, views expressed in this article reflect the author's opinions.

2. Dambrot v. Central Michigan University, 839 F.Supp. 477 (E.D. Mich. 1993); UWM Post, Inc. v. Board of Regents of the University of Wisconsin System, 774 F.Supp. 1163 (E.D. Wis. 1991); Doe v. University of Michigan, 721 F.Supp. 852 (E.D. Mich. 1989). Likewise, in a fourth legal challenge to another campus hate speech code, the university agreed to rewrite its code to bring it into conformity with the First Amendment. Wu v. University of Connecticut, No. Civ. H-89–649 PCD (D. Conn. 1990). The ACLU represented the parties that successfully challenged the hate speech codes in all these cases except *Dambrot*.

3. R.A.V. v. City of St. Paul, 112 S.Ct. 2538 (1992).

4. See Lawrence at 481.

5. In Lawrence's composite view, traditional civil libertarians display the following "typical" propensities. They argue that all speech should be absolutely protected (see Lawrence at 436, 438, 449, 457, 461, 473–74, 476–77), at least if it "stops short of physical violence" (*id.* at 449). They maintain that no face-to-face insults or fighting words are protected free speech, unless they are racial in nature (see *id.* at 436–37, 476). They might support "less protection" for captive audiences "when they are held captive by racist speakers" (*id.* at 438). They do not acknowledge that racist speech inflicts real harm (see *id.* at 448, 457, 458, 478). They are more committed to the values reflected in the Constitution's free speech clause than to those reflected in its equal protection clause (see *id.* at 448, 461, 477–78). They do not support, and indeed "often" oppose, "group expressions of condem-

nation" of racist speech (see *id.* at 477). They "typically . . . elect[ ] to stand by" while universities draft constitutionally vulnerable hate speech regulations (see *id.* at 477). They "wait [to] attack [such] poorly drafted and obviously overbroad regulations" (*id.* at 478 n.162).

The foregoing stereotypes are presented through unsupported assertions and are belied by the facts recited throughout this chapter. Lawrence also makes incorrect and misleading statements specifically about the ACLU and its members, which are also countered throughout this chapter. See *id.* at 473, 478 & nn.163–64.

Lawrence qualifies his depiction of the "traditional" civil libertarian or ACLU member in one important respect: he repeatedly suggests that civil libertarians and ACLU members who are members of minority groups (or perhaps women) differ from others in their positions on free speech and equal protection issues. See *id.* at 466 (distinguishing "[m]ost blacks" from "many white civil libertarians"); see also *id.* at 458–59, 461 & n.113, 473–74, 477–78 & nn.163–64.

Such racial (and gender) stereotyping is both factually inaccurate and antithetical to equality principles. The inaccuracy is illustrated by the fact that the ACLU's policy concerning free speech and equality on campus (see Appendix) was adopted unanimously, without dissent from any of the many National Board members who are African American, members of other minority groups, or female.

6. See Lawrence, at 450 & n.82, 481, citing Stanford University, "Fundamental Stanford Interpretation: Free Expression and Discriminatory Harassment" (June 1990). At various points in his article, Lawrence endorses regulations of broader scope. However, he stresses his proposed variation of the Stanford code, which would apply to "all common areas" and would "not . . . protect[ ] persons . . . vilified on the basis of their membership in dominant majority groups." Lawrence at 450 n.82. Therefore, throughout the remainder of this chapter, references to the regulation endorsed by Professor Lawrence refer to this formulation, unless expressly indicated otherwise.

7. See Lawrence at 438–49.

8. See *id.* at 449.

9. *Id.* at 436 n.27.

10. Thomas Grey, who drafted the Stanford code, said "his rule probably wouldn't apply to one of the most publicized racial incidents at Stanford, when a white student left on a black student's door a poster of Beethoven drawn as a black caricature." Gottlieb, "Banning Bigoted Speech: Stanford Weighs Rules," *San Jose Mercury-News,* Jan. 7, 1990, at 3, col. 1. The broader variation of the Stanford code that Lawrence endorsed (see Lawrence at 450 n.82) apparently would have applied to this Stanford incident (see *id.* at 456 n.101), but not to the incident endured by his sister or to his boyhood ordeal.

11. Lawrence at 480.
12. I owe this formulation to Ira Glasser, executive director of the ACLU (and a non-lawyer).
13. *Id.* at 449. See also *id.* at 438, 457, 461, 473–74, 476–77.
14. See T. Emerson, *The System of Free Expression,* 337–38 (1970) (" '[F]ighting words' can be considered the equivalent of knocking a chip off the shoulder—the traditional symbolic act that puts the parties in the role of physical combatants."); L. Tribe, *American Constitutional Law,* § 12–10, at 852–53 (2d ed., 1988) ("[I]t is not difficult to recognize the genuine dilemma that law enforcement officers may confront when violence is incipient; although free speech would be suppressed, silencing the speaker is certainly preferable to a blood bath").
15. See, e.g., F. Haiman, *Speech and Law in a Free Society* (1981). Haiman states:

> [I]t is my contention that in *all* of the circumstances in which antagonistic crowds or individuals respond or threaten to respond violently to communicators, the *audience* should be held responsible for its behavior, and not the speaker. . . . [V]iolent *reaction,* by definition, is born in the psyche of the respondent. The idea to attack the communicator is not implanted or urged by the speaker, as might an idea to commit illegal acts be initiated and advocated by one who incites a supportive audience. . . .
>
> . . . [I]f hostile audiences are not held responsible for their own behavior . . . they will soon learn that they have the power to exercise a "heckler's veto" over the speech of their antagonists.

> *Id.* at 258; see also *id.* at 20–23, 132–35, 253–54, 256–58.
16. For example, the Stanford code applies only to intentionally insulting words "addressed directly" to an individual or small number of individuals. In contrast, the University of Michigan rule, which was held to violate the First Amendment, did not require either that the penalized words be intentionally insulting or that they be addressed to specific individuals. Moreover, the Michigan rule originally proscribed speech that "[c]reates an intimidating, hostile, or demeaning environment." The same overbroad, vague language was contained in the University of Wisconsin rule, which was also held unconstitutional.
17. The reference is to an American neo-Nazi group's efforts, in 1977–78, to gain permission to demonstrate peacefully in Skokie, Illinois, a community with a large Jewish population, including many Holocaust survivors. For the judicial opinions rejecting arguments that Skokie residents should be protected from such personally odious expressions, see Collin v. Smith, 578 F.2d 1197, 1205–7 (7th Cir.), *cert. denied,* 439 U.S. 916 (1978); Village of Skokie v. National Socialist Party, 69 Ill. 2d 605, 612–18, 373 N.E. 2d 21, 23–25 (1978). For an excellent account of both the specific Skokie controversy and the general issues it raised, see A. Neier, *Defending My Enemy: American Nazis, the Skokie Case, and the Risks of Freedom* (1979).
18. I use the term "minorities" to encompass groups differentiated by various

characteristics, including race, ethnicity, religion, sexual orientation, and physical disability. I recognize, however, that the term "minorities" may "impl[y] a certain delegitimacy in a majoritarian system" and in fact describes groups that in the aggregate are a majority. Williams, "Alchemical Notes: Reconstructing Ideals from Deconstructed Rights," 22 *Harv. C.R.-C.L. L. Rev.* 401, 404 n.4 (1987).

19. See C. Lawrence, "Presentation at ACLU Biennial Conference," at 7.

20. Dorsen, "Is There a Right to Stop Offensive Speech? The Case of the Nazis in Skokie," in *Civil Liberties in Conflict*, 133–34 (L. Gostin, ed., 1988).

21. Regarding speech that is an essential element of unlawful conduct, the *ACLU Policy Guide*, at Policy No. 16, states that "[T]here is . . . [a] need for the regulation of selling practices to minimize fraud, deception, and misinterpretation. . . . If the sale or transaction is one that can be validly regulated or prohibited, then communications that are an integral part of such a sale or transaction can be regulated."

Regarding speech that can cause an immediate injury by its very utterance, see *ACLU Policy Guide*, at Policy No. 6 (accepting limitations on expression that creates "clear and present danger" of immediate unlawful action); *id.* at Policy No. 37 (recognizing that, under strictly limited circumstances, certain lawsuits may be brought for libel and invasion of privacy through speech without violating First Amendment).

Regarding captive audiences, the *ACLU Policy Guide*, at Policy No. 43, states:

[T]he First Amendment is not inconsistent with reasonable regulations designed to restrict sensory intrusions so intense as to be assaultive. Reasonable regulations are those that apply only to time, place and manner without regard to content. . . . What constitutes a "reasonable" regulation will necessarily vary depending upon such factors as (1) the size of the . . . area involved, (2) the duration [or] frequency with which an individual is in the area . . . , or (3) the extent to which alternatives exist so that the individual can reasonably be called upon to avoid the area. . . . Assaultive sensory intrusions are those that are objectionable to the average person because of an excessive degree of intensity, e.g., volume or brightness, and which cannot be avoided.

In larger public spaces . . . all communication is permitted unless it interferes with the primary purpose of the space. . . .

In open public areas . . . people are able to move away from communication which they consider offensive. So long as there is ample public space[ ] where communication is unrestricted, the government may creat [sic] and maintain reasonably limited sanctuaries in public places where people can go for quiet contemplation.

22. L. Tribe, § 12–19, at 949–50 n.24. For an argument that the captive audience concept should be construed narrowly, see Haiman, "Speech v. Privacy: Is There a Right Not to Be Spoken To?," 67 *Nw. U.L. Rev.* 153, 184 (1972). Haiman argues:

[H]uman beings have a significant ability mentally to reject many assaultive stimuli. The process known as "selective perception" enables us to generally choose what we wish to assimilate from the multitude of sensory bombardments surrounding us. . . . [W]e also have a strong tendency to screen out or distort messages that are inconsistent with . . . our current beliefs.

Given these tendencies . . . one might argue that the possibilities of unwelcome messages penetrating the psychological armor of unwilling audiences are so small that we ought to be worrying more about how to help unpopular communicators get through to reluctant listeners than how to give further protection from speech to those who already know too well how to isolate themselves from alien ideas.

23. Rowan v. United States Post Office Dep't, 397 U.S. 728, 738 (1970).
24. See, e.g., Erznoznik v. Jacksonville, 422 U.S. 205, 210 (1975); Cohen v. California, 403 U.S. 15, 21 (1971).
25. *Cohen,* 403 U.S. at 21.
26. See, e.g., *Rowan,* 397 U.S. at 737; Kovacs v. Cooper, 336 U.S. 77, 87 (1949).
27. See Consolidated Edison Co. v. Public Serv. Comm'n, 447 U.S. 530, 542 (1980).
28. See, e.g., Keyishian v. Board of Regents, 385 U.S. 589, 603 (1967); Shelton v. Tucker, 364 U.S. 479, 487 (1960); Sweeney v. New Hampshire, 354 U.S. 234, 250 (1957).
29. Cornelius v. NAACP Legal Defense and Educ. Fund, 473 U.S. 788, 803 (1985).
30. Organization for a Better Austin v. Keefe, 402 U.S. 415, 420 (1971); see also Frisby v. Schultz, 487 U.S. 474, 485 (1988).
31. See Board of Trustees v. Fox, 492 U.S. 469 (1989). The district court in the same case had characterized these dormitories as "limited public forums." Fox v. Board of Trustees, 649 F.Supp. 1393, 1401 (N.D.N.Y. 1986).
32. Keyishian v. Board of Regents, 385 U.S. 589, 603 (1967).
33. See Schmidt, "Freedom of Thought: A Principle in Peril?," *Yale Alumni Mag.,* Oct. 1989, at 66 ("On some other campuses in this country, values of civility and community have been offered by some as paramount values of the university, even to the point of superseding freedom of expression. Such a view is wrong in principle, and, if extended, disastrous to freedom of thought").
34. Joseph Grano stated:

One of the harms posited in the University of Michigan case was that some students found the speech at issue so upsetting that they had difficulty concentrating on their studies. The same harm could be posited, of course, in many other circumstances. During the Vietnam War, for example, the frequent and often caustic antiwar protests, which sometimes even expressed support for those whom the United States was fighting, may have extremely upset students who had served in the battle, who had lost family members or friends in the war, or who simply believed that an unwavering loyalty was owed to their country. Similarly, many students, especially on segregated campuses in the South, may have been deeply disturbed by the civil rights protests gripping the nation and many universities during the Sixties.

Grano, "Free Speech v. the University of Michigan," *Academic Questions,* Spring 1990, at 17.

35. See, e.g., Contreras v. Crown Zellerbach Corp., 88 Wash. 2d 735, 741, 565 P.2d 1173, 1176 (1977).
The ACLU's policy endorsing restrictions on a limited category of verbal sexual harassment on campus is confined to situations that involve "the abuse of power."

36. See First Nat'l Bank v. Bellotti, 435 U.S. 765, 785 (1978); Madison Joint School Dist. No. 8 v. Wisconsin Employment Relations Comm'n, 429 U.S. 167, 175–76 (1976).

37. See Lehman v. City of Shaker Heights, 418 U.S. 298, 305 (1974); American Booksellers Ass'n v. Hudnut, 771 F.2d 323, 333 (7th Cir. 1985), *aff'd,* 475 U.S. 1001 (1986).

38. Lawrence at 450 n.82.

39. See Hentoff, "Stanford and the Speech Police," *Washington Post,* July 21, 1990, at A19, col. 1. Hentoff stated:

> During a debate in the Faculty Senate, Professor Michael Bratman offered a hypothetical: in angry exchange with a white student, a black student calls him a "honky SOB." I assume, said Bratman, that language would be prohibited.
> "No," said Professor [Robert] Rabin [a law professor who chairs the Student Conduct Legislative Council, which propounded the code]. The proposed speech standard takes the position, Rabin explained, that the white majority as a whole is not in as much need of protection from discriminatory harassing speech as are those who have suffered discrimination.
> "Calling a white a 'honky,'" Rabin said, "is not the same as calling a black a 'nigger.'"

40. The University of Michigan based its rule on yet another approach, which focused on stigmatization and victimization of students, interference with academic efforts, and the creation of an intimidating or hostile educational environment. In Doe v. University of Mich., 721 F.Supp. 852 (E.D. Mich. 1989), this rule was held to violate the First Amendment.

41. 120 L. Ed. 2d 305 (1992).

42. *Id.* at 323.

43. 315 U.S. 568 (1942).

44. 405 U.S. 518, 523 (1972) (where appellant had said to police officers, "White son of a bitch, I'll kill you," "You son of a bitch, I'll choke you to death," and "You son of a bitch, if you ever put your hands on me again, I'll cut you all in pieces," Court reversed conviction under law that it found overbroad in light of *Chaplinsky*).

45. See, e.g., Karlan v. City of Cincinnati, 416 U.S. 924 (1974); Rosen v. California, 416 U.S. 924 (1974); Kelly v. Ohio, 416 U.S. 923 (1974); Lucas

v. Arkansas, 416 U.S. 919 (1974); Brown v. Oklahoma, 408 U.S. 914 (1972); Lewis v. New Orleans, 408 U.S. 913 (1972); Rosenfeld v. New Jersey, 408 U.S. 901 (1972).

46. See, e.g., Eaton v. City of Tulsa, 415 U.S. 697, 699 (1974) (per curiam); Hess v. Indiana, 414 U.S. 104, 109 (1973) (per curiam).

47. Compare Cafeteria Employees Local 302 v. Angelos, 320 U.S. 293, 295 (1943) (use of word "fascist" is "part of the conventional give-and-take in our economic and political controversies" and hence protected under federal labor law) with *Chaplinsky*, 315 U.S. at 573–74 (conviction affirmed on ground that words "God damned racketeer" and "damned Fascist," when addressed to police officer, were likely to provoke violent response).

48. See, e.g., Gard, "Fighting Words as Free Speech," 58 *Wash. U. L.Q.* 531, 536 (1980) (hereafter Gard) (post-*Chaplinsky* Supreme Court decisions have rendered fighting words doctrine "nothing more than a quaint remnant of an earlier morality that has no place in a democratic society dedicated to the principle of free expression"); Shea, " 'Don't Bother to Smile When You Call Me That'—Fighting Words and the First Amendment," 63 *Ky. L.J.* 1, 1–2 (1975) ("majority of the U.S. Supreme Court has gradually concluded that fighting words, no matter how narrowly defined, are a protected form of speech").

49. See Gard at 580.

50. H. Kalven, *The Negro and the First Amendment*, 14–15 (1965).

51. Z. Chafee, *Free Speech in the United States*, 151–52 (1941), at 151.

52. See, e.g., Gregory v. City of Chicago, 394 U.S. 111 (1969); Cox v. Louisiana, 379 U.S. 536, 550 (1965); Terminiello v. Chicago, 337 U.S. 1 (1949).

53. Gard at 580.

54. *Id.* at 548. *Accord id.* at 568. Compare Lawrence, at 437 n.29 ("[T]here is no evidence that the continued usage of [the fighting words doctrine] has led down the slippery slope to rampant censorship").

55. See, e.g., Lewis v. City of New Orleans, 415 U.S. 130 (1974) (state court upheld conviction on basis of fighting words doctrine in situation in which police officer said to young suspect's mother, "[g]et your black ass in the goddamned car," and she responded, "you god damn mother fucking police—I am going to [the Superintendent of Police] about this"); Street v. New York, 394 U.S. 576 (1969) (black man who protested against shooting of civil rights leader James Meredith by burning the American flag and saying, "If they let that happen to Meredith we don't need an American flag," was convicted under statute that criminalized words casting contempt on United States flag; Supreme Court rejected contention that conviction could be justified on fighting words rationale, *id.* at 592); Edwards v. South Carolina, 372 U.S. 229, 236 (1963) (state court upheld convictions of civil rights demonstrators for holding placards stating "I am proud to be a Negro" and "Down with Segregation"; Supreme Court rejected contention that convictions could be justified on fighting words doctrine); Waller v. City of St. Petersburg, 245 So. 2d 685 (Fla. Dist. Ct. App. 1971), *rev'd*, City

of St. Petersburg v. Waller, 261 So. 2d 151 (Fla. 1972) (black man was convicted after shouting "pig" at passing police car, and state supreme court upheld conviction based on fighting words doctrine).

56. Lawrence at 453 n.92.
57. See Gard at 22.
58. Gard at 564.
59. Lawrence recognizes the potential danger that any speech-restricting precedent "would pose for the speech of all dissenters," and that such a danger "might . . . include general societal tolerance for the suppression of speech." Lawrence at 458 & n.106.
60. Gard at 578 (emphasis added).
61. 485 U.S. 46 (1988).
62. *Falwell,* 485 U.S. at 55.
63. It is particularly noteworthy that David Riesman, who published an influential series of articles advocating group defamation laws in 1942, subsequently changed his position. See Riesman, "Democracy and Defamation: Fair Game and Fair Comment II," 42 *Colum. L. Rev.* 1282 (1942); Riesman, "Democracy and Defamation: Fair Game and Fair Comment I," 42 *Colum. L. Rev.* 1085 (1942); Riesman, "Democracy and Defamation: Control of Group Libel," 42 *Colum. L. Rev.* 727 (1942). But see S. Walker, *In Defense of American Liberties: A History of the ACLU,* at 330 n.23, 437 (1990).
64. 343 U.S. 250 (1952).
65. 376 U.S. 254 (1964).
66. 110 S.Ct. 2695 (1990).
67. The Illinois statute provided, in pertinent part: "It shall be unlawful . . . to . . . publish . . . in any public place . . . any . . . publication [which] . . . exposes citizens of any race, color, creed or religion to contempt, derision or obloquy." *Ill. Rev. Stat.,* chap. 38, para. 471 (1949). Although the Supreme Court held this law constitutional in 1952, the Illinois legislature repealed it in 1961.
68. Tanenhaus, "Group Libel," 35 *Cornell L.Q.* 261, 279–80 (1950).
69. See Amsterdam, "Perspectives on the Fourth Amendment," 58 *Minn. L. Rev.* 349, 435 (1974) ("The dangers of abuse of a particular power are, certainly, a pertinent consideration in determining whether the power should be allowed in the first instance").
70. See L. Tribe, § 12–10, at 856 (although the Constitution probably permits legislation punishing words that cause hurt by their mere utterance, such legislation "would be constitutionally problematic—the potential for content-specific regulation is always great").
71. See, e.g., West Virginia State Bd. of Educ. v. Barnette, 319 U.S. 624, 641 (1943); Boyd v. United States, 116 U.S. 616, 635 (1886).
72. Walter Dellinger tellingly made this point about another proposed exception to the First Amendment of an ostensibly limited nature—for physical desecration of the U.S. flag:

What would this proposed act of constitutional revision do to the moral legitimacy of the stance our Constitution has taken (and will continue to take) in defense of expression that offends many Americans as deeply as flag burning offends the great majority of us? . . . Once we have quickly passed the Twenty-seventh amendment to protect the sensibilities of those who revere the flag, what do we say to those who are particularly offended by, but must continue to tolerate, the burning of crosses by hooded members of the Ku Klux Klan, a brazen reminder of the era of lynching and terror? And what do we say to those who find themselves silenced and marginalized by sexualized (but not constitutionally "obscene") portrayals of women? What enduring Constitutional principle will remain unimpaired that will legitimately surmount these claims . . . ?

"Hearings on Measures to Protect the Physical Integrity of the American Flag, Before the Senate Committee on the Judiciary," 101st Cong., 1st sess. 553 (1989) (statement of Walter Dellinger).

73. United States v. Eichman, 496 U.S. 310, 318 (1990) (footnote omitted).
74. As a private institution, Stanford University is not directly bound by First Amendment standards. However, many private academic institutions make policy choices to adhere to standards that are consistent with their notions of academic freedom.
75. Gard at 563–64.
76. The Stanford code also may fail to satisfy the Court's strict parameters for the fighting words doctrine in other respects. First, it does not expressly require that the prohibited speech "must constitute a personally abusive epithet," the first criterion set forth in Gard's list. Based on his analysis of cases that address the fighting words doctrine, Gard concluded that "the utterance must constitute an extremely provocative personal insult" in order to comport with free speech principles. Gard, at 536.

Although the Stanford code may comply with the Court's second and third requirements, by prescribing that the prohibited speech must be "addressed directly to the individual or individuals whom it insults or stigmatizes," both of these elements have been construed so strictly that they may not be satisfied by this provision. Some judicial rulings indicate that the second requirement, the face-to-face element, "is not satisfied by mere technical physical presence, but contemplates an extremely close physical proximity." Gard, at 559. The third requirement has been interpreted to mean that "the offensive words must be descriptive of the *particular* person and addressed to that person." Gard, at 561 (emphasis added). The Stanford code does not require that the prohibited words describe the individual to whom they are addressed. Instead, under the Stanford code, the words may convey hatred for broad groups of people.
77. That regulation provided that, in certain "[e]ducational and academic centers," individuals were subject to discipline for:

Any behavior, verbal or physical, that stigmatizes or victimizes an individual on the basis of race, ethnicity, religion, sex, sexual orientation, creed, national origin, ancestry, age, marital status, handicap or Vietnam-era veteran status, and that . . .

[i]nvolves an express or implied threat to ... or has the purpose or reasonably foreseeable effect of interfering with an individual's academic efforts, employment, participation in University sponsored extra-curricular activities or personal safety. . . .

Doe v. University of Mich., 721 F.Supp. 852, 856 (E.D. Mich. 1989). As originally adopted and implemented, the regulation also sanctioned speech that "[c]reates an intimidating, hostile, or demeaning environment for educational pursuits, employment or participation in University sponsored extra-curricular activities." *Id.* After the regulation was legally challenged, however, the university announced that it was withdrawing that section on the ground that "a need exists for further explanation and clarification" of it. *Id.*

Lawrence contends that it is unfair to judge the Stanford code in light of the experience under the Michigan rule, arguing that the latter was "clearly overbroad," and asserting that "it is difficult to believe that anyone at the University of Michigan Law School was consulted in drafting" it. Lawrence, at 477 n.161 & 478 n.162.

It is ironic that, in this particular context, Lawrence seeks to focus the debate solely on the Stanford code. As previously observed, throughout his article he repeatedly defends alternative hate speech regulations that are not only broader than Stanford's but also broader than Michigan's. Moreover, his proffered rationales would justify sweeping prohibitions. Therefore, perhaps Lawrence should not be so quick to protest that the Michigan code was "obviously overbroad." Lawrence, at 478 n.162.

In any event, the University of Michigan did consult with law school faculty members, including Lee Bollinger and Theodore St. Antoine, as well as university counsel and other lawyers. The university also received comments from numerous other individuals and groups, including the ACLU, in its drafting process. See Letter from Henry W. Saad (counsel to university in *Doe* litigation) to Honorable Avern Cohn, at 2 (Aug. 17, 1989). Therefore, Lawrence's unsubstantiated assertion that the ACLU and "[t]raditional civil liberties lawyers typically have elected to stand by" while universities draft clearly unconstitutional rules (Lawrence at 477) is directly belied by the Michigan experience.

78. 721 F.Supp. 852 (E.D. Mich. 1989).

79. See *Doe*, 721 F.Supp. 865. The court cited the following examples of protected speech that had been subjected to the policy: a statement by a graduate student in the School of Social Work, in a research class, expressing his belief that homosexuality was a disease and that he intended to develop a counseling plan for changing gay clients to straight *(id.)*; the reading of an allegedly homophobic limerick, which ridiculed a well-known athlete for his presumed sexual orientation, by a student in the School of Business Administration during a class public-speaking exercise *(id.)*; and a statement by a student during an orientation session of a preclinical den-

tistry class, widely regarded as especially difficult, that he had heard that minorities had a hard time in the course and that they were not treated fairly (*id.* at 865–66).

80. Lawrence at 478 n.162.
81. UWM Post, Inc. v. Board of Regents of the University of Wisconsin System, 774 F.Supp. 1163, 1180 (E.D. Wis. 1991).
82. Gottlieb, "Banning Bigoted Speech: Stanford Weighs Rules," *San Jose Mercury-News,* Jan. 7, 1990, at 3, col. 1.
83. Other examples of legitimate academic discourse condemned as "hate speech" include the following: a group of students complained that a faculty member had created a hostile atmosphere by quoting racist comments originally made at the turn of the century, even though the professor said that was not his intention (see Statement of the Washtenaw County Branch, American Civil Liberties Union on the University of Michigan Policy, "Discrimination and Discriminatory Harassment by Students in the University Environment" 4, May 25, 1989); another group of students contended that the former students' complaint about the professor had itself created a hostile atmosphere (see *id.* at 5); a law student suggested that judicial decisions reflecting adverse stereotypes about blacks should not be studied in law school courses (see Shaw, "Caveat Emptor," *N.Y.L. Sch. Rep.,* Apr. 1989, at 3); a Jewish professor was penalized for suggesting to his black students that they should celebrate the anniversary of their ancestors' liberation from slavery under the Thirteenth Amendment, just as Jews celebrate their ancestors' liberation from slavery during Passover (see Hentoff, "Campus Court-Martial," *Washington Post,* Dec. 15, 1988, at A25, col. 2; students complained about a professor's statement that black students are not sufficiently critical of human rights violations by black African governments (see McKinley, "Minority Students Walk Out Over a Teacher's Remarks," *New York Times,* Oct. 4, 1989, at B3, col. 5).
84. Regarding the chilling effect of a University of Connecticut anti-hate speech rule, which the ACLU successfully challenged, see Brief of Amicus Curiae in Support of Plaintiff's Motion for Preliminary Injunction, at 9–10 and n.10, Wu v. University of Conn., No. Civ. H-89–649 PCD (D. Conn. Jan. 25, 1990) (submitted by ACLU). In its brief, the ACLU stated:

> [A] student could plausibly fear prosecution for voicing an opinion that members of the Unification Church . . . are "cultists"; that Zionists are "imperialists" or that Palestinians are "terrorists"; that evangelical ministers are "hustlers" and their followers are "dupes"; or that homosexuals are "sick." . . . [A] homosexual rights activist could perhaps be prosecuted for declaring that Catholics are "bigots" if they follow their Church's teaching that homosexuality is a sin. . . . Similarly, a black activist student leader might reasonably hesitate to characterize other black students, who are deemed insufficiently supportive of black causes, as "Uncle Toms."

85. As Justice Harlan observed in Cohen v. California, 403 U.S. 15, 26 (1971), "We cannot indulge in the facile assumption that one can forbid a particular

word without also running the substantial risk of suppressing ideas in the process."

86. Affidavit of John Doe in Support of Plaintiff's Motion for Preliminary Injunction at para. 14, Doe v. University of Mich., 721 F.Supp. 852 (E.D. Mich. 1989) (No. 89–71683).

87. Keyishian v. Board of Regents, 385 U.S. 589, 603 (1967). See also West Virginia State Bd. of Educ. v. Barnette, 319 U.S. 624, 642 (1943) ("If there is any fixed star in our constitutional constellation, it is that no official, high or petty, can prescribe what shall be orthodox in politics, nationalism, religion or other matters of opinion").

88. See Letter from William Cohen to George Parker, chair of the Student Conduct Legislative Council of Stanford University (March 10, 1989), reprinted in *Stanford Univ. Campus Rep.*, Mar. 15, 1989, at 18.

89. See Lawrence at 438–44.

90. Gitlow v. New York, 268 U.S. 652, 673 (1925) (Holmes, J., dissenting).

91. Abrams v. United States, 250 U.S. 616, 630 (1919) (Holmes, J., dissenting).

92. *Id.* at 630–31.

93. 395 U.S. 444 (1969) (per curiam).

94. *Id.* at 447.

95. L. Tribe, § 12–8, at 838 n.17.

96. In a widely quoted dissent, Justice Holmes championed this rationale for free speech as "the theory of our Constitution":

> [W]hen men have realized that time has upset many fighting faiths, they may come to believe even more than they believe the very foundations of their own conduct that the ultimate good desired is better reached by free trade in ideas—that the best test of truth is the power of the thought to get itself accepted in the competition of the market, and that truth is the only ground upon which their wishes safely can be carried out.

Abrams v. United States, 250 U.S. 616, 630 (1919) (Holmes, J., dissenting). See also Cohen v. California, 403 U.S. 15, 24 (1971); *New York Times Co. v. Sullivan*, 376 U.S. 254, 270 (1964).

97. See *Cohen*, 403 U.S. at 24 ("[N]o other approach [than protecting free speech] would comport with the premise of individual dignity and choice upon which our political system rests").

98. See L. Bollinger, *The Tolerant Society: Freedom of Speech and Extremist Speech in American Society* (1986).

99. R. Smolla, *Free Speech in an Open Society* (1992).

100. Terminiello v. Chicago, 337 U.S. 1 (1949) (ACLU appeared amicus curiae).

101. See Delgado, "Words That Wound: A Tort Action for Racial Insults, Epithets, and Name-Calling," 17 *Harv. C.R. -C.L. L. Rev.* 133, 179–80 (1982):

[A]n epithet such as "You damn nigger" would almost always be found actionable, as it is highly insulting and highly racial. . . . "Boy," directed at a young black male, might be actionable, depending on the speaker's intent, the hearer's understanding, and whether a reasonable person would consider it a racial insult in the particular context. "Hey, nigger," spoken affectionately between black persons and used as a greeting, would not be actionable. An insult such as "You dumb honkey," directed at a white person, could be actionable . . . but only in the unusual situations where the plaintiff would suffer harm from such an insult.

Id. See also UWM Post, Inc. v. Board of Regents of the University of Wisconsin System, 774 F.Supp. 1163, 1180 (E.D. Wis. 1991):

[T]he University of Wisconsin–Whitewater found that a white student had not violated the UW Rule where he called a black student "nigger" as part of a verbal exchange which led to a physical confrontation. . . . The University explained that there was no violation because: "[The white student] was raised in a racially mixed neighborhood in Chicago. It was common for both blacks and whites in this environment to refer to blacks who were not respected, liked or appreciated as 'nigger.' As [the white student] stated, 'it's like calling someone an ass or names like that.' [The black student] agreed and stated that this kind of language/name calling exists in his neighborhood as well. [He] also stated that he did not think [the] intent [of the white student] was to demean him personally or racially."

102. For example, during a discussion about the University of Wisconsin hate speech policy, even its advocates disagreed as to whether it would (or should) apply to the following hypothetical situation: A white student sits down next to a black student and says, "I want you to know that I'm a racist and hate the idea of blacks being here at the University," but does not use any racist epithet. Telephone interview with Eunice Edgar, executive director of ACLU of Wisconsin (Nov. 14, 1989).

103. See Lawrence at 460. It should be stressed, though, that this expression would not be encompassed by either the Stanford code or Professor Lawrence's variation on it.

104. See letter from Gerald Gunther to George Parker, chair of the Student Conduct Legislative Council, Stanford University (Mar. 10, 1989), reprinted in *Stanford Univ. Campus Rep.*, Mar. 15, 1989, at 17 (hereafter Gunther letter):

[L]est it be said that I unduly slight the pain imposed by expressions of racial or religious hatred let me add that I have suffered that pain. I empathize with others who have, and I rest my deep belief in the principles of the First Amendment in part on my own experiences.

I received my elementary education in a public school in a very small town in Nazi Germany. I was subjected to vehement anti-Semitic remarks, from my teacher, my classmates and others. "Judensau" (Jew pig) was far from the harshest.

105. See A. Neier at 2–3 (recounting his childhood as a Jew in Hitler's Germany, his narrow escape from the Nazi death camps, and the extermina-

tion of almost all his relatives, beyond his immediate family, during World War II).

106. Gunther stated:

> My own experiences have certainly not led me to be insensitive to the myriad pains offensive speech can and often does impose. But the lesson I have drawn from my childhood in Nazi Germany and my happier adult life in this country is the need to walk the sometimes difficult path of denouncing the bigots' hateful ideas with all my power yet at the same time challenging any community's attempt to suppress hateful ideas by force of law.

Gunther letter.

107. Aryeh Neier, reflecting on his role in the Skokie incident, recalled:

> The most frequently repeated line of all in the many letters about Skokie that I received was: "How can you, a Jew, defend freedom for Nazis?" . . . The response I made . . . most often began with a question: "How can I, a Jew, refuse to defend freedom, even for Nazis? . . ." Because we Jews are uniquely vulnerable, I believe we can win only brief respite from persecution in a society in which encounters are settled by power. As a Jew, therefore . . . I want restraints placed on power . . . I want restraints which prohibit those in power from interfering with my right to speak, my right to publish, or my right to gather with others who also feel threatened. . . . To defend myself, I must restrain power with freedom, even if the temporary beneficiaries are the enemies of freedom.

A. Neier at 4–5.

108. Lawrence at 456.

109. 347 U.S. 483 (1954).

110. 461 U.S. 574 (1983).

111. See Lawrence at 438–49.

112. 391 U.S. 367 (1968).

113. United States v. Eichman, 496 U.S. 310 (1990); Texas v. Johnson, 491 U.S. 397 (1989).

114. One can imagine situations in which racially segregated schools would not convey the message of white supremacy, which Lawrence views as the central meaning of school segregation. See Lawrence at 441, 462–64. Yet, under *Brown,* such schools surely would still violate the equal protection clause. For example, a black student who had been raised in a different culture marked by black supremacy, and then moved to the U.S. and attended a racially segregated school, might well interpret school segregation as conveying the message of white inferiority. Would *Brown* not demand that this student should nonetheless attend a desegregated school? As another example, a community might come to view racial diversity much the way it now regards religious diversity, so that the choice to attend a racially segregated school would be viewed as conveying no more stigmatizing a message than the choice to attend a religiously segregated school. Would *Brown* not insist, nevertheless, that no public schools could

be racially segregated, even if the option of attending them was completely voluntary? See Green v. County School Bd., 391 U.S. 430 (1968) (rejected "freedom-of-choice" plan for desegregation).

115. Norwood v. Harrison, 413 U.S. 455, 471 (1973).
116. Board of Educ. v. Allen, 392 U.S. 236, 248 (1968).
117. See, e.g., Wallace v. Jaffree, 472 U.S. 38, 70 (1985).
118. 496 U.S. 226 (1990).
119. *Id.* at 250 (emphasis added).
120. Bob Jones Univ. v. United States, 461 U.S. 574 (1983).
121. Lawrence at 448.
122. 377 U.S. 218, 233 (1964).
123. Equally unpersuasive is Lawrence's attempted reliance on cases upholding prohibitions upon race- or gender-designated advertisements for employees, home sales, and rentals (see Lawrence at 449 & n.81, 464 n.123). As the Supreme Court ruled, in Pittsburgh Press Co. v. Human Relations Comm'n, 413 U.S. 376, 391 (1973), such advertisements constituted integral elements of the prohibited discriminatory conduct—e.g., refusing to hire women. *Id.* at 388–89. Therefore, these advertisements fit within the general category of speech that may be regulated on the ground that it constitutes an essential element of an unlawful act.
124. Lawrence at 452 n.87.
125. 337 U.S. 1 (1949).
126. 403 U.S. 15 (1971).
127. Winters v. New York, 333 U.S. 507, 510 (1948).
128. *Terminiello,* 337 U.S. at 4–5 (citations omitted).
129. It is noteworthy that these two ringing endorsements of constitutional protection for offensive, provocative speech were written by justices at opposite ends of the Court's ideological spectrum. The agreement on this issue between Justice Douglas, a noted liberal, and Justice Harlan, a respected conservative, indicates that their views represent a solidly entrenched consensus about free speech tenets.
130. *Cohen,* 403 U.S. at 26 (emphasis added).
131. Rutzick, "Offensive Language and the Evolution of First Amendment Protection," 9 *Harv. C.R.-C.L. L. Rev.* 1, 18 (1974).
132. Lawrence at 463 n.119.
133. Lawrence at 480.
134. C. Lawrence, Presentation at ACLU Biennial Conference, Madison, Wisconsin, June 16, 1989, at 30.
135. A. Neier at 170–71.
136. Lawrence at 480 n.166.
137. The three affiliates that have challenged university hate speech rules are located in Connecticut, Michigan, and Wisconsin. All three are engaged in ongoing efforts to counter race discrimination, of which I will describe a few examples. In a pathbreaking case under the Connecticut Constitution,

the Connecticut ACLU (along with the NAACP Legal Defense Fund) is challenging the de facto maintenance of two separate and unequal public school systems in the Hartford area: one for low-income, minority students in Hartford and one for more affluent, white students in Hartford's suburbs. The Connecticut affiliate also successfully challenged racial discrimination in the hiring and promotion of minorities within the state police department, and has taken various initiatives to counter police brutality against minority citizens. The Michigan ACLU, along with the NAACP, is challenging the 1992 legislative reapportionment scheme for the Michigan House and Senate as unconstitutionally diluting minority votes. The Wisconsin ACLU is co-counsel in a challenge to the practice of "red-lining" homeowners insurance in the Milwaukee area (to exclude coverage for areas with large minority populations), which resulted in the first appellate court ruling that this practice violates the current Federal Fair Housing Act. The Wisconsin affiliate also has fought against various discriminatory measures aimed at Chippewa Indians and Hmong immigrants.

138. See Lasson, "Racism in Great Britain: Drawing the Line on Free Speech," 7 *B.C. Third World L.J.* 161, 166, 171–73 (1987) (Democratic National Party chairman Kingsley Read was tried under Race Relations Act in 1978 for referring in a public speech to "niggers, wogs, and coons," and for commenting on an Asian who had been killed in a race riot, "One down, a million to go." The judge instructed the jury that Read's words were not in themselves unlawful, and the jury acquitted Read).

139. See, e.g., Raines, "London Police Faulted as Racial Attacks Soar," *New York Times*, Mar. 24, 1988, at A1, col. 1.

140. See Stein, "History against Free Speech: The New German Law against the 'Auschwitz'—and Other—'Lies,' " 85 *Mich. L. Rev.* 277 (1986). Stein argues that although there was an article in the German Criminal Code in 1871 that punished offenses against personal honor, "[T]he German Supreme Court . . . consistently refused to apply this article to insults against Jews as a group—although it gave the benefit of its protection to such groups as 'Germans living in Prussian provinces, large landowners, all Christian clerics, German officers, and Prussian troops who fought in Belgium and Northern France.' " *Id.* at 286 (footnotes omitted).

141. Sandra Coliver, "Hate Speech Laws: Do They Work?" in *Striking a Balance: Hate Speech, Freedom of Expression and Non-Discrimination*, 373– 74 (Sandra Coliver, ed., 1992); see also Kevin Boyle, "Overview of a Dilemma: Censorship Versus Racism," in *Striking a Balance*, 3 ("The South African laws against racial hatred were used systematically against the victims of its racist policies. In Eastern Europe and the former Soviet Union laws against defamation and insult were vehicles for the persecution of critics who were often also victims of state-tolerated or sponsored anti-Semitism").

142. See Plaintiff's Exhibit Submitted in Support of Motion for Preliminary

Injunction at 1, Doe v. University of Mich., 721 F.Supp. 852 (E.D. Mich. 1989) (No. 89–CV-71683–DT) (black student used term "white trash" in conversation with white student); *id.* at 5 (at beginning of preclinical dentistry course, recognized as difficult, faculty member led small group discussion, designed to "identify concerns of students"; dental student said that he had heard, from his minority roommate, that minorities have a difficult time in the course and were not treated fairly; the faculty member, who was black, complained that the student was accusing her of racism).

143. These students wrote graffiti, including a swastika, on a classroom blackboard, and said they intended it as a practical joke.

144. His allegedly offensive remark was the question why black people feel discriminated against; after being charged, he explained that he was attempting to complain that black students in his dormitory tended to socialize together, with the result that he felt socially isolated.

145. See Lawrence at 466 (noting "cruel irony" in Stanford's refusal to punish white students for hanging racist poster in a dormitory, while punishing black students who engaged in peaceful sit-in to protest that refusal).

146. *Id.* at 450 n.82.

147. Just one such problem is how "dominant majority groups" would be defined. Would they be defined in the context of the particular academic community—for example, at Howard Law School, blacks would probably fit this definition, and at Cardozo Law School, Jews would—or in the context of the larger society?

148. For example, when the American Nazi party finally was allowed to march in Illinois in 1978, following the government's and Anti-Defamation League's attempts to prevent this demonstration, two thousand onlookers watched the twenty Nazis demonstrate.

149. See S. Walker, at 59–62 (the ACLU's content-neutral defense of free speech for the Ku Klux Klan—which in the 1920s dominated many state legislatures, played a major role at the 1924 Democratic National Convention, and staged a massive march on Washington, D.C.—led to a decline in the Klan's influence by exposing its vicious plans to public view). See also Neier, at 34: "The Nazis deter the expression of anti-Semitism in forms that might be more palatable to the American public and, therefore, more threatening to the Jews. Other anti-Semites must impose restraints on themselves for fear of being bracketed with the almost universally hated Nazis. A strong Nazi movement would be a great danger to Jews in the United States; a weak Nazi movement with no potential for growth has its uses."

150. 491 U.S. 397 (1989).

151. *Id.* at 419.

152. In response to a letter demeaning women that a student club had circulated, Derek Bok, president of Harvard University, argued that this letter should not be suppressed. He then issued the following public criticism of the letter:

The wording of the letter was so extreme and derogatory to women that I wanted to communicate my disapproval publicly, if only to make sure that no one could gain the false impression that the Harvard administration harbored any sympathy or complacency toward the tone and substance of the letter. Such action does not infringe on free speech. Indeed, statements of disagreement are part and parcel of the open debate that freedom of speech is meant to encourage; the right to condemn a point of view is as protected as the right to express it. Of course, I recognize that even verbal disapproval by persons in positions of authority may have inhibiting effects on students. Nevertheless, this possibility is not sufficient to outweigh the need for officials to speak out on matters of significance to the community— provided, of course, that they take no action to penalize the speech of others.

Bok, "Reflections of Free Speech: An Open Letter to the Harvard Community," *Educ. Rec.*, Winter 1985, at 6.

153. See, e.g., Neier at 170 (Illinois ACLU, which had represented neo-Nazi group seeking to demonstrate, also assisted anti-Nazi groups in securing their First Amendment rights to counter-demonstrate).
154. Samuel Walker, *Hate Speech: The History of an American Controversy* (Univ. of Nebraska Press, 1994), 126.
155. Lawrence at 466.
156. See Lamont v. Postmaster General, 381 U.S. 301 (1965).
157. Neier at 110.
158. Lawrence at 466.
159. *Id.* at 467.
160. This paragraph and the following paragraph are drawn in large part from Gale and Strossen, "The Real ACLU," 2 *Yale J.L. & Feminism* 161, 174–76 (1990).
161. See H. Kalven, at 4.
162. M. L. King, "Letter from Birmingham Jail," in *Why We Can't Wait*, 76 (1964).
163. Shuttlesworth v. Birmingham, 394 U.S. 147 (1969).
164. See, e.g., NAACP v. Claiborne Hardware Co., 458 U.S. 886 (1982); Gregory v. Chicago, 394 U.S. 111 (1969); Cox v. Louisiana, 379 U.S. 536, 550 (1965); Edwards v. South Carolina, 372 U.S. 229 (1963).
165. See Brown v. Oklahoma, 408 U.S. 914 (1972) (during political meeting in university chapel, appellant, a Black Panther, had referred to specific policemen as "mother-fucking fascist pig cops"; Supreme Court summarily vacated conviction under law which it found unconstitutionally over-broad); Gooding v. Wilson, 405 U.S. 518, 523 (1972) (where appellant, a black demonstrator, had made several threatening statements to police officers, including "White son of a bitch, I'll kill you," Court reversed conviction under law that it found unconstitutionally overbroad); see also Lewis v. New Orleans, 415 U.S. 130 (1974) (where police officer said to young suspect's mother, "Get your black ass in the goddamned car," and suspect's mother responded, "You god damn mother fucking police—I am going to [the Superintendent of Police] about this," lower courts upheld

mother's conviction on fighting words doctrine, but the Supreme Court reversed).

166. Karst, "Equality as a Central Principle in the First Amendment," 43 *U. Chi. L. Rev.* 20, 43–44 (1975).
167. Murphy, "Opinion, The Supreme Court Flag-Burning Decision: The Symbol versus the Reality," *Higher Educ. & Nat'l Aff.*, Sept. 25, 1989, at 5.

5. The First Amendment and the Art of Storytelling

Anthony P. Griffin

We often hear that storytelling is a lost art and that we spend little time in developing the art, less time in listening, and a pittance of our time in preserving the truths of the storyteller. I admit, I ain't no storyteller, I'm a lawyer. But I have heard enough stories to fill reams of books. Some of the stories are humorous, some are sad, some make you grab your stomach, hold your head, and scream with joy, laughter, and anger all at the same time. Maybe I am a storyteller. Maybe the art of lawyering, if done right, is part storytelling, part myth making, part myth destruction.

The three short stories that follow are about life. Some of what is written is true. Some of the stories arise from everyday interactions. Some of them are dreams that we have all had. All of them are about our words, our likes, our hates, and our right to say them. I hope that they anger you; I hope that they capture your imagination; I hope that they help you think, laugh, and cry. I hope that it conveys a slice of our lives.

ACT I

But My Brother Is Not That Heavy

Whether we regulate hate speech is an issue that causes each side to stand on its moral soapbox and bespeak doom for the society's freedoms. The soapbox of equality has it that before we, as a society, can obtain true equality, we must regulate hate speech (thoughts) and hateful acts (acts predicated on one's hate for the victim of the crime). The argument of equality is compelling, comforting, and well intended. It allows those understanding the pain of racism to relax in the vigilant fight to expose, destroy, and challenge racism's institutionalized status. Those feeling the sting associated with the words of Skinheads, the Nazis, and the Klan feel more secure with the silencing of such "words that wound." Those of us who have been reared in an environment where the differences are clearly demarcated, defined, and made a part of the culture, idiom, and expectations are supposedly required to accept these new tenets of equality without dispute, debate, or exposure. We are told that the soapbox is well constructed, is not missing nails, and is capable of bearing the weight of any of its advocates.

It is not as if the King has no clothes. He does. In fact, the King's clothes are quite attractive, they're multicolored, all inclusive, and fit the King quite well. The problem is they are the King's clothes. The cloth appears to be of quality fabric. The fabric is of such a nature that it allows its admirers to feel comfortable and protected. The fabric colors are rich in the people's history and sense of self-worth. The garments are constructed by craftspersons who possess great pride in them, but ignore that the clothes were constructed for the King and not for them.

The craftspersons, as they construct their garments, understand the First Amendment about as well as the rest of us. They know that the First Amendment is quite simplistic and they can cite line and verse the admonitions that "Congress shall make no law respecting an establishment of religion, or prohibiting the free exercise thereof; or abridging the freedom of speech, or of the press; or the right of the people peaceably to assemble, and to petition the Government for a redress of grievances." They argue, "But this is a good King!" They implore, "The First Amendment is a breathing, living document and as such contemplates the importance of equality in our society and the victims of hate feeling safe. They explain, "We will not have true equality, until and unless we regulate the hatemongers, and protect our minorities from the rhetoric of hate." They work diligently to complete the King's clothes in time for his speech in the great hall. The soapbox's construction went quicker than they had thought, so they must speed up production of the remaining portion of the King's wardrobe.

When the King begins his speech, some Troublemakers inquire gently as to whether *his words that wound* argument is nothing more than an attack on the First Amendment. The King is at first stung by such an accusation. He gathers himself, and then conveys his emotional conviction of wanting to stop racism, wanting to stop the Nazis as they march, wanting to stop the Klan—"because I am a good King, I am one of you." The crowd rises from its seats and cheers the King's wonderful words. One of the Troublemakers rises and starts to walk down the aisle to examine the King's garments. The King, noticing the Troublemaker's approach, cites the First Amendment and speaks of an undying belief in the viability of the document. "They have every right to speak. I too am a civil libertarian, but that does not mean that the First Amendment should preclude a citizen from being protected from the hate of the Skinheads. I am one of you." The King's soapbox begins to shake, but before he can fall, a number of citizens whom the Troublemaker recognizes, but can't focus on because of the flurry of activity, prop up the soapbox. After the King regains his composure, the Troublemaker recognized that it was not his enemy who protected the King, but the Troublemaker's own friends. Amens ring out through the hall.

The Troublemaker screams in disgust: "But he has no clothes!"

The friends state the obvious: "But he does and they are pretty! We constructed them out of the history of oppression. Our attack is not against you, but the Klan."

The Troublemaker listens.

"Our attack is not against you, but the Nazis."

The Troublemaker thinks: "But it says that Congress shall make no law abridging the freedom of speech or press or the right of the people to assemble peaceably, and to petition the Government for a redress of grievances."

"Our attack is not against you, but the Skinheads."

The Troublemaker begins to speak and is promptly told by the King that he is out of order. The Troublemaker's friends continue: "Freedom is contextual. We don't have the freedom to shout 'fire' in a crowded theater. Our courts have not extended protection to obscenity. We treat commercial speech differently than we treat other forms of speech. Our First Amendment privileges are not absolute as they stand now. And my friend, the protection of the historically oppressed from the pains of hate is a commendable, compelling state interest. Our attack is not against you, but those anti-abortion protestors. You aren't one of them, are you?"

Stung by the words, the Troublemaker in a rapid manner addresses those surrounding the King: "That is not what this is about. Whether I am, or not, is not the question. If I worship a rock, that is my privilege. Whether I agree or disagree with you, the King can't tell me in what manner, and how I should think!"

A voice from behind the King calmly states the obvious, revealing the not-so-obvious: "My, you are upset. Why not be rational? Why are you forsaking your friends for *them?* You are right, you do have a free speech right, but the King seeks to attack our enemies. This King seeks to stop those who show up on our televisions taking advantage of religion. Who are these people and who are their members? This King does not seek to attack you, but attacks *hate.*"

The Troublemaker looks around the stage and notices that some are becoming impatient. The King is whispering in the direction of a couple of them.

"Whose hate? " he asks.

"Their hate."

"Who is 'their?' "

"The Nazis, the Klan, the Skinheads."

"Who else? "

"You know."

"I know what? Who else? Who else are you seeking to regulate?"

"We are not seeking to regulate anyone. All we asked our King for was appropriate legislation that prevents the use of words in a manner that would have a tendency to harm its victims. The legislation would be based on a reasonable-person test, that is, that the words would be prohibited if a reasonable person found the words to be insulting, harmful, or hateful."

The King continues to whisper in the direction of a few. Others work to shore up his soapbox.

The Troublemaker's reply is a fast one: "But who decides?"

The return is faster: "We do!"

"But who is we? Is it the King? Is it the King's men? When the King dies, we still have the law, don't we?"

The Troublemaker's friends hear only one of the four questions asked, or, in any event, only answer one: "Yes, we would still have the law. We would have the law to be protected from the hate. We would pass the law to assure that in the future our children, your children, and others historically oppressed wouldn't have to suffer from the pangs of hate that prevent the full attainment of equality."

The Troublemaker notices some of *the friends* exiting stage left after speaking to the King. They seem to have left with a sense of purpose. The Troublemaker continues to speak: "Do you obtain equality without fair housing?"

The answer is obvious: "No!"

"Do you obtain equality without speaking to economic deprivation and the lack of jobs?"

"No."

More people leave the stage.

"Do you obtain equality with such a gross disparity of wealth?"

Silence rings throughout the hall.

"Do you obtain equality when the laws are interpreted unevenly, leading to higher arrest, higher detentions, and higher convictions of the historically oppressed? Does the passage of this *thought legislation* make us feel good, but ignore the real societal problems that we face? So what, I don't get called a name in the process. So, I am screwed with acts of kindness, I am still being screwed. Will you please answer my questions!"

The answer is a consistent one: "But he is a good King."

The King's clothes glisten under the lights, the King's face does not. As the Troublemaker starts to mouth *Congress shall make no law*, the friends who had left the stage reach him. Their intent seems clear. Their words are even clearer: "You are upset, calm down. It is not that important. You have to understand that we, too, believe in the First Amendment and understand that *those people* have a right to speak, organize, assemble and pray, but *they* have no right to spew *their* hate. We know you feel strongly about it, but calm down. *They* have a history of violence and therefore *they* have forfeited the right to speak. The Constitution simply does not apply to *them*. So please calm down. And by the way, the King asked that you come with us, you are being requested to leave the hall."

"What?! "

"You are being asked to leave. If you don't leave quietly, you will be arrested."

The Troublemaker looks upon the stage and notices that the King's smile has returned. The soapbox is still shaky, but there are now more props around it and more nails driven in the props than in the soapbox itself. The contrast brings a smile to the Troublemaker's face. Looking about the stage, the Troublemaker notices that the friends working on the soapbox and those listening to the King had taken on the dress of the King's men. The Troublemaker is not sure what to make of this. Before he can consider this further, a voice interrupts his thoughts.

"You have been asked to leave. You have insulted the King. You have insulted his clothes. The King said that a *reasonable person* could consider your words to be hateful in nature with a tendency to intimidate, oppress, and cause fear in the intended listener. Please leave."

The Troublemaker is perplexed: *"Do you now have the power of arrest?"*

One of the persons surrounding the Troublemaker responds, even though the question was not directed at her: "The King has given us the power."

The Troublemaker looked in the direction of the King, who looks a little more impatient. The Troublemaker cannot determine whether it was because of the delay in leaving or because the King's props have now grown twice as large as his soapbox.

Turning back to those within reach, the Troublemaker assures them that he will leave, adding, "You really do need to get the King a new soapbox. I think that he may fall."

"Yes, it *is* strange. The King has hired the best skilled laborers, the best carpenters, the best designers, and no one has been successful in constructing a soapbox to hold the King. He is not that heavy. He only wants the soapbox to show his new clothes and to tell the citizens about our new legislation. But that is not the point. You must leave and you must leave now."

As the Troublemaker exits the hall, a loud sound resonates behind him. Others standing in the foyer area run back toward the hall.

The Troublemaker smiles and leaves the building without turning back.

ACT II

The Softer Sex

As the graying, fortyish, slightly overweight comedian slouched in his chair, he listened as his agent and his lawyer explained that he would not be able to perform at the state-supported institution. The comic wondered why. He knew that during the last few years he had not visited the college campuses and had concentrated on writing for the bevy of television shows purporting to portray black life in America. He had grown tired of the incessant babbling of the television industry, and he wondered if he had lost his edge. He wanted to return to the college circuit. Now he was being told that he could not, at least not with the material that had made him a noted social commentator. He couldn't believe what he was being told.

Jamaal Wedgeable looked down and admired his shoes, but continued to listen. He had always been consistent in his work and life. Profane, challenging, biting, and humorous, he was also one who loved comfort, the niceties of life, and soft, comfortable shoes. He saw nothing inconsistent about this. In fact there wasn't. His art was to integrate a broad social view and life's diversity into his humor. He understood the nature of his craft: he was a comic.

The others in the room were oblivious to his daydreaming. He stared out the window and noticed the clouds beginning to move over the city. He wondered whether his lawyer was joking as he explained that new limits were being placed on his craft.

"Are you saying that I can't curse?"

"No, we are not saying that."

"Then what are you saying?"

"We are saying that you can't perform at any state-supported institutions. I know that it's upsetting to you, I know that it seems preposterous, but the university is within its rights to ban your appearance and speech."

Jamaal could feel his pressure rise and his temper flair. He couldn't believe his ears. He knew that his lawyer was a long-term ally, but his words flew from him: "You on my side or what? You my lawyer, or what? What the hell you mean the university is within its right? This letter says that 'because of your past history of using hateful speech, the

University will not approve your appearance before the student body.'
This shit is illegal."

The lawyer, ten years Wedgeable's senior, had been the comedian's
counsel for the last fifteen years. In their more youthful years, they had
spent considerable time visiting the pubs of the Village and making
themselves obnoxious with their stares, suggestive comments, and alco-
holically induced "cuteness" directed at what they called the softer sex.
They never explained what they meant by the softer sex; they would just
smile at each other, emit a hearty laugh, and order another beer. Over
the last ten years, they communicated mostly by letters, by contracts,
and had an occasional telephone call with respect to a pending legal
issue. Since Jamaal had moved to Los Angeles, the distance prevented
the type of male bonding that had been the foundation of their rapport.
Larry, the lawyer, was Jewish and spent the earlier years of his career
working for the Lawyers Committee on Civil Rights and teaching at
Yale.

As Jamaal spoke, Larry picked at his cuticles but felt the sting of
Jamaal's words. "Whose side you on anyway?" The translation of words
from mouth, to ears, to brain made him hear, "You are selling me out,
Larry!" As Jamaal continued to speak, Larry remained absorbed by his
cuticles and pretend not to be bothered, and Jamaal's agent remained
silent.

The year was 2003. Ten years earlier, the Supreme Court had declared that the state possessed the power to regulate hateful speech. The
question was the balancing of free speech against hateful speech. These
three men, in some sense, had participated in shaping the course and
scope of the public dialogue and, in fact, had prevailed in getting their
desired position heard, ruled on, and adopted by the nation's highest
Court. They felt a sense of pride and comfort at the time. As they sat in
Larry's comfortably appointed office, the clouds moving over the city set
an appropriate mood.

Jamaal's agent, Allen Brown, was a former general counsel for the
National Association for the Advancement of Colored People. He was
Jamaal's age, had kept himself fit over the years, and teased Jamaal
profusely about his graying and receding hairline and growing paunch,
to which Jamaal would respond in the most basic terms: "You think
you funny, huh!" In 1993 Allen had argued, written, and encouraged
the regulation of hate speech, particularly that of the Ku Klux Klan.

In 1993, Larry had worked for the Lawyer's Committee on Civil Rights and filed an amicus brief with the Supreme Court in another case where free speech was an issue. He sought to regulate the Nazis. Larry was also a member of the Anti-Defamation League's task force that helped to formulate hate speech legislation in a number of states.

In 1993, Jamaal was doing some standup, some writing, and he joked about the damn Klan, those asshole Nazis—everybody laughed then. The clouds continued to move in, the wink of the sun's rays now barely visible. Jamaal wondered whether it was going to rain.

Larry sought to remind Jamaal of the Court's decision: "Remember, the issue was a rather hot one. The question revolved around the limits of speech. The issue was whether speech could be hateful, scornful, vile, vicious, and aggressive, and if it could be regulated when there was an absence of violence."

Jamaal interjected: "I remember, but we were attacking the Klan, the Nazis, the *assholes.*"

Larry continued: "But that is why I say that the university is within its rights to prevent you from speaking. Remember, when the Supreme Court ruled ten years ago, the opinion was applauded by the NAACP, the Anti-Defamation League, Jewish Defense League, the Lawyer's Committee on Civil Rights, and most civil rights organizations in the country. Some of us saw it as a method to curtail Nazi activities in the country; some of us saw it as a method to stop the Klan's actions in Cincinnati, Ohio, and Vidor, Texas. In fact, African American groups had encouraged the solicitor general's office to enter an appearance supporting the government's restrictions. And if I am remembering it right, we sought to protect the historically disadvantaged, and the descendants of slavery."

Jamaal never did have the patience for lawyer gobbledygook. "What does that have to do with me! I'm a comic, not a Klansman, fuck Hitler with his wickedly great ass!" Jamaal laughed at his own joke.

Larry continued steadfastly. "It has everything to do with us. Remember, we argued that the government should have the right to regulate hateful speech. The Court took us to heart."

The weight of history began to weigh on Larry's shoulders. He slouched forward as he talked. Visually, his salt-and-pepper hair contrasted nicely with the wallpaper, as if the decorator decided on the color by taking swabs of his hair. Now silent, Larry began to daydream.

Larry had watched the development of the law and noticed that almost immediately after the Court's decision, the bantering of hate groups in the public forum had ceased. He and Allen celebrated every time a Klan rally was banned or a Nazi was arrested for espousing hate. He remembered feeling a sense of purpose and thanking God for making him a lawyer.

Larry remembered how, with every arrest, he experienced a greater sense of comfort. He remembered dreaming that with every banned speech, particularly on the campus of state-supported institutions, the long-fought fight for equality was being won. Larry also knew of reports that said that Nazis' and Klans' memberships had, in fact, increased since the Supreme Court's decision. He didn't want to understand why.

Jamaal continued to ask, "But what does that have to do with me?"

"Everything. Remember 1995, when the Court banned all forms of hate speech? Remember 1996, when the Court banned all anti-abortion protests? Remember, we applauded."

Allen, who had remained quiet, walked toward the window and looked out over the city. He wistfully echoed the comments. "I remember. And Jamaal, I think Larry is right. The current state of the law allows the university to ban your speech. I disagree with the Court, but that is the current state of the law."

Jamaal couldn't believe his ears. "But I am not a Klansman!"

Larry, now standing next to Jamaal, interrupted: "But *that is not the point.*"

Jamaal rose from his seat and reminded his buddies that the letter banned him because of hate speech. "What hate speech?" he wanted to know.

Drawing on his training with the NAACP, Allen abandoned his role of agent for a minute. He remembered some of the heated meetings that had helped craft the speech codes that were now law: He patiently sought to explain. "In response to the Supreme Court's decisions, state-supported institutions have enacted speech codes. These speech codes prevent use of racist words, like 'nigger,' the use of anti-Semitic words, and/or any word or words that can be considered derisive. These speech codes also attack any words that may be deemed to be sexist, hateful, or paint another in a negative manner."

In response Jamaal added, "But I don't eat tofu. I am a comic. I engage in social commentary. I use offensive words. I make people uncomfortable. I want people to relive controversy and embarrassing moments. Words wound, heal, and make us learn, laugh, and cry. I don't eat tofu and this whole notion of using nice words is crazy, this can't be legal."

Everybody laughed. His buddies knew what he meant, but they could not agree with him. They could sense Jamaal's frustrations and said nothing about their own.

Jamaal continued: "It is insulting for you to tell me that somehow the government can define my humor. I am not spewing hate. Sure, I talk about short people, fat people, ugly people, and colored people. I use words. I use contrast. I use diversity to help my audience grow, but this also helps me grow. This doesn't make any sense. This letter can't be constitutional, this has to be challenged."

Larry had listened, fumbled with his pencil, and looked for the words to explain to his friend the limits on free speech. "That's right, you use words and somebody has to define the words you *can* use."

Jamaal, not to be deterred, intoned, "Nigger."

Without hesitation, Larry shot back, "Hate speech."

"Hate speech! What the hell you talking about, hate speech?"

"The Court has said that the state may ban and regulate hate speech. Hate speech is considered any speech that has a chance of harming. It is considered any speech whose history is one of being discriminatory in origin."

Jamaal added another one: "Cunt."

Allen turned from his window perch. "Not at a state institution."

Jamaal did not back away and added, "But you can be a good cunt or a bad cunt." No one would touch Jamaal's joke. Jamaal didn't care and laughed at his own joke. As he finished his chuckle, he returned to his seat, hiked his pants, caught a glimpse of his most comfortable shoes, and intoned, "This is censorship."

Larry, looking even more uncomfortable, took the lawyer's path to comfort and tried to explain the Court's rulings. "No, it is not censorship, you have to understand, the law is developmental. When we stopped the Klan, we cheered. Remember?"

Allen provided the response: "I remember."

"When we stopped the Nazis, the Jewish groups gave us awards."

Jamaal then responded in the style and manner of a backup singer: "I do remember."

Larry continued in his effort to explain: "Then we were able to enjoin and stop any sort of hateful speech from anti-abortion groups. The Court's intervention allowed women to exercise their right of choice."

Jamaal continued the sing-sing interaction. "I don't disagree, but again, that's the Nazis, that's the Klan, that's those Bible-toting hypocrites. I believe in the choice. I am a comic. What has that got to do with me!" Jamaal laughed and added, "Tina Turner, 1984."

Allen retorted, "That's 'What's Love Got to Do with It?' "

Jamaal quickly responded, "Yeah, yeah, but I think it's 'What's That Got to Do with Me.' Positive K, 1992." Jamaal bellowed a hearty laugh. Larry and Allen missed the generational humor.

Allen looked at Jamaal and explained, "But you use words."

Larry continued: "The Court has found that for equality to work as a concept, equality should be just that. The Court has taken up the fight for equality and adopted a purist stance. Affirmative action was abolished under the notion that all are now equal and on an equal footing."

Jamaal blew his answer across the room at Larry. "Bullshit! The last time I checked I was still considered black! We have not gotten that far, we are not on equal footing, even in 2003!"

Larry continued: "The Court has used the speech-equality debate to restrict the use of hostile words, vile words, and hateful words. Words that have a tendency to hurt. Words that have a historical meaning."

The amused tone left Jamaal's voice. "But all words have historical meaning. All words can hurt, all words can be vile. Some words may be hostile to others, hateful to you, but music to my ears. What right does the government have to tell me when I can exercise my humor? I can't believe my ears. You two were raised in the civil rights and civil liberties communities. How dare you so easily explain away our freedoms under the notion of equality, under the notion that it makes us feel good, under the notion that it is safe? Life is not safe. Each of you is my friend, but how can you equate me to the Klan and the Nazis?"

Larry, sensing the truth in Jamaal's attack, explained, "That was not the intent. We had sensed an opportunity to further develop the rights of the disadvantaged. Remember, Thurgood had just died, the NAACP was redefining itself, and we had just suffered through twelve years of Republican rule in the White House. There was a sense of virility with the passage of the Civil Rights and Women's Equity Act of 1991. There was a sense of opportunity with a new administration. There was a sense that free speech had gone too far when Nazis and Klan groups were using it as an excuse to harass black families, to hold parades mocking our religious values or even seeking to inject their hate in the public debate. We fought along the side of state governments to stop their marching, to stop their speaking, and to regulate the hate speech. It was our feeling that the First Amendment could withstand this intrusion. The Court had treated obscenity differently. A policy decision had to be made that hate speech was no different, just as harmful to its victims, and just as much a state's compelling interest. As I said, the Court accepted our argument and then took two steps we didn't expect."

Allen then aided with a history lesson. "The Court, in the tradition of the First Amendment, and partly in the tradition of the Reagan legacy, ruled that all speech could be regulated. We silenced the Klan, we silenced the Nazis, we silenced Khallid Abdul Muhammad's outrageous hatemongering, but we have silenced you also. It is my feeling that is the price that we have to pay for equality."

Jamaal had historically been the more vocally hostile of the three. He could feel his skin become flush with anger. He looked down at his paper-sack brown skin and could see that his hands were a shade darker. He couldn't believe his ears, but his mind began to move fast with the paradox of what he was being told. But he lived and breathed humor and chuckled to himself.

"Damn, this shit is funny. I give up my free speech rights because you want to silence the Klan. Let those fools speak then. You are telling me that because you want to regulate hateful words, then I can't use the wonders of words to educate, to challenge, to make people laugh. Who died and made you assholes God? This letter is unconstitutional and I want it challenged. I am not willing to check my free speech rights at the front door. Damn, this shit is funny! How 'bout me designating you, Allen, as God, and you, Larry, as his helper? Or do you, brethren of the law, want to fight over your roles?"

Jamaal's comment hit its mark; Larry's anger flared. "I don't think that's funny. You don't understand. You didn't make those comments ten years ago when we were silencing the Klan, or the Nazis, or the damn Bible nuts."

Allen turned and watched the clouds begin to weep.

Jamaal, undeterred, continued: "I *do* understand. I understand *perfectly*. Words do wound, but they also educate, salve, heal, and bring humor, diversity, and understanding. There is no way I am willing to give the right away to you as a Republican or to you as a Democrat. There is no way I am willing to define my craft on whether you as a government official think that it's funny or not. Hell, you may be the brunt of the joke! Don't you think that your government friend is going to find the speech hateful, to find it lacking in social meaning, to find that it is vile if it's spoken against him, the brunt of the joke? Answer my question, lawyer!" Jamaal didn't chuckle as he drew the line in the sand.

Allen continued to look out over the city, the rain at sunset coming down in a symphony of colors—gray, orange, red, white, and black. It seemed so perfect for this discussion.

Larry knew Jamaal was angry. He felt a sense of desperation and wanted to be elsewhere than in this conversation. He understood his client-friend's anger, but he continued. "You really don't understand. The only way we will be able to have true equality is to regulate the hate."

Jamaal exploded. "Regulate the hate, how? How in the hell do you regulate the hate? So you tell the Skinheads to speak kindly of you, do you honestly believe that they will? So you drive them underground, do you think their silence makes them stop hating? The damn Nazis have been banned in parts of Europe, they still attack. Their membership grew when forced underground. It was not their words that hurt Larry, it was their acts of violence. I don't know, Larry, I don't know . . ." His voice trailed off.

Both Larry and Allen interrupted the thought and in unison spoke the obvious. "But you didn't complain when it was occurring."

"I know, but I ain't no damn skinhead. I ain't no damn Nazi and that wasn't part of the deal."

Larry interrupted and explained, "That became a part of the deal. When we sought to regulate hate, to regulate thoughts, historically we can't pick and choose good speech from bad speech. The state institution is right."

Jamaal exploded, "Fuck you, Larry! How in the hell can they be right when they write that because of my past performances they feel that I have engaged in hate speech and in all likelihood will engage in hate speech in the future? I haven't performed on a college campus nor have I done standup work in at least five years. This seems as if they are prejudging me on something somebody told them, something they read, or something I said in the past."

Allen turned back toward the window, wiped his eyes with his handkerchief, and watched the water splash and swirl as the traffic passed through the streets below. He hoped his friends did not see him wipe. He listened.

Larry explained the legal term for the university's act: "It is called a prior restraint. At one time it was illegal for the government to exercise a prior restraint on any form of speech. It was illegal to engage in a prior restraint of the press, or the publication of books or even pure speech. The Supreme Court, until the passage of the thought legislation, had ruled that to allow prior restraints chilled the right of free speech and was in violation of the First Amendment. In order to regulate hate legislation, the Courts have allowed your past speech, your past acts, your history—like the Klan, like the Nazis, like the Skinheads—to become one of the variables in preventing the speech. The Courts have stated that if the university provides a hearing, within a reasonable time, to determine the context of the speech, then such a hearing is in compliance with due process and does not violate your free speech rights."

Jamaal shot back, "But the hearing is scheduled after my performance date."

"I know that, but your failure to show at the hearing will waive any right to complain you may have. Your performance will subject you to arrest."

Allen said nothing; he reached for his handkerchief again.

"You are telling me that I must produce for them a text of my performance. I have no text; this is comedy. I work with concepts. I work with the diversity of life. *Through diversity there is humor, through humor there is diversity.* That's what Dick Gregory said, that's what I believe. This prior restraint bullshit is just that, bullshit. How can we debate, argue, learn, if you control what is said? Tell me, how can we? Tell me, lawyers, tell me!"

Larry said nothing. Allen left his window perch and took his seat. Jamaal continued to rail uncontrollably. "I blame both of you. Why didn't you warn me that this would happen? Why didn't each of you tell me that my rights were tied to some idiot in sheets? I may have understood and I may have been willing to let that idiot speak as long as you didn't silence my right to tell others that the idiot was wrong! Why didn't you tell me when we were arresting the Nazis for marching that you were also arresting me?!"

Jamaal wheeled and turned in Allen's direction. "Allen, when is the last time the NAACP has run the risk of marching in a state that was hostile to the NAACP? It's been since 1997, or was it 1998? Is the failure to march, the failure to speak in recognition that you have let the chickens out of the coop? What about our friend in the White House— he was defeated, wasn't he? What about our friends on the bench—they resigned, took other jobs, didn't they, or they just ran off and fucking died! But why didn't you warn me that they were going to use the same rules against me?"

Speaking to no one in particular, but just anguishing over life's contradictions, Jamaal began to talk to himself. "Damn, where have I been for the last ten years? There is not a comic in this country that doesn't insult someone. Some may be insulted because of too much profanity, or some may feel some insult because the comic is too damn nice. Yeah, that's funny, *damn and nice* in the same sentence. Where is the line drawn? Obviously it has been drawn pretty broadly since the last time I checked." Jamaal looked up and screamed, "Fuck you, Larry! And fuck you, too, Allen!"

Allen covered his face with the handkerchief. The years of trying to structure an appropriate response to the developments of law now flooded his emotions. He didn't care if Larry or Jamaal saw, understood, or spoke to his tears. The rain was now blowing against the window and played a slow tap dance against the backdrop of what was now silence.

Larry thought of his rabbi explaining that there was a Nazi complaint that one of the rabbi's speeches, given six months ago, fell within the purview of the Hate Speech Act. The rabbi said the state was taking the investigation seriously. No one spoke, no one needed to. The phone did not ring, even though Larry sat there wishing that it would.

Jamaal took his seat as if exhausted by it all; he didn't notice the scuff marks on his shoes; they were not there when this conversation had begun. Jamaal didn't care; he held his hand against his mouth and counted to himself as he watched Allen wipe and Larry refuse to look. The rain continued to pitter, or was it patter, against the window. Jamaal laughed to himself, thought that this would be a wonderful routine for his next standup performance. The rain now pittered and pattered.

Jamaal rose, reached for Allen's hand, and said, "It's all right man, I'm going to perform anyway. You know, I can't let this good material go to waste. And since I am in the city, how 'bout a beer?" Larry looked up and mentioned the Village. They all smiled a manly smile.

As Larry reached for his suit coat, he looked to Jamaal. "I think you're right. I think that the law should be challenged. I'm willing to defend your right to speak. I'm willing to defend your right to be funny. I'm willing to defend your right to insult, to vilify, and to wound, heal, and expand the discussion. And after we defend your right, and win, we will defend the rights of those damn Nazis."

The rain began to abate as they left the building. They got into the taxi, each anticipating smoothing things over at the bar with a few beers, each with the words of their history on his lips. "The softer sex. Yeah!"

ACT III

And Peace Be with You, My Child

Grandmother was always a good storyteller. You never knew whether the story was the truth or not. You never knew whether the characters were real or a by-product of her imagination born from the miles and miles of picking peas under the Texas sun. You never knew and I think that was the point. She could tell a story with words, with language so clean—oh no, she didn't curse—and so cutting, that you could see the blood rise from her victim's wounds.

Grandmother was patient, up until the time she got sick. Her patience allowed her to be a healer, a listener, and, yeah, a good storyteller. At the time, I didn't know why she started telling me a story that day. I don't know if it related to telling me that she thought I did right in revealing that my bag of cotton had already been weighed and a mistake was being made. When she began the story, I didn't know, and she didn't say. Of course I didn't ask—that would have been disrespectful.

She just sat on the porch cleaning her teeth with the wooden stick that took on the appearance of a tooth brush because of the soft, frayed ending created from chewing the wood. It must have worked, she didn't have cavity one. The brilliance of the sun was starting to abate and the evening's breeze began to heal.

I had told my Grandmother the summer past that I wanted to be a lawyer. She said nothing then, but I knew she was listening. After I finished, she asked me whether I had finished my chores. I said that I had. It was now a new summer and as she began to tell her story, I knew that she had remembered my dreams.

She adjusted her thick, caramel-colored hose and told me about this colored lawyer who had agreed to take a case representing the Grand Dragon of the Ku Klux Klan. Yes, "colored": Grandmother wasn't and didn't pretend to be politically correct. I don't know if I showed it or not, but my interest immediately piqued when she mentioned anything about a lawyer. I didn't know my grandmother was *hype*.

Baby, he wasn't a young lawyer, had been practicing his craft for close to twenty years. He had taken his share of controversial cases, cases that helped people, cases that made him money and cases where he didn't get paid at all. They tell me he was a good lawyer.

He got this call from these white people. The organization was called the American Civil Liberties Union. They say that they didn't know he was colored. He said that he had never met the caller. He knew the Klan. He knew that they hated his people, talked of his people's destruction, and he had Klan hate mail that he had received over the years for cases that he had taken, defended, or prosecuted. Baby, they say it took him only twenty seconds to decide to take this Grand Dragon's case. They tell me that he said it would be an honor.

Well, folks were shocked at this. They knew that the state of Texas was after the Klan's membership list. They knew that the state may have been wrong to make such a request. They knew that colored people had fought to keep their membership list private during the movement. They knew that at one time it wasn't safe for colored people to admit that they could read, write, and no less say that they were a member of the NAACP. Some didn't understand what was going on, but asked, "Why him? He is a colored man."

Well, baby, not to make this too complicated, this colored lawyer was the general counsel for the NAACP in the state of Texas. Word had it that he was the best at his craft—you know, we have to be twice as good. I've told you that before, haven't I?

I nodded as quickly as I could so that my Grandmother would continue.

Well, if I haven't told you, you have to be twice as good.

He took the case. Some said that he was a fool. Some said that he sold his people out. Some called for his firing as general counsel.

Now, baby, Texas is a big state, but it wasn't big enough for this news. Some laughed at the thought of a colored lawyer representing the Grand Dragon of the KKK. The white people down at the Cotton Gin said that he was going to get that Klansman off and then get hung for dinner. They laughed. I didn't think it was so funny and told them so. They said they were only joking. Some of the colored citizens thought him to be like Bob Ryan, a white folk's nigger. He heard the whispers.

It was still summer when all of this occurred. They say that heat makes us act a little bit crazier. I say the moon controls the emotions to a greater extent than the sun. Newspaper folks traveled to Galveston to ask the colored lawyer whether he had lost his senses. They kept waiting for him to say "Uh, yes sur"; they kept waiting for him to shuffle; they kept waiting for him to split some verbs and to conjugate some "be's"; they kept waiting for him to give a speech about how there was no racism, that colored people were treated fairly and that he didn't know what discrimination was and had never seen it.

Grandmother chuckled to herself as she finished the last line.

He never gave them any of that. He said it was the right thing to do. He said that folks we hate have constitutional rights, too. He said that an issue was being made out of his race and he felt insulted by it. He said that a white lawyer could represent the Klan, the Nazis, and any black person and no one would complain. He said that his people's criticism was misplaced and that his race should not preclude him from defending the Constitution. No one wanted to hear that. They looked at this colored lawyer physically and saw youth; they looked at his skin and saw color; they listened to him talk and didn't hear what they expected.

"He's from Texas, isn't he?"

"He's from a small town, isn't he?"

"He will be overwhelmed by the lights, the comments, the threats, the attacks, won't he?"

He pretended that it didn't bother him.

Baby, I don't remember what year this was, but they say it was also the summer in which this colored lawyer was to receive an award from a group of colored citizens. They were to name him Citizen of the Year.

When the lawyer learned of the award, he thought about not appearing. The committee kept calling. He agreed to attend. He discouraged others from attending. He expected to appear, accept the award, and leave immediately. He thought that the award was for his work on civil rights cases, cases he worked on so that colored people could have a meaningful right to vote. He was partly right.

As this colored lawyer entered the convention center, he noticed that hundreds of people were present. He noticed that there were news cameras all about. He heard talk about his representation of the Grand Dragon. He pretended that it didn't bother him. He also heard that the next day the NAACP planned to remove him from the general counsel position.

As he walked into the center, he watched faces. Some smiled. Some looked away. Some conveyed disgust. He could pretend no more. He began to think about what was occurring. His years of trial work were beginning to elude him; he did not know this at the time.

As the program started, he couldn't remain in his seat. Baby, they say he traipsed such a trail to and from his seat to the bathroom that they are still trying to get the carpet to stand back up. They tell me that he would enter the bathroom, pretend to empty his bladder, look at his eyes and engage in idle conversation. He sought to control his emotions. He had never been so affected.

Baby, they say he began to talk to himself. Not as a crazy man would, but as we all do to reassure ourselves. He began to stroke his own hand. He begin to wonder why the news cameras kept following him. He became angry that the cameras followed. He thought about leaving and going back to his office, but he didn't. As the time for his award got nearer, he rewalked his now established line to the toilet and pretended to let his water run—he had none; he checked his eyes.

I understand the city manager for his city gave him the award. The lawyer had guessed wrong. The city manager talked about the voting cases, but also talked about the Klan. The colored lawyer's insides screamed! Not here! Not now! How am I going to explain my decision? No one will understand. Well, he walked up to the podium, hoping that he wouldn't trip. He watched his shoes as he walked. He avoided stepping on any cracks.

As he began to explain his beliefs he looked about the crowd. His mind wandered. As he began to explain his dislike for the Klan, he saw only disbelief. His mind panicked. As he began to explain that constitutionally free speech meant speech for those who speak unkindly of us, he became angry.

They say his anger was because he resented being portrayed as being someone who had no sense of his community. They say his anger was because he resented being portrayed as someone who had missed the constitutional mark. They say that he feared that attacking the Klan's rights meant that we were attacking our rights.

As this colored lawyer looked out over the crowd, he felt his emotions taking advantage of him. He couldn't leave and go back to the bathroom to check his eyes. He paused for a moment. As he began to speak, he felt his voice deserting him. He paused for a period, slightly longer than a moment. He looked out at the audience, he could not see them. He could not hear them. He looked down and saw a napkin being handed to him. He didn't know who handed him the napkin. He accepted the gift without protest.

This colored lawyer had never cried in public. Not at his grandparents' funerals, not at his nephew's funeral, not at any of his friends' untimely deaths, and not in any of the many trials that he had made his reputation on. They say life is strange in that way, but he could not control his tears on this day. He made it through, he spoke of the beauty of speaking one's mind, he hung his head in embarrassment and anger.

As he left the convention center, others stopped him, stroked his hand, his shoulder, and said it was all right. He couldn't respond. His mind was confused as to why he cried. He wanted to leave and return to his office to complete a project. They wouldn't get out of the way. He didn't force them, waiting compliantly.

When he arrived at his car, a car pulled up alongside and a fellow lawyer exited and hugged him and they both began to cry. He kept apologizing for crying. He said he cried out of anger, but he didn't know why he cried. She said it was all right.

Back in his car, he drove a short five blocks to his office, and entered with the intent of working. Baby, they say life's plans sometimes go astray. He went straight to the bathroom and blew his nose. Then he walked to the closet, grabbed a blanket and laid on the floor and finished his cry. They say he didn't work that night on legal work. He slept and he thought.

As he rose that next morning he knew that the project would have to *wait another day. He also knew that sleep and thoughts and tears had helped him identify his fear. He feared being disowned by his own. No matter how great the principle, life's most basic want and desire still affected him. He still was angry at his emotions for running out on him.*

Baby, this colored lawyer wiped his face with a cool towel. He smiled at the world and thought how he could explain that some principles are greater than those things that divide us. I will tell you that honesty is one of them. By the way, I am proud of you for telling that man the truth about the cotton.

My chest burst with pride when Grandmother said that.

The other is what that colored lawyer was saying. If you understand that, you will be a good lawyer.

EPILOGUE

Oh, I'm sorry. I forgot to explain that free speech protects us all. It protects those who say kind words, it protects those who are not so kind, it protects our friends, our enemies, and ourselves. Free speech allows for the symphony of ideas to play in the marketplace.

I must also apologize—I forgot to tell you that Act I was told in a genderless format. No *his* or *her,* no use of the *possessive* for our Troublemaker, because the Troublemaker can be any one of us. He/she/it can be black/brown/blue-black/white/yellow/beige/copper or any of the arrays of colors, speeches, or cultures that life's diversity represents.

And while we are engaging in admissions, one more. Act III is an adaptation of the time I represented the Grand Dragon of the Texas Knights of the Ku Klux Klan and the organization itself. The dispute is described accurately. The Texas Human Rights Commission, a state agency, requested the Klan's membership list in order to investigate who attended Klan rallies and who protested against the integration of public housing in Vidor, Texas. Act III represents a slice of one set of emotions that greeted my decision to defend the rights of those we hate. I say that it is but a slice, in that because of my cloudy ears and eyes and weakened vocal cords, I did not notice the crowd standing; I was told later that the crowd stood at least four times in support. I say that it is but a slice, in that I fail to convey the conversations that took place with loved ones after I returned to the office.

Yes, contained in all fiction is a slice of all of our lives. Therefore, if I have made you angry, so be it. If the profanity makes you pray for my soul, thank you. If you have laughed without understanding the importance of protecting the speech of your enemies, then I have failed. And, if it is not clear that we tend to believe in free speech when it is our own, but have a difficult time understanding this most simplistic concept when it is exercised by those whose speech is vile, or makes us angry, then I have failed. I hope that I have not.

6. Since When Is the Fourteenth Amendment Our Route to Equality? Some Reflections on the Construction of the "Hate-Speech" Debate from a Lesbian/Gay Perspective

William B. Rubenstein

The places where the law does not go to redress harm have tended to be the places where women, children, people of color, and poor people live.
— Mari Matsuda, "Public Response to Racist Speech: Considering the Victim's Story," 87 *Mich. L. Rev.* 2320, 2322 (1989)

The big lie about lesbians and gay men is that we do not exist. . . . America [is] a dream that ha[s] no room for the existence of homosexuals.
— Vito Russo, *The Celluloid Closet: Homosexuality in the Movies* (1987), xii

In her groundbreaking article, "Public Response to Racist Speech: Considering the Victim's Story," [1] Mari Matsuda made a conscious decision to focus solely on racist—and to a lesser extent on anti-Semitic—speech. She explains her exclusion of other types of "hate-speech":

The serious problems of violent pornography and anti-gay and anti-lesbian hate speech are not discussed in this article. While I believe these forms of hate speech require public restriction, these forms also require a separate analysis because of the complex and violent nature of gender subordination, and the different way in which sex operates as a locus of oppression. They are, therefore, beyond the scope of this piece. . . . The claim that a legal response to racist speech is required stems from a recognition of the structural reality of racism in America. [2]

I concur with Professor Matsuda's conclusion and believe that the question of whether—and what—legal response is required to combat anti-gay/lesbian speech must start from a recognition of the structural reality of the oppression of lesbians and gay men in the United States. My purpose here, then, is not to propose where lines should be drawn to develop speech codes that comply with the First Amendment nor to propose some grand speech code of my own.

Rather, what I hope to begin[3] to explore in this chapter is a basic understanding of one portion (that involving lesbian/gay sexuality) of the way "sex operates as a locus of oppression," which—as Professor Matsuda makes clear—is a necessary background to the decision about whether and how to limit gay-related hate speech. In section 1, I outline one understanding of how homophobia operates in our society. Through this description, I attempt to show the central place that the suppression of speech has played (and continues to play) in the oppression of lesbians and gay men. In section 2, I outline my understanding of how the legal system has worked or not worked to redress the harm that has been inflicted upon lesbians and gay men. My point in this part is to demonstrate how our equality has been achieved—when at all—almost exclusively through the First Amendment, while our Fourteenth Amendment claims—which are almost necessarily premised upon the "speech acts" of coming out—have largely failed.

Drawing on these themes, in section 3 I will deconstruct the principle understanding of the hate speech debate in the United States—namely, that those who would regulate hate speech value equality and the Fourteenth Amendment above all else and thus are willing to accept restrictions on speech and the First Amendment to achieve equality, while those who oppose the regulation of hate speech are said to value free speech above all else, and thus will not tolerate restrictions on speech even if such restrictions were to promote equality. Because lesbian and gay equality has almost exclusively been safeguarded by the First Amendment, while lesbian/gay Fourteenth Amendment claims have been defeated by the very speech-act of "coming out," the experience of lesbians and gay men in this country contradicts the understanding of the First and Fourteenth Amendments constructed by the hate speech debate.

After deconstructing the governing analysis, I offer some tentative conclusions in part 4 about the implications of this effort on the question of whether—and/or how—we ought to regulate hate speech.

Before I embark on this journey, I would like to begin with two caveats concerning my institutional affiliation. Although I am the director of the ACLU's Lesbian and Gay Rights Project, my remarks are my own. They are of course informed by my experience with the ACLU. I do not want to suggest, however, that what follows is the organization's official position on hate speech, to the extent there even is such a thing.[4] Nonetheless, I feel compelled to add that I am anything but embarrassed or defensive about my association with the ACLU on this or any other issue.

Professor Charles Lawrence, in his important work on hate speech,[5] harangues those (he labels as "civil libertarians") who deplore racist speech but believe it cannot be regulated consistent with the First Amendment and yet do little else to combat its effects:

> There is much in the way many civil libertarians have participated in the debate over the regulation of racist speech that causes the victims of that speech to wonder which side they are on. Those who raise their voices in protest against public sanctions of racist speech have not organized private protests against the voices of racism. It has been people of color, women, and gays who have held vigils at offending fraternity houses, staged candlelight marches, counter-demonstrations and distributed flyers calling upon classmates and colleagues to express their outrage at pervasive racism, sexism, and homophobia in their midst and to show solidarity with its victims.
>
> Traditional civil libertarians have been conspicuous largely in their absence from these group expressions of condemnation.

While Professor Lawrence's message is an important one in the context of lesbians and gay rights, it is also important to acknowledge the work that "civil libertarians" such as the ACLU undertake to achieve equality for lesbians and gay men. Put simply, we undertake far more such legal work than any other organization in the United States, straight or gay.[6] This is not to say that the ACLU's commitment to lesbian and gay rights has always been strong and unwavering. It has not. Nor is it to say we do enough. And, as with too many organizations, the lesbian/gay rights work of the ACLU is too often handled solely by lesbians and gay men, who must too often explain to their non-gay counterparts why certain issues are "civil liberties" issues or cajole these colleagues to do more. Nonetheless, I strongly believe a sufficiently strong prima facie case exists to shift the burden of proof to those who would more widely regulate (homophobic) speech. Such proponents of speech restrictions might properly be asked: Other than proposing restrictions on speech, what have you done for lesbian/gay rights lately? As much as the ACLU?

Having made my necessary disclaimers and defenses, let me proceed to sketch one basis upon which lesbians and gay men approach the hate speech debate.

1. ONE UNDERSTANDING OF THE OPERATION OF HOMOPHOBIA IN AMERICAN SOCIETY

The experience of lesbians and gay men in the United States is centrally one of silence. A resounding, deafening, mind-boggling silence. Perhaps the most eloquent expression of this silence was written by the late Vito Russo in his brilliant study of lesbian and gay images in American film:

In her book on women in film, *From Reverence to Rape,* Molly Haskell says that "the big lie" is that women are inferior. The big lie about lesbians and gay men is that we do not exist. The story of the ways in which gayness has been defined in American film is the story of the ways in which gayness has been defined in America. In Eldridge Cleaver's *Soul on Ice,* Beverly Axelrod says, "Our tragedy does not derive from our fantasy of what homosexuals are but from our fantasy of what America is. We have made each other up." As expressed on screen, America was a dream that had no room for the existence of homosexuals. Laws were made against depicting such things on-screen. And when the fact of our existence became unavoidable, we were reflected, onscreen and off, as dirty secrets.[7]

The oppression of silence is possible because sexual orientation is not, like race or gender, visually identifiable: individuals must take on a lesbian/gay identity through some speech or speech act known as "coming out."[8] Because taking on a lesbian/gay identity involves coming out, society can oppress gay people most directly simply by ensuring that such expressions are silenced.

The silencing oppression is experienced by gay people on both a personal and societal level. A nearly universal "coming out" experience for lesbians and gay men is that after they tell their family, or straight friends, that they are gay, no one—no one—ever, ever, mentions it again. Ever. Or, a typical family reaction is, "That's fine dear, I just don't want to know about it." Our life, our love, a central aspect of our identity, is something people closest to us in the world "just don't want to know about."

A friend of mine, for instance, made the mistake of coming out to his parents in the context of a discussion about his possibly moving back to his hometown, a medium-sized city in the Midwest. While heretofore his parents would have been thrilled by his return, suddenly they were not. His mother asked him quite simply, "Would you be living that life-style if you moved back here? Because if you were, we wouldn't want you to live here." She explained, "While we will always love you, we don't want to see that." He patiently attempted to explain to her that there was no difference between "that life-style" and him; there was always just him, now taking on an openly gay identity, and living his life. But his mother did not want to know about his homosexuality—she wanted to silence the aspect of his identity that made her uncomfortable.

Society operates in a similar fashion. As Vito Russo makes clear in the passage quoted above, popular images of lesbians and gay men are nonexistent, or, when they do exist, are abhorrent. Everywhere heterosexism is enforced as the norm—any picture of any couple in any advertisement for any product is always a heterosexual couple; if a single picture is used in an advertisement it is almost exclusively an image of a single woman depicted in a manner so as to appeal to straight men.

Indeed, society cares much more about open expressions of lesbian and gay identity than it does about lesbian and gay sexuality itself. The United States military's pre-1994 regulations, for example, enforced the exclusion of lesbians and gay men through a three-prong policy:[9] individuals were ousted from the military for stating that they were gay, for engaging in homosexual acts, and/or for participating in homosexual marriages.[10] The first prong of this policy—expressions of gay identity—had no exception; conversely, the second prong, engaging in homosexual acts, had exceptions for youthfulness, drunkenness, mistake, etc.[11] Congress's new "don't ask, don't tell" law embodies this same principle, as it's nickname implies.

Throughout the legal system one finds greater regulation of lesbian and gay identity than of homosexual sexual activity.[12] Sodomy laws, for example, are rarely directly enforced against gay people.[13] However, lesbians and gay men routinely lose their jobs with little legal redress where they dare to come out publicly,[14] or they are punished for their openness through the deprivation, for instance, of the right to custody of or visitation with their children.[15] Censorship in American society is also uniquely aimed at lesbian and gay speech.[16] As Nan Hunter has written:

[S]odomy may be about privacy, but homosexuality is not. The primary rationales for discrimination, as well as the arenas in which it occurs and is experienced, concern public perceptions, not private events. The issue that has generated most of the current judicial debate—the military's personnel policy declaring homosexuality to be incompatible with military service—is about secret versus public identity. . . . The military does not seek to justify its policy on the ground that private sexual acts render gay and lesbian service members inept, but on the grounds that public opprobrium toward homosexuals would imperil morale, discipline and recruitment if homosexuals were openly part of the armed forces. In numerous other cases, the asserted state interest used to justify discrimination was a fear that equal treatment would be perceived by the public as an endorsement of homosexuality. It is the public process of creation, assignment and use of sexual identity—not the right to keep private conduct secret—on which future litigation will focus.[17]

By focusing on "silencing" as being at the core of homophobia, I do not mean to downplay the other very real means by which lesbian and gay men are oppressed in this society. Anti-gay violence, for instance, is perhaps the most pervasive—and still most accepted—form of hate-related conduct in the United States. Silence is central, though, because even anti-gay violence is rarely directed at someone until he or she has taken on a lesbian or gay identity or is publicly perceived as being lesbian or gay. The violence, then, can be seen as a means of silencing the public identity, the true subject of the attack.

2. LESBIANS/GAY MEN AND THE AMERICAN LEGAL SYSTEM

There is no space here to set forth a definitive history of the fight for lesbian and gay rights in this country. Rather, what follows is an attempt to delineate two lines of legal argument that have been made on behalf of lesbians and gay men: one flowing from the First Amendment and involving free speech and association, and the other flowing from the Fourteenth Amendment and involving that amendment's promise of equal protection under the laws. I select these types of claims because they are at the center of the great debate about hate speech. What I hope to demonstrate here is that the experience of lesbians and gay men in this country contradicts the basic understanding of the First and Fourteenth Amendments in that our equality has been achieved almost exclusively through the First Amendment, while our Fourteenth Amendment claims—which are almost necessarily premised upon "speech" or "speech acts"—have largely failed.

A. First Amendment Claims for Lesbians and Gay Men

The birth of what is referred to as the "modern" gay rights movement is typically traced to the riots at the Stonewall Inn in New York City on the nights in 1969 following the death of Judy Garland, when lesbians and gay men (largely drag queens of color) resisted the theretofore routine harassment at the hands of the police. Lesbian/gay life would never again be the same. According to this story, gay life is divided into two eras: "before Stonewall," which is meant to date back to the stone age, and the twenty-five years since Stonewall.

Stonewall—and the surrounding social events of the late-1960s—did signal a new rise in lesbian and gay consciousness and self-identity. While lesbians and gay men in the United States had been organizing to overcome their oppression for decades before Stonewall, the early 1970s saw an explosion of lesbian and gay social activism. Central to this activism was the need for lesbians and gay men to speak out; to do so, they had to be able to meet and form associations for the purpose of fighting back. Not surprisingly, as such groups formed they were very often met with government repression and attempts to squelch the rise of this activism.

Accordingly, in the immediate aftermath of Stonewall, a series of First Amendment cases challenged government restrictions on lesbian and gay organizations. For example, there is a whole line of cases that traces the formation of lesbian and gay student groups on college campuses and these groups' fights for university recognition.[18] Without exception, the final decisions in each of these cases vindicated the rights of the lesbian and gay litigants. An important aspect of these cases from the perspective of the hate speech debate involves the arguments put forward by the opponents of the gay organizations. Typically, in the litany of their contentions was an argument that the gay meeting "offended" students on the campus. The courts in these cases correctly rejected such arguments, safeguarding the students' rights regardless of how "offensive" their meeting was to others.[19]

These cases are mirrored by similar cases outside the university that also uphold the association of lesbians and gay men on First Amendment grounds and ranged from First Amendment protections for gay bars to the protection of a gay high school student to bring a male date to his high school prom.[20] Similarly, the First Amendment has been used to prohibit governmental publications from denying the existence of lesbian and gay groups and events.[21]

In each of these cases, the First Amendment enabled lesbians and gay men to overcome the central oppressive function of invisibility: lesbian and gay groups were "recognized"; lesbian and gay bars were validated; lesbian and gay names were listed in directories; speech itself—by and about lesbians and gay men—was liberated and sent out into the world.

This is not to say that the First Amendment has always worked perfectly for lesbians and gay men. There are a number of serious internal and external limitations on its applicability. First, the First Amendment is triggered only where "state action" exists, although anti-gay silencing is not so limited.[22] Instances of private censorship—an encyclopedia's failure to include an entry on gay life, for example— are not actionable. Second, even where there is state action, the First Amendment applies only to conduct that is speech, to association that is political. Claims for lesbian/gay litigants have failed where courts have ruled that the speech at issue, such as coming out, was not "political," and thus not protected by the First Amendment.[23] Third, the First Amendment does not extend to protect speech that will cause "imminent lawless conduct"; some courts have ruled that gay organizations will lead to outbreaks of sodomy and are therefore appropriately subjected to state regulation.[24] Similarly, some lesbian/gay expression is considered obscene and therefore beyond the protection of the First Amendment.[25] First Amendment rights are also limited in the sense that the amendment is not absolute—where the government has a compelling state interest in policing such rights, they can be curtailed. Moreover, where First Amendment rights clash with other First Amendment rights, someone must prevail. Lesbian/gay litigants have lost cases on these grounds as well.[26] Finally, sometimes the First Amendment just does not work. There have been absolutely outrageous instances of courts refusing to recognize our First Amendment rights. For instance, after Ohio's secretary of state refused to permit the incorporation of Cincinnati's Gay

Activist Alliance, his decision was upheld by every level of the Ohio state judiciary and *certiorari* was denied by the United States Supreme Court.[27]

Nonetheless, the First Amendment has been the only consistent friend of lesbian and gay rights litigators since Stonewall. With rare exceptions, when a case is properly framed as a First Amendment case, lesbian and gay plaintiffs prevail. This is not to say that the amendment is perfect, nor that there are not occasionally bad opinions, nor that it covers all contingencies. But it does work. The First Amendment is premised upon an ideal—currently absent from Fourteenth Amendment jurisprudence—that the judiciary should protect even those ideas it finds deplorable. It finds ours deplorable, but has, in a series of important cases, protected us nonetheless.

B. Fourteenth Amendment Claims for Lesbians and Gay Men

It may be easier to appreciate the value of the First Amendment when the alternatives are considered. The primary alternative for equality claims for gay people has been the Fourteenth Amendment, in both its due process and equal protection components. Any hope that the rights of lesbians and gay men would be protected through the due process clause's right to privacy were dashed by the Supreme Court's 1986 decision in the *Hardwick* case, which held that the right to privacy does not cover homosexual sodomy.[28]

In its place, the primary argument for lesbian and gay rights in the 1980s has been the equal protection clause. Unfortunately, the Fourteenth Amendment has provided very little—if any—equality for lesbians and gay men. There have been only a scattered few federal court decisions extending heightened judicial scrutiny to classifications based on sexual orientation, and most of these have been overturned or vacated.[29] There are no definitive, final circuit court opinions applying heightened scrutiny to discrimination against lesbians and gay men, and, indeed, at least six federal circuit courts have considered such arguments and ruled just the opposite.[30] What's worse, I know of only one case in the history of the United States in which a lesbian or gay man has won a final decision from a federal court based on the Fourteenth Amendment.[31] One. And in that case, the court's equal protection ruling is so confused that it is nearly incomprehensible. One, poorly reasoned, and hence of-little-precedential-value, opinion.

The jurisprudence of lesbian and gay rights under the Fourteenth Amendment has been so bad that courts have permitted prejudice itself to be used as a rational reason for discriminatory governmental actions, failing even to see the circularity in their conclusions. The central point of the equal protection clause is to require the judiciary to step in when the democratic processes have yielded results that are discriminatory because of the biases of majoritarian rule. In such instances, the courts' task is to force the government to come forward with at least some rational reason for the classifications and distinctions it is drawing. Obviously, it should not be sufficient for the government to step forward and say, "We are discriminating against this group because we do not like them." Rather than offering a rational basis, such an argument merely restates the question. But this is precisely what the courts have permitted the state to get away with in cases involving lesbians and gay men. In *High Tech Gays*,[32] for example, the Ninth Circuit permitted the alleged fact that the KGB targeted homosexuals as potential security risks to be used as the rationale for special scrutiny of lesbian/gay security clearance applicants. Not only did the court here defer to the prejudice, but given the choice between trusting the KGB or gay people, it chose the KGB.[33]

3. DECONSTRUCTING THE HATE-SPEECH DEBATE

My main point about hate speech concerns the structure that currently frames the debate over regulating it, which purports to pit free speech against equality and thus the First Amendment against the Fourteenth. Those who would police hate speech to correct the harms that such speech causes its victims are said to value equality above all else. They are said to be willing to compromise the First Amendment to achieve greater equality in certain carefully prescribed circumstances. Those who would not police hate speech are said to be governed by a different narrative, one that values free speech above all else, even equality, and thus they are said to not be willing to accept limitations on the First Amendment even to achieve Fourteenth Amendment equality.

This structure does not feel right to me. Reading this debate from the perspective of someone who works full-time for equality for lesbians and gay men, I do not experience this First Amendment/Fourteenth Amendment distinction to comport with the speech/equality distinction. As explained earlier, the Fourteenth Amendment has provided very little, if any, equality for lesbians and gay men, while, by contrast, the First Amendment has been the only consistent friend of lesbian and gay rights litigators since Stonewall. But more importantly, I do not find that "equality" belongs only to the Fourteenth Amendment and "speech" only to the First. The pureness of these legal categories collapses under the experience of lesbians and gay men: First Amendment cases are about equality and equal protection cases are about speech.

First Amendment cases are about equality. In the First Amendment cases in which gay litigants prevail, the narrative that can be weaved about these cases goes much farther than the vindication of free speech. When a state university, for instance, denies a gay student group the right to meet on campus, it is not just striking a blow at free association, although it is indeed doing that. Rather, the university is sending out a message that lesbians and gay men are less equal than other persons. When the First Amendment vindicates our rights of association, we are made whole, we have been *equalized* to the other student groups. When people read in the student newspaper that courts have forced the university to recognize the lesbian/gay group, they do not think, "Another victory for freedom of association." They think, "The queers won; they beat the school." The message that goes forth in the popular imagination is one of vindication, triumph, equality. The First Amendment is not just about free speech, then, but includes within it a narrative of equal rights. Indeed, a typical rendering of the principle of the First Amendment might go something like this: "While a state university does not, for example, have to recognize student groups, once it begins doing so, it cannot treat groups differentially or unequally based on the content of the group's message." Thus, I cherish the First Amendment not only because it protects free speech, but also because it is the most direct and powerful instrument of *equality* for lesbian and gay persons.

Fourteenth Amendment cases are about speech. Conversely, this amendment is not just about equality for lesbians and gay men. In fact, as noted above, it has rarely been about such equality at all. However, it is important to note that for lesbians and gay men, a Fourteenth Amendment case rarely arises in the absence of speech or a speech act because sexual orientation is typically not visually identifiable. In most cases, a lesbian or gay man must "come out" to be recognized as being gay; coming out inevitably involves speech or a speech act, and thus most Fourteenth Amendment cases flow from and contain a speech component.

Interestingly, it is often this very speech-act component that is used to defeat the claim of equality for lesbians and gay men. Courts often rule that gay people are not being discriminated against because of who they are, but rather because of the very act of self-identification, of speaking out about being gay;[34] the speech act is used to defeat the claim of status-based equal protection. In this sense, the courts appear to be placing the burden of the protection of gay rights clearly within the First Amendment.

4. THE IMPLICATIONS OF THE DECONSTRUCTION OF THE HATE-SPEECH DEBATE

But so what? What are the implications of this for the hate speech debate itself? What are the implications for lesbian and gay rights? Here are some tentative thoughts.

Implications for the hate speech debate. Mari Matsuda, quoted at the outset of this piece, stated that her "claim that a legal response to racist speech is required stems from a recognition of the structural reality of racism in America."[35] In this piece, I have attempted to sketch an understanding of the structural reality of homophobia in America and in so doing I have outlined a number of ways in which gender operates as a locus of oppression in a different way than race does.[36]

The structure of homophobia I have outlined here leads me to have grave concerns about restrictions on hate speech, even when those restrictions are supposedly made to further the equality of lesbians and gay men. I am cautious, first, because allowing limitations on free speech might well limit *our* ability to speak freely, and in this instance, therefore, particularly limit our ability to come out, to undertake the very act of self-identification central to overcoming lesbian/gay oppression. Second, I am also cautious because I worry that allowing limitations on the primary instrument of gay equality may well limit the equality itself.[37]

Nonetheless, I do feel some hate speech must be regulated. Some hate speech is so harmful to lesbians and gay men that restrictions on it don't much threaten the realization of our own First Amendment/equality rights. This speech is speech that has certain key characteristics, for example, it must be targeted at a specific individual or identifiable group of individuals and is intended to frighten, coerce, or unreasonably intimidate its target. This is a fairly standard intimidation statute that can constitutionally and rightfully be enforced.

Even this I say with trepidation, however, because even as I say it, I see it being used against lesbians and gay men. Consider, for example, Ohio's "importuning" statute. Ohio defines the crime of "importuning" as soliciting a person of the same sex to engage in sexual activity, knowing that such solicitation is offensive to the other person; the statute provides punishments of up six months in jail and/or a $1,000 fine.[38] The underlying sexual act is not a crime in Ohio; only the solicitation, and only "offensive" solicitations for sex, and only when made to a person of the same gender.[39] As such a statute shows, hate speech regulation can yield more power to the government, to the majority, to the oppressors—power I am very hesitant to yield because I feel it is inevitable that the power will ultimately and inevitably be used against oppressed minorities.

In sum, my experience litigating on behalf of lesbians and gay men makes me reluctant to be a party to placing limitations on the First Amendment—and this is my main point. I hesitate to be a party to limitations on the First Amendment not because I am deeply mired in some narrative of free expression (although I have been accused of worse), but rather because the First Amendment is our instrument, at present our strongest tool, of constitutional equality. It's what we've got and I believe we should guard it carefully.

Implications for lesbian and gay rights. I believe that the challenge set forth by Mari Matsuda, to which I begin to respond in this piece, presents interesting questions about the relationships between different categories of oppression—between, for instance, sexual orientation and race. Matsuda suggested that the consideration of constitutional rights, and balancing them, might be different in the context of sexual orientation than it is in the context of race, and here I have outlined a view of homophobia that might lead one to constitutional determinations distinct from those made in the racial context.

But I experience as threatening the conclusion that race and sexual orientation do not necessarily go hand in hand. Most of the arguments for equality for lesbians and gay men are based on arguments from the model of racial civil rights in this country—arguments from the Fourteenth Amendment. If each oppression takes its own distinct form and thus each form must seek its own unique solutions—if what works for one may not necessarily work for the other—what does this mean for lesbian/gay rights? Is it possible that valuing Fourteenth Amendment equality at the expense of First Amendment speech in the race context might simply make more sense than it does in the context of sexual orientation? How could that be, though, unless hate speech directed at lesbians and gay men stings less than hate speech directed at African Americans?

I don't purport to have the answers to these questions posed by Matsuda. But I do agree that their implications are worth exploring. A much deeper and more varied analysis of how sex operates as a locus of oppression and a more in-depth exploration of the constitutional ramifications are fertile ground for further inquiry.

Lest it be thought that I am prepared to sever the fight for lesbian/gay rights from the structure of the fight for racial justice and the Fourteenth Amendment, I will end by stating that my primary conclusion is that we need new thinking about our claims under the Fourteenth Amendment. Specifically, I believe we need to tie our Fourteenth Amendment claims more closely to the unique structure of homophobia—silencing—more closely, in legal terms, to the opponent of silencing, the First Amendment.

In her article, "Life after *Hardwick*,"[40] Nan Hunter sets forth this challenge. Hunter observes that while most future litigation for lesbian and gay rights will be premised on the Fourteenth Amendment, each of the criteria for stricter scrutiny of equal protection claims "history of group discrimination, a status of relative political disempowerment and the indicia of identifiable group status itself . . . raises problems that are unique to lesbian and gay rights claims."[41] Hunter specifically zeroes in on the immutability prong of equal protection jurisprudence, writing that "[b]iological immutability is not an absolute prerequisite to invalidating classifications on the basis of the trait. Aliens can and do become citizens; persons can and do alter their religious group affiliations. Neither group is penalized for the refusal to change, even though change is possible."[42]

With regard to religious affiliation, Hunter notes that it is "independently protected under the Free Exercise Clause of the First Amendment."[43] The structure of equal protection claims for religious groups then derives some, if not all, of its power from the protection of religious freedom in the First Amendment. In concluding that the oppression of lesbians and gay men is centrally about speech, I am led to believe that we ought to consider creating an equal protection jurisprudence for lesbian/gay identity that derives its power from the protections of free speech and association in the First Amendment.[44] Heightened scrutiny under the equal protection clause is triggered not only by suspect classifications but also by governmental actions that burden fundamental rights. To the extent we can convince judges that homosexual identity is centrally about speech, we may be able to convince them that state actions that discriminate on the basis of sexual orientation burden the fundamental right to speak and thus should be strictly scrutinized.[45]

In sum, then, rather than end on a note of great despair about the Fourteenth Amendment because it still remains an unfulfilled promise for lesbians and gay men, I will end on a note of optimism about it. If we can escape rigid thinking about the First and Fourteenth Amendments, such as that found in most of the writing about hate speech, and if we can appreciate the complexities of these two constitutional guarantees, perhaps we can find a way for the Fourteenth Amendment to work as a guarantor of equality. One way of doing this is to use the First Amendment as the vehicle.

Notes

This chapter grew out of my participation in a symposium at Tulane Law School on October 4, 1991, entitled, "Legal Restrictions on Homophobic and Racist Speech: Collateral Consequences for the Lesbian and Gay Community." My remarks at that symposium were published at 2 L. & Sexuality: A Review of Lesbian and Gay Legal Issues 19 (1992). For the purposes of this publication, I have expanded and updated those remarks.

1. 87 *Mich. L. Rev.* 2320 (1989).
2. *Id.* at 2331–32 (footnotes omitted).
3. This exploration is only a beginning for a variety of reasons. First, there are time and space limitations. Second, I do not believe that a task as encompassing as setting forth a basic understanding of the oppression of lesbians

and gay men can be accomplished in a single article, nor, third, from a single perspective. My description, therefore, is not only tentative but necessarily limited by my particular worldview and situation. Much more work must be undertaken in this area to ensure a full context for the hate speech debate.

4. While there is a national ACLU policy related to "Free Speech and Bias on College Campuses," ACLU affiliates are clearly divided on the issue. See Nadine Strossen, "Regulating Racist Speech on Campus: A Modest Proposal," 1990 *Duke L.J.* 484, 487 n. 11 (1990).

5. Charles Lawrence, "If He Hollers Let Him Go: Regulating Racist Speech on Campus," 1990 *Duke L.J.* 431 (1990).

6. The ACLU's 1993 dockets comprised more than 125 lesbian/gay rights matters in nearly forty states around the U.S. Eight ACLU attorneys, including five with the national Lesbian and Gay Rights/AIDS Project, work full-time on lesbian and gay (and AIDS) issues. In addition to these dedicated staff members, all of the fifty-two ACLU affiliates also undertake regular educational efforts, advocacy, lobbying, and litigation on lesbian/gay issues in their states. All of the lesbian/gay cases that were decided by the Supreme Court in the 1980s—the Georgia sodomy case, *Bowers v. Hardwick*, 478 U.S. 186 (1986); the CIA gay employee case, *Webster v. Doe*, 486 U.S. 592 (1988); and the gay Olympics case, *San Fran. Arts & Athletics, Inc. v. U.S.O.C.*, 483 U.S. 522 (1987)—were ACLU cases.

7. Vito Russo, *The Celluloid Closet: Homosexuality in the Movies* (New York: Harper and Row, 1987), xii.

8. The exception to this are those individuals who are presumed to be homosexual based on their deviation from gender role stereotypes. Thus, effeminate men and masculine women are presumed to be gay men and lesbians because society confuses sexual orientation with gender roles.

9. See United States Army Regulation 135–175 (1981).

10. This last prong is fascinating in that lesbians and gay men cannot legally marry anywhere in the United States. Such a ceremony, therefore, is solely one of religious significance and would thereby appear to be beyond the state's power to police. But see *Shahar v. Bowers*, 836 F. Supp. 859 (N.D. Ga. 1993) (upholding firing of lesbian by state attorney general for engaging in same-sex marriage). See also *Goldman v. Weinberger*, 475 U.S. 501 (1986).

11. Compare U.S. Army Regulation 135–175, § VII (Separation for Homosexuality), ¶ 2–39(a) with ¶ 2–39(b) (1981).

12. See William B. Rubenstein, " 'Homosexuality Per Se': The Search for Articulations of Homophobia in Judicial Text" (unpublished essay).

13. Where sodomy laws are applied against lesbians and gay men, it is typically because the gay person has taken on an openly gay identity. See "Interview with Michael Hardwick (by Peter Irons)," in *Lesbians, Gay Men, and the Law*, 125–31 (Rubenstein, ed., 1993) (showing why police were in Michael Hardwick's bedroom in an incident that gave rise to *Bowers v. Hardwick*,

478 U.S. 186 [1986]). Kendall Thomas examines this extensively in "Beyond the Privacy Principle," 92 *Columbia L. Rev.* 1431 (1992).

14. See, e.g., *Rowland v. Mad River Local School District, Montgomery County, Ohio,* 730 F.2d 444 (6th Cir. 1984), *cert. denied,* 470 U.S. 1009 (1985); *Singer v. U.S. Civil Service Commission,* 530 F.2d 247 (9th Cir. 1976), *vacated,* 429 U.S. 1034 (1977). See, generally, *Lesbians, Gay Men, and the Law,* 243–375 (Rubenstein, ed., 1993).

15. See, e.g., *In re J. S.& C.,* 324 A.2d 90 (Ch. Div. 1974), *aff'd,* 362 A.2d 54 (App. Div. 1976). See, generally, *Lesbians, Gay Men, and the Law,* 475–562 (Rubenstein, ed., 1993).

16. See, e.g., *Finley v. N.E.A.,* 795 F.Supp. 1457 (C.D. Cal., June 9, 1992). Cf. *GMHC v. Sullivan,* 792 F.Supp. 278 (S.D. N.Y., 1992). See, generally, LaMarche and Rubenstein, "The Love That Dare Not Speak," *The Nation,* November 5, 1990.

17. Nan D. Hunter, "Life after *Hardwick*," 27 *Harv. C.R.-C.L. L. Rev.* 531, 551–52 (1992) (citation omitted).

18. See, e.g., *Gay and Lesbian Students Ass'n v. Gohn,* 850 F.2d 361 (8th Cir. 1988); *Gay Students Services v. Texas A & M University,* 737 F.2d 1317 (5th Cir. 1984); *Gay Lib v. University of Missouri,* 558 F.2d 848 (8th Cir. 1977), *cert. denied sub nom. Ratchford v. Gay Lib,* 434 U.S. 1080 (1978), *reh. denied* 435 U.S. 981 (1978); *Gay Alliance of Students v. Matthews,* 544 F.2d 161 (4th Cir. 1976); *Gay Students Organization of the Univ. of New Hampshire v. Bonner,* 509 F.2d 652 (1st Cir. 1974); *Student Coalition for Gay Rights v. Austin Peay University,* 477 F.Supp. 1267 (M.D. Tenn. 1979); *Wood v. Davison,* 351 F.Supp. 543 (N.D. Ga. 1972).

19. It is worth noting that notwithstanding societal advances and the overwhelming legal precedent in this area, these cases continue into the 1990s. The ACLU is currently involved in litigating such a case in Alabama and in securing the rights of a lesbian/gay student group in Idaho.

20. See, e.g., *Fricke v. Lynch,* 491 F.Supp. 381 (D. R.I. 1980) (prom date); *Cyr v. Walls,* 439 F.Supp. 697 (N.D. Tex. 1977) (gay conference); *In re Thom, Lambda Legal Defense & Educ. Fund, Inc.,* 337 N.Y.S.2d 558 (1972), *rev'd and remanded sub nom. Application of Thom,* 347 N.Y.S.2d 571, *on remand,* 350 N.Y.S. 2d 1 (1973) (legal advocacy group); *One Eleven Wines & Liquors, Inc. v. Division of Alcoholic Beverage Control,* 235 A.2d 12 (N.J. 1967) (bar). See, generally, *Lesbians, Gay Men, and the Law,* 209 (Rubenstein, ed., 1993).

21. See, e.g., *Toward a Gayer Bicentennial Comm. v. Rhode Island Bicentennial Found.,* 417 F.Supp. 632 (D. R.I. 1976); *Alaska Gay Coalition v. Sullivan,* 578 P.2d 951 (Alaska 1978); *Gay Activists Alliance v. Washington Metropolitan Area Transit Auth.,* 5 Med. L. Rep. (BNA) 1404 (D. D.C. 1979).

22. See, e.g., *Hatheway v. Gannett,* 459 N.W. 2d 873 (Wisc. App. 1990) (private newspaper refuses to run advertisements with the words "lesbian" and "gay"); *Loving v. Bellsouth Advertising & Publishing Corp.,* 339 S.E.

2d 372 (Ga. Ct. App. 1985) (Yellow Pages, a private enterprise, not obligated to accept advertising from a gay bookstore). See also *San Francisco Arts & Athletics, Inc. v. United States Olympic Comm.*, 483 U.S. 522 (1987) (no state action from injunction forcing the Gay Olympic Games to cease using the word "Olympics").

23. See, e.g., *Rowland v. Mad River Local School District, Montgomery County, Ohio*, 730 F.2d 444 (6th Cir. 1984), *cert. denied*, 470 U.S. 1009 (1985).

24. See, e.g., *Gay and Lesbian Students Association v. Gohn*, 656 F.Supp. 1045 (W.D. Ark. 1987), *rev'd, Gay and Lesbian Students Ass'n v. Gohn*, 850 F.2d 361 (8th Cir. 1988).

25. *See* Nan D. Hunter, Sherryl E. Michaelson, and Thomas B. Stoddard, *The Rights of Lesbians and Gay Men*, 11–12 (3d ed., 1992) (describing prosecution of Cincinnati art museum for display of Robert Mapplethorpe photographs depicting, inter alia, gay sexuality). *Cf. New York v. Ferber*, 458 U.S. 747 (1982) (child pornography can be regulated by state because it is obscenity not protected by the First Amendment).

26. See, e.g., "Judge Rules Scouts Can Block Gay Man As a Troop Leader," *New York Times*, May 23, 1991, B13.

27. *State ex rel. Grant v. Brown*, 313 N.E.2d 847 (1974) *(per curiam), appeal dismissed and cert. denied sub nom. Duggan v. Brown*, 420 U.S. 916 (1975).

28. *Bowers v. Hardwick*, 478 U.S. 186 (1986). A separate line of cases from the late 1960s through the late 1970s established a tentative principle under the due process clause that government discrimination against lesbians and gay men—in, for instance, the employment setting—had to have a rational nexus to the requirements of the job. See, e.g., *Norton v. Macy*, 417 F.2d 1161 (D.C. Cir. 1969). These cases have subsequently been read as being limited to situations in which the litigant had a protected liberty or property interest at stake, and thus this line of cases has waned as the Supreme Court has throughout the 1980s limited such instances. In fact, the court's decision in *Norton v. Macy* does not appear to require the presence of a property or liberty interest, and thus it could still provide the basis for a broad constitutional theory for lesbian/gay rights.

29. *Watkins v. United States Army*, 873 F.2d 1428 (9th Cir. 1988), *withdrawn on reh'g, Watkins v. United States Army*, 875 F.2d 699 (9th Cir. 1989) (en banc), *cert. denied*, 111 S.Ct. 384 (1990); *High Tech Gays v. Def. Indus. Sec. Clear. Office*, 668 F.Supp. 1361 (N.D. Cal. 1987), *reversed*, 895 F.2d 563 (9th Cir. 1990); *Jantz v. Muci*, 759 F.Supp. 1543 (D. Kan. 1991), *reversed*, 976 F.2d 623 (10th Cir. 1992), *cert. denied*, 113 S.Ct. 2445 (1993).

30. See, e.g., *Jantz v. Muci*, 976 F.2d 623 (10th Cir. 1992), *cert. denied*, 113 S.Ct. 2445 (1993); *High Tech Gays v. Defense Industry Security Clearance Office*, 895 F.2d 563 (9th Cir.), *reh'g and reh'g en banc denied*, 909 F.2d

375 (9th Cir. 1990); *Woodward v. United States*, 871 F.2d 1068 (Fed. Cir. 1989), *cert. denied*, 110 S.Ct. 1295 (1990); *Ben-Shalom v. Marsh*, 881 F.2d 454 (7th Cir. 1989); *Padula v. Webster*, 822 F.2d 97 (D.C. Cir. 1987); *Baker v. Wade*, 769 F.2d 289 (5th Cir. 1985), *cert. denied*, 478 U.S. 1022 (1986); *Rich v. Secretary of Army*, 735 F.2d 1220 (10th Cir. 1984).

31. *Doe v. Sparks*, 733 F.Supp. 227 (W.D. Pa. 1990).
32. *High Tech Gays v. DISCO*, 895 F.2d 563 (9th Cir. 1990).
33. I am indebted to Nan Hunter for this observation.
34. See, e.g., *McConnell v. Anderson*, 451 F.2d 193 (8th Cir. 1971); *Singer v. U.S. Civil Service Commission*, 530 F.2d 247 (9th Cir. 1976); *Shahar v. Bowers*, 836 F.Supp. 859 (N.D. Ga. 1993).
35. See n. 1, *supra*.
36. This is in no way meant to further the impression that lesbians and gay men are all white and that all people of color are heterosexual. To suggest that race and sexuality operate as loci of oppression in different ways is not to suggest that both may not be in operation at the same time.
37. Moreover, when one understands the First Amendment as being about equality as much as it is about speech, one can see that when the First Amendment vindicates hate speech against its restricters, it places the imprimatur of equality on that speech as well. This is what Nadine Strossen has referred to as "making a first amendment martyr" out of the speech we do not like. The content of that person's speech becomes "equalized" when it has to be vindicated by the federal courts. Why put ourselves in the position that we are equalizing the speech of our oppressors?
38. Ohio R.C. § 2907.07(B).
39. In rejecting a claim that this statute was unconstitutionally vague or overbroad (though construing the statute to apply solely to "fighting words"), the Ohio Supreme Court noted that the "type of expression proscribed . . . may have been acceptable in a more barbarous age when human dignity had not reached the level expected by citizens in our modern society." *State v. Phipps*, 389 N.E. 2d 1128 (Ohio 1979).
40. See n. 17, *supra*.
41. Hunter, supra n. 17, at 547.
42. *Id.* at 549–50.
43. *Id.* at 550 n.79.
44. Janet Halley has undertaken a much more sophisticated elaboration of a related theme in her article, "The Politics of the Closet: Toward Equal Protection for Gay, Lesbian and Bisexual Identity," 36 *U.C.L.A. L. Rev.* 915 (1989).
45. This theme is alluded to in several judicial decisions. For example, in his dissent from the denial of certiorari in *Rowland v. Mad River Local School District, Montgomery County, Ohio*, 470 U.S. 1009, 84 L.Ed. 2d 392 (1985), Justice Brennan wrote: "[P]etitioner's [coming out] 'speech' is perhaps better evaluated as no more than a natural consequence of her sexual

orientation, in the same way that co-workers generally know whom their fellow employees are dating or to whom they are married. Under this view, petitioner's First Amendment and equal protection claims may be seen to converge, because it is realistically impossible to separate her spoken statements from her status." *Id.* at 397 n.11. See also *Fricke v. Lynch,* 491 F.Supp. 381, 387 n.5, 388 n.6 (D. R.I. 1980).